HOW A ... STATES

# OXFAM INTERNATIONAL

Oxfam International is a confederation of 13 organisations working together with over 3,000 partners in more than 100 countries to find lasting solutions to poverty and injustice. With partners and allies, Oxfam International acts in solidarity with people living in poverty, especially women, to achieve their rights and assert their dignity as full citizens. It will support them to hold governments, corporations, and international organisations (including Oxfam) to account for their responsibilities. Oxfam International supports local, national, and international organisations and social movements of active citizens to demand justice, particularly gender justice, and to change ideas and beliefs, policies and practices to achieve improvements in people's lives.

Oxfam America, Oxfam Australia, Oxfam-in-Belgium, Oxfam Canada, Oxfam France - Agir ici, Oxfam Germany, Oxfam GB, Oxfam Hong Kong, Intermón Oxfam (Spain), Oxfam Ireland, Oxfam New Zealand, Oxfam Novib (Netherlands), and Oxfam Québec.

www.oxfam.org

# FROM POVERTY
# TO POWER

## HOW ACTIVE CITIZENS AND EFFECTIVE STATES
## CAN CHANGE THE WORLD

DUNCAN GREEN

**Oxfam**
International

First published by Oxfam International in 2008

© Oxfam International 2008

ISBN 978-0-85598-593-6

A catalogue record for this publication is available from the British Library.

The information in this publication is correct at the time of going to press.

Published by Oxfam International, Oxfam International Secretariat, Suite 20, 266 Banbury Road, Oxford OX2 7DL, United Kingdom www.oxfam.org

This publication is distributed in print for the publisher by Oxfam GB and is available from:

BEBC Distribution, PO Box 1496, Parkstone, Dorset, BH12 3YD, UK
Tel: +44 (0)1202 712933; fax: +44 (0)1202 712930; email: oxfam@bebc.co.uk

USA: Stylus Publishing LLC, PO Box 605, Herndon, VA 20172-0605, USA
Tel: +1 (0)703 661 1581; fax: +1 (0)703 661 1547; email: styluspub@aol.com

West Africa: EPP Books Services, Accra, Ghana Tel: +233 (21) 778347;
email: epp@eppbookservices.com www.eppbookservices.com
ISBN 978-9988-0-7507-1

East Africa: Fountain Publishers Ltd., Kampala, Uganda Tel: +256 (41) 259163/251112;
email: fountain@starcom.co.ug www.fountainpublishers.co.ug
ISBN 978-9970-02-809-2

India: Academic Foundation, New Delhi, www.academicfoundation.com
ISBN 978-81-7188-700-2

South Africa: Jacana, www.jacana.co.za
ISBN 978-1-77009-580-9

For details of local agents and representatives in other countries, consult www.oxfam.org.uk/publications. This website contains a fully searchable database of all Oxfam publications and facilities for secure on-line ordering.

Or contact Oxfam Publishing, Oxfam House, John Smith Drive, Cowley, Oxford, OX4 2JY, UK Tel +44 (0)1865 472255; fax (0)1865 472393; email: publish@oxfam.org.uk

For translated editions go to www.oxfam.org.uk/publications

Cover design: Coralie Bickford-Smith

Printed by Information Press, Eynsham.
Inners printed on recycled paper made from 100% post-consumer waste.
Cover printed on 100% recycled paper.

Oxfam GB is a registered charity, no. 202 918, and is a member of Oxfam International.

# CONTENTS

# LIST OF FIGURES

# LIST OF TABLES

# LIST OF BOXES

# LIST OF ACRONYMS

| | |
|---|---|
| AIDS | acquired immune deficiency syndrome |
| ART | antiretroviral treatment/therapy |
| ARV | antiretroviral |
| ASEAN | Association of South-East Asian Nations |
| AU | African Union |
| CAP | Common Agricultural Policy |
| CDM | Clean Development Mechanism |
| CEDAW | Convention on the Elimination of All Forms of Discrimination Against Women |
| CERF | Central Emergency Response Fund |
| CGIAR | Consultative Group on International Agricultural Research |
| CSO | civil society organisation |
| CSR | corporate social responsibility |
| DAC | Development Assistance Committee (of the OECD) |
| DFID | Department for International Development (UK) |
| ECOSOC | United Nations Economic and Social Council |
| ECOWAS | Economic Community of West African States |
| EFA | Education for All |
| EITI | Extractive Industries Transparency Initiative |
| EPA | Economic Partnership Agreement |
| EPZ | export-processing zone |
| EU ETS | European Union Emissions Trading Scheme |

| | |
|---|---|
| FAO | Food and Agriculture Organization of the United Nations |
| FDI | foreign direct investment |
| FTA | free trade agreement |
| G7 | the seven richest nations (USA, UK, Germany, Japan, Italy, France, and Canada) |
| G8 | G7 nations + Russia |
| GATS | General Agreement on Trade in Services |
| GATT | General Agreement on Tariffs and Trade |
| GAVI | Global Alliance for Vaccines and Immunization |
| GBS | general budget support |
| GCAP | Global Call to Action against Poverty |
| GCE | Global Campaign for Education |
| GDP | gross domestic product |
| GNP | gross national product |
| HIPC | Heavily Indebted Poor Country |
| HIV | human immunodeficiency virus |
| ICC | International Criminal Court |
| ICRC | International Committee of the Red Cross |
| IDP | internally displaced person |
| IFI | international financial institution |
| IFRC | International Federation of the Red Cross and Red Crescent Societies |
| IHL | international humanitarian law |
| ILO | International Labour Organization |
| IMF | International Monetary Fund |
| INGO | international non-government organisation |
| IPCC | Intergovernmental Panel on Climate Change |
| LDC | least developed country |
| MDG | Millennium Development Goal |
| MDRI | Multilateral Debt Relief Initiative |
| MSF | Médecins Sans Frontières |

| | |
|---|---|
| NAFTA | North American Free Trade Agreement |
| NGO | non-government organisation |
| OCHA | UN Office for the Co-ordination of Humanitarian Affairs (UN) |
| ODA | overseas development assistance |
| ODI | Overseas Development Institute, UK |
| OECD | Organisation for Economic Co-operation and Development |
| ORT | oral rehydration therapy |
| PRGF | Poverty Reduction and Growth Facility (IMF) |
| PRSP | Poverty Reduction Strategy Paper (IMF and World Bank) |
| SAP | structural adjustment programme |
| SAPRI | Structural Adjustment Participatory Review Initiative |
| SARS | severe acute respiratory syndrome |
| SMEs | small and medium-sized enterprises |
| SWAP | sector-wide approach |
| TNC | transnational corporation |
| TRIMS | Trade-Related Investment Measures |
| TRIPS | Trade-Related Aspects of Intellectual Property Rights |
| UNCAC | United Nations Convention Against Corruption |
| UNCTAD | United Nations Conference on Trade and Development |
| UNDP | United Nations Development Programme |
| UNFCCC | United Nations Framework Convention on Climate Change |
| UNHCR | United Nations High Commissioner for Refugees |
| UNICEF | United Nations Children's Fund |
| WFP | World Food Programme |
| WHO | World Health Organization |
| WIPO | World Intellectual Property Organization |
| WTO | World Trade Organization |

# ACKNOWLEDGEMENTS

The word 'editor' hardly does justice to Mark Fried's enormous contribution to this book. He has used his unique combination of editorial skills and deep knowledge of development to shape the text, spot gaps, and propose improvements – all this with unfailing patience and good humour. Seemingly infinite reserves of stamina and good humour have also allowed Anna Coryndon to manage the project from its conception, through Byzantine consultations, to final product, her extraordinary eye for detail spotting whenever things were starting to unravel. It has been a delight to work with them both.

I would like to thank Oxfam for ensuring that I had the time and resources to get this job done. In particular Phil Bloomer, and before him Justin Forsyth, offered unswerving support and brilliant advice throughout. Others who played a crucial role include John Ambler, Jan Bouke Wijbrandi, Becky Buell, Sam Bickersteth, Marjolein Brouwer, James Ensor, Gonzalo Fanjul, Lot Felizco, Jeremy Hobbs, Richard King, Adam Leach, Luk Tak Chuen, and Chris Roche. Space forces me to be selective – the full list of those I would like to thank is on the book's website. Dozens of Oxfam specialists, and others, have also contributed background papers and case studies – these are listed on page 497.

Outside Oxfam, numerous academics and others have offered expert advice. They include Saamah Abdallah, Chris Adam, Supriya Akerkar, Sabina Alkire, Peter Bakvis, Catherine Barber, Stefan Baskerville and first year students at University College, Oxford, Nicholas Bayne, Jo Beall, David Booth, Saturnino M. Borras Jr, Diana Cammack, Ha-Joon Chang, Celine Charveriat, Martha Chen, Anuradha Chenoy, John Clark, Paddy Coulter, Chris Cramer, James Darcy, Michael Ellis,

Rosalind Eyben, Julian Filochowski, Sean Fox, Verena Fritz, John Gaventa, Jonathan Hellin, Mark Heywood, Rolph van der Hoeven, Richard Jolly, Jonathan di John, Roman Krznaric, David Lewis, Matthew Lockwood, Ian MacAuslan, Ruth Mayne, Branko Milanovic, Jamie Morrison, Sarah Mulley, Karma Nabulsi, Peter Newell, Sheila Page, Jenny Pearce, Jeff Powell, the staff and students of Queen Elizabeth House, Oxford, Vicky Randall, Amartya Sen, Frances Stewart, Pablo Suarez, Jim Sumberg, Michael Taylor, Kevin Watkins, David Woodward, Andrew Wyatt, and Roger Yates. The author assumes full responsibility for all opinions and any errors.

Finally, I would like to thank my family, Catherine, Calum, and Finlay, for putting up with a self-obsessed author in the house (again).

Duncan Green,
*Oxfam GB*
*Oxford, April 2008*

A list of the NGOs, civil society organisations, and networks supported by Oxfam that are mentioned in this book is available on the book's website: www.fp2p.org

# FOREWORD

George Bernard Shaw argued more than 100 years ago (in the preface to his 1907 play *Major Barbara*) that, 'The greatest of evils and the worst of crimes is poverty'. This certainly goes well beyond noting the fact that poverty is a huge tragedy, which ruins the lives of a great many people across the world. The immense tragedy of poverty is obvious enough: lives are battered, happiness stifled, creativity destroyed, freedoms eradicated by the misfortunes of poverty. But Shaw was not talking, on this occasion, about the hardship of poverty, or the misfortune that goes with it. He was commenting on the causation and consequences of poverty – that it is bred through evil and ends up being a crime. Why so? And how is that evil bred?

The classic view that poverty is just a shortage of income may be well established in our minds, but ultimately we have to see poverty as unfreedoms of various sorts: the lack of freedom to achieve even minimally satisfactory living conditions. Low income can certainly contribute to that, but so can a number of other influences, such as the lack of schools, absence of health facilities, unavailability of medicines, the subjugation of women, hazardous environmental features, and lack of jobs (something that affects more than the earning of incomes). Poverty can be reduced through expanding these facilities, but in order to guarantee that, what is needed is an enhancement of the power of people, especially of the afflicted people, to make sure that the facilities are expanded and the deficiencies removed.

People remain unempowered as a result of a variety of complex processes. The predicament of the poor need not be the result of deliberate cultivation of asymmetry of power by identifiable 'evil-doers'. But no matter how the deprivations develop, the gross asymmetries do not correct themselves. Quiet acceptance – by the victims and by others – of the inability of a great many people to achieve minimally effective capabilities and to have basic substantive freedoms acts as a huge barrier to social change. And so does the absence of public outrage at the terrible helplessness of millions of people. Thus the social evil draws not just on those who positively contribute to keeping people down, but also on all the people who are ready to tolerate the thoroughly unacceptable predicaments of millions of fellow human beings. The nature of this evil does not relate principally, even primarily, to the diagnosis of specific evil-doers. We have to see how the actions and inactions of a great many persons together lead to this social evil, and how a change of our priorities – our policies, our institutions, our individual and joint actions – can help to eliminate the atrocity of poverty.

This book from Oxfam explores many different ways in which poverty is being fought through the empowerment of the people whose deprivations relate ultimately to their helplessness in a badly organised world. Under the lead authorship of Duncan Green, the book discusses a number of different types of initiative across the world that have enhanced and expanded the powers of the powerless and through that have reduced the unfreedoms that characterise the poverty of the deprived. In bringing about these changes, the state obviously can – and does – have an important role to play, and yet the state is not the only responsible agency that can make a difference, nor is it the only instrument for tackling the general evil that society tends to tolerate and accept. If the evil of poverty and the crime associated with it can come through the actions and inactions of a great many persons, the remedy too can come from the co-operative efforts of people at large.

What the book calls 'active citizenship' can be a very effective way of seeking and securing solutions to these pervasive problems of powerlessness and unfreedom. The reader is told about various efforts to enhance the power of the unempowered, varying from the pursuit of women's rights in Morocco to the international campaign to ban landmines around the world. They can all make a huge difference in fighting intolerable and unacceptable deprivations. One case study after another is invoked, presented, and investigated to show how changes can be brought about through deliberate and organised efforts.

This book, which I hope will be widely read, is important for at least three distinct reasons. First, through discussing the ways and means of reducing and removing deprivation, the case studies bring out the role of powerlessness in generating deprivation and the effectiveness of empowerment in overcoming widespread deprivations.

Second, studies of this kind serve as much-needed correctives to the growing tendency to think of poverty removal mainly in terms of economic growth. There has certainly been some success in many countries in the world in reducing the proportion of people with very low incomes through economic growth, a success that is significant enough even though the achievements are often exaggerated. But the attraction – even the intoxication – of this success has also contributed to the mistaken understanding that (1) raising income is the uniquely privileged way – indeed the only secure way – of removing the unfreedoms of poverty (this downplays the role of general enhancement of economic, social, and political opportunities) and (2) high economic growth must necessarily be a sure-fire method of raising the incomes of the poor (this understates the social changes that are needed for expanding the freedom of the deprived to get a reasonable share in market-based aggregate economic growth). It is critically important, as a corrective, to clarify, with actual illustrations, that poverty has many dimensions, and that the removal of deprivation calls for much more than economic growth (important as it is).

Third, the recounting of a number of successful initiatives in removing deprivation through empowerment helps also to confront the pervasive pessimism that has become so common these days concerning the possibility of deliberately bringing about the changes that are needed. An exaggerated belief in the frailty of public efforts – whether of the state or of active citizens – generates a climate of cynicism and provides comfortable grounds for inaction and torpor, even when the widespread deprivations and sufferings are fairly well recognised. The recounting of what is actually being achieved – and how these achievements come about – can be very important as an antidote to inactivity based on exaggerated pessimism.

George Bernard Shaw may have chosen unusual words to characterise poverty as an 'evil' and a 'crime', but underlying that verbal choice is clearly a call for action, through a more forceful social analysis of the nature and causation of poverty that can lead to more determined efforts to eliminate the iniquity of poverty. In telling us what can be achieved by ordinary people through organised action, this book generates hope even as it enhances understanding of what is involved in the removal of poverty. The world does need hope as well as the know-how, and we have reason to be grateful for what we get from this important study of a rich collection of collaborative social action.

Amartya Sen,
*Honorary Adviser, Oxfam,*
*March 2008*

# PART ONE

# INTRODUCTION
## THE UNEQUAL WORLD

# THE UNEQUAL WORLD

Massive poverty and obscene inequality are such terrible scourges of
our times – times in which the world boasts breathtaking advances
in science, technology, industry, and wealth accumulation – that they
have to rank alongside slavery and apartheid as social evils.

NELSON MANDELA, LONDON, 2005

From cradle to grave, a person's life chances are dominated by the
extraordinary levels of inequality that characterise the modern world.
A girl born in Norway will almost certainly live to old age.[1] If she is
born in Sierra Leone, however, she has a one in four chance of dying
before her fifth birthday. A Norwegian girl can expect to go to a good
school, followed by university, and to be healthy and cared for right
through to old age. In Sierra Leone only two in three girls start school
at all, and many drop out along the way, deterred by having to find
'user fees' levied by the school or by the low standards of education, or
forced to stay home to care for their brothers and sisters, or to go out
to work to feed the family. Only one in four women is able to read and
write. University is an impossible dream.

The extent of global inequality is breathtaking. The income of the
world's 500 richest billionaires exceeds that of its poorest 416 million
people.[2] Every minute of every day, somewhere in the developing
world, a woman dies needlessly in childbirth or pregnancy, and 20
children are killed by avoidable diseases such as diarrhoea or malaria.[3]
Governments spend least on health care where the need is the greatest.[4]

2

Ending inequality's 'lottery by birth' is perhaps the greatest global challenge of the twenty-first century. And it is one that concerns all nations, since in a globalised world, poverty and suffering do not remain confined within borders, but spill over in the form of conflict, migration, and environmental degradation.

The world as a whole is far more unequal than any single country. Such grotesque unfairness would probably precipitate social and political meltdown were it to occur within a single country. One consequence of globalisation is that the world is increasingly coming to resemble just that: a single community bound together by ever-improving transportation and communications links. The political price of continued inequality can only rise.

According to a calculation by Oxfam based on income-distribution data held by the World Bank, if global inequality could be reduced to even that of Haiti (one of the most unequal countries in the world), the number of people living under $1 a day would be halved to 490 million. Go further, and achieve a distribution of income of a middle-ranking country (in terms of inequality), say Costa Rica, and $1-a-day poverty falls to 190 million – a fifth of the current total.

Even within countries, inequalities are grotesque across the whole spectrum of life chances. Children born into the poorest 20 per cent of households in Ghana or Senegal are two to three times more likely to die before the age of five than children born into the richest 20 per cent of households. In the UK, the government's Scientific Reference Group on Health Inequalities found that life expectancy in the country's wealthiest areas is seven to eight years longer than in the poorest areas.[5]

Inequality compounds, and often stems from, discrimination based on gender, race, or caste. Black Brazilians are twice as likely as white Brazilians to die a violent death, and are only one-third as likely to go to university.[6] In Guatemala, the number of children of European descent dying before they reach their fifth birthday is 56 in every 1,000, compared with 79 of every 1,000 indigenous children. In the Indian states of Uttar Pradesh and Bihar, primary school enrolment for scheduled caste and scheduled tribe girls is 37 per cent, compared with 60 per cent for girls from non-scheduled castes.[7] Among boys from non-scheduled castes, 77 per cent are enrolled.[8]

For poor people, such inequalities cancel out the benefits of living in a better-off society. Average income is three times higher in Brazil than it is in Viet Nam. Yet the poorest 10 per cent of Brazilians earn less than the poorest 10 per cent of Vietnamese.[9] Here too, rich countries have nothing to brag about. The infant mortality rate among indigenous Canadians is, on average, two to three times the national rate, and the average indigenous person will die 20 years earlier than the average Canadian.[10]

Regionally, Latin America is renowned for a level of inequality that is 'extensive, pervasive, and resilient' [11] and for the exceptional slice of national wealth that is owned by the very rich. Statistics show the USA to have a similarly skewed (and worsening) distribution of income and wealth.[12] Research in Africa suggests that, at least in terms of income, inequalities are as high as in Latin America, a finding that may surprise those who assume that, at African levels of poverty, all are more or less equal. Asia contains countries with low levels of inequality (Taiwan, Viet Nam) and others such as China, where inequality is rapidly approaching Latin American, US, and African levels.[13]

Nowhere is the injustice of inequality more evident than in the phenomenon of 'missing women'. Due to discrimination against girls and women, the world's female population is lower than it should be compared with males; discrimination starts even before birth through selective abortion and then continues as girl children are neglected with respect to nutrition and health care (compared with their brothers). Recent estimates put the number of missing women at 101.3 million – more than the total number of people killed in all the wars of the bloody twentieth century. Eighty million of these are Indian or Chinese: a staggering 6.7 per cent of the expected female population of China, and 7.9 per cent of the expected female population of India.[14]

## WHY INEQUALITY MATTERS[15]

Oxfam and other NGOs have long highlighted the moral repugnance of the world's yawning social and economic divides. There is something deeply unjust about a system that allows 800 million people to go hungry, while an epidemic of obesity blights millions of lives in rich countries (and increasingly, in cities in developing countries).

Extreme inequality provokes outrage and condemnation, because it violates the widely held notion that all people, wherever they are, enjoy certain basic rights. Addressing inequality is essential if countries are to live up to their obligations under the international human rights framework established by the UN, to guarantee equal civil and political rights and to pursue the 'progressive realisation' of economic, social, and cultural rights.[16]

Yet inequality and redistribution have been out of fashion with rich-country decision-makers for many years and warrant barely a mention in the Millennium Development Goals (MDGs), which emerged during the course of the 1990s.[17] In sway to the Washington Consensus view that 'a rising tide lifts all boats', rich-country leaders believed that economic growth alone would be enough to address poverty. By 2005, the manifest failure of that approach prompted a rash of high-profile publications from the World Bank, and the UN argued that tackling inequality is one of the most urgent tasks of our time.[18]

Academic literature used to stress the positive potential for inequality to reward 'wealth creators' and so encourage innovation and economic growth. Now economists argue that it is *equality* that is good for growth and makes that growth more effective at reducing poverty:

**Inequality wastes talent.** If women are excluded from top jobs, half the talent of any nation is squandered. By one estimate, if all states in India were to perform as well as the best (Karnataka) in eradicating gender discrimination in the workplace, national output would increase by a third.[19] When banks refuse to lend to poor people, good economic opportunities are wasted.

**Inequality undermines society and its institutions.** In an unequal society, elites find it easier to 'capture' governments and other institutions, and use them to further their own narrow interests, rather than the overall economic good.

**Inequality undermines social cohesion.** 'Vertical inequality' between individuals is linked to rises in crime, while 'horizontal inequality' (for example, between different ethnic groups) increases the likelihood of conflicts that can set countries back decades.

5

**Inequality limits the impact of economic growth on poverty.** A one-percentage point increase in growth will benefit poor people more in an equal society than in an unequal one.

**Inequality transmits poverty from one generation to the next.** Most cruelly, the poverty of a mother can blight the entire lives of her children. Each year in developing countries around 30 million children are born with impaired growth due to poor nutrition during foetal development. Babies born with a low birth weight are much more likely to die, and should they survive, are more likely to face a lifetime of sickness and poverty.[20]

While inequality has received greater attention in recent years, rich-country decision-makers have shied away from the idea of wide-spread redistribution of the kind that occurred in Europe after the Second World War or in the New Deal in the USA. The World Bank argues for equality of *opportunity* (for example, access to education, freedom from discrimination, equality before the law), but mentions greater equality of *outcome* only in relation to avoiding absolute deprivation. The redistribution of assets, through progressive taxation or radical land reform, is treated with great caution and its risks (for example, deterring investors) are continually stressed. When the rich world talks about development, it is more comfortable talking about poverty than about inequality, and it prefers inequality to redistribution.

Moreover, inequality holds the key to the poverty that exists around the world. The idea of ending poverty is not new, but the difference is that the global economy now has the resources to actually do so. The twentieth century delivered extraordinary progress in health, education, democracy, technology, and economic growth. Each year, the global economy churns out some $9,543 worth of goods and services per man, woman, and child – 25 times the $365 per annum that defines the 'extreme poverty' of a billion human beings.[21] There is more than enough to go round. According to the UN, $300bn a year would lift everyone on the planet above the extreme poverty line of $1 a day.[22] That is just a third of each year's global military spending.

## POVERTY, THE HUMAN CONSEQUENCE OF INEQUALITY

At the sharp end of the skewed distribution of power, assets, and opportunities are the billion people who live in extreme poverty. Poverty is about much more than a low income, something that becomes particularly clear when people living in poverty are asked to define it for themselves. It is a sense of powerlessness, frustration, exhaustion, and exclusion from decision-making, not to mention the relative lack of access to public services, the financial system, and just about any other source of official support. The academic Robert Chambers talks of the world being divided into 'uppers' and 'lowers', a description that fits numerous aspects of poverty, whether women's subjugation by men, the power imbalances between ethnic groups, or those between social classes.[23]

The many dimensions of poverty reinforce one another. Poor people are discriminated against, but many people are also poor because they suffer discrimination. In South Asia, households that face discrimination because of religion, ethnicity, or caste are significantly more vulnerable to labour market exploitation and debt bondage than other economically poor families.

In 2000, the World Bank published *Voices of the Poor*, a remarkable attempt at understanding poverty from the inside, based on discussions with 64,000 poor people around the world.[24] What emerged from these interviews was a complex and human account of poverty, encompassing issues that are often ignored in academic literature, such as the need to look good and feel loved, the importance of being able to give one's children a good start in life, or the mental anguish that all too often accompanies poverty. The overall conclusion was that, 'again and again, powerlessness seems to be at the core of the bad life'.

The reverse of such 'multi-dimensional' poverty is not simply wealth (although income is important), but a wider notion of well-being, springing from health, physical safety, meaningful work, connection to community, and other non-monetary factors. That is why good development practices build on the skills, strengths, and ideas of people living in poverty – on their assets – rather than treating them as empty receptacles of charity.

7

Although this multi-dimensional view of poverty is widely accepted in theory, in practice, attention centres on income poverty, most commonly defined by the international 'extreme poverty' line of $1 a day, which forms the basis of the first MDG, that of halving the proportion of the world's population living in extreme poverty by 2015.[25] Anyone living below that line is judged to be unable to feed themselves properly. The $2-a-day 'poverty line' is seen as the minimum required to provide food, clothing, and shelter.

Extreme income poverty is falling over time. Between 1990 and 2004 the number of people worldwide in developing countries living on less than $1 a day fell from 1.25 billion to 980 million. The proportion of people living in extreme poverty fell from nearly a third (32 per cent) to 19 per cent over the same period.[26] However, the rate of improvement has slowed in recent years.[27]

The nature and location of poverty is also changing. The UN notes 'an increased tendency for people to rotate in and out of poverty, a rise in urban poverty and stagnation in rural poverty, and increases in the proportion of informal workers among the urban poor and in the number of unemployed poor'.[28] In 2007, the earth's urban population overtook its rural population for the first time in human history, driven mainly by growth in cities in developing countries. Of the three billion urban residents in the world today, one billion live in slums, and are vulnerable to disease, violence, and social, political, and economic exclusion. UN-Habitat estimates that the world's slum population will double in the next 30 years, outpacing the predicted rate of urbanisation.[29]

Globally, achievements in reducing income poverty can be attributed largely to the economic take-off of China and India. Despite worsening inequality, China in particular has made extraordinary progress, reducing the proportion of its people living in extreme poverty from two-thirds in 1981 (634 million people) to just one in ten (128 million people) in 2004. Many countries have shown how to grapple successfully with the other dimensions of poverty. Egypt has sustained one of the fastest declines in child mortality rates in the world since 1980. Bangladesh, Honduras, Nicaragua, and Viet Nam have also achieved rapid progress.[30]

Such advances should of course be celebrated and learned from, but should not be allowed to mask the plight of numerous countries and sectors in which progress has been slow or non-existent – and in many cases, poverty has been getting worse. In sub-Saharan Africa, the ranks of extremely poor people increased by 58.3 million between 1990 and 2004.

Beyond income poverty, too, the glass is not even close to half full. Compared with the position in 1990, there are 30 million fewer children of primary school age out of school now, but more than 70 million still do not receive an education, 57 per cent of them girls. Today, there are 2.8 million fewer child deaths than there were in 1990, but more than 10 million children still die each year.[31] Almost all such deaths are preventable. Every minute, two children die from malaria alone.[32]

The rapid scale-up in global immunisation since 2001 through the Global Alliance for Vaccines and Immunization has also brought down the death toll, saving an estimated half-a-million lives. Yet diseases such as measles, diphtheria, and tetanus, which can be prevented with a simple vaccination, account for two to three million childhood deaths every year. For every child who dies, many more will fall sick or will miss school, trapped in a vicious circle that links poor health in childhood to poverty in adulthood. Like the 500,000 women who die each year from pregnancy-related causes, more than 98 per cent of the children who die each year live in poor countries.[33] That some poor countries have brought an end to such pain and suffering makes these deaths all the more unacceptable.

Poor health is compounded by dirty water. Another 1.2 billion people have gained access to clean water over the past decade, but a further 1.1 billion still lack access to safe water and 2.6 billion have no access to improved sanitation.[34] Diseases transmitted through water or human waste are the second biggest cause of death among children worldwide, after respiratory tract infection. The overall death toll: an estimated 3,900 children every day.[35]

Hunger combines with ill health to weaken the bodies and under-mine the futures of poor people. More than 880 million people, including one in four pre-school children, are undernourished, even though the world has enough food for its whole population. The appalling toll is both human and economic – for every year that hunger remains at such levels, premature death and disability rob developing countries of around $500bn in lost productivity and earnings.[36]

While poverty has been falling since 1980, HIV and AIDS have spread their grip across the poorest countries in the world, and AIDS has become a disease that mainly strikes women in developing countries. In 2007, an estimated 2.1 million people died from the disease, and another 2.5 million became infected with HIV. Almost all of these deaths were in the developing world, with 77 per cent of them in Africa. Some 33.2 million people are now living with HIV – 22.5 million of them in sub-Saharan Africa.[37]

Some of the billion people who live on less than $1 a day are worse off than others. Many of them move in and out of poverty, according to the vagaries of the weather, personal circumstances, and the economy. An Oxfam survey of slum dwellers in the Indian city of Lucknow showed that over a three-year period, out of 424 households, 110 stayed poor, 162 stayed above the poverty line, and the remainder – just over a third – moved in and out of poverty.[38]

Worldwide, some 340–470 million people constitute the 'chronically poor', trapped below the poverty line with little immediate prospect of escape. Chronic poverty exists in all regions, but is heavily concentrated in South Asia and sub-Saharan Africa. Chronic poverty particularly affects children, older people, and people with disabilities, who face layers of social discrimination, often based on ethnicity, religion, or language.[39]

Multiple deprivations reinforce one other. Indigenous children sent to schools that use a language foreign to them fail to acquire the education needed to find decent jobs and earn their way out of poverty, even when racial prejudice does not deny them equal opportunities. For these people, reducing the extent of their social and political exclusion and their vulnerability to shocks is more pressing than economic growth (since many of them are jobless and are likely to remain so).

## ACTIVE CITIZENSHIP AND EFFECTIVE STATES

As Nelson Mandela says, poverty and extreme inequality rank alongside slavery and apartheid as evils that can be vanquished. This book argues for a radical redistribution of opportunities, but also of power and assets, to break the cycle of poverty and inequality.

People living in poverty certainly need opportunities, such as access to decent education, health care, water, and sanitation, and assistance to help them cope with the shocks of everyday life. Poor people need power over their own destinies and over the factors that influence them, such as party politics, the justice system, and the markets for land, labour, and goods and services.

In recent memory, a combination of pressure from below and enlightened leadership from above has produced some remarkable exercises in redistribution. In several East Asian countries, for example, elites have embraced the long-term case for equality, to prevent social division and to stoke a thriving economy. Taiwan and Viet Nam have combined astonishing growth with high levels of equity. Indonesia and Malaysia have managed to reduce inequality over an extended period through government-led redistribution and generation of employment.[40]

In Brazil under the governments of Fernando Henrique Cardoso and Luiz Inácio Lula da Silva, popular movements have carried business elites along in redistributing wealth and opportunity in a hitherto appallingly unequal society. In the past decade Brazil has managed to lower its world inequality ranking from second to tenth by a mixture of good economic management (for example, controlling inflation, which customarily hits poor people hardest) and redistributing income to poor people through various government schemes such as the *Bolsa Família* (Family Stipend), which pays poor families a monthly stipend if they ensure that their children attend school and are vaccinated.[41] Lula's first term saw the poorest 10 per cent of the population increase their incomes by 7 per cent a year, while the incomes of the richest 10 per cent stagnated. As a result, some five million Brazilians were lifted out of poverty, and inequality fell to its lowest level in 30 years.[42] A similar story of progress built on popular pressure and state action could be told of South Africa since the end of apartheid.

11

This book explores these and other efforts to grapple with inequality and poverty in three key areas: politics, markets, and vulnerability. In each case it finds that development, and in particular efforts to tackle inequality, is best achieved through a combination of active citizens and effective states.

By active citizenship, we mean that combination of rights and obligations that link individuals to the state, including paying taxes, obeying laws, and exercising the full range of political, civil, and social rights. Active citizens use these rights to improve the quality of political or civic life, through involvement in the formal economy or formal politics, or through the sort of collective action that historically has allowed poor and excluded groups to make their voices heard. For those who do not enjoy full rights of citizenship, such as migrants or (in some cultures) women, the first step is often to organise to assert those rights.

By effective states, we mean states that can guarantee security and the rule of law, and can design and implement an effective strategy to ensure inclusive economic growth. Effective states, often known as 'developmental states', must be accountable to citizens and able to guarantee their rights.

Why focus on effective states? Because history shows that no country has prospered without a state than can actively manage the development process. The extraordinary transformations of countries such as South Korea, Taiwan, Botswana, or Mauritius have been led by states that ensure health and education for all, and which actively promote and manage the process of economic growth. After 20 years of erosion by deregulation, 'structural adjustment programmes', and international trade and aid agreements, many states are weak or absent. But there are no shortcuts, and neither aid nor NGOs can take its place; the road to development lies through the state.

Why active citizenship? Because people working together to determine the course of their own lives, fighting for rights and justice in their own societies, are critical in holding states, private companies, and others to account. Active citizenship has inherent merits: people living in poverty must have a voice in deciding their own destiny, rather than be treated as passive recipients of welfare or government action. What is more, the system – governments, judiciaries, parliaments, and companies – cannot tackle poverty and inequality by treating

12

people as 'objects' of government action or other action. Rather, people must be recognised as 'subjects', conscious of and actively demanding their rights, for efforts to bear fruit.

Active citizens, of course, are not limited to people living in poverty. Members of the middle class often play a vital role in supporting grassroots organisations, helping them deal with those in power, and challenging entrenched attitudes and beliefs among elites.

Most development practitioners acknowledge the centrality of citizenship and the state. However, in practice, for many NGOs development is about citizenship only, while for many official donor agencies and government ministries development is only about the state. The former elevate active citizenship to be synonymous with progress, while the latter reduce it to periodic elections and 'consultation' by government. Similarly, the latter elevate the state to the be-all-and-end-all of development, while the former eschew it as beyond their remit. In Oxfam's experience, both are central to the pursuit of any development worth the name.

The focus on active citizens and effective states underlines the need to grapple with the central role of politics in development. Too often, discussions about development are conducted on the basis of policies rather than politics. Advocates adopt an 'If I ruled the world, I would do X' approach, often portraying political leaders and movements in developing countries as irritants or obstacles. At best, politics is reduced to the depoliticised issue of 'governance'. Yet it is such leaders and movements that change societies, for better or worse, and understanding and engaging with politics is essential.

This book argues that active citizenship and effective states are compatible, as well as desirable. The challenge is to combine them as early as possible in a country's development. However, the relationship between the two is complex. They march to different rhythms, the steady grind of state machineries contrasting with the ebb and flow of civil society activism. In many cases, long-term development requires an element of deferred gratification, requiring businesses to reinvest rather than skim off profits, rich people to accept redistribution of wealth and income for the sake of national stability and growth, and poor people to limit demands for the improved wages and social spending that they so desperately need.

This in turn requires a 'social contract', a deal, whether explicit or implicit, that builds confidence and trust between citizens and the state. The nature of active citizenship and effective states, and their interaction, is explored in Part 2, which discusses the factors that contribute to active citizenship: the concept of rights, attitudes and beliefs, essential services, and access to information. This section also addresses property rights, corruption, and the spread of democracy.

There is an argument for including the private sector as a third pillar in this scheme, alongside state and citizens, interacting with the others both positively and negatively. The private sector creates jobs and products, transfers knowledge and technology, and contributes taxes to the state. Crucially, it drives the economic growth that is so vital to long-term development. However, over-powerful corporations can also undermine states (for example, through bribery or inappropriate lobbying) or citizenship (by denying labour rights).

This book instead portrays a flourishing private sector as one objective of the interaction between effective states and active citizens, arguing that, between them, they can create enabling conditions for the kind of equitable, sustainable private sector activity and economic growth on which development relies. The private sector, along with the critical role of markets in tackling poverty and inequality, is discussed in Part 3, which sketches out the sort of economics needed to deliver real development, and its implications for rural livelihoods, labour, and growth models.

A particularly important role for citizens and states is dealing with vulnerability. People living in poverty are more vulnerable than those who are well-off to personal disasters such as sickness or job loss, or at a community level to weather events, earthquakes, or outbreaks of conflict that invariably cause the greatest suffering among the poorest people.

A holistic effort to reduce vulnerability should be based on supporting and strengthening the self-organisation of poor people, and providing protection, whether at state or international level – what we term 'human security'. Vulnerability and the search for such security are discussed in Part 4, which explores the increasing interest in social protection policies, the nature of and responses to hunger and famine, the growing impact of climate change on poor people and communities, and other risks such as HIV and AIDS, natural disasters, and violence and conflict.

While the history of development success shows that the crucible of change is primarily national and local, such change takes place in an increasingly globalised world of ever tighter political, economic, and cultural ties. In such a world, rich countries, societies, and corporations carry a great responsibility. The deeply inequitable forms of global governance must be overhauled so that global phenomena such as climate change, capital flows, migration, conflict, and trade and investment are managed in the interests of human sustainability. In other areas, powerful governments and international institutions should do *less*: for example, refraining from imposing particular economic policies on developing countries, and recognising that effective states and active citizens are the main actors in the drama of development and must be allowed to experiment, fail, learn, and succeed.

Citizens and states in rich countries should concentrate on putting their own houses in order, cracking down on their current harmful activities, such as the arms trade, restrictions on the free flow of knowledge and technology, corporate malpractice, the forced liberalisation of trade and capital markets, and grotesque levels of planet-destroying carbon emissions. This 'stop doing harm' agenda should be complemented by 'global citizenship' – active solidarity by people and governments in the rich world with the struggles of poor people and their communities within developing countries. How this might be undertaken in the international systems for finance, trade, aid, humanitarian relief, and climate change is addressed in Part 5.

The combination of citizens and state is not intended to be a blueprint, still less an intellectual straitjacket. As this book stresses, different countries have followed diverse paths to development. But Oxfam's experience on the ground suggests that some such combination lies at the heart of most, if not all, attempts to build a humane and sustainable development path, and is likely to play a vital role in tackling inequality and poverty during the course of the current century.

Perhaps the best way to illustrate the complex and subtle interplay between citizens and states is through concrete experiences of change. This book takes eight such examples at community, national, and

15

global levels, and explores 'how change happens', using an approach sketched out in the Annex. This is a 'work in progress', and suggestions on how to improve its methodology are particularly welcome.

## THIS BOOK

*From Poverty to Power* is partly the author's personal reflection, part conversation – the result of prolonged discussion within Oxfam and with numerous other development professionals, including some with views very different from our own. Given its origins, the content of the book inevitably concentrates on those areas in which Oxfam has most experience, and draws out a common story from that experience in the field.

The book is not a comprehensive statement of Oxfam's current thinking or of Oxfam's agreed official policies – for these, readers may consult Oxfam International's strategic plan[43] – but is intended as a contribution to an evolving debate. In that spirit, readers wishing to join in the conversation should visit the Oxfam website.[44]

Beyond the moral outrage aroused by so much needless injustice and suffering, this book is driven by the additional urgency of the development challenge today, when the planet's ecosystem itself is under threat. We need to build a secure, fair, and sustainable world before we pass the point of no return. As Martin Luther King Jr. presciently wrote 40 years ago:

> *We are confronted with the fierce urgency of now. Human progress is neither automatic nor inevitable... In this unfolding conundrum of life and history there is such a thing as being too late... We may cry out desperately for time to pause in her passage, but time is deaf to every plea and rushes on. Over the bleached bones and jumbled residues of numerous civilizations are written the pathetic words: Too late.* [45]

This book is predicated on the belief that it is not too late, provided leaders, organisations, and individuals act. Starting today.

PART TWO

# POWER AND POLITICS

# THE POLITICAL ROOTS OF DEVELOPMENT

Jeronima Quiviquivi is a force of nature. Surrounded by the youngest of her six children, sitting outside her new house on the edge of the indigenous village of Monteverde in the muggy heat of a tropical afternoon, she recalls the struggles of her people, the Chiquitano Indians of lowland Bolivia.

> *My father never realised about our rights. We just did what the*
> *white people told us – only they could be in power, be president. We*
> *couldn't even go into the town centre – people swore at us. But then*
> *we got our own organisation and elected our own leaders and*
> *that's when we realised we had rights.*

Organising themselves at first under the guise of a soccer league – the only way they could meet and talk with Chiquitanos from other villages – the indigenous activists of Monteverde fought for things that mattered to them: land, education, rights, a political voice. Moments of confrontation helped build a common history: bursting into the local government offices to seize the files proving that the unpaid labour they were forced to provide had been outlawed years before; a march on the distant capital, La Paz, which bolstered their sense of common identity with Bolivia's highland indigenous majority (see case study on page 31).

Now the Chiquitanos have seized the positions of what was once white power: they have their own mayors and senators and, in La Paz, South America's first ever indigenous president, Evo Morales.

And with power came the promise of precious land: after a ten-year campaign, on 3 July 2007 the Chiquitanos of Monteverde clinched an agreement with the government that granted them a 'land of communal origin' of 1m hectares.

The course of this epic struggle also transformed relationships at home. Jeronima's husband, himself a local leader, now looks after the kids when she has a meeting. 'We used to meet separately as women, but now we meet with the men – we're no longer afraid,' she says.

The Chiquitanos' journey out of marginalisation underlines the central role of power and politics in development. The interplay between individuals, families, communities, and states can open paths to rights, security, and prosperity, or it can condemn communities to vulnerability and poverty. Power and politics will determine whether the world can build on the extraordinary pace of political and social change of the twentieth century in order to eradicate extreme poverty and tackle inequality and injustice.

At the core of power and politics lie citizens and effective states. By 'citizens' we mean anyone living in a particular place, even if they are not formally eligible to vote, such as migrants or children. By 'effective states', we mean states that can guarantee security and the rule of law, design and implement an effective strategy to ensure inclusive economic growth, and are accountable to and able to guarantee the rights of their citizens. The interaction between active citizens and effective states, with its complexity, its cross-class alliances, its peaks and troughs, and its many contradictions will be discussed below.

At an individual level, active citizenship means developing self-confidence and overcoming the insidious way in which the condition of being relatively powerless can become internalised. In relation to other people, it means developing the ability to negotiate and influence decisions. And when empowered individuals work together, it means involvement in collective action, be it at the village or neighbourhood level, or more broadly.[1] Ultimately, active citizenship means engaging with the political system to build an effective state, and assuming some degree of responsibility for the public domain, leaving behind simple notions of 'them' and 'us'. Otherwise, in the memorable phrase of the French philosopher Bertrand de Jouvenel, 'A society of sheep must in time beget a government of wolves'.[2]

Active citizenship includes, but is not confined to, political activism. It comprises any individual action with social consequences, which may include participation in faith groups or neighbourhood associations, 'social entrepreneurship' directing business activities to social ends, and a panoply of other social organisations, if their benefits extend beyond the purely personal or familial. Necessarily it is blurred at the edges – and is distinct from the broader concept of 'social capital' (which includes any social network), being distinguished by its transformatory character and its engagement with the structures of power, in particular the state.

Such an assertion of power is both an end in itself – a crucial kind of freedom – and a means to ensure that the different institutions of society (the state, the market, the community, and the family) respect people's rights and meet their needs, via laws, rules, policies, and day-to-day practices. Institutions often discriminate against women, indigenous communities, disabled people, and other specific groups. Yet when individuals join together to challenge discrimination, they can transform the institutions that oppress them. In contrast with portrayals of poor people as passive 'victims' (of disasters, or poverty, or famine) or as 'beneficiaries' (of aid), in this development vision poor people's own 'agency' takes centre stage. In the words of Bangladeshi academic Naila Kabeer, 'From a state of powerlessness that manifests itself in a feeling of "I cannot", activism contains an element of collective self-confidence that results in a feeling of "we can".' [3]

Across the world, Oxfam has seen social, political, and economic activism by people living in poverty achieve profound and lasting improvements in their lives. It constitutes a central means of combating deep-rooted inequalities by redistributing power, voice, opportunities, and assets to those who historically have lacked all four. Activism is more often local than national, and more often national than global, although increasingly it takes place on all three levels. It is often about resisting imposed changes, which in the process may create positive alternatives. It usually addresses the allocation of resources, such as land, public spending, or credit. And it nearly always pursues reforms rather than revolution, although the reforms pursued are often radical, and the accumulation of reforms can, over time, constitute a revolution.

Nevertheless, activism alone is not enough. Of all the institutions that exercise power over people's lives, it is the state that is capable of channelling the power of individual initiative and the market toward long-term development goals.

In the interaction between states and citizens lie the seeds of developmental success and failure. That interaction includes both the formal politics of elections, parliamentary debate, and party activism, and the wider engagement of active citizenship.

Development is seldom peaceful. When a country transforms itself, social and economic structures change rapidly, new classes are born, and new wealth is accumulated at historically unprecedented rates. Losers and winners in this upheaval often come to blows. It took centuries for this social and economic transformation to manifest itself in today's industrialised countries, yet in developing countries a shock of a similar magnitude has been telescoped into a period of decades.[4]

In some countries, this process of 'creative destruction' has led to a viable and dynamic capitalism. In others, it has led to 'spoils politics' – the theft of resources by unproductive classes – and a descent into anarchy. The nature and political evolution of the state is crucial in determining which path a country follows.

Effective, accountable states are essential for development. States ensure health, education, water, and sanitation for all; they guarantee security, the rule of law, and social and economic stability; and they regulate, develop, and upgrade the economy. There are no short cuts, either through the private sector or social movements, although these too play a crucial role.

A central challenge for development is thus how to build states that are both effective and accountable, able to tackle poverty and inequality in all their forms (not just income), and ensure the respect for rights that allows active citizenship to flourish. Effectives states are critical in reducing vulnerability to shocks and enabling poor people and communities to benefit from the market, as will be discussed elsewhere.

However murky their origins, modern-day states are duty-bound by international law to uphold people's rights, and are increasingly evolving into this role under pressure from citizens' movements and

the international community. For this reason, politics writ large –
the interface of citizens and states – is the focus of this part of the
book, which examines the challenges of political action, as well as
evidence of progress towards ever greater freedom.

# I HAVE RIGHTS, THEREFORE I AM

The highest manifestation of life consists in this: that a being governs
its own actions.

ST THOMAS AQUINAS, THIRTEENTH CENTURY

An old development saying runs: 'If you give a man a fish, you feed
him for a day. If you teach him how to fish, you feed him for a lifetime.'
Fine and good, except that, as the case study on the fishing communities
of Tikamgarh on page 146 shows, he must have rights to fish the pond
in the first place. Moreover, as a village leader from Cambodia points
out, 'A man is just as likely to be *a woman*'. She adds:

> That woman already knows how to fish. She would like her river
> left alone by illegal logging companies or fish poachers. She would
> prefer that her government not build huge dams with the help of the
> Asian Development Bank, dams that have damaged her livelihood.
> She would prefer that the police not violently evict communities to
> make way for the dam. She doesn't want charity. She would like
> respect for her basic rights. [5]

Feeling that one has a right to something is much more powerful than
simply needing or wanting it. It implies that someone else has a duty
to respond. Rights are long-term guarantees, a set of structural claims
or entitlements that enable people, particularly the most vulnerable
and excluded in society, to make demands on those in power, who are
known in the jargon as 'duty-bearers'. These duty-bearers in turn have

a responsibility to respect, protect, and fulfil the rights of 'rights-holders'. Rights therefore are naturally bound up with notions of citizenship, participation, and power.

Rights alone are not enough, however. In the words of Indian economist Amartya Sen, individuals need capabilities – rights and the ability to exercise them – an ability that is undermined when people are poor, illiterate, destitute, sick, lack vital information, or live in fear of violence. Having the 'right' to go to school is of no use to girls if the pressure of domestic tasks, prejudice in the home or community, or coming last in line at family meal-times means that they must spend their days hungry, carrying water, cleaning, or looking after younger siblings. Capabilities determine what people can do, and who they can be.[6] The ability to achieve material security through productive labour is a crucial aspect of such capabilities.

All rights are necessarily related to responsibilities, constituting the web of moral connections and obligations that binds society together. All people, however poor, have responsibilities towards their communities, but powerful individuals and organisations, notably governments, bear a particular burden of responsibility if we are to build a society based on equity and fairness.

## THE ROOTS OF RIGHTS

The idea that all people are of equal dignity and worth, and have natural rights, developed in Western Europe in the seventeenth and eighteenth centuries as a tool to protect individuals from the arbitrary power of the state. Some authors speak of two 'human rights revolutions': the first around the period of the US Declaration of Independence (1776) and the French Declaration on the Rights of Man and the Citizen (1789); the second linked with the post-Second World War era of globalisation with the Universal Declaration of Human Rights (1948) which, for the first time in history, acknowledged human rights as a global responsibility.[7] That second revolution is still under way, as human rights frameworks expand with new treaties that address gender, ethnicity, and the rights of children. It forms the basis of the emerging system of global governance and international law (see Part 5).

Progress in human rights became one of the hallmarks of the second half of the twentieth century, with the spread of democracy and decolonisation leading to a massive expansion in the proportion of the world's population that exercised some degree of say in the organisation of society. The advent of mass literacy and improvements in health meanwhile strengthened their ability to exercise those rights.

Human rights can be grouped into three distinct generations: civil and political, or so-called 'negative' rights such as freedom from torture, which the state must guarantee; economic, social, and cultural, or 'positive rights', such as the right to education, which the state must finance and actively promote; and finally collective rights, such as self-determination, which the state must respect. Most recently, the UN has tried to extend the notion of rights to non-state actors such as corporations.[8]

From universal franchise and the abolition of slavery onwards, new forms of rights have initially been viewed by those in positions of power as unreasonable or unjustified, but have slowly been absorbed into the mainstream consensus. The latest candidates are the culturally contentious issues of equal rights for women and for children.

For many years after the UN Declaration, the rhetoric of human rights was reduced to a weapon in the propaganda battles of the Cold War. As the economist J.K. Galbraith once joked, 'Under capitalism, man exploits man. Under socialism, it is the other way around.' Neither side had much time for human rights. The West pointed the finger at socialist countries for denying civil and political rights. The East criticised the capitalist countries for their failure to secure economic and social rights for all citizens and for supporting cruel dictators such as Zaire's Mobuto Sese Seko or Chile's Augusto Pinochet. There was little active interaction between the worlds of rights and development.

The end of the Cold War brought convergence, with many development practitioners combining the two disciplines into what became known as a 'rights-based approach' to development. By reuniting economic and social rights with political and civil rights, this approach aimed to build a comprehensive vision of a new, just, and viable 'social contract' between state and citizen.[9]

25

The worlds of human rights and development feel very different. Put crudely, lawyers and scholars dominate the former, and economists and engineers the latter. While this can lead to communication problems between two sets of mutually impenetrable jargon, both sides have much to learn from one another. According to the UN:

> *The tradition of human rights brings legal tools and institutions – laws, the judiciary, and the process of litigation – as means to secure freedoms and human development. Rights also lend moral legitimacy and the principle of social justice to the objectives of human development. The rights perspective helps shift the priority to the most deprived and excluded. It also directs attention to the need for information and political voice for all people as a development issue – and to civil and political rights as integral parts of the development process.*
>
> *Human development, in turn, brings a dynamic long-term perspective to the fulfilment of rights. It directs attention to the socio-economic context in which rights can be realised – or threatened. Human development thus contributes to building a long-run strategy for the realisation of rights. In short, human development is essential for realising human rights, and human rights are essential for full human development.* [10]

Sometimes making use of the international human rights system, citizens in many countries have successfully pressed governments to pass laws protecting rights. One of the leaders in this field has been India, which in recent years has seen several groundbreaking initiatives on the rights to food and information.[11] Numerous countries now have ombudsmen to whom citizens can appeal if they believe their rights have been violated. Most countries now also recognise the rights of children. Such laws, often introduced in response to UN conventions, exert a permanent 'drip-drip' impact on attitudes and practices. These subterranean shifts in notions of rights occasionally explode into the political daylight when groups of citizens seek political redress, as witnessed by events in recent decades in La Paz, Kiev, Berlin, Tehran, and Manila, where mass demonstrations of people demanding their rights overthrew governments and ushered in eras of rapid change.

## RIGHTS AND POVERTY

Oxfam starts from the premise that poverty is a state of relative powerlessness in which people are denied the ability to control crucial aspects of their lives.[12] Poverty is a symptom of deeply rooted inequities and unequal power relationships, institutionalised through policies and practices at the levels of state, society, and household. People often lack money, land, or freedom because they are discriminated against on the grounds of one or more aspects of their personal identity – their class, gender, ethnicity, age, or sexuality – constraining their ability to claim and control the resources that allow them choices in life.

One in seven people in the world – about 900 million people – experiences discrimination on the basis of ethnic, linguistic, or religious identities alone.[13] These excluded groups form the hard core of the 'chronic poor'. Some unequal power relationships are due to age-old injustices. In the Indian state of Uttar Pradesh in northern India, for instance, close to 80 per cent of women require their husband's permission to visit a health centre, and 60 per cent have to seek permission before stepping outside their house. Other such relationships are the more recent result of economic globalisation and imbalances in negotiating power between rich and poor countries.

The underlying purpose of a rights-based approach to development is to identify ways of transforming the self-perpetuating vicious circle of poverty, disempowerment, and conflict into a virtuous circle in which all people, as rights-holders, can demand accountability from states as duty-bearers, and where duty-bearers have both the willingness and capacity to fulfil, protect, and promote people's human rights.

A rights-based approach rejects the notion that people living in poverty can only meet their basic needs as passive recipients of charity. People are the active subjects of their own development, as they seek to realise their rights. Development actors, including the state, should seek to build people's capabilities to do so, by guaranteeing their rights to the essentials of a decent life: education, health care, water and sanitation, and protection against violence, repression, or sudden disaster. Less gritty issues such as access to information and technology are no less important in the long run.

Such a rights-based approach anchors the debate about equity and justice in principles endorsed by the international community and codified in international law. In an era when nations are subject to a multiplicity of forces affecting the state's capacity to address the needs of its citizens, the human rights framework helps governments and citizens to pursue justice.[14] A rights-based approach compels Oxfam and other rights-based agencies to 'raise the bar' on their own accountability, lest they unwittingly perpetuate outmoded notions of charity, overlook discrimination and exclusion, and reinforce existing imbalances of power.

## RIGHTS AND POWER

People's capacity to realise their rights, and states' capacity to fulfil them, are of course dependent on their relative power. Inequality in power drives the motor of social and economic inequality in the lives of poor and rich alike. Power resembles a force field that permeates households, communities, and society at large, shaping both the interactions and innermost thoughts of individuals and groups. And like a force field, it is often only detectable through its impact on events.

Development policies and practitioners sometimes act as if power did not exist. When aid donor and recipient nations agreed the Paris Declaration on Aid Effectiveness in 2005, they used the words 'partner' and 'partnership' 96 times, but 'power' not once, ignoring the deeply unequal power relationships between rich and poor countries.[15] Understanding power and how it shapes the lives and struggles of both powerful and powerless people is essential in the effort to build the combination of active citizenship and effective states that lies at the heart of development.

Power is often understood merely in terms of one person's ability to achieve a desired end, with or without the consent of others, but it comes in at least four different forms:

- Power *over*: the power of the strong over the weak.
  This power is often hidden – for example, what elites manage to keep off the table of political debate.
- Power *to*: meaning the capability to decide actions and carry them out.

- Power *with*: collective power, through organisation, solidarity, and joint action.
- Power *within*: personal self-confidence, often linked to culture, religion, or other aspects of collective identity, which influence what thoughts and actions appear legitimate or acceptable.

Power is real, but conceptually slippery. Any individual or group of people has multiple relationships, in which they are more or less powerful. Nobody is entirely powerless: a mother has power over her children, but may be at the mercy of a violent male partner. Her children in turn have power over their younger siblings. Moreover, changing the distribution of power is not always a 'zero sum game': one person acquiring power need not require another person to lose power in equal measure.

A rights-based approach supports poor people to build up their power by addressing both their self-confidence – 'power within' – and their organisation – 'power with'. Visits to Oxfam's programmes on the ground reveal dozens of gripping personal stories of how contact with outside agents – NGOs, activists, inspirational leaders, academics, or others – has helped to catalyse a process of personal transformation in which, as with the Chiquitanos in Bolivia (see page 31), the scales fell from people's eyes and they became aware of their rights. According to Chiquitano activist Miguel Rivera, 'A sense of our rights came from outside, from political leaders and ILO Convention 169 [on indigenous rights]. It was important, it made our indigenous part wake up.' [16]

Previously marginalised people and groups then have the 'power within' to demand their rights by challenging elites with 'power over' them, and assert their rights by acquiring the 'power to' do the things they need to improve their lives.[17] Many of the best-known development initiatives, such as India's Self Employed Women's Association (SEWA), have followed this 'bottom up' process.

'Power with' is not always progressive, as a long tradition of 'uncivil society', from the Russian pogroms to the genocide in Rwanda, attests. More importantly, 'power over' is not always malign. To achieve lasting improvements in people's lives requires harnessing the state's 'power over', not doing away with it.

Within families, communities, and nations at large, people in positions of power are usually better resourced, connected, organised, and skilled in pursuing their interests, and can use that power to maintain privileges and exclude others from the charmed circle. Economic power and political power are always interwoven. Elites in all countries have historically gone to extreme, often bloody, lengths to maintain and even increase their dominance. That structures and practices on issues such as the lack of transparency or accountability reinforce these inequities is no accident: efforts to reform them meet dogged, sometimes violent, resistance. Redistributing economic and political power more fairly is often the first step towards disrupting this self-perpetuating cycle of inequality.

The founder of the British National Health Service, the Welsh radical Aneurin Bevan, believed that 'the purpose of getting power is to give it away', and indeed those in power may opt to share it, for a combination of altruistic and selfish reasons. In the end, though, harnessing power for development depends not on the virtues or calculations of individual leaders, but on a combination of public watchfulness and institutional checks and balances, such as the division of powers, rule of law, and an independent media – all based on the guarantee of rights.

Asserting rights can be slow, legal, and peaceful, but often it involves moments of confrontation and struggle, when the powerful resist, often with force, and the newly empowered refuse to back down. In some of the epic struggles for justice in recent times, such as the fight against apartheid in South Africa, violent confrontation lasted for decades and became a crucible in which a new collective national identity was forged. Even when such dramatic events are over, the struggle and negotiation for the fulfilment of rights continues.

## HOW CHANGE HAPPENS CASE STUDY
## A REVOLUTION FOR BOLIVIA'S CHIQUITANO PEOPLE

On 3 July 2007, after 12 years of unremitting and often frustrating struggle, the Chiquitano people of Bolivia – a group numbering some 120,000 people – won legal title to the 1m-hectare indigenous territory of Monteverde in the eastern department of Santa Cruz. Evo Morales, the country's first indigenous president, and several ministers attended the ceremony. So did three elected mayors, ten local councillors (six women, four men), a senator, a congressman, and two members of the Constituent Assembly – all of them Chiquitanos.

Such an event would have been unthinkable even a generation ago. Until the 1980s, the Chiquitanos lived in near-feudal conditions, required to work unpaid for local authorities, landowners, and the Church, and prevented from owning land.

The Chiquitanos are best known outside Bolivia as an indigenous group that survived some of the worst impacts of colonisation on Jesuit *reducciones* (missions), where they became adept baroque musicians and built extraordinary churches that still attract tourists to the region. Their story was told in the 1986 film *The Mission*.

In the nineteenth century the Bolivian government colonised the eastern lowlands. During the ensuing 30-year rubber boom, thousands of Chiquitanos and other indigenous peoples were enslaved on rubber estates. Despite the radical revolution that swept the highlands in 1952, in the isolated East, indigenous families continued to be bought and sold along with the estates where they worked.

Change began to stir in the 1980s, as indigenous identity slowly began to replace the class-based peasant identity promoted by the nationalism of the 1952 revolution. For the first time, the Chiquitanos began to identify themselves as indigenous people, with their own particular demands, and rapidly built their own Chiquitano Indigenous Organization (OICH), representing more than 450 communities. As one elderly woman explained: 'Only a short while ago did we begin calling ourselves Chiquitano Indians…We look alike, we were all handed over to the bosses… they called us *cambas* or peasants until not long ago.'

CASE STUDY

31

This process was unexpectedly boosted by the structural adjustment policies of the 1980s, which dramatically reversed three decades of state intervention and improvements in social rights, and galvanised protest movements across Bolivia. Following the lead of other social movements, lowland peoples organised a march to the capital La Paz in 1990, which, as one participant put it, 'demonstrated that the indigenous peoples of the East exist'. Literally and politically, indigenous people were on the move.

The 1990s saw some unorthodox measures within the hard-line Washington Consensus policies, including a new law that greatly facilitated participation in local government, and an acceleration of agrarian reform, all of which helped boost indigenous movements.

In January 1995, the Chiquitanos presented their first legal demand for title to Monteverde under a new concept, 'Original Community Territory'. A year-and-a-half later, a second indigenous march won parliamentary recognition for the concept. Years of tedious legal procedures followed. However, by the time of the third march of indigenous peoples from the East in 2000, ferment was growing across the country. Privatisation of water services in the city of Cochabamba led to a fully fledged uprising, which chased the water company from the city and triggered a wave of protest nationwide.

At another march in 2003, the Chiquitanos put forth national demands and established national alliances. 'We met with one of the high-lands leaders,' recalls Chiquitano leader, now Senator, Carlos Cuasase, 'and we said, "Look brother, you have the same problems that we do, the same needs." We agreed not only on [the law to nationalise] hydrocarbons but also to defend the rights of indigenous people of both highlands and lowlands.'

After protests toppled President Sánchez de Lozada in October 2003, identity documents became easier to obtain and candidates were allowed to run independently of traditional political parties, which led to major gains for indigenous peoples in the 2005 municipal elections. In December of that year, Bolivia elected Evo Morales as its president. People who had never before dreamed of serving in high-level posts became ministers. The new foreign affairs minister was an indigenous leader without higher education, the justice minister had previously been a leader of the home workers' union, and the water minister was previously the leader of urban organisations in El Alto and worked as a carpenter. Other ministers came from unions and NGOs. The election marked a sea-change in the fortunes of Bolivia's indigenous peoples, including the Chiquitanos.

Three further factors help to explain why change happened in Bolivia. First, the discovery of large reserves of natural gas contributed to a general perception that the country was on the threshold of a historic opportunity. Second, the historical memory of the country's indigenous peoples allowed them to draw strength from deep traditions of identity and resistance. Third, vibrant social institutions such as trade unions, neighbourhood associations, and indigenous organisations were able to catalyse popular unrest.

Political strategy was also essential. Aware of Bolivia's history of military coups followed by violent repression, Chiquitano leaders sought to emphasise the country's equally strong tradition of negotiation. Their main intent was to pressure the national government to fulfil its role as the duty-bearer of rights, and they insisted on legal procedures despite the tricks of adversaries and delays of judges. The challenges now are to implement the indigenous rights framed in the new constitution, to manage indigenous territory sustainably, and to prepare a new generation of men and women leaders.

*Sources: E. Caceres (2007) 'Territories and citizenship, the revolution of the Chiquitanos', background paper for Oxfam International; Diakonia, La Paz (2006) 'Género, etnicidad y participación política', García Linera. For a short chronology of the Original Community Territory legal process up to 2001, see Artículo Primero, vol. V, no. 19, 2001.*

CASE STUDY

# I BELIEVE, THEREFORE I AM

One person with a belief is equal to a force of 99 who have only interests.
JOHN STUART MILL, NINETEENTH-CENTURY ENGLISH ECONOMIST
AND PHILOSOPHER

Maria da Penha Nascimento was an imposing figure; a big, confident woman who had risen to become president of the Alagoa Grande Rural Workers' Union in Brazil's drought-prone and poverty-ridden Northeast. She recounted her life story, the words half lost in the drumming of a sudden downpour. A broken home, starting work aged seven, a mother who died from TB when she was 12, early marriage, and the struggle to feed her six children: the story of countless poor women. Then came transformation when she joined the union, inspired by a charismatic woman leader named Margarida Maria Alves. When Margarida was assassinated, probably by local landowners, Penha (as she was universally known) took over.[18]

There are thousands of women like Penha across Latin America and in every other region of the world, inspirational grassroots activists breathing vigour into social and political life. What motivates them is belief, in themselves, in a better future, in the struggle for justice and rights, and in the dignity of women and men everywhere.

## ATTITUDES AND BELIEFS

Development is often framed in dessicated terms such as interest groups, economic growth, institutional evolution, or technological change, while ignoring the central importance of attitudes and beliefs – people's views and the values that underpin them. Development is at least as much about passion as about calculation. In terms of their impact on development, attitudes and beliefs are deeply ambiguous: they can empower or disempower, mobilise or pacify. In the right circumstances, they can build a public ethos among the powerful, or open the door to the 'power within' that lies at the heart of active citizenship.

Attitudes and beliefs help to explain why people so often act in ways that contradict the idea of 'rational choice'. Even the simple act of casting a vote owes much more to belief in the importance of democracy, or of a citizen's duty, than to self-interest – only a negligible number of votes actually change the outcome of an election. Across the world, citizens and political leaders act out of conviction, not just out of self-interest. They set up or take part in organisations, work tirelessly to improve their own lives or those of other poor and excluded people. Often the work involves genuine sacrifice, of time, foregone opportunities, or physical safety. Meeting and talking with activists is one of the greatest honours of working for an organisation like Oxfam.

When it comes to attitudes, more grizzled activists – and parents – have always moaned about the lack of commitment of the young. In the eighth century BC, Hesiod observed: 'I see no hope for the future of our people if they are dependent on the frivolous youth of today, for certainly all youth are reckless beyond words'. The good news is that, in poor countries, surveys suggest that such grumbling is misplaced: in China, India, Nigeria, Viet Nam, and Zimbabwe, young people are at least as interested in politics as older people. In Indonesia and Iran, interest in politics is highest among the young, and steadily declines with age.[19] In rich countries, there has been a steady rise in the percentage of the population that has taken part in a demonstration, a strike, a consumer boycott, or a petition, even as conventional party activism has declined.[20] Such youth activism has a lasting impact. Participating early in life is a good predictor of ability and willingness to engage in the future.[21]

The attitudes and beliefs of elites are crucial to any effort to build the combination of active citizens and effective states. Do the wealthy believe that only fools pay taxes? Do they feel any personal responsibility for reducing poverty and inequality? With high walls, private schools, private medical care, and university education overseas, the rich in many countries can insulate themselves to a remarkable degree from the poverty and inequality that surround them.[22] However, individual members of the elite often 'defect' to become leaders of social movements and NGOs, bringing with them their skills and connections, and a crucial understanding of how those in power operate. Others who remain in elite circles can play a crucial role in developing a public ethos that emphasises human rights and the role of the state as servant, rather than master, of its citizens.

Some of the most deeply held beliefs in many countries relate to identity, such as gender or ethnicity. Such beliefs often rationalise and reinforce deep inequalities in treatment, whether at the hands of individuals or the law. Changing attitudes and beliefs is a crucial part of the struggle for development. In South Asia, the We Can campaign has achieved notable successes in changing attitudes to domestic violence, using a model of people-to-people contact, rather than the more standard strategy of targeting governments for funds or legislation (see page 276).

## RELIGION AND ACTIVE CITIZENSHIP

Perhaps the most powerful force in shaping attitudes and beliefs is religion. In many communities, poor people trust their local church, mosque, or temple more than any other institution.[23] While secularisation has been a notable feature of European life over the past 50 years, in much of the rest of the world religious institutions remain at the centre of community life. Many countries have seen a rise in religious fervour, perhaps because faiths can bring solace and security, especially when livelihoods and cultures are challenged by globalisation or emigration from settled rural communities to the chaos of the shanty town.

Although public attention often focuses on conflicts and divisions between faiths, perhaps more remarkable is how much they have in common (see Box 2.1). When representatives of nine world faiths –

Bahá'ís, Buddhists, Christians, Hindus, Jains, Jews, Muslims, Sikhs, and Taoists – attended a World Faiths and Development Conference in 1998, they revealed a startling degree of consensus about some of life's deepest truths:

- Material gain alone cannot lead to true development: economic activities are inter-related with all other aspects of life.
- The whole world belongs to God. Human beings have no right to act in a harmful way to other living creatures.
- Everyone is of equal worth.
- People's well-being and their very identity are rooted in their spiritual, social, and cultural traditions.
- Social cohesion is essential for true development.
- Societies (and the world) must be run on the basis of equity and justice.[24]

This convergence can be seen in the co-operation between faiths across the developing world, where Oxfam, a secular agency, supports and works with partner organisations from a number of faiths, who share common goals of rights and social justice.

---

## BOX 2.1
## THE GOLDEN RULE

**Brahmanism:** 'This is the sum of duty: do naught unto others which would cause you pain if done to you.'
(Mahabharata 5, 1517)

**Buddhism:** 'Hurt not others in ways that you yourself would find hurtful.' (Udana-Varga 5,18)

**Christianity:** 'Do unto others as you would have done unto you.'
(Jesus, quoted in Luke 6:31)

**Confucianism:** 'Surely it is the maxim of loving-kindness:
do not unto others that you would not have them do unto you.'
(Analects 15, 23)

**Islam:** 'No man is a true believer unless he desireth for his brother that which he desireth for himself.'
(Azizullah – Hadith 150)

**Jain:** 'A man should treat all creatures in the world as he himself would like to be treated.'
(Wisdom of the Living Religions, #69 – I:II:33)

**Taoism:** 'Regard your neighbour's gains as your own gain and your neighbour's loss as your own loss.'
(T'ai Shang Kan Ying P'ien)

**Zoroastrianism:** 'That nature alone is good which refrains from doing unto another whatsoever is not good for itself.'
(Dadistan-i-dinik 94-5)

Besides framing attitudes, beliefs, and personal behaviour, the impact of religion crosses over into the social world. Many faiths directly promote active citizenship. Jubilee 2000, the debt campaign across 40 countries that persuaded the rich creditor nations to cancel billions of dollars of debt owed by the world's poorest countries, was based on the biblical concept of the Jubilee – every fiftieth year – in which those enslaved because of debts are freed, lands lost because of debt are returned, and community torn by inequality is restored. Many of the 70,000 Jubilee 2000 protestors that ringed the G8 meeting in Birmingham, UK in 1998 and forced debt onto the agenda were conventional church-goers who saw a direct relationship between the debt issue and scriptural calls for social justice.

In Southern Africa, many of the powerful and charismatic women who typically run community projects helping those living with HIV or orphaned by AIDS are active church-goers and draw on their faith for inspiration and energy in what is often an exhausting and thankless task. Across Latin America, radical Catholics have made a 'preferential option for the poor', leading movements against oppressive governments. This prompted one notorious right-wing death squad in El Salvador to print bumper stickers urging its followers to 'be a patriot, kill a priest'. The killers went even further, assassinating San Salvador's Archbishop Romero in 1980 because of his public stand against military repression. In Iran, Muslim clerics led the popular insurrection against the Shah and his notorious secret police in 1979.

However, a profound ambiguity characterises the interaction between faith and politics. While Marx saw religion as 'the opium of the people', blinding them to the true nature of their oppression, and Gramsci saw it as a means through which elites could construct and maintain their domination, Durkheim portrayed it as a way of building collective identity that promotes social cohesion and stability.[25] In different places at different times, religion can encourage activism, conformity, or hatred.

Nowhere is this contradictory role more evident than in relation to women's rights. Fundamentalists of virtually all religions view the emancipation of women as profoundly disturbing, their influence giving rise, for example, to the curious alliance of the Vatican, the Iranian government, and the US government to block international progress on sexual and reproductive rights. At the same time, organised religion is undergoing change, often at the behest of women activists. In the cases of Islam and Catholicism, reinterpretation of scriptures has moved in parallel with changing attitudes and beliefs, with women's rights leading to a new popular approach to the faiths, despite the opposition of the religious hierarchies (see the case study on Morocco on page 67).

# I READ, THEREFORE I AM

Daybreak in a shanty town brings ample evidence of the central importance of essential services in the lives of poor people. Children in miraculously pristine school uniforms emerge from the dingiest of shacks; women set off to the standpipe to collect the day's water, or drag off sick and coughing infants to wait in the inevitable queue at the local clinic. Unseen are those excluded from such services: girls kept home from school to carry out the domestic chores; disabled or elderly people who need particular assistance to take part in public life.

The provision of decent public services is one of the key roles of an effective state, both in terms of building a dynamic economy, and in securing its own legitimacy. Social investment in health, education, clean water, and sanitation is not a luxury for countries that have achieved growth, but is in fact a precursor of that growth, and also makes it much more likely that growth and its proceeds will be equitable.[26] Such services are the basic building blocks of a decent life, enshrined as universal rights by the United Nations.

Improvements are often cumulative: one study in Nigeria found that providing health facilities for illiterate mothers increased their children's life expectancy at birth by 20 per cent, while providing education without health facilities raised it by 33 per cent – but providing health care and education together led to a whopping 87 per cent increase in life expectancy.[27] According to poor women with whom Oxfam works in India, literacy enables them to 'be more intelligent, fill in forms, read letters from our parents after we get married, be able to leave the village (we can't read the destination on the bus!), get a good match, find a government job'. [28]

Essential services improve the quality of life, enable poor communities to become active participants in society at large, and boost the economy. Properly funded, well-managed, quality public services are a crucial means of combating inequality, redistributing power and voice across the generations. In contrast, underfunded, poor-quality public services further marginalise the most excluded members of society, entrenching inequality.

Public services have a significant impact on gender inequality. An absence of good-quality essential services has a doubly negative impact on women and girls. First, when public services have to be paid for, men and boys consistently have greater access to them. Boys are the ones for whom families find school fees, and the cost of treatment for sick fathers comes before spending on sick mothers. Second, in the absence of essential public services, it is women and girls who all too often have to take up the slack. It is they who have to trudge for miles to get water, and it is an army of home-based women carers across the world who have to take up the burden of care for relatives in the absence of public provision. Free public services and the emancipation of women are two sides of the same coin.

Workers providing public services are often among the more active citizens, beyond their immediate roles as providers of education or health care. In rural communities, the teacher is often an important local figure, and the school one of the few visible manifestations of the state. Public sector trade unions are often highly active in broader politics, and in some countries have faced severe repression.

Nevertheless, despite the essential role of public services in development, millions of people are still dying, sick, or out of school because there are not enough teachers, nurses, or doctors in poor countries. Oxfam estimates that two million more teachers and 4.25 million more health workers must be recruited across the developing world to make health and education for all a reality. Aid donors are failing to plug the gap: only 8 cents in each aid dollar is channelled into government plans that include the training and salaries of teachers and health workers.[29]

Even where public services exist, they often fail to address the diverse needs of women, poor, elderly, and disabled people, people living with HIV or AIDS, or from particular ethnic or religious groups. This may be due in part to the fact that government officials are overwhelmingly male, relatively well-off, able-bodied, and from an ethnic majority – which highlights the importance of involving a representative range of citizens in shaping policies and in delivering services.

Health is discussed in Part 4, while this section explores education, water and sanitation, and fertility control, as well as the roles of citizens and states in providing essential services.

## EDUCATION

Education is crucial in breaking the cycle of poverty. It is a right in itself, and it equips individuals to lead full lives, understand the world, and ultimately gain the self-confidence to make themselves heard. Good-quality education is emancipatory, a path to greater freedom and choice, and opens the door to improved health, earning opportunities, and material well-being. On average, each additional year of formal schooling increases a worker's wages by 5–10 per cent, and the skills gained can transform the quality of life for generations to come.[30]

Over the past ten years, Brazil has managed to reduce its historically extreme inequality to its lowest level in 30 years, in large part by providing education to poor people, along with social protection schemes.[31] Schooling is the single most powerful way to break the transmission of deprivation from one generation to the next. When such services are paid for by progressive taxation, the impact in reducing inequality is all the greater.

Conversely, the absence of education perpetuates inequalities. Children are less likely to receive an education if they are girls, live in rural areas, or are poor. When all three sources of exclusion coincide, the results can be startling. In Guinea, a boy living in an urban area, with an educated mother and belonging to the wealthiest quintile, is 126 times more likely to attend school than a rural girl from the poorest quintile with an uneducated mother.[32]

Educating women and girls is particularly important because it enables them to challenge inequality with men, within the family and in wider society. Educated women tend to have healthier children and smaller families, suggesting that education is linked to greater bargaining power in marriage. Education makes it more likely that a woman can earn money of her own, which means she is more likely to be able to remain single if she chooses, or to leave an abusive or unhappy relationship. Education can also break down the stereotypes of women's and men's roles in society which restrict the horizons of both girls and boys, and girls in particular can gain the self-confidence to challenge discrimination.

Globally, significant progress is being made in reducing the number of children of primary-school age who are not enrolled in school. Between 1999 and 2006 the number fell by around 21 million to 72 million.[33] The spread of primary education has halved levels of illiteracy since 1970, greatly improving the quality of life of millions of poor people. Still, some 780 million adults (one in five worldwide) lack basic literacy, and two-thirds of them are women.[34] The Millennium Development Goal of achieving gender parity in primary enrolment by 2005 (the only MDG to specifically target inequality) was missed by a wide margin.

The glass is half full in other areas: enrolment in secondary school is increasing rapidly, although there is still a long way to go, especially in sub-Saharan Africa and South Asia. Perhaps the most extraordinary progress has been in university and other higher education, where worldwide the number of students enrolled rose 43 per cent between 1999 and 2004 to 132 million. Three-quarters of this growth took place in developing countries, with China alone accounting for 60 per cent.[35]

Key reasons behind the increases in school enrolment achieved over the past decade, particularly for girls, include the removal of school fees, economic growth, and urbanisation (which reduces the cost to the state of providing schools). Public pressure has also played a role: national grassroots campaigns in 120 countries, co-ordinated by the Global Campaign for Education, obliged governments to spend significantly more on primary education.[36] Education budgets increased in two-thirds of countries for which data are available. In Kenya the national coalition of education groups, Elimu Yetu (Our Education), played a pivotal role in making free primary education a central election issue, ensuring it was introduced in 2002; the result was that 1.2 million children went to school for the first time.[37]

Quality is also crucial. Class size, the quality and availability of textbooks, curriculum content, and teacher motivation all determine whether and what a child learns in school. There is a world of difference between a dispiriting 'chalk and talk' session with an underpaid, demotivated, and poorly trained teacher in an overcrowded classroom and an exciting, empowering class geared to the culture, experiences, and interests of the children involved. A quality education is a transformative process that respects children's rights, encourages active citizenship, and contributes to building a just and democratic society.

Studies show that employing and training more teachers is *the* critical issue in delivering quality education. Smaller class sizes and the quality and morale of the teacher are critical elements in improving educational outcomes. A classroom without a teacher is useless, but a teacher without a classroom can start to educate children. Uganda's near-doubling of net enrolments, from 54 per cent to over 90 per cent by 2000, was preceded by an increase in teachers' salaries from $8 to $72 per month from 1997. Governments also ensured that rural facilities were well staffed, often by requiring publicly trained workers to work in rural areas.

In Sri Lanka, all teachers are expected to work for three to four years in 'difficult schools'. In the Gambia the government is building new housing in remote areas and establishing a 'teacher housing loan scheme' to help female teachers with the costs of decent accommodation. In Nicaragua, thousands of volunteers helped in a hugely successful national literacy campaign.[38]

## WATER AND SANITATION

Of course I wish I was in school. I want to learn to read and write…
But how can I? My mother needs me to get water.

YENI BAZAN, AGE 10, EL ALTO, BOLIVIA

'By means of water', says the Koran, 'we give life to everything.' Access to clean water and sanitation is a basic right, and is essential in allowing people to live decent, dignified lives. The proportion of people using drinking water from improved sources has risen in the developing world, reaching 80 per cent in 2000, up from 71 per cent in 1990, while 1.2 billion more people gained access to sanitation.[39] As a result, the reduced threat of infectious disease has contributed to there being two million fewer child deaths per year today than in 1990. But this still leaves many people paying a terrible toll. Nearly 5,000 children die every day due to dirty water, 1.1 billion people have inadequate access to water, and 2.6 billion lack basic sanitation.

Inequality in access to water and sanitation is extreme. Most of the 1.1 billion people lacking access to clean water use much less than the minimum threshold of 20 litres a day, often as little as five litres, while in high-income areas of cities in Asia, Latin America, and Africa, people use several hundred litres a day. Paradoxically, piped water supplied to middle- or high-income households is often cheaper than water bought by the bucket from private tankers. People living in the slums of Jakarta, Manila, and Nairobi pay five to ten times more per unit than those in high-income areas in their own cities – and more than consumers pay in London or New York. Other inequalities compound the problem of unequal access: women tend to attach more importance to sanitation than do men, but female priorities carry less weight in household budgeting.

Beyond the obvious direct link to health, access to clean drinking water can save hours of back-breaking toil for women, particularly in rural areas. These are hours that could be spent learning a skill, earning money, enjoying the company of friends or family, or simply sleeping at the end of an exhausting day. Until they escape the drudgery of water collection, women cannot hope to live better lives than their mothers, or to save their own daughters from the same fate.

The case for action on water and sanitation is unanswerable. Economically, every $1 spent in the sector generates another $8 in costs averted and productivity gained. A major UN study put the economic losses in sub-Saharan Africa at about 5 per cent of GDP ($28bn a year) and concluded: 'No act of terrorism generates economic devastation on the scale of the crisis in water and sanitation.'[40] In human terms, access to safe water and flush toilets significantly reduces child death rates. Yet as with other public services, action has been held back by bad advice, Northern arm-twisting and self-interest, and in some cases by public attitudes and beliefs.

Despite some positive results, the dogmatic insistence of aid donors that only privatisation will improve water provision (discussed in Part 5) has led to sharp price rises, excluding poor people and triggering at least one 'water war' of protest, in Bolivia. The polarised debate over privatisation has sidelined the more necessary discussion of how to ensure access for poor people and communities. Public providers, who still deliver over 90 per cent of water in developing countries, include both dismal failures and outstanding success stories. Learning the lessons of good public sector reform is a vital part of delivering water to poor people.

Sanitation is often given little attention in national debates, due to a taboo on public discussion of the topic, leading to less spending. In Malawi, for example, while government spending on health and education has grown as a share of GDP, spending on water and sanitation has declined.[41]

Like education and health care, water and sanitation services are a focus of grassroots activism, via self-help initiatives and efforts to convince authorities to act. Some of the greatest progress has come in India and Pakistan, where slum dweller associations have helped to bring sanitation to millions of people. Success on water and sanitation in countries such as China, India, Lesotho, and Brazil show that one of the keys is developing demand for sanitation, rather than pursuing 'top down' engineering solutions. Progress lies in the interaction between citizens' movements and effective states.

## CONTROL OVER FERTILITY

One essential service is rarely considered vital by government planners or economists, and is therefore most often overlooked: reproductive and sexual health care. If women are to realise their full human rights, and nations are to ensure broader health and well-being, women must be able to decide what happens to their own bodies in terms of sexuality and child-bearing. Failure to provide reproductive and sexual health care, and to uphold women's access to these services, accounts for nearly one-fifth of illness and premature death, and one-third of the illness and death of women of reproductive age.[42] Control over fertility, along with economic opportunity, women's education, and changes in attitudes and beliefs, is central to ending discrimination against women.

46

Currently public and private spending in the developing world meets the needs of more than 500 million women for a modern contraceptive method. These family planning services and supplies prevent 187 million unintended pregnancies each year, avoiding 60 million unplanned births and 105 million abortions. This has measurable health benefits, including 2.7 million fewer infant deaths and 215,000 fewer pregnancy-related deaths, and has reduced maternal mortality worldwide by 30 per cent.[43]

Beyond their medical impact, family planning programmes also have far-reaching social, economic, and psychological benefits for women. Being able to control fertility enables poor women to make life choices that are simply unavailable if they have to undergo frequent, unplanned pregnancies and then provide and care for children. If a woman can control the number of children she has, and the timing of their births, she can make choices to balance her role as a mother with other roles, spending time in paid work or community life, rather than relying on men to earn money and represent her.

Before modern contraceptive methods became available, women in many societies found ways to space births, such as taboos on sex while breast-feeding. However, even such 'weapons of the weak' depend on women's relative power. Based on research in India and China, Amartya Sen established a link between women's power and control over fertility. In India, women's education and economic independence turn out to be the 'best contraceptive', leading to smaller family sizes, while real income per capita shows almost no impact on family size. Comparing India's record with China's notorious 'one child' policy, Sen finds that 'coercion of the type used in China has not been used either in Tamil Nadu or Kerala and both have achieved much faster declines in fertility than China….The solution of the population problem calls for *more* freedom, not less.'[44]

## STATE VERSUS PRIVATE

In guaranteeing access to decent health care, education, drinking water, and sanitation, there is no substitute for the state.[45] This has been as true historically as it is today. In the late nineteenth century, London was awash with infectious diseases, including dysentery and typhoid. Child death rates were as high then as they are now in much of sub-Saharan Africa. Faced with the inefficiencies, costs, and corruption of private sector water provision, the British state stepped in to create public water and sanitation systems.[46] In the nineteenth century in Germany the national health system unified multiple insurance schemes under one equitable system. Compulsory public education was extended across Europe, North America, and Japan in the early part of the twentieth century, and these welfare states expanded further after the Second World War.

The state does not have to be the end provider of every school, clinic, or water pipe. In practice, these are often delivered by NGOs, religious groups, and private companies. Community-based workers, both paid and voluntary, in areas such as health and veterinary services have proved an effective way to rapidly improve coverage in Lesotho and South Africa.[47] But the state must ensure that civil society providers are part of a single coherent system. Governments sometimes achieve this by funding the running costs and regularly monitoring them to maintain standards. Successful examples have combined regulation and incorporation of other providers with a significant scaling up of state provision.[48]

In Armenia, NGOs stepped into the breach when the state health system effectively collapsed after the fall of the communist government in 1991. Support to Communities (STC), a local NGO, set up a simple health financing scheme, asking people to contribute small amounts to fund local clinics, a nurse, and a functioning water system. The intention was to create a model that the state could eventually take up and replicate. STC rapidly won the trust of communities and spread the scheme across dozens of villages in remote areas before moving on to lobby the Armenian government to expand it across the country.

In contrast, when China phased out free public health care in favour of profit-making hospitals and health insurance schemes, household health costs rose forty-fold, and progress on tackling infant mortality slowed. Services that were once free are now paid for through health insurance, which covers only one in five people in rural China.[49]

The good news is that advances both in technology and in our understanding of how to provide services mean that success is now within reach of even the poorest countries. Sri Lanka, Malaysia, and Kerala state in India, for example, have within a generation made advances in health and education that took industrialised countries 200 years to achieve.

## POLICIES THAT WORK

Sri Lanka is classed as a 'lower-middle income country', yet its maternal mortality rates are among the lowest in the world. When a Sri Lankan woman gives birth, there is a 96 per cent chance that she will be attended by a qualified midwife. If she or her family need medical treatment, it is available free of charge from a public clinic within walking distance of her home, staffed by a qualified nurse. Her children can go to primary school free, and education for girls is free up to university level.

Compare that with oil-rich Kazakhstan, where investment in public services has lagged far behind increases in per capita income. Even though Sri Lanka has 60 per cent less income per capita, a child in Kazakhstan is nearly five times more likely to die in its first five years and is far less likely to go to school, drink clean water, or have the use of a latrine.

Oxfam's experience around the world suggests that successful governments get results by ensuring that essential services work for women and girls, abolishing user fees for primary health care and education, and subsidising water and sanitation services. Other policies that have been shown to work include building long-term public capacity to deliver services, expanding services into rural areas, investing in teachers and nurses, and strengthening the social status and autonomy of women as users and providers of services.

Any type of fee charged at a primary health care or education facility has such an injurious impact on poor people that such fees should be abolished. The World Bank, which advocated the imposition of user fees in the 1980s and early 1990s, has since revised its position, at least in terms of its public messaging. It no longer supports user fees in education, although its position on user fees in health is more ambiguous. A growing number of governments receiving debt relief are using the proceeds to abolish fees, such as Zambia, which announced the end of user fees for its rural population in 2006.

In water services, user fees can encourage sustainable use of a finite resource. It is crucial, however, that the structure and affordability of water tariffs are managed in order to achieve equitable access for poor people. In Porto Alegre, Brazil, water consumption is subsidised, with the first 10,000 litres discounted to the price of 4,000 litres. In Uganda, the water utility NWSC provides community water points that are managed by private individuals, where the price of water is publicised at the tap and is much lower than that of water provided by private vendors.[50]

Too often, economists focus on the efficiencies of production and allocation under existing structures and constraints, and ignore deeply embedded discrimination against poor people, and poor women in particular. Overcoming the exclusion of women first of all requires the acknowledgement of their rights. Measures such as promoting women as health and education workers, at the front line of delivering services, will also encourage other women and girls to use those services. In Mali, *animatrices*, local women who work with parents to convince them of the importance of sending girls to school, have achieved some notable successes. In Palestine, where the vast majority of teachers are women, net primary enrolment rates are among the highest in the Middle East and 97 per cent of girls go on to secondary school.

Women's access to services can also be boosted by ensuring that social protection payments put cash in their hands (see Part 4). Mexico's PROGRESA programme reaches over 2.6 million rural households and links cash benefits and nutritional supplements to mandatory participation in health and education programmes. Several design features directly target women. Mothers are designated as beneficiaries and receive the cash transfers. The entire family – primarily pregnant and lactating mothers and children under five years – is required to follow a schedule of clinic visits, and women attend monthly health education lectures. Children must achieve an 80 per cent rate of school attendance, and financial incentives are slightly higher for girls' attendance. PROGRESA has had a positive impact on child and adult health, has increased household food expenditure, and has increased women's control over their additional income.[51]

There are several reasons for optimism that the kinds of investment and changes in policy needed to provide all citizens with the building blocks for a decent life will be forthcoming. In virtually every country where Oxfam works, it has seen a seemingly irreversible spread of literacy, activism, and elected government, and with them a growing voice from citizens pressing for improved essential services. Urbanisation may generate environmental and social problems such as overcrowding, but it makes providing toilets and taps, clinics and classrooms much easier. Surveys show that elites in developing countries grasp the role of decent education systems in creating the basis for national development, although, interestingly, they do not appear to draw the same conclusions with regard to health.[52]

# I SURF, THEREFORE I AM

Knowledge is power.

FRANCIS BACON

For two decades the people of Sunder Nagri, a slum on the north-eastern edge of the Indian capital, Delhi, had to make do without sewers, as local officials kept promising to clean things up. In 2005, making use of the country's new Right to Information law, local businessman Noshe Ali was able to discover what everyone in Sunder Nagri had already guessed – that there were no plans to dig any sewers. Armed with that knowledge, Ali convinced the city's chief minister to authorise a budget. Work started within a year.

Not long after, a local woman followed Ali's example. Asked to hand over 800 rupees ($20) for birth certificates for her two daughters, she refused, and instead used the Right to Information law to find out what was delaying her application, and which official was responsible. Rather than face public shaming, the local government quickly gave her the birth certificates.[53]

## ACCESS TO KNOWLEDGE AND INFORMATION

Access to information is no abstract debate; it is an essential tool of citizenship. Knowledge expands horizons, allows people to make informed choices, and strengthens their ability to demand their rights. Ensuring access to knowledge and information is integral to enabling poor people to tackle the deep inequalities of power and voice that entrench inequality across the world. At a national level, the ability to absorb, adapt, and generate knowledge and turn it into technology increasingly determines an economy's prospects.

Poor people's access to information has increased greatly in recent decades, driven by rising literacy levels and the spread of radio, television, mobile telephony, and the Internet. By 2007, there were twice as many mobile phone owners in developing countries as in industrialised countries, and subscriber growth rates in Africa were running at 50 per cent per year. Mobile phones have transformed poor people's access to finance, market information, and each other.[54]

To some extent, legislation has also progressed: just over a decade ago, freedom of information was guaranteed in only a handful of countries. Now more than 50 countries have freedom of information laws, and 15–20 more are considering them.[55] In the words of Internet pioneer Stewart Brand, it appears that 'information wants to be free'.

Mobile phones, email, and the Internet have also transformed the way that civil society organisations and NGOs operate, especially at an international level. Global networks can spring up almost overnight, sharing information on particular issues, while blogs and websites can reach new audiences without passing through the filter of traditional media. This massive increase in connectivity has drastically reduced the costs of networking and coalition building (albeit at the cost of over-stuffed inboxes).

Free and responsive media can raise public awareness on issues of rights, but can also provoke reprisals. Iraq, Algeria, Russia, and Colombia are currently the most deadly countries for journalists.[56] In many African countries the media have effectively tackled stigma and discrimination on HIV and AIDS, through popular drama series such as South Africa's *Soul City*, and promoted debate on social issues, such as rape and domestic violence.[57] In Armenia, *My Rights*, a television series that uses mock trials to depict real-life disputes in the courts, became a surprise number-one show, increasing public awareness and scrutiny of the legal system. When the electricity went off in one village a few minutes before *My Rights* was due on air, townspeople marched on the mayor's office and accused local officials of trying to keep them (literally and figuratively) in the dark.[58]

53

Despite the hype surrounding the Internet, as of late 2007 Africa and South Asia still had only five Internet users per 100 people.[59] Beyond personal face-to-face and telephonic communication, poor people remain largely reliant on government- or corporate-dominated broadcast media for access to information. As many as 45 countries block content in a manner that reduces transparency and responsiveness.[60] Governments use bribery to control the media. One revealing study found that Peru's notorious Fujimori government in the 1990s paid television channel owners bribes about 100 times larger than those it paid to judges and politicians. The strongest potential check on the government's power, warranting the largest bribe, were the news media.[61]

In radio, often the main source of information for poor people, the low cost of entry for new stations has diluted state or corporate control. Community broadcasters are now well established across most of Latin America, reaching otherwise excluded groups, and are spreading rapidly across Africa. Radio provides one of the few sources of information in unofficial languages – a major issue when it comes to empowering poor communities, given that most people living on $1 a day do not speak their country's official language.[62] Quechua, a language spoken by some ten million people in Bolivia, Ecuador, and Peru, is rarely heard on television and is completely absent from the Internet. By contrast, 180 radio stations offer programmes in Quechua.

The forces driving greater access to information are strong, thanks to a combination of demand (improved literacy, more assertive citizens, the spread of elected government) and supply (technologies that make knowledge more widely and cheaply available). Despite the concentration of media ownership in the hands of a few global titans, the coming years should see poor people gain greater access to knowledge and information, through an increasingly diverse set of traditional and new channels.

Access to information can help poor people influence decisions that affect their lives. In the Pacific, the Solomon Islands Natural Resources and Rights Coalition helps local communities gain access to logging agreements and other government documents so that they can fight for their rights over forests. Public access to information can also prompt the state to become more effective, as evidenced in the Indian example cited above.

## THE PROMISE OF TECHNOLOGY

When oral rehydration therapy (ORT) was developed at Bangladesh's International Centre for Diarrhoeal Disease Research in the late 1960s, the *Lancet*, a leading medical journal, hailed it as possibly the most important medical discovery of the twentieth century. Until then the only effective remedy for dehydration caused by diarrhoea was providing sterilised liquid through an intravenous drip, which cost about $50 per child, far beyond the budgets and facilities of most developing-country health centres. In comparison, ORT sachets sell at less than 10 cents apiece. Scientists found that ORT led to a 25-fold increase in a child's ability to absorb the solution, compared with water alone, saving hundreds of thousands of lives.[63]

Technology is knowledge embodied in machines or processes, and holds out the allure of a fast and apparently painless track to development. The capacity of countries to create knowledge and turn it into technology increasingly determines their economic prospects. However, despite the gee-whizz enthusiasm of optimists, technology is dogged by issues of power and politics that severely hamper its ability to help poor people build their capabilities. Nor is technology always benign. After working on the Manhattan Project to develop nuclear weapons during the Second World War, Albert Einstein observed, 'Technological progress is like an axe in the hands of a pathological criminal.'

Technological progress often exacerbates inequality. At least initially, those with power and a voice are often better placed to acquire and adapt new technologies, which helps skew global research and development (R&D) priorities towards the needs of the wealthy, both in terms of issues and funding. Only 1 per cent of the new medicines brought to market between 1975 and 1996 were for the treatment of tropical diseases. Ten years later, and despite some philanthropic efforts, that disparity remains: only 10 per cent of the overall world health research budget of $50bn–$60bn is spent on the diseases that affect 90 per cent of the world's population.[64]

The failure to develop an effective microbicide against HIV is one example of the distortion in global research priorities. In part because pharmaceutical companies cater to rich-country markets, where for many years the pandemic affected primarily male homosexuals, their research efforts have centred on male-controlled prevention methods. In sub-Saharan Africa, where the target population is primarily heterosexual and women's bargaining power over sex is limited, a prevention method that could be controlled by women and would not block procreation is an urgent need. Recent initiatives have sought to fill the gap, but a breakthrough is still years away. Likewise, an affordable female condom that could protect millions of women from HIV infection has still not been developed.

The Bill & Melinda Gates Foundation, among others, hopes to help correct this bias by offering grants to fund R&D for neglected diseases. The UK, Canada, and other governments are offering what they call 'advance market commitments': a guarantee to buy bulk supplies of new vaccines in order to encourage research. The basic idea is not new. In 1714 the British government offered £20,000 – a fortune at the time – to whoever could invent a way of measuring longitude at sea. The offer worked: by 1735 the clockmaker and inventor John Harrison had produced an accurate maritime chronometer.[65]

Research is increasingly dominated by the private sector. In agriculture, five large multinational companies – Bayer, Dow Agro, DuPont, Monsanto, and Syngenta – spend $7.3bn per year on agricultural research. This is more than 18 times the budget of the publicly funded Consultative Group on International Agricultural Research.[66] Left to its own devices, private sector research will respond to future opportunities for profit, not public need (although the two may coincide), so tropical diseases or improved varieties of the staple foods of poor communities, such as cassava and sorghum, are likely to be overlooked in favour of high-value, high-profit products.

R&D may benefit people living in poverty, even when it is dominated by the wealthy and run by the private sector. But it is less likely to improve their prospects than R&D geared more closely to their needs, and may run greater risks. Biotechnology, for example, may well produce drought-resistant strains of seeds that become an essential tool for adapting to climate change. However, it could also erode the genetic diversity on which developing-country farmers rely, and place excessive power in the hands of transnational corporations through their control of seed strains.

Unless regulated by governments, private sector-driven R&D is likely to widen the technological divide between 'haves' and 'have-nots'. An effective state, motivated and supported by other actors, could reorient the focus of technological development towards the needs of poor people by regulating research and funding of higher education and R&D. Active citizens, in both North and South, could contribute to this outcome by pressuring private companies and states to include poor people in the benefits of new technology.

Above all, the emphasis must be on the development of 'appropriate technologies', which address the needs of the poorest and most excluded people, and respect the sustainability of the ecosystem upon which they depend. India's M.S. Swaminathan, winner of the 1987 World Food Prize, applied Mahatma Gandhi's words to this point: 'Recall the face of the poorest and the weakest person you have seen, and ask yourself, if the steps you contemplate are going to be of any use to him.' [67]

Besides reorienting the focus of global R&D, developing countries face the challenge of developing their own capacities to create knowledge, which are stymied today by the flight of qualified professionals, lured away by better pay and working conditions in wealthy countries. Unless this global problem is addressed, the higher-education systems of developing countries will continue running up a down escalator in order to build their science base. The issue of migration is taken up in detail in Part 5.

More worrying even than the brain drain is an emerging pattern of global governance of knowledge that is biased against poor people and poor countries. Enshrined in 'intellectual property rights' (IPR) legislation at both national and global levels, increasingly aggressive IP rules drastically reduce the flow of technology to poor countries, while requiring them to waste scarce funds and personnel on administering a regime that only benefits foreign companies. By inflating the price of all technology-rich products, the IP regime constitutes a harmful tax on economic development. Like migration, this problem is addressed in Part 5.

# WE ORGANISE, THEREFORE WE ARE

Never doubt that a group of concerned citizens can change the world – indeed, it is the only thing that ever has.

MARGARET MEAD, ANTHROPOLOGIST

The first sign of the squatters is a huge red flag flapping above a depression in the hills a few hundred yards away. Across two barbed wire fences and an arid, sandy hillside lies the cluster of huts thrown up a number of weeks ago by 40 landless families. They have called the encampment 'Hope' (Esperança). Already the inhabitants are making the first improvements: tiles are starting to replace plastic sheets on the roofs of the huts, whose walls are made from branches tied together with twine. To provide safety in numbers, 500 people originally occupied the site. When ten armed policemen promptly arrived to evict them, the children stood in front with stones; behind them came the women and adolescents, followed by the men armed with their primitive farming tools. The policemen backed off without a fight, allowing the squatters to get on with planting their first crops of yams and fennel.[68]

The red flag belongs to Brazil's Landless Workers Movement, the MST. The MST leads landless peasants in well-organised invasions of wasteland or uncultivated farmland. Standing amidst newly ploughed furrows thirsty for rain, one of the squatters explains: 'People came here for land. We weren't interested in riches – land created people and

58

people must live from it. The owner says the land is his, but if he doesn't even farm it, how can that be?'

The MST is a social movement that is one of thousands of civil society organisations (CSOs) across the developing world, whose political activity takes place outside the channels of formal politics. CSOs include highly institutionalised groups, such as religious organisations, trade unions, or business associations; local organisations such as community associations, farmers' organisations, or cultural groups; and looser networks such as social movements.[69] They form a vital part of the interaction between active citizens and effective states, which can redistribute power, voice, and opportunity. They also exemplify a tradition of creating moral, political, and economic foundations for communities. A history of social change would show that much of what we think of now as the role of the state was first incubated in such experiments in Utopia, away from bureaucracies and politicians.[70]

In seeking change, citizens have always come together, either to achieve strength in numbers or to reduce the likelihood of repression. CSOs include groups focused purely on self-help at a local level, charities simply trying to help excluded groups in society, and others with a more transformatory agenda working for social and political change: for example, by taking direct action, as in the case of the MST, or representing their members' interests, as in the case of trade unions. Others (like Oxfam) lobby and campaign, conduct research, or act as watchdogs on those in power. Today, vibrant social movements are seen by many as a vital part of any real democracy and 'an arena where the possibilities and hope for change reside'.[71] According to the UN, it is estimated that one person in five participates in some form of CSO.[72]

The rise of civil society has been driven by both long-term and short-term factors. In the long term, the spread of literacy, democracy, and notions of rights have prompted a rise in active citizenship. CSOs, which function beyond the individual or household level but below the state, can play a role in complementing more traditional links of clan, caste, or religion that have been eroded by the onset of modernity. In the long run, coming together in CSOs helps citizens rebuild the stock of trust and co-operation on which all societies depend.[73] It should be remembered, however, that some citizens' groups seek to reinforce discrimination, fear, and mistrust; called 'uncivil society' by some, their activities can sometimes spill over into violence, as in the case of religious or racist pogroms or paramilitary organisations.

## CIVIL SOCIETY AND CHANGE

Many CSOs see themselves as 'change agents'. Often their work is painstaking and almost invisible, supporting poor people as they organise to demand their rights, pushing the authorities for grassroots improvements such as street lighting, paved roads, schools, or clinics, or providing such services themselves, along with public education programmes on everything from hand washing to labour rights. However, in recent years, civil society's most prominent role, at least as reflected in the global media, has been in helping to install elected governments in place of authoritarian regimes. Since the 1980s, successive waves of civil society protest have contributed to the over-throw of military governments across Latin America, the downfall of communist and authoritarian regimes in Eastern Europe and Central Asia, the removal of dictators in the Philippines and Indonesia, and the end of apartheid in South Africa.

According to Freedom House, a US government-funded foundation, civic resistance has been a key factor driving 50 out of 67 transitions from repressive or dictatorial to relatively 'free' regimes in the past 33 years; the majority of these countries managed to effect a lasting transition from dictatorial regimes to elected governments.[74] Tactics have included boycotts, mass protests, blockades, strikes, and civil disobedience. While many other pressures contribute to political transitions (involvement of the opposition or the military, foreign intervention, and so on), the presence of strong and cohesive non-violent civic coalitions has proven vital.

One example is the Georgia Young Lawyers Association (GYLA), a network of some 1,000 lawyers, established in 1992. The GYLA provides free legal advice to poor people, but also targets government malpractice. As a founding member of the movement known as 'Kamra' ('Enough'), it played a crucial role in triggering the protests that toppled the corrupt regime of President Eduard Shevardnadze in 2003 by winning a court case against the government over election irregularities, based on evidence provided by its own 200 election monitors.

Compared with the steady hum of the state's machinery, civil society activity waxes and wanes, coming into its own in moments of protest and crisis, and often falling away after a victory – such as winning a change in the law, or the election of a more progressive government that promptly recruits key civil society leaders. In such circumstances, many CSOs find it difficult to move from a strategy of opposition to one of engagement. Other CSOs, notably those sponsored by religious institutions, are much more stable, outlasting all but a handful of governments, but even they experience cycles of activism and silence.

Less dramatic than mass protest, but equally important, civil society can demonstrate broad public support for policy changes, thus making it easier for political leaders to act and resist pressure from those who would rather maintain the status quo. In the late 1990s, for example, the Maria Elena Cuadra Women's Movement in Nicaragua collected 50,000 signatures calling for better working conditions in the country's export-processing zones, prompting the minister of labour to enforce the law and convincing factory owners to adopt a voluntary code of conduct.

Civil society also plays an important, if less visible, role in more closed political systems, such as one-party states. A study in Viet Nam revealed a virtuous circle of state and NGO investment in training and education, improved communications (for example, an upgraded road, funded by the World Bank, which allowed easier contact between villages and the district authorities), and pressure from the central government for local authorities to encourage popular partici-pation in poverty reduction efforts. As a result, both villagers and local authorities gained confidence and began to exchange opinions and ideas more openly. Women in particular became much more vocal after receiving training in agricultural methods and making more reg-ular trips away from the village.[75]

Much of the long-term impact of CSOs is based on the slow build-ing of people's skills and capabilities, fostering changes in attitudes and beliefs. In Serbia, for example, a network of groups is seeking to strengthen the negotiating and lobbying skills of the Roma popu-lation, the poorest community in Europe, in part by ensuring that more women and young people join and assume leadership positions.

The bedrock of civil society is formed of local groups concerned primarily with the welfare of their fellow citizens, like the General Assistance and Volunteer Organization (GAVO). This organisation was founded in 1992 by a dozen young men from different sub-clans in Berbera, their hometown in the arid region of the Horn of Africa known as Somaliland. Their childhoods had been shattered by civil war, and they hoped that through volunteer action they might begin to address some of the town's pressing social problems.

Acting on the advice of their Koranic teacher to help the most destitute of their fellow citizens, they started with patients at the local psychiatric hospital suffering from war trauma: trimming their hair and nails, taking them out to a cool plateau on Fridays, washing their clothes. Shunned by many who associated mental illness with sorcery, the hospital received no government or private funding. GAVO's volunteers used popular theatre to educate the community, and reached beyond the boundaries of family and clan to raise money, breaking social taboos in the process.

Within four years, GAVO had managed to set up an out-patient clinic, help demystify mental illness, and garner steady donations from local merchants and municipal authorities. Then, aware of their own limited scope, they began to lobby for changes in government policy regarding children's rights.

Paradoxically, organisations like GAVO are often viewed by funders as being of little significance to development. They are local, usually 'traditional' rather than 'progressive', and distant from grand challenges on the national level. Yet such groups provide opportunities for communities and ordinary citizens to discuss and act on some of the difficulties they face. Though small-scale, they can be instrumental in the development of a democratic culture and of skills needed for addressing national challenges. GAVO travelled on just such a trajectory – from charity to service provision to public outreach to outright advocacy.

Civil society is often at its most active in the burgeoning shanty towns and suburbs of cities. With better access to schooling, and with exchanges of opinions and information on every street corner, urbanites are more likely to get involved in CSOs. Cities are vividly political places, dense with social movements demanding housing, schools, clinics, or decent water and sanitation. Protest and conflict abound, between workers and employers or service providers and users.

## ALLIANCES AND PARTICIPATION

In practice, civil society is a complex political and social ecosystem, including grassroots social movements, established organisations such as churches and trade unions, and NGOs made up of more middle-class activists. Alliances between such dissimilar organisations are both fruitful and fraught, with 'turf wars' and frequent accusations of co-option or of NGOs 'speaking on behalf of' (and claiming funds for) groups they do not represent.

One regular source of tension is over whether to pursue the tactics of 'outsider' confrontation, for example mass street protests, or less visible 'insider' engagement, such as lobbying. An outsider strategy based on mass mobilisation often needs stark, unchanging messages, but these can alienate officials and political leaders, and limit the insiders' access to decision-makers. Conversely, an insider strategy muddies the waters with compromises, undermining mobilisation and raising fears of betrayal and co-option. Yet both are necessary and a joint 'insider–outsider' strategy can be highly effective.

CSOs are not immune from the wider inequalities in society. Men often dominate, as do powerful groups based on ethnicity or caste. CSOs of hitherto marginalised groups have often emerged as splinters from CSOs serving the general population, when women, or indigenous or HIV-positive people, found that their specific concerns continually evaporated from the agendas of mixed organisations.

Active participation has intrinsic merits, creating strong bonds of belonging and common purpose. As one woman told researchers in Pakistan, 'Before the organisation was formed, we knew nothing and were completely ignorant. The organisation has instilled a new soul in us.'[76] Participation can build a sense of self-confidence and involvement, enabling excluded groups and individuals to challenge their confinement to the margins of society.

However, participation is not without costs. CSO activism can involve exhausting rounds of meetings, voluntary toil, and confrontations with impervious or insulting authorities. People keep going out of commitment and belief, be it political, religious, or simply a sense of duty. In Latin America, women activists talk of the exhaustion of their 'triple day' of paid work, running a home, and then spending any remaining time engaged in community work.

Moreover, participation in civil society organisation brings risks of repression or worse. Across the developing world, activists who challenge existing power structures face attacks by police, hired thugs, and paramilitaries – or from irate husbands and fathers. In many countries, women activists can face a violent backlash at home, as their activism leads them to challenge traditional inequalities, or simply means they cannot have dinner on the table at the expected hour.

Beyond the personal benefits (and costs) of participation, a strong civil society obliges political parties to compete for the public's support, and to offer social progress, rather than co-option. In Ghana, political leadership, independent media, and a strong network of civil society organisations have helped build up a politics of interest groups, including urban youth, cocoa farmers, native authority elites, professional and business elites, and unionised workers. The shift to a more stable state was demonstrated when the incumbent party lost the 2000 presidential election and an orderly transition ensued. The ruling party retained power in 2004, but elections were seriously contested. Steady improvements in literacy, access to information, and levels of social organisation may help other countries to follow suit.

Civil society can play a crucial role in 'keeping the demos in democracy'.[77] Even the cleanest and most transparent electoral systems can be undermined by undemocratic institutions – corporate lobbyists, clientilist political networks, and the like. For these practices, sunlight is the best antiseptic, in the form of civil society scrutiny and activism. In recent years, civil society organisations have tried to ensure that government spending tackles inequality and poverty. Such 'budget monitoring' work involves painstaking analysis of both what is promised and what is delivered, and advocacy to influence the way that budgets are allocated. In Israel, the Adva Centre, an NGO founded by activists from different social movements working on equal rights for Mizrahi Jews, women, and Arab citizens, uses a combination of analysis, parliamentary lobbying, popular education, and media campaigns.

In Guatemala, the Social Spending Observatory was established in 2004 to challenge the secrecy surrounding the budget process, publishing quarterly analyses of government spending. The Observatory's work has highlighted the lack of spending among the country's impoverished indigenous majority. In South Africa and elsewhere, 'gender budget monitoring' projects specifically highlight the impact of budget decisions on women, while monitoring programmes such as those in Uganda have identified and publicised episodes of corruption.

The rapid spread of cheap communications technology has enabled CSOs to 'go global'. A good example is the Via Campesina, which links together peasant and landless movements around the world.[78] Another is Social Watch, an international NGO watchdog, made up of national citizens' groups from 50 countries. Based in Uruguay, Social Watch monitors progress on governments' international commitments on poverty eradication and equality.[79] Other groups link up through the World Social Forum, a regular event, which at its fourth such meeting in Mumbai in 2004 brought together over 130,000 civil society activists from around the world.

In recent years, North–South alliances of CSOs have successfully pushed issues to the top of the political agenda at meetings of the G8, the World Bank, and the WTO. Landmark initiatives, such as the International Criminal Court and International Landmines Treaty, were spearheaded by joint efforts of concerned citizens and NGOs, while sustained campaigns have sought to improve the respect of transnational corporations for labour rights and reduce the damage they cause to local communities and environments. Over the next few years, international campaigning of this nature will be crucial in pressuring governments to make and keep the commitments needed to reduce carbon emissions, as well as cover the rising costs of adaptation to climate change in poor countries. As Amnesty International's 'prisoners of conscience' work has also shown, Northern campaigners can be invaluable allies for activists in the South who face repression and torture at the hands of the authorities.

The great attention attracted by CSOs is viewed by some with concern, as a 'reification' that downplays the historically much more significant contribution of trade unions and political parties. Western governments and private philanthropists have poured money into CSOs, especially the kinds of organisations they recognise: urban, middle class-led, and modern, such as credit associations, women's groups, law societies, business associations, or local development NGOs. They have sometimes given succour to CSOs that are little more than vehicles for relatively educated people to access funds when other jobs are scarce. In the process, they have ignored kin, ethnic, religious, or age-based groups, even though these often have deeper roots among much larger numbers of people, especially in the poorest communities.

Being ignored by funders may be no bad thing. Some donor governments deliberately use funding to defuse radical social movements that threaten vested interests. Other donors undermine the potential of CSOs by making them administrators, rather than irritants. According to two authorities on the subject, 'Donor civil society strengthening programmes, with their blueprints, technical solutions, and indicators of achievement, run the risk of inhibiting and ultimately destroying that most important of purposes of civil society, namely the freedom to imagine that the world could be different.'[80]

Active participation contrasts sharply with the idea that people should express themselves simply through what they consume ('I shop, therefore I am') or how they vote, and with a more technocratic vision of citizens as passive consumers of state services delivered by wise and well-trained administrators.

At its best, an active and progressive civil society can be profoundly transformatory, enhancing the lives of both participants and society as a whole, empowering poor people to demand change and to hold their rulers accountable. Over time, active citizenship can make states more effective. When states are absent, civil society organisations can step into the breach to keep at least some level of services operating. But CSOs are not a magic path to development, nor are they a substitute for responsive, effective states capable of delivering tangible and sustained improvements in people's lives. In practice, development requires both.

## HOW CHANGE HAPPENS CASE STUDY
**WINNING WOMEN'S RIGHTS IN MOROCCO**

In 2004 women's organisations in Morocco won a remarkable victory when Parliament unanimously approved a new Islamic Family Code that radically strengthened the rights of women. The reforms included the right to decide legal matters without the guardianship of a male, equal responsibility over the household and children, and the need for consent from both husband and wife to dissolve a marriage.

Activists had sought reforms since the early 1960s, but in 1992 the Union de l'Action Feminine (UAF) launched a grassroots campaign to change the set of family laws known as the *Moudawana*. They collected more than a million signatures on a petition and won the first legislative amendments the following year. Though major issues such as polygamy and divorce were left virtually untouched, a father could now no longer compel his daughter to marry. Activists saw these early reforms as a critical success, ensuring that the *Moudawana* could no longer be portrayed as sacred and unalterable.

Women's rights groups continued to mobilise, opting to work within the framework of Islam, arguing that the conservative interpretation enshrined in family law ran counter to the true spirit of the Koran. Activist Rabéa Naciri recalls: 'We chose not to separate the universal human rights framework from the religious framework. We maintained that Islam is not opposed to women's equality and dignity and should not be presented as such… Islamic law is a human and historical production, and consequently is able to evolve, to fulfil the current needs of Muslim men and women.'

A key moment in the campaign was the victory of the socialist opposition in the 1997 election. The political opportunity for women's voices to be heard further increased when the liberal King Mohamed VI assumed the throne in 1999. In an address to Parliament, the King publicly supported women's quest for equality. Seizing the moment, women's rights activists came together to create a Plan of Action for the Integration of Women in Development (PANIFD in the French acronym), which included the key tenets of the UN's Beijing Platform

CASE STUDY

67

and won the endorsement of Prime Minister Abderrhamane el-Youssoufi.

Conservatives and political Islamists quickly formed an opposition grouping, the National Group for the Protection of the Moroccan Family (Organisme national pour la protection de la famille Marocaine), and launched their own campaign through mosques and in the popular media. Religious conservatives argued that any revision of the law would go against Islam, while political Islamists blamed attempts at reform on Western influence. Soon thereafter, the government withdrew its support for PANIFD.

Women's groups, however, redoubled their efforts, culminating in a demonstration in 2000 that brought tens of thousands of women and men onto the streets of Rabat. A counter-march held in Casablanca at the same time brought out similar numbers of opponents.

Following the demonstrations, King Mohamed VI asked 40 important female leaders from women's organisations and political and social movements to meet and make recommendations. He then created a Royal Commission responsible for the reform of the *Moudawana*, composed of religious scientists, lawyers, sociologists, and doctors. Significantly, three members of the Commission were women from highly respected professions. The King's guidelines were that their proposals should be coherent with the founding principles and spirit of Islam, follow any Islamic legal tradition as long as it was in favour of the family and of harmony, and fulfil Morocco's international human rights obligations.

After two years of delays, the Commission held nine months of open hearings in 2004, meeting to analyse the old *Moudawana* and discuss proposals put forth by different constituencies and, finally, to prepare recommendations to the King. All the while, the PANIFD campaign continued lobbying the Commission and reaching out to the public. Activists made use of real cases of women who had experienced domestic violence, repudiation, or early marriage under the old laws, asking men if they wanted their daughters protected from such injustices.

On 3 February 2004, the legislation to reform the *Moudawana*, the new Family Code, was passed unanimously by Parliament. Women gained important legal autonomy and were afforded more equality in the areas of divorce, legal custody, marriage, and family relations. The reinterpretation of the *Moudawana* challenged dominant modes of thinking about women's rights and their relations within the family.

In the campaign for *Moudawana* reform, activists employed an astute 'insider–outsider' strategy, combining mass demonstrations and public awareness campaigns with lobbying of the Commission. The campaign not only contributed to a better quality of life at home for Moroccan women, but also paved the way for further progressive reforms.

*Source: A. Pittman and R. Naciri (2007) 'Cultural Adaptations: The Moroccan Women's Campaign to Change the Moudawana', Institute for Development Studies, available at: www.ids.ac.uk/ids/Part/proj/pnp.html*

CASE STUDY

# I OWN, THEREFORE I AM

For millions of Indians, the Ganges is a holy river, but to the people of the riverside slum of Sanjay Nagar in the pilgrim city of Allahabad, this means the annual threat of eviction, as their shacks are bulldozed to make way for celebrants coming to bathe. The shacks are mud-walled, with plastic roofs held down by ropes; the mud path is carpeted with discarded sandals, and pigs root among piles of rubbish; the air is rank. But at least Sanjay Nagar offers shelter; the fear of eviction is a nagging insecurity in the hearts of the residents. 'When we're evicted,' says one, 'we have to lie low, sleep rough, and then come back, but we never know if we'll be able to rebuild.' Now the area is slated for 'beautification', and this time the eviction may be final.

One of the most agonising aspects of living in poverty is not having secure rights to your own house or land, something often taken for granted in the North. In India, Ghana, Cambodia, and Bolivia, more than 50 per cent of all urban residents live in informal settlements, and the United Nations expects the number of people living in urban areas without secure property rights to reach 1.5 billion by 2020.[81] More than 6.7 million people worldwide were evicted from their homes in 2001–02, according to the Centre for Housing Rights and Evictions, most of them in urban areas.[82]

Eviction comes at the hands of powerful landlords or the authorities and is often brutal. In Zimbabwe in 2005, Operation Murambatsvina, literally meaning 'drive out the rubbish', forced an estimated 700,000 urban residents from their homes in the capital city of Harare, affecting up to 2.4 million people overall. Bulldozers and demolition squads run by youth militia demolished self-help housing, while street vendors and others operating in the informal economy were arrested and their businesses destroyed.[83]

## PROPERTY RIGHTS AND DEVELOPMENT

The notion of a 'right' to property is controversial. Property rights are not included in human rights treaties, but the right is acknowledged in Article 17 of the Universal Declaration of Human Rights: 'Everyone has the right to own property alone as well as in association with others. No one shall be arbitrarily deprived of his property.'

Property rights are perhaps best seen as a means to an end – a way to reduce the vulnerability of the poor. Rich people have other ways to defend their property, as the razor wire and 'armed response' warning signs outside the more opulent residences in South Africa suggest, but poor people need legal protection from depredation. The absence of property rights can stymie efforts to tackle inequality and exclusion.

Many economists argue that secure property rights hold the key to broader development, encouraging investment in land or construction. The link between property rights and growth, however, is weak,[84] and history is full of counter-examples: most recently China has successfully experimented with a complex mixture of private, public, and hybrid ownership patterns, often with relatively unclear property rights. Furthermore, the dispossession of some landholders (violating certain existing property rights) has in many cases been beneficial for economic development. For example, in rapid and far-reaching land reforms in South Korea and Taiwan beginning in 1949, all agricultural land above a very low ceiling was compulsorily acquired by the state at below-market prices and sold to tenants at an artificially low price. By any account, such enforced transfers were not consistent with well-defined property rights, but they set the stage for a broad expansion of the economy.[85]

Most recently, Peruvian economist Hernando de Soto has become something of a *cause célèbre* for his beguiling argument that property rights offer an escape route from poverty, enabling poor people to 'breathe life into dead assets' by using their houses or land as collateral to obtain credit and kickstart a business. He even puts some rather dubious numbers on such assets, extrapolating from studies in five large cities to arrive at an eye-popping global estimate of $9.3 trillion in 'dead capital' owned by the poor – a figure on a par with the combined value of the world's 20 largest stock markets.[86]

De Soto's thinking has been taken up with enthusiasm by politicians across the spectrum. A 2005 housing policy document from the South African government, 'Breaking New Ground', complains that the 1.6 million new houses funded by the state since 1994 have not become 'valuable assets' for poorer people, and emphasises the need for improved access to title deeds so that poor people can participate in residential property markets.[87]

What many of De Soto's followers fail to appreciate is his insistence that effective property-rights systems grow out of customary law or other initially non-statutory systems, such as those developed by squatters and settlers. His more zealous acolytes too often ignore the subtle and complex forms of land use and implied property rights already in operation among poor people and impose legalistic 'off-the-shelf' regimes.

In Papua New Guinea (PNG) over 97 per cent of land is under such traditional 'customary' title, and there is a significant push, including from the Australian government and the World Bank, to reform land-ownership systems on the premise that customary title is an impediment to development. However, research from the Australian National University shows that in recent decades agricultural production in PNG – both domestically marketed food and export crops – has expanded steadily under customary tenures, while mostly declining under registered titles. Individual land titles have not helped producers with the problems and shocks they faced (including declining world prices, inability to switch from one commodity to another as the market changed, poor transport infrastructure, and security issues), whereas smallholders under customary tenure systems have been able to adapt more readily to changing circumstances and constraints.[88]

Customary laws did not develop in a political or social vacuum, however. They often reflect the interests of the more powerful groups in society, and are determined by many of the same structures that generate poverty and exclusion, usually at the cost of women, marginalised ethnic groups, and the poorest communities and castes.

Moreover, the claim that distributing formal land titles will open the floodgates to credit has proved false. Commercial banks do not like lending to poor people, and poor people are often reluctant to risk putting up their precious new titles as collateral. Recent comparative studies in slum areas in Buenos Aires and de Soto's home city of Lima compared families with and without titles to their homes and found that land-owning families had no better access to credit.[89] A study of a community in Western Kenya seven years after land titles had been handed out there found that only 3 per cent of the 896 titles had been used to secure loans.

Distributing land titles that can be bought and sold can deter those who would steal land at gunpoint and can provide poor people with options, but it can also lead to rising inequality, as large landlords or farmers buy out their poorer neighbours. The replacement of communally owned lands by individual farm plots in Mexico in the 1990s led to a rapid process of land concentration.[90] Similarly, dismantling regimes based on common property often serves as a legal vehicle for removing people in order to gain access to logging, mining, or other resources, as has occurred in Laos.

The simplistic approach of privatising and handing out land titles to individuals is clearly inadequate, even though it is often funded by donors and fits the electoral ambitions of populist politicians. An effective state needs to ensure that property rights are secure, are equitable, and recognise multiple claims – for example, so that both husbands and wives enjoy equal rights via joint titling. Property therefore should be registered at individual, family, or community levels. Under pressure from organised slum dwellers, municipal governments are increasingly recognising the need to strengthen property rights as a means of formalising the urban economy and ensuring better provision of water and sanitation. Neighbourhood associations and federations of urban poor people are playing a major role in some cities, surveying urban land and negotiating their rights to occupy it.[91]

## LAND REFORM

'Land and Liberty!' ran the battle cry of Emiliano Zapata that inspired Mexico's peasantry to rise up in the Mexican revolution of 1910–17. And the resulting reforms help to explain Mexico's relative prosperity in the decades that followed. Land reform was a central feature of revolutions in China, Russia, Cuba, and Viet Nam, and the first step on the path of economic transformation in several East Asian 'tiger' economies. Especially in predominantly peasant societies, land reform can transform power relations and get at the root of social and economic inequality (see Table 2.1).

Skewed land ownership is a core driver of inequality – women grow between 60–80 per cent of the food produced in most developing countries, yet own less than 2 per cent of the land.[92] Land empowers: research in Kerala, India, found that almost half of women who owned no property reported physical violence compared with only 7 per cent who did own property. Other studies have shown that women who do not own land are statistically more likely also to be infected with HIV.[93] Indigenous groups like Bolivia's Chiquitanos (see the case study on page 31) see control over traditional territories as a core part of their identity. Redistributing land can also boost the economy. Farmers who are secure on their land are more likely to invest in upgrading production, and may find it easier to borrow money.

Struggles over land can be particularly acute following a disaster. Earthquakes, droughts, or wars drive people off their land and, in the aftermath, powerful local elites and businesses often look to seize land whose ownership is poorly defined. Women left widowed are frequently dispossessed, sometimes by their own family members. Resisting such pressures and ensuring a fair distribution of land is a vital role for the state and others after such shocks.

The rise of powerful indigenous and landless movements in countries such as Bolivia, Brazil, India, and the Philippines has brought land reform back onto the agenda in recent years after it disappeared in the 1980s, when development orthodoxy saw it as intolerably interventionist for the state to be involved in redistribution.

The results can be spectacular. In Cambodia from 1998–2001, unprecedented co-operation between government and civil society

## Table 2.1: Great land reforms of the twentieth century

| Countries (in descending order of scale of beneficiaries) | Years of reform acts | Beneficiary households as percentage of total agricultural households (%) | Redistributed land as percentage of total agricultural land (%) |
|---|---|---|---|
| China | 1949–56 | c. 90 | 80 |
| South Korea | 1945, 1950 | 75–77 | 65 |
| Cuba | 1959–65 | 60 | 60 |
| Ethiopia | 1975, 1979 | 57 | 76 |
| Iraq | 1958, 1971 | 56 | 60 |
| Mexico | 1915, 1934, 1940, 1971 | c. 55 | 42 |
| Tunisia | 1956, 1957, 1958, 1964 | 49 | 57 |
| Iran | 1962, 1967, 1989 | 45 | 34 |
| Peru | 1969, 1970 | 40 | 38 |
| Algeria | 1962, 1971 | 37 | 50 |
| Yemen, South | 1969, 1970 | 25 | 47 |
| Nicaragua | 1979, 1984, 1986 | 23 | 28 |
| Sri Lanka | 1972, 1973 | 23 | 12 |
| El Salvador | 1980 | 23 | 22 |
| Syria | 1958, 1963, 1980 | 16 | 10 |
| Egypt | 1952, 1961 | 14 | 10 |
| Libya | 1970–75 | 12 | 13 |
| Chile | 1967–73 | 12 | 13 |
| Philippines | 1972, 1988, 1994 | 8 | 10 |
| India | 1953–79 | 4 | 3 |
| Pakistan | 1959, 1972 | 3 | 4 |
| Morocco | 1956, 1963, 1973 | 2 | 4 |

*Source:* M. Riad El-Ghonemy (1999) 'The Political Economy of Market-Based Land Reform', UNRISD Discussion Paper 104. See source for details of the types of land holdings included in individual country totals.

led to the country's first national land policy, which tried to reconcile the needs of peasants, squatters, indigenous peoples, and commercial investors. Over a million land titles have been handed out, and the land rights of many women have been secured for the first time ever.[94] In the Philippines, land reform in public and some private land took off in the mid 1990s during the presidency of Fidel Ramos, a former general and defence minister. An analysis by two Filipino academics points to a powerful combination of active citizenship and an effective state: 'a high degree of social pressures from below and a high degree of independent state reform initiatives from above, and then the high degree of interaction between the two'. In the Philippines this is known as the '*bibingka* strategy', after a traditional delicacy, a rice cake that is cooked by fire lit both above and below it.

Elsewhere, land reform has had a chequered record. In Zimbabwe, productive white-owned farms have been handed over as rewards to government supporters who had little farming experience, with devastating effects on agricultural output. Elsewhere, land reform has failed because it has not guaranteed access to vital services such as credit, infrastructure, or extension services. In many countries land reforms have run out of steam in the face of dogged and often violent resistance from local elites, lack of state commitment, and the sheer bureaucratic and legal complexities of enforcing land titles and redistribution across hundreds of thousands of small farms. Even in the Philippines, these have remained constant challenges. In such situations, the slow pace of reform breeds a simmering resentment, which occasionally explodes into protests and land occupations.

Where land reform has successfully transformed economies and societies, it has required strong, independent states that are able to face down local elites. Success also requires mobilised organisations of landless workers or peasant farmers, able to channel demands and ensure that the reform process meets their needs.

Donors and many governments have responded to the recent resurgence in interest in land reform by introducing so-called 'market-led' policies. These seek to avoid forced redistribution by the state in favour of 'willing buyer, willing seller' approaches, whereby large farmers agree to sell their land to peasants and landless workers, often with the state stepping in to facilitate the sale, for example by advancing funds to small farmers to buy the land. The alternatives, either compulsory purchase or seizing land without compensation, arouse ferocious opposition from landowners and their allies, and can greatly increase opposition to reform.

Market-led approaches have been widely criticised for ignoring issues of social justice: the beneficiaries are often not 'the poorest of the poor', they enter their new lands saddled with debt, and the approach often recognises only individual titles, ignoring other, often more widespread, customary land tenure systems. In practice, governments often square the circle by handing out publicly owned land at low or no cost.

## WOMEN'S PROPERTY RIGHTS

In wealthy countries, property rights were one of the first goals fought for by first-wave feminists in the nineteenth century, and today they remain central to many organisations of poor women across the world.[95] In many countries, a combination of attitudes and beliefs and legal discrimination in both 'modern' and 'customary' law excludes women from owning land. Women rarely possess full rights over land, instead being forced to negotiate as secondary claimants through male relatives – fathers, brothers, husbands, or sons. Women usually cannot inherit the matrimonial home on the death of their husband. Formalisation of customary law often means that a piece of land with multiple users becomes the property of a single owner, usually male. For example, the Kenyan Court of Appeal ruled in 1988 that a wife's interests under customary law cease to exist once her husband becomes the formally registered owner.[96] The unpalatable option for many women is often between being a second-class citizen under customary law or being completely invisible under formal systems.

The impact of the denial of property rights affects all women. Making a living depends on having a place to live, and – depending on what you do to survive – on having some land to farm, a room to run a business from, money to pay for materials and equipment, and someone to look after the children. Yet without legal rights to own property, regardless of marital status, most women living in poverty in developing countries depend on their relationships with men to deliver these things. Hence their livelihoods are precarious. If the relationship sours, or if the man falls ill and dies, how are they and their children to survive?

The worst affected are women in charge of households, whose numbers are rising through a combination of widowhood (due to conflict or HIV and AIDS) and family breakdown. The plight of the burgeoning number of widows is illustrated by the case of Mrs Chilala, a 78-year-old Zambian widow. Upon the death of her husband in 1990, her brother-in-law began to bury dead bodies on her land to scare her away from the area, so that he could seize her land.[97]

Conflicts over land are likely to intensify in coming decades. In the cities, booming populations will force the poorest and most marginalised into ever more unsafe and precarious places, exacerbating the gulf between the 'have homes' and the homeless. In the countryside, climate change and environmental degradation are likely to reduce the amount of fertile land available, while the advent of biofuels and other new crops will increase land prices and squeeze poor people off their farms. Ever more assertive movements of peasants, landless workers, and indigenous peoples are unlikely to back down from their demands. How states and citizens' movements deal with the pressure cooker of land conflict will play an important role in the future development of many of the world's poorest countries.

# I VOTE, THEREFORE I AM

Whether in Florida, Lagos, or Nairobi, elections can be chaotic events. Over the course of a day, a single common act unites the citizens of a country, unleashing hopes and fears, unity and division, fair play and foul. Stolen or fraudulent elections can trigger instability and violence. But stand back, and perhaps the most astonishing aspect of the spread of elections, however flawed, is that they happen at all.

Governments elected by universal suffrage were perhaps the most notable political innovation of the twentieth century. In 1900, New Zealand was the only country with a government elected by all its adult citizens. By the end of the century, despite a number of severe reversals (including fascism and communism and succeeding waves of military coups against elected governments), there were ostensibly 120 electoral democracies in place (out of 192 existing countries), of which some 85 were thought to be 'full' democracies, in the sense that they provided respect for the rule of law and civil and political rights.[98]

The pace of democratisation has accelerated in recent decades. After Portugal in 1974, democracy spread first to Greece and Spain and subsequently to Latin America, where elected civilian governments replaced military rulers in nine countries between 1979 and 1985. The mid 1980s and early 1990s saw democratisation in the Philippines, South Korea, Taiwan, Bangladesh, and Nepal. The fall of the Berlin Wall in 1989 and the collapse of the Soviet Union in 1991 prompted competitive elections in most of the former Soviet bloc, while Benin and South Africa opened the floodgates to a further wave of regime change in Africa in 1990. More than two-thirds of Africans now live in countries with democratic, multi-party election systems – and African governments took the lead in opposing an anti-democratic coup in Togo in 2005.[99]

However, much of what passes for democracy is a pale reflection of the term's etymological origins in 'people power'. In many countries, democracy exists as a thin veneer of Western concepts, a set of formal institutions that do not translate into real democratic practice or culture on the ground. Multi-party elections can provide a smoke-screen that obscures overbearing executive power, limitations on press freedom, and human rights abuses that strip democracy of its meaning.

These so-called 'exclusionary democracies' are deeply unpopular: only 10 per cent of 50,000 people polled worldwide in 1999 thought that their governments 'responded to the people's will'.[100] The indignity of political exclusion was memorably summed up by a peasant farmer in Baluchistan, Pakistan, who told researchers, 'During elections, they [the politicians] visit us individually to pocket maximum votes, but afterwards they avoid us and we feel evil-smelling. First they hug us, and later our sweat and grime repels them'.[101]

Yet poor people persist in their support for elected government over any alternative, echoing Winston Churchill's aphorism that 'democracy is the worst form of Government … except all those others that have been tried'.

## DEMOCRACY AND DEVELOPMENT

Democracy is desirable in itself. An international survey in 2005 found that eight out of ten citizens in a cross-section of countries believed that democracy was the best system of government.[102] Other regional surveys found that 69 per cent of Africans and an increasing proportion of Latin Americans believe that democracy is 'always preferable' to other political systems.[103]

Such preferences are reflected in international law. Article 21 of the Universal Declaration of Human Rights grants every individual 'the right to take part in the government of his [sic] country, directly or through freely chosen representatives.…The will of the people shall be the basis of the authority of government; this will shall be expressed in periodic and genuine elections which shall be by universal and equal suffrage and shall be held by secret vote or by equivalent free voting procedures.'

More than any other political system, democracy has a track record of promoting and protecting individual political rights and civil liberties, such as freedom of speech and association, and these in turn help to entrench democratic values and foster democratic politics, paving the way for the enjoyment of economic, social, and cultural rights. Democracy is not necessarily benign: emerging democracies in the USA, Argentina, and Australia committed something close to genocide against indigenous groups. Without a wider range of state institutions being in place (see Part 4), elections (which can seriously challenge existing power structures) can trigger violence, as in recent attempts at democratic transitions in Lebanon, Afghanistan, Kenya, and the Palestinian Authority, while elections in Algeria, Burundi, and Yugoslavia in the 1990s led directly to major civil wars.[104]

More than periodic elections, democracy is best understood as a cluster of devices and institutions, some of which point in contradictory directions, and all of which are continuing to evolve. It is the checks and balances that these different institutions –legislature, judiciary, executive, media, and civil society – exert on each other that determine the degree to which democratic regimes respect the rights of all their citizens.[105] When competitive elections are introduced in a situation of weak or non-existent institutions, as in the Democratic Republic of the Congo, it can trigger an outbreak of 'spoils politics' and political meltdown, undermining efforts to build the state.

Democracy is made possible by greater equality, and in turn promotes equality and seems to encourage governments to focus on the prosaic needs of their citizens, rather than on glory or plunder. Studies find a clear link between democracy and the greater provision of primary education. Once income effects are excluded, democracies spend 25–50 per cent more than autocracies on public goods and services.[106] Democracy also has an equalising effect on power relations between men and women. Conversely, where democracies fail to address inequalities, civic involvement and voter turnout fall.[107]

Where flawed democracies allow a majority to dominate and exclude a minority, they can also aggravate inequality.

Amartya Sen famously established that no famine has ever occurred in a functioning democracy, but any deeper link between democracy and economic well-being is much more disputed. The decades of democratisation have not produced a growth rebound – quite the contrary. In many regions, new democracies proved unexpectedly willing to introduce harsh structural adjustment measures that hurt both growth and equity.[108] The economies of democracies in Latin America and Africa have stagnated, while China, Viet Nam, Indonesia, and South Korea have taken off economically under authoritarian governments.

Because democracies require an element of consent – defeated candidates must accept their defeat – it can be more difficult for democratic governments to pursue radical change, such as redistribution through land reform, even where it is required to trigger economic take-off (as in Taiwan and South Korea). By the same token, a democratic regime is less likely to get away with the sort of radically anti-poor reforms that were implemented by the Pinochet dictatorship in Chile, when opponents such as trade unionists were killed, jailed, or exiled as part of its free market overhaul of the economy. That very inertia can be a blessing: one study found that although democracies have grown more slowly in economic terms than some non-democratic countries, they have grown more steadily over long periods, avoiding the booms and busts that invariably hit the poor hardest and ratchet up inequality.[109]

Economist Ha-Joon Chang believes that 'market and democracy clash at a fundamental level. Democracy runs on the principle of "one man (one person), one vote". The market runs on the principle of "one dollar, one vote".' Chang points out that 'most nineteenth century liberals opposed democracy because they thought it was *not* compatible with a free market.[110] They argued that democracy would allow the poor majority to introduce policies that would exploit the rich minority (e.g. a progressive income tax, nationalisation of private property), thus destroying the incentive for wealth creation'.[111]

Perhaps he exaggerates (many liberals believe that the independence and security given by a market and property are needed to make democracy work), but the relationship between market and democracy does more closely resemble a difficult and stormy marriage than the blissful partnership portrayed by many Northern governments.

Overall, the most plausible hypothesis is that economic growth more often prompts democracy than vice versa. For example, in South Korea, economic growth gave rise to a new, educated business elite who resented the heavy-handed involvement of the state in their affairs, a process many observers expect to be repeated in China as its middle class grows. The hypothesis, however, raises uncomfortable questions: does fighting for democracy in poor countries bring more freedom, but at the cost of less growth? And in terms of a broad under-standing of development, is that acceptable? Does the search for growth justify autocratic government and the denial of rights? Since democracy appears earlier or later in different countries' development and has different impacts on poverty, inequality, and growth, the real challenge is to understand how institutions, events, geography, and politics interact to determine these outcomes.

## PARLIAMENTS AND POLITICAL PARTIES

The workings of elected legislatures are often overlooked, but are essential in the construction of effective, accountable states. Historically weak 'rubber stamp' affairs in many countries, parliaments, or congresses are often unrepresentative and frequently beholden to powerful political leaders for their jobs – a surefire way to curb over-troublesome opposition. Women are notoriously under-represented, occupying only 17.1 per cent of parliamentary seats worldwide in 2007. The most equitable parliament in the world at present is Rwanda's lower house, where women hold nearly 49 per cent of the seats.[112] Legislative bodies are often starved of funds and the basic skills needed to carry out their functions, and often isolated from the civil society organisations, media, private sector, and trade unions that could help them carry out their jobs.

Parliaments have in some cases started to assert themselves, for example by providing oversight of budget processes in Tanzania, or restraining presidents from overturning the constitution to seek a third term in Nigeria. Elsewhere they have demanded the right to scrutinise loan agreements with international institutions and have

started to attract the attention of donors (among Northern government organisations, USAID has the most established track record of
funding the strengthening of legislatures). Over 40 countries have also
adopted quota laws to regulate the selection or election of women to
political office, and the average proportion of women in national
parliaments has doubled since 1995.[113]

Opinion polls show that they are almost universally despised by
the public, and they are often close to invisible in the literature on
development, but political parties play a vital role in linking citizens
and state. Development is not only about individual freedom of
choice, but also about making difficult choices at the collective level.
Parties bring together and sift the constellation of public needs and
desires, reconciling conflicts as they endeavour to win support from a
wide selection of groups. Following an election victory, the winning
party seeks to translate public desires into policy. In office, the party
becomes a focus of accountability and a channel for influencing
government. Social movements and poor communities lobby parties,
as well as civil servants and political leaders. Indeed, parties such as
Brazil's PT (Partido dos Trabalhadores, the Workers' Party) grew
largely out of the country's vibrant social movements and trade
unions and still retain strong links with both.

However, many political parties fail to live up to this ideal, and are
mere vehicles for individuals or elites to enrich themselves or to gain
power. Party politics often seems to belong in the gossip columns,
with a focus on personalities – who's in, who's out, who's rifling
the state's coffers – rather than on policies. Patronage politics easily
fragments parties along ethnic, tribal, regional, or religious lines, as
local 'big men' use state resources to buy support and power. In
Malawi and Tanzania, for instance, the proliferation of parties has
merely fragmented patronage politics, leading to serious political
instability as rival parties vie for power.[114] New parties appear
overnight, and wax or wane with the fortunes of their leaders. In other
countries, dominant presidents make the increasing number of
parties in parliament largely irrelevant.

Most political parties fall somewhere between these extremes, and
often reflect the state of civil society and its capacity to oblige parties
to offer collective rather than individual benefits. Their willingness

and ability to perform a useful democratic function rise or fall with time, as weak party systems grow stronger and strong ones crumble. Given their key role in democracy, strengthening political parties is an important step in linking citizens and states. Crucial issues include internal party democracy, transparency (for example, in the use of funds and election of leaders), and party and campaign financing – issues that are at least as pressing in the North as in the South.

No political system is fixed: state and party systems are constantly evolving, some becoming stronger and more accountable, others falling under the sway of autocrats or the spell of riches. Strengthening democracy by demanding progress in political systems (and preventing backsliding) is an essential task in the effort to build effective states, both for national citizens, and for those outsiders seeking to promote development and justice.

# I STEAL, THEREFORE I AM

Poor people hate corruption. When asked what defines poverty, they frequently cite not lack of income, but their helplessness to resist demands for bribes from the police and civil servants. Such corruption generates a profound sense of powerlessness and exclusion, undermining efforts to build active citizenship.

Economically, corruption has the biggest relative impact on the poorest people. In Romania, a World Bank study showed that the poorest third of families pay 11 per cent of their income in bribes, while the richest third pay just 2 per cent.[115] Corruption is widespread in rich and poor countries alike. The US Attorney General has declared health-care fraud to be the country's 'number two crime problem' after violent crime, costing billions of dollars each year.[116] In many countries, private companies pay substantial bribes to obtain government contracts. Across the developing world, informal 'fees' are charged for water, education, and health services.[117]

Corruption is the abuse of entrusted power for private gain. Corruption for need (sometimes known as petty corruption) contrasts with corruption for greed (grand corruption). They have different impacts on poor people and on countries at large, and require different remedies.

Petty corruption includes the charging of illegal, often small, fees by service providers, and state employees failing to turn up for work. This is poor people's most direct experience of corruption in the developing world. Poverty fuels corruption, as starving people find it

86

difficult not to sell their votes for a bag of flour, and under-paid civil servants often fail to resist the temptation of a bribe. But attitudes and beliefs also play a role. Oxfam staff in East Africa, Indonesia, and Central America report a widespread belief in these regions that people in positions of influence should help their families and home community, a mindset that often leads to public tolerance of what elsewhere would be seen as unacceptable graft.

Poverty encourages petty corruption and, conversely, development diminishes the threat it poses. Development increases the capacity of the government to collect taxes, pay decent wages, and spend more on detecting and punishing malfeasance among officials – all of which help to make corruption less corrosive of the system. In Cambodia and the Czech Republic, salary top-ups for health workers, combined with commitments to codes of ethical good practice, led to a decline in informal bribe payments and greater access to health services for poor people.[118] Unions and professional associations play an important role as partners in developing professional standards and in engaging workers in improving services.

The huge variations between countries at similar levels of development suggest that more can be done than merely waiting for growth to help make the problem manageable. Japan exhibits similar levels of corruption to much poorer Chile, according to Transparency International's 2007 Corruption Perception Index, while Uruguay ranks well ahead of Italy, despite having only one-seventh of its income per capita.[119]

Grand corruption is different. It not only affects national budgets, as in the case of presidents Mobutu (Zaire) and Suharto (Indonesia), each of whom stole billions, but also the private sector, where 'asset stripping' by executives and owners robs industry of its ability to invest, develop, and compete. More subtly, close ties between members of socio-economic elites can lead to politicians and officials setting policies that favour their friends and family members in the private sector, rather than the economy as a whole. In sectors such as oil and gas, arms, and construction, sizable bribes are routinely paid by large firms to state officials in exchange for contracts, while numerous privatisation programmes have provided the pretext for large-scale transfers of wealth from the state to well-connected members of the elite.

## THE CURSE OF WEALTH

A fundamental factor contributing to grand corruption is a country's reliance on natural resources. The great Uruguayan writer Eduardo Galeano termed it the 'curse of wealth'. Abundant deposits of oil, gas, or minerals act as poison in the bloodstream of politics, creating incentives for get-rich-quick power-mongering, rather than the long-term investment and hard slog that has underlain the success of resource-poor countries such as South Korea or Taiwan whose only economic asset was their people. In Nigeria, by contrast, $300bn in oil revenues has 'disappeared' since the 1960s,[120] leaving little tangible impact on a nation virtually devoid of paved roads, in which over 70 per cent of the population live on less than $1 a day.[121]

Natural resources can sever the 'social contract' between state and citizen. When a government can rely on royalties from oil, it need not tax citizens to raise revenue, and so need not cultivate public legitimacy but instead retains power through bribery. In such circumstances, democracy can be a double-edged sword. A study by Paul Collier of Oxford University found that, where countries have both competitive elections and 'checks and balances' in the form of free media and an independent judiciary, natural resources generally benefit the economy, because governments are forced to be more accountable and effective. However, take away the institutional checks and balances, and competitive elections seem to unleash even worse corruption and chaos, as parties jostle to get their hands on the wealth. In such countries, economic growth is even lower than under authoritarian regimes. The implications for the future of Iraq are sombre.[122]

Natural resources are not a developmental death sentence, however. The way Botswana has managed its diamond wealth stands in stark contrast with the devastation wrought by 'blood diamonds' in Angola, Sierra Leone, and the DRC, while Malaysia has graduated from tin and rubber production to microwaves and mobile phones. What matters is having, or creating, sufficiently strong and accountable institutions to cope with the money coming out of the ground.

Effective states can resist the lure of spoils politics and build long-term development based on revenue from natural resource windfalls. Norway charges an estimated 75 per cent tax rate on its oil and has used it to build up a 'Petroleum Fund' to provide long-term financing for its welfare state even after the oil runs out. In contrast, Bolivia, which has suffered from the 'curse of wealth' for 400 years,[123] was charging just 18 per cent tax on its oil and gas when in 2003 popular unrest prompted changes of government and a new tax level of 50 per cent. Bolivia's new leaders subsequently turned to Norway for advice, and the two governments signed a co-operation agreement in 2007 to strengthen public institutions in the energy sector.

Strong citizens' organisations too can play a fundamental role. The Extractive Industries Transparency Initiative – a global effort to require oil and gas companies to publish    at they pay to governments, and for governments to disclose what they receive[124] – convinced Nigeria to sign on, leading to the country's first independent audits of oil and gas revenues, which recovered an extra $1bn in tax revenue.[125] Such transparency enables civil society watchdog organisations to track revenue trails, reducing the opportunity for corruption.

Some of the best results in anti-corruption efforts have come from active citizens holding their governments to account. In India, the Right to Information movement has scored some notable successes. In Chile, groups monitor party political funding; in Malawi, citizens' groups tour schools, making sure that textbooks paid for by foreign aid actually arrive. In Uganda, a public information campaign on education spending galvanised citizens' scrutiny of government finances and substantially increased the amount of money reaching schools,[126] and an anti-corruption group named and shamed a corrupt official who had pocketed £15,000 earmarked for a road upgrade. He was arrested and forced to hand back the money. On a larger scale, bilateral aid is being used to strengthen state institutions that can address corruption, such as the police and the judiciary.

Corruption is not the central issue in development: corrupt countries can still prosper, as the history of Northern countries shows. But corruption undoubtedly squanders resources and makes it harder to build trust and dialogue between citizens and states. Conversely, attacking corruption, whether by encouraging citizen watchdogs or improving the wages and conditions of state employees, or simply by enforcing the rule of law without favour, can strengthen the combination of active citizens and effective states that lies at the heart of development.

# I RULE, THEREFORE I AM

In the early 1960s, the Democratic Republic of the Congo (formerly Zaire) had a national income per capita twice that of South Korea. Both countries had hungry, illiterate populations; both received substantial US aid; both were devastated by conflict. Since then, Korea has become one of the great development success stories of recent times, transforming the lives of its people, while the DRC has slid further into economic decline and civil war. In large part, this divergence can be put down to the presence or absence of an effective, development-oriented state.

Even though in historical terms the state is a comparatively recent creation, it is hard to imagine successful development without it. States ensure the provision of health, education, water, and sanitation; they guarantee rights, security, the rule of law, and social and economic stability; they regulate, develop, and upgrade the economy. A central challenge for development is to build states that are both effective and accountable.

The state is not the only source of authority. In many countries, traditional structures of chiefs, elders, clans, and churches sit alongside formal state systems of governors and mayors, while civil society and the private sector are additional sources of power. In some places, the state's writ barely extends beyond the capital city. Nor is the nature of the state static, which is perhaps just as well, as its origins are often bloody. In the words of social historian Charles Tilly, 'war made the state and the state made war'.[127]

Over time, some states have remained mired in this world of raw power and gangsterism, more master than servant, while others have evolved through bargains struck between classes or other interest groups – for example, the right to raise taxes in exchange for defending the national territory. Bodies of law and institutions have come to act somewhat independently of interest groups, bringing rules and disciplines to the running of society, and providing the services deemed essential for development. In all countries, the state remains a work in progress, a place of constant power battles and shifting alliances where reverses are as frequent as advances in terms of redistribution of power, voice, assets, and opportunities.

Overall, the tendency has been for the state to grow. As long ago as the twelfth century, Ch'en Liang, the influential Chinese political thinker, wrote that the human heart is 'mostly self-regarding, but laws and regulations can be used to make it public-minded. This is why the prevailing trend in the world is inevitably moving towards laws and institutions'.[128] As the state's role has expanded, it has accounted for an ever greater proportion of the economy. In 1870, states typically absorbed around 11 per cent of GDP in developed countries. This rose to 28 per cent in 1960 and 42 per cent in 2006.[129]

In his novel *Nineteen Eighty-four*, written at the onset of the Cold War, George Orwell pictured a bleak future of a 'big brother state', 'a boot stamping on a human face, forever'. In fact, in the twentieth century some 170 million people were killed by their own governments, four times the number killed in wars between states.[130] Today, however, the worst deprivation and suffering often coincide with states that are weak or almost non-existent: half of all children who are out of school, and half of those dying before the age of five live in states currently defined as 'fragile'.[131]

Public recognition of the central role of the state ebbs and flows. According to Thandika Mkandawire, an eminent Malawian academic, 'The African state is today the most demonized social institution in Africa, vilified for its weaknesses, its over-extension, its interference with the smooth functioning of the markets, its repressive character, its dependence on foreign powers, its ubiquity, its absence'.[132] In the 1980s and 1990s, followers of the Washington Consensus argued that the state was part of the problem, not the solution (see Part 5). Since the turn of the twentieth century, such market fundamentalism has subsided and, to differing degrees, aid donors and the Washington institutions have turned their attention to how to ensure that states are effective and accountable, rather than absent.

How can states best deliver development? One thing is clear. The Nobel prize-winning scientist Linus Pauling once remarked, 'The best way to have good ideas is to have lots of ideas, and then to discard the bad ones'. The same holds true for states. Successful institutions evolve out of specific national realities, and successful states evolve by doing, failing, and learning, not by importing institutions or policies from elsewhere.

Despite the widespread assumption in the North that developing countries lag behind Europe and North America along a historical continuum, the political cultures of most poor countries are anything but young. Many are based on ancient religious and cultural traditions that are reflected in their political institutions. Geoff Mulgan, who was an adviser to British Prime Minister Tony Blair, observes that while the West emphasises the structures of good government – for example, institutional checks and balances on power – other traditions from China and India have richer insights into how moral principles can be internalised in the minds of rulers and officials. Witness East Asia's strong tradition of meritocratic civil service and the cultivation of learning, both based on Confucian ideals, in part to prevent the formation of permanent elites.[133]

Many lessons can be learned from studying the most successful developing countries in recent years, 'Asian tigers' such as Taiwan, South Korea, Singapore, Malaysia, Viet Nam, China, and others. Although these countries differ hugely in size, economy, and politics, they have several common features that suggest what an economically successful state needs to do:

**Govern for the future:** Governments and officials in these states were intent on transforming the country, rather than merely achieving short-term results or skimming off wealth for a few individuals. Civil servants were largely selected on merit rather than because of personal or party connections.

**Promote growth:** All these states actively intervened in the economy, building infrastructure and directing credit and support to those industries they deemed to be 'winners'. Crucially, they were also able to drop 'losers': if companies or sectors failed to perform, the state withdrew support and let them founder. By promoting domestic savings and investment, they were able to minimise their dependence on fickle sources of foreign capital.

**Start with equity:** South Korea and Taiwan began their take-offs after the Second World War with 'pre-distribution' in the shape of radical land reforms, Malaysia with an affirmative action programme in favour of the economically excluded ethnic Malay population.

**Integrate with the global economy, but discriminate in so doing:** The tigers used trade to generate wealth, but protected fledgling industries. Governments actively promoted national firms, engaging selectively with foreign investment rather than bowing to US and European demands that they accord foreign companies the same treatment as local ones. These economic development policies are discussed in greater detail in Part 3.

**Guarantee health and education for all:** Development is synonymous with healthy and educated populations, not least because an industrial economy requires a skilled and fit workforce. In recent decades, many developing countries (not just in East Asia) have made enormous advances in health and education.

A study of East Asia's successes also debunks some common myths: many economies grew despite high levels of corruption; countries such as China and Viet Nam have not guaranteed Western-style 'property rights' deemed essential by the World Bank and others; and Malaysia and Viet Nam overcame the 'resource curse' of abundant mineral and agricultural wealth that is often seen as a death sentence for developing countries.

## BOX 2.2
## ARE EFFECTIVE STATES COMPATIBLE WITH ACTIVE CITIZENS?

The rise of strong states over the past two centuries is littered with famous names such as Napoleon (France), Cavour (Italy), Bismarck (Germany), Atatürk (Turkey), Mao Tse Tung (China), Stalin (USSR), Chiang Kai-shek (Taiwan), Jawarhalal Nehru (India), Jomo Kenyatta (Kenya), and Sukarno (Indonesia), as well as some not so famous ones like Seretse Khama of Botswana and Lázaro Cárdenas of Mexico.

These leaders inspired a sense of national pride and identity, but their fame seldom stemmed from their commitment to democracy. The most notorious among them sought to establish total state control by crushing any independent action by citizens.

Effective states in East Asia and elsewhere have typically taken off with little initial recognition of human rights or democracy, although this has often improved later on; in Latin America, active social movements and political organisations have rarely been accompanied by effective states. Are the two mutually exclusive? Or is this a case of 'selection bias' – those countries that have had both have already ceased to be poor, and so disappear from the development radar? Many of the most successful transformations in the past century, such as those of Sweden and Finland, have been triggered by social pacts within a democracy, showing what the elusive combination of active citizens and effective states can achieve. Data are limited and beset with measurement problems, but seem to suggest a positive correlation between active citizenship and effective states. Although this does not prove which came first, it at least suggests that they are not mutually incompatible.[134]

In any case, backing authoritarianism in the hope that it could deliver economic growth was never a safe bet. For every Lee Kuan Yew in Singapore or Chinese Communist Party, there have been dozens of autocrats who ignored both citizens and business leaders and drove their economies into the ground. Moreover, the authoritarian road to development is getting harder. The spread of democracy makes it much harder for today's autocrats to achieve legitimacy, either at home or in the eyes of the international community. Widespread awareness of rights means that economic growth alone, while necessary, will not guarantee legitimacy, much less bring about the deep transformations that constitute real development.

## THE POLITICS OF EFFECTIVE STATES

States reflect the history and nature of the society in question. One of the hallmarks of effective states is that they possess economic and political elites willing to participate in building the nation by investing in people, infrastructure, and production. Such elites are sometimes corrupt but confine themselves to skimming off a percentage, aware that to be sustainable, even corruption requires a flourishing economy.[135] By contrast, building effective states becomes extraordinarily difficult when elites are dominated by get-rich-quick politicians and business leaders, or by those unwilling to risk investing at home and who instead park their wealth abroad. This so-called 'national bourgeoisie question' bedevils much of Latin America and Africa.

The glue that binds powerful elites into a national project can stem from history, fear, culture, ideology, leadership, or national pride. In East Asia, war, occupation, and defeat gave rise to nationalism in Japan and communism in China, while the uprooting of existing elites and the persistence of an external threat were important in South Korea, Taiwan, and Hong Kong. Cultural traditions of paternalism and commitment to education undoubtedly helped, although their importance is often exaggerated. Culture is an endlessly malleable concept: prior to South Korea's take-off, Confucianism's respect for authority and hierarchy was held up as one explanation for its *failure* to develop. And effective states have arisen in many cultures: 'African' or 'Latin American' values cannot explain why Botswana or Uruguay were able to build effective states while others around them did not.

Successful states manage a difficult balancing act. They must keep at arm's length groups seeking to 'capture' the state for their own short-term gain, yet must remain deeply integrated into society in order to understand the needs and possibilities of the economy. This 'embedded autonomy' [136] requires a skilled civil service, based on meritocratic appointments and able to experiment and learn from its mistakes as it seeks to build the institutions – economic, social, or political – needed for development.

Where would-be developmental states have failed, it is often because such autonomy could not be maintained. In Latin America, many of the businesses that initially flourished behind tariff barriers failed to invest and increase productivity, but proved adept at lobbying governments for subsidies and continued protection. Latin American governments turned out to be ineffectual at picking winners, but the losers proved masters at picking governments.

States need *legitimacy* in the eyes of most citizens, who accept the state's right to rule in exchange for their ability to seek protection and claim rights. In this, states often resemble banks, which cocoon themselves in pompous buildings and rituals to create an illusion of solidity and to win public confidence, since without that they are remarkably fragile. In the political equivalent of a run on a bank, the astonishing collapse of communist states in Eastern Europe in the early 1990s shows what happens when such legitimacy is lost. In order to manage conflicts within society peacefully, states also need the active support of the most powerful citizens, such as business, ethnic, and religious leaders, or of regional power brokers.

Legitimacy is based on an underlying 'social contract' between state and citizen – a deal, whether explicit or not, that builds confidence and trust between citizens, businesses, and the state by establishing the rights and responsibilities of each. The state's responsibility to protect gives it the right to conscript or to impose martial law. Its responsibility for public welfare gives it the right to raise taxes. Its responsibility for justice bestows the right to arrest and imprison.

Even non-democratic regimes need to achieve a degree of legitimacy to survive over time. In Indonesia, the Suharto regime (1967–98) achieved significant legitimacy for many years, despite its military origins and authoritarian character, by ensuring the basic delivery of education and health services and paying attention to rural development.

Three revealing tests of a state's effectiveness and legitimacy are its ability to manage an impartial system of justice, raise taxes fairly, and spend revenue wisely. In recent years, state spending has been transformed by the trend towards decentralisation, which is aimed at bringing it closer to its citizens.

## ACCESS TO JUSTICE

The relationship between development and institutions such as the law is double-edged. Laws are agreed by leaders and parliaments dominated by elites; Rousseau believed that 'laws are always useful to those who possess and injurious to those who have nothing'.[137] Discrimination, for example against 'non-citizens' such as migrants, or women, can be enshrined in law. In Pakistan, the evidence in court of a Muslim woman is worth half that of a man.[138]

Nevertheless, Oxfam's experience in numerous countries is that access to justice, in the shape of the law and the courts, can be a vital tool for protecting and empowering poor people. For example, enforcing legal guarantees of ownership of land or housing is a crucial issue in ensuring that poor people do not suffer arbitrary expropriation or eviction.

Across the developing world, a gulf exists between laws and practice, since poor people face difficulties in getting the judicial system to take up their cause. Information is unobtainable, the police are hostile or unhelpful (particularly to women and ethnic minorities), and judges are more likely to find in favour of their rich friends and neighbours than of 'upstart' social activists. Labyrinthine legal systems are particularly impenetrable for illiterate people, or indigenous groups without a good command of the official language. And justice costs money: 'If we look for justice in the courts, we make ourselves even poorer – we have to sell a piece of land or some of our things', explains one Guatemalan villager.

Although justice claims to be rules-based and 'blind', in practice activism is often essential to force the judicial system to respond. In South Africa, women's organisations trying to use the legal system to confront domestic violence have found that demonstrators singing and dancing outside the courthouse greatly improve their chances of success.[139]

In the face of such a systemic failure, numerous NGOs and legal aid organisations around the world fight to obtain access to justice for poor people and their organisations. Sometimes they win. In Yemen, the volunteer lawyers of the Yemeni Women's Union (YWU) provide free legal support to poor women in prisons, courts, and police stations, and in 2004–05 won the release of 450 female prisoners. An advocacy campaign mounted by the YWU also led to changes in the law, which had previously forbidden women to leave prison unless collected by a male guardian, and to the opening in 2005 of Yemen's first ever female-staffed detention centre, where women report feeling much less at risk.

## TAXATION

The eighteenth-century philosopher Edmund Burke once observed that 'Revenue is the chief preoccupation of the state. Nay more it is the state.'[140] Taxation not only raises revenue for public spending to fight poverty, it can redistribute wealth and opportunities in order to diminish inequality. Taxation is also central to public accountability. As noted elsewhere in this book, until governments depend on their publics for their wages, it will always be an uphill struggle to force them to listen.

Curiously, taxation is an all but invisible issue in many poor countries, for whom tax represents a 'chicken and egg' problem. Without tax revenue, states struggle to pay civil servants, while a competent civil service is needed to collect tax. There are only about 700 taxpayers in the whole of the DRC (population 59 million), and they provide 90 per cent of domestic revenue.[141] Poorer African and Latin American countries have traditionally depended on resource revenues and taxes on imports, but the latter has declined precipitously due to trade liberalisation.

The nature of taxation is crucial if it is to effectively address inequality. Poor people spend a larger slice of their income on food, clothing, and other essentials, so taxes on income, profits, or property tend to favour redistribution more than taxes on consumption. Recent tax reforms in Latin America, prompted by World Bank advice, have increased value-added tax (VAT) and reduced more progressive taxes, while East Asia has done precisely the opposite.[142] The Bank's logic that VAT is easier to collect, especially when many workers and properties are in the informal economy, has led to poor people paying more than their fair share. Such regressive taxation may help explain the persistence of Latin America's stark inequality – or perhaps, conversely, it points to an ongoing lack of political consensus in deeply divided societies. The shift to VAT at the behest of aid donors is likely to make taxation more visible as a political issue over the coming years, as is the growth of civil society scrutiny of government spending.

South Africa, remarkably, has maintained both a high tax take and a high proportion of socially progressive income and corporate taxation through the transition from apartheid to majority rule. The country collects over three times as much income tax as Brazil – a sign of an underlying 'culture of compliance' by business and white elites, despite the political turbulence of the past 20 years.

Chile's progressive tax system resulted from a unique pact negotiated during the transition from military to civilian rule in 1990. The civilian government held intensive discussions with a wide range of players regarding the 'social debt' owed to the many people impoverished by the economic transformations imposed under the dictatorship. The result was an agreement to increase personal and corporate income tax and VAT, with the extra revenue earmarked for greater social spending.[143]

## DECENTRALISATION

In recent decades, many of the more innovative changes to state structures have occurred through a process with a deeply unenticing name: decentralisation. Under way in some 80 per cent of countries by the end of the 1990s,[144] decentralisation pushes power and decisions down from national to local levels and has become the vogue for both good and bad reasons. On the positive side, proponents argue that it brings power closer to the people, ensuring that local decisions match local needs. Less positively, some governments see decentralisation as a politically acceptable way to evade the demands of national CSOs, especially trade unions, and to reduce the size of the state.

In Southern Peru, Quique Quilla, the mayor of the rural town of Sandia, reckons that the municipality can build schools for half the cost incurred by central government, and says that the population's new involvement and understanding of local administration has changed the nature of local politics: 'Candidates for mayor no longer come along and promise impossible marvels like in the old days – people know what is possible,' he says. Mr Quilla also worries about resources being spent on status symbols such as the impressive but largely empty sports stadia that dot Peru's hinterland rather than the less glamorous business of water, sanitation, or street lighting.

In a limited number of cases – most notably in parts of Bolivia, Brazil, and India – decentralisation has had a remarkable impact, setting in motion a process of citizen demand and government response that has resulted in more effective and accountable states. Bolivia's 1994 Popular Participation Law devolved funds and responsibilities to municipalities and set up local oversight committees of representatives from local groups. The simple decision to allocate public spending on a per capita basis led to the share of funds being channelled to the country's three largest and politically best-connected cities falling from 86 per cent to 27 per cent, and allowed indigenous organisations and others to acquire a far greater say in the workings of the state.[145]

Perhaps the best-known case of decentralised citizen participation is the Participatory Budget process in Brazil, which was developed initially in the city of Porto Alegre but then spread to some 140 Brazilian municipalities by 2000. Meetings that are open to everyone rank spending priorities and elect delegates. The results are impressive: after local communities across Porto Alegre gave top priority to water and sanitation, the number of households with access to water services increased from 80 per cent in 1989 to 98 per cent in 1996, while the proportion of the population served by the sewerage system increased from 46 per cent to 85 per cent.[146]

In India, decentralisation combined with affirmative action has led to an upsurge in women's leadership. A 1992 constitutional amendment required that at least one-third of seats in local councils (*panchayat*) be allocated to women. Around 40 per cent of the women elected have come from families below the poverty line, triggering shifts in public spending on water, community toilets, the promotion of school attendance for girls, and other essential services.[147]

However, in many other cases, decentralisation has made little difference to poor people, and in some cases may have made matters worse. Powerful local elites can hijack the process and devolve graft, rather than power. Local governments, particularly in poor areas, often have neither the money nor the technical expertise to provide quality services. Decentralisation that assigns responsibilities without matching them with resources undermines the redistributive role of national public spending and may increase inequality, as rich areas find it far easier than poor ones to raise revenue from their inhabitants.

Like other tools of development policy, decentralisation requires well-organised, confident social movements that can press for accountability and avoid co-optation by local elites, as well as government commitment and capacity to move funding and technical resources to the local level: in other words, an active citizenry and an effective state.

## TRANSFORMING WEAK STATES

In many parts of the developing world, states bear little resemblance to the effective models described above. With a few notable exceptions, in sub-Saharan Africa, Central America, and Central Asia states have failed to deliver more than brief bursts of development before sliding back.

Bad governance is not a life sentence: numerous states that once would have been branded 'failing' have turned things around. Malaysia went from a post-independence meltdown of ethnic rioting to being an industrial giant. Economist Ha-Joon Chang points to his own country, South Korea, where in the 1960s government officials were sent by the World Bank to Pakistan and the Philippines to 'learn about good governance'.[148]

In Africa, Botswana showed that decolonisation and the 'curse' of massive deposits of diamonds could be turned into development success, while Mauritius has successfully diversified out of sugar dependence into textiles, finance, and tourism (see the case study on page 192). More recently, Ghana and Tanzania have strengthened their public institutions, while Rwanda, Mozambique, and Viet Nam have successfully rebuilt their economies after devastating conflicts.

In the Horn of Africa, Somaliland has demonstrated that change is possible in even the most unpromising of circumstances. After declaring independence from the conflict-ridden and collapsing state of Somalia in 1991, Somaliland has achieved remarkable internal stability based on a combination of presidential and parliamentary elections and traditional councils of elders. It has developed an innovative, community-based approach to peace-building and has harnessed interest and resources from its large international diaspora.

A recent study of efforts to rebuild African states after conflicts concluded that the prospects for stability depend fundamentally on the nature of the political coalition in power.[149] Whether or not the political settlement resolves the differences that led to war, either through real compromise or by the clear victory of one group over others, appears to be crucial. Thus clear victories in civil wars in Uganda, Ethiopia, and Rwanda ushered in periods of stability and state-building, while a negotiated settlement that excluded key parties in the Congo left a weak government. This could also apply to the cases of real compromise in the settlement of El Salvador's civil war, or to the exclusion of parties from the more recent peace agreement in Afghanistan. If this is true, it offers a lesson about how to resolve conflicts: an incomplete negotiated settlement may temporarily reduce human suffering but condemn a country to prolonged instability.

Success in state-building often depends on seizing a moment of political and social consensus after a war, an economic crisis, or a return to democracy to strengthen state institutions, through means such as galvanising the economy (Viet Nam, Mozambique), tax reform (Chile), or rewriting the national constitution (Brazil). Countries' ability to seize that moment invariably depends on domestic politics and institutions. These manage tensions, guarantee (or undermine) stability, and create (or destroy) an 'enabling environment' for businesses. Above all, they respect (or deny) rights, and reduce (or exacerbate) inequality and poverty.

None of this is easy. The German philosopher Georg Hegel described the state as a 'work of art'. As works of conscious design, the greatest constitutions and states stand comparison with the finest achievements of civilisation in visual arts, music, philosophy, or poetry.

They are the collective manifestation of the human imagination, and often surpass individual achievements in the extent to which they have transformed people's lives.[150]

The inter-relationships between active citizenship, effective states, and democracy are complex and constantly evolving. Citizen capacities are often built through state action – providing access to education, health, and information, for example. And state institutions are built, shaped, and then re-shaped through the actions of citizens thus empowered. Formal democracy may enhance the voice and power of citizens, but this depends on the nature of the democratic process: it can also exclude poor and marginal communities, and produce a sense of resignation, rather than empowerment.

# FROM POVERTY TO POWER

Development is about transforming the lives and expectations of a nation's inhabitants, an ambition that goes far beyond simply increasing monetary income. Although the past 60 years have seen enormous progress, huge and urgent challenges remain in tackling injustice, inequality, and needless suffering. The starting point for this effort must be guaranteeing that all people enjoy their basic rights and the ability to exercise them (capabilities). People living in poverty must take or create power over their own lives and destinies. To develop, countries need educated, informed, and healthy citizens and a state both willing and able to provide the essential services on which their well-being depends. The state must also ensure that both the quality and quantity of economic growth meets developmental needs.

Globalisation has complex implications for the politics of building effective states. Most tangible are the increasing constraints it imposes on the economic policies that states can use, which are discussed in Part 5.

However, its political impact is more insidious. The most globally integrated segment in almost every developing country is the political and economic elite. People in this group consume more imported goods, travel more widely, and read the *Financial Times* or the *Herald Tribune*. Their children absorb international culture from MTV and the Internet, and often leave to study at European or North American universities, before returning to lead their countries. To what extent does such integration weaken the sense of national identity and purpose that historically has played a crucial role in building effective states?

On one level this is nothing new: developing-country elites have often been bag carriers for the colonial powers, weakening their own role in building national identities. But global integration raises this to a new level. The danger is that elites across the developing world are becoming most at home shopping in Miami or mixing with the powerful in Washington, New York, or London, and less willing or able to help build development in their own countries.

If this is true, the authoritarian road to state-building is likely to prove even less effective in the future. Elites will use power to extract wealth, rather than invest it. Autocracies will look more like Myanmar than South Korea. A politics of development based on active citizens and political and economic inclusion will become more essential than ever in building the effective, accountable states that remain the key to development.

PART THREE

# POVERTY AND WEALTH

# AN ECONOMICS FOR THE TWENTY-FIRST CENTURY

A day spent in a village or shanty town in the developing world rapidly dispels any notion that people might be poor because they are work-shy. Women rise early to prepare food and get children ready for school, often before heading out to their own paid work in offices, markets, or as cleaners and cooks. Men labour in construction or as porters of goods or people. In the countryside, farming and agricultural labour demand long hours of back-breaking toil in harsh conditions.

Despite all this effort, and the huge wealth generated by the global economy, hundreds of millions of men and women remain desperately poor. Why? This section seeks an answer by exploring the nature of markets – the web of economic interactions that binds individuals, communities, and nations together. At their best, markets are mighty engines, generating wealth and transforming the lives and expectations of people throughout society. At their worst, they exclude poor people, exacerbate inequality, and degrade the natural world on which we all depend.

The problem is not with markets *per se* – Amartya Sen once remarked that 'To be generically against markets would be almost as odd as being generically against conversation' [1] – but with the rules and institutions that govern them. The impact of markets on poverty and inequality depends on whether poor people can exert influence over the way they operate. When small producers, farmers, or workers organise, they can use their increased scale and bargaining power to reduce costs, negotiate better prices or wages, and expand their sales.

When they are organised, people can also convince authorities to alter the structure and rules governing markets to ensure that they get a fair deal. To marshal the power of markets to meet the grand challenges of this century will require action by both states and citizens, and a new approach to the main tool used to understand markets: economics. Time is short: the global economy needs to move rapidly to a 'smart' course of pro-poor, sustainable growth, or else climate change and natural resource constraints will become increasingly disruptive, undermining growth and exacerbating poverty and inequality.

## ECONOMICS

Economics is a broad but divided discipline, comprising dozens of schools of thought covering almost every aspect of human existence and spanning the political and philosophical spectrum. However, this rich diversity of analysis and insight is seldom visible in the economic debates at the centres of power.

For much of the twentieth century, two such schools, the neo-classical and the Keynesian, battled for intellectual supremacy and for the ear of decision-makers. In recent decades, the neoclassical school has been in the ascendant. Within the neoclassical school, there have been many thoughtful efforts to engage with the deep nuance and complexity of development, but in practice, economic policy making is often dominated by a much cruder, 'dumbed-down' version that argues for simplistic solutions to complex problems (liberalise, privatise, avoid a fiscal deficit at all costs). While some economists undoubtedly pander to this need for simple messages, others squirm. The International Monetary Fund's disastrous response to the Asian financial crisis of the late 1990s drove an exasperated Joseph Stiglitz (Nobel laureate turned World Bank chief economist) to lament the 'third-rank students from first-rate universities' who were running the Fund.[2]

The dominance of this version of the neoclassical school rests not solely on the frequently inquisitorial attitude it takes toward other approaches, but also on the simple, compelling, yet deeply flawed picture it offers of the world: that of people and institutions as individual actors relentlessly pursuing their own self-interest.

Assuming human society to consist of atomistic, utility-maximising individuals with fixed preferences enables neoclassical economists to develop the complex mathematical models that give their discipline the appearance of an 'objective' science. Such models in turn allow policy makers to make predictions – implement policy Y and the economy should grow by X – which then justify the allocation of scarce resources, although economists themselves often place heavy health warnings on any effort to predict the future.

The assumptions behind these models often ignore the complexities of real life, in which attitudes, beliefs, and social and political relations influence behaviour as much as does individual self-interest.[3] Markets are often assumed to be natural, when in fact they are governed by detailed rules on contracts, access to credit, competition, collective bargaining, and so on. Such rules are not arrived at in a political vacuum: they reflect the relative strength of those involved in, or excluded from, negotiating them. Prevailing attitudes about the value of particular work are also fundamental, and are often unquestioned by conventional economic thinking.

By making income a proxy for utility (or happiness), the neoclassical approach views development primarily as being about generating rising incomes, and sheds little light on how markets can achieve development in the broader sense, based on rights and dignity.[4] Even within the realm of income, the conventional view focuses on absolute rather than relative incomes, either at a national or individual level, thus often downplaying issues of equity.[5] In this view of the world, poverty reduction takes place as a spin-off of wider economic growth and redistribution, as an afterthought rather than as a central tenet of economic policy making.

Two essential shortcomings of the use of mainstream economics in development are, first, its failure to measure and value unpaid work in the home, rearing children or caring for the sick and elderly; and second, its tendency to downplay environmental degradation. Both failings spring from a reluctance to engage with the non-monetary economy, and both must be remedied if policies are to achieve environmental and social sustainability.

## THE FEMINIST CRITIQUE

Mainstream economics fails to measure or value the production and distribution of goods and services that lie outside the monetised economy, notably unpaid work, such as child care, collecting fuel wood and water, or preparing food – precisely the activities that occupy the time and energies of most poor women and which are essential to sustain society.[6]

While social sustainability is valued in a general way, unpaid work is not recognised in national accounts, even though it subsidises the paid work that does get counted, since it has to be done each day if the formal economy is to continue running. A UN report on measures of unrecorded economic activities in 14 countries shows that unpaid work in households is of the same magnitude as paid work in the market.[7] Estimates of the value of household work as a proportion of GDP vary from 35 per cent to 55 per cent.[8]

All this has huge implications for development policy, as well as for women's rights. The time that unpaid caring work 'takes away' from paid work is considered a drag on the 'real economy' rather than a contribution to it. Therefore only those who can work full-time for their entire lives – mostly men – are considered 'real workers', deserving of decent wages and benefits. The reality is that an increasing number of households are ever more reliant on the lower earnings of women.

This critique is not specifically or uniquely about women. However, the gap between the real and perceived contribution of unpaid labour perpetuates inequality between women and men, and it can result in discrimination against women in public policy and investment decisions. Conventional economic analyses often end up recommending infrastructure projects that address the need for irrigation but not for household water supplies, credit programmes that give loans for oxen but not for corn-grinding mills or fuel-efficient stoves, or labour policies that set minimum wages but do not guarantee a right to maternity leave.

The fact that women and men do different kinds of work springs from a combination of inequality in power, built on social norms and institutions (known as patriarchy), and natural difference (women give birth and breast-feed). The different value attributed by society to the work of women and men is by no means immutable and ought to be changed, since it is both an outcome and a driver of systematic bias against women, transmitted through culture, the family, markets, and the state.

Differences between women and men in terms of what they consume also matter. Women on average choose to spend a higher proportion of their incomes on education and health care, which enhances the well-being and capabilities of their families. Research from many different contexts in both the developing and the developed world shows a correlation between the proportion of money controlled by women and improved child health.[9] Men are likely to spend a higher proportion of income on themselves, but are also more likely to invest in longer-term enterprises, including small businesses, which do not bring immediate benefits to the family but may pay off handsomely in the long run.

By ignoring gender-based differences, policy makers may exacerbate gender inequality. In parts of sub-Saharan Africa, for example, women have generally been more adversely affected by trade liberalisation. Because of their relative disadvantages in gaining access to credit, new technologies, and marketing networks, as well as their relative 'time poverty', women are slower than men to take advantage of new export opportunities.[10] At the same time, liberalisation has increased competition from imports in the domestic food market, where women farmers play a predominant role. In households in which women's bargaining power is weak, men may pressure women to spend more time on cash crop production, while retaining control over the proceeds.

To date, feminist economics has not moved into the mainstream, despite overwhelming evidence that gender equity produces a more prosperous and efficient economy, and despite women's increasing refusal to act as an infinite resource to be exploited without cost. If development is to succeed in reducing poverty and inequality, economics must acknowledge household politics and incorporate as a positive contribution the work invested in caring for the next generation. The global spread of women's rights shows how fast attitudes about women's 'proper' role are changing. Conventional economic thinking needs to catch up.

## THE ENVIRONMENTAL CRITIQUE

Unlike feminism, environmental thinking, the second major lacuna in conventional economics, has moved rapidly from the margins to the mainstream over recent decades, and is reflected in national legislation, the appointment of environment ministers, new academic disciplines, international agreements such as the Kyoto protocol, and massive public awareness. The driving forces behind such change have been the growing and incontrovertible evidence of serious environmental damage and the efforts of active citizens around the world to push the environment higher up the agenda of policy makers.

As long ago as 1987, the concept of 'sustainable development' came to prominence through the Brundtland Report, which defined it as 'development that meets the needs of the present without compromising the ability of future generations to meet their own needs'.[11] While vague, the definition cleverly brought together two fundamental issues: the environmental degradation that so commonly accompanies growth in the market economy, and the need for such growth to alleviate poverty.[12] To solve this apparent contradiction, policy makers need to stop assuming that the natural environment is infinite and begin taking the cost of damaging it into account.

One way to do this is called 'full cost accounting' (FCA). Under FCA, goods and services are priced to reflect their true costs (including environmental and other social costs). Thus the true cost of a vehicle would include its environmental impact and the cost of final disposal, in addition to the cost of manufacture. With full cost accounting, natural resources would be factored into calculations of a country's GDP, natural resources would be redefined as assets on company ledgers, and damage to the environment would be built into a product's cost.

World Bank economists used just such an approach when they estimated the depletion of natural resources and pollution damage in Bolivia in 2003. They found that what conventional economic analysis would have said was a national savings level of 12 per cent of total economic output was actually a net loss of nearly 4 per cent.[13] In China, losses from pollution and ecological damage have ranged from 7–20 per cent of GDP in every year over the past two decades – not even counting the 300,000 deaths per year that are attributed to air pollution.[14]

While the environment matters to everyone, the environment-friendly policies resulting from full cost accounting would especially benefit poor people, whose livelihoods are more directly connected to the natural resource base. Farmers facing drought, fishing communities struggling with falling stocks or dried-up rivers, or slum dwellers at risk of flooding, landslides, and pollution do not need experts to tell them that their environments are deteriorating. For low-income countries, environmental damage is proportionately more costly, since natural resources make up a greater share of their national wealth.[15]

Because of their social and economic roles, women in particular would benefit, as they are often at higher risk and more vulnerable than men to the impacts of environmental degradation. When environmental hazards damage the livelihoods and health of impoverished communities, commonly accepted gender roles place the burden of maintenance, care, and recovery most heavily on women.

Incorporating environmental costs into economic analysis should oblige a fundamental rethink of the role of growth in economic development. Although there is some evidence that the intensity of natural resource use (for example, energy use per unit of GDP) falls after a country develops past a certain point,[16] such declines are outpaced by overall growth in the economy. In other words, there is very little evidence of a genuine 'decoupling' of economic growth from resource use. As of 2003, Cuba was the only country in the world that managed to live within its environmental footprint while achieving high levels of human development.[17] This was probably due to its unique combination of sound environmental management, excellent health and education provision, and an inability to generate sustained growth in the market economy.

Meanwhile, China and India are pursuing rapid GDP growth in much the same ways that Europe and North America did before them. Their success is driving massive increases in consumption (of grain, meat, steel, oil, and timber) and a sharp rise in greenhouse gas emissions. By acting as the 'world's factory', China also allows the countries that consume its goods to outsource their carbon emissions. As a result, China is expected to overtake the USA as the world's number one emitter of carbon dioxide ($CO_2$) sometime within the next few years.

The global ecosystem simply cannot sustain additional billions of people all trying to live like wealthy Americans, even if they subsequently move on to a less resource-intensive, post-industrial lifestyle. According to an estimate by the UN's *Human Development Report*, if all of the world's people generated greenhouse gases at the same rate as Canada or the USA, we would need nine planets to absorb the impact.[18]

Added urgency comes from improved understanding of the non-linear nature of environmental change. Environmental processes are rife with thresholds, or 'tipping points'. When thresholds are crossed, environmental change can become catastrophic and even irreversible. Cod stocks in the Grand Banks off Canada still show few signs of recovering more than 15 years after their sudden collapse and the closure of the fishery in 1992. Scientists now believe that a 2°C rise above pre-industrial levels in average global surface temperatures is the threshold at which dangerous effects on geophysical and biological systems would become likely (see Part 4).

Changing the model of development is a huge task, not least because any new paradigm must avoid 'kicking away the ladder' from countries and communities still struggling to emerge from poverty. It is both politically and morally untenable to say 'the Indians must not have fridges and cars' when rich countries have them in abundance. Instead, a balance must be found that reduces the environmental intensity of rich economies, guarantees fairer access to the world's resources between rich and poor, and preserves the environment.

The good news is that sustainability has become, within a few decades, one of the burning issues of the age, high on the agendas of world leaders and publics alike. But the politics are daunting. The powerful actors who run the economy – corporations, investors, and governments – must be convinced to act in concert and, in many cases, against their own short-term self-interest.

## ASSESSING DEVELOPMENTAL IMPACTS

As employed by policy makers, both neoclassical and Keynesian economics fail to take non-monetary aspects of development and well-being into account. By incorporating unpaid labour, damage to nature, and other essential elements, conventional economic analysis can be broadened to address the much wider range of impacts that policies and institutions have on people and on development. There are at least eight core areas to be considered (shown in Figure 3.1):

**Orthodox economic activity:** growth, return on investment, price stability;

**Income poverty:** wages, government transfers;

**Environmental sustainability:** land (forests, soil), water, air (marine and freshwater systems), climate change;

**Equity:** horizontal (ethnic, geographical), vertical (income, assets), gender;

**Social sustainability:** caring, child rearing, household;

**Vulnerability:** to individual or collective shocks;

**State effectiveness:** human capital formation, tax revenue, administrative capacity;

**Rights and citizenship:** civil, political, economic, cultural.

## FIGURE 3.1: ASSESSING DEVELOPMENTAL IMPACTS

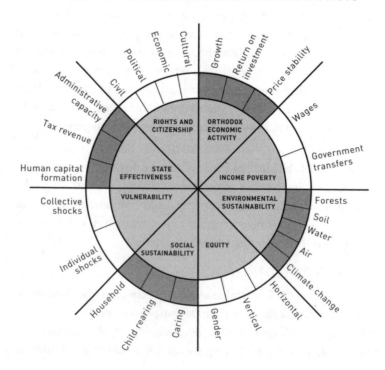

Only the first two core areas (economic activity and income poverty) are customarily covered by conventional economic policy making; the remaining six are usually ignored or downplayed. Yet all need to be considered if the real impact of a given policy or institution on human well-being is to be understood.

For example, a government considering whether to promote exports by creating export-processing zones or encouraging export agriculture would still need to think about growth, return on investment, and price stability, as well as wages and government transfers. But in addition, policy makers would have to address the other six areas. Contemplating the impact on land, air, water, and climate change might raise concerns about water use, pesticide run-off, or the rising carbon emissions from transport. Regarding equity, a government may have to consider whether its actions would benefit the coast more than the interior, or would exclude ethnic minorities not plugged into the market economy, or whether they would enhance women's employment and wages. Similarly, on unpaid labour, it may discover that liberalisation could increase women's role in the paid workforce and require state action to support child rearing.

In the areas of vulnerability, citizenship, and state effectiveness, other equally important considerations would arise. How would vulnerability to individual shocks such as unemployment, or collective ones such as the sudden loss of market access, be mitigated? Would trade union rights be undermined or strengthened? How would the government pay for services, given the low levels of taxation needed to attract investors? Is the government committed to and able to promote industrial upgrading, whether through technical support, finance, or other industrial policies?

The neoclassical approach offers a litmus test, often return on investment or impact on GDP, to provide a 'right' answer. This broader framework instead reflects the messiness of reality: accounting for wealth and well-being, rather than solely for growth, means internalising the costs of resource use, unpaid labour, and other so-called 'externalities' into everyday economic thinking, and moving the emphasis from flows of goods and services in markets to their impact on welfare and sustainability. This approach includes far more attention to issues of insecurity and inequality, which are central to well-being but are largely marginal to discussions of growth in the market economy.

One approach to implementing such an 'economics for the twenty-first century' is to try to expand the number of factors considered in a numerical calculation of the relative costs and benefits of different policy options, for example by moving towards full cost accounting. This retains the core attraction of economics as a discipline: attaching numbers enables policy makers to say 'Option A is better than option B'. Factors such as active citizenship, an effective state, the enjoyment of rights, or a wider sense of well-being are hard to measure, however, and may end up being squeezed to the margins of debate. As Einstein once observed, 'Everything that can be counted does not necessarily count; everything that counts cannot necessarily be counted.'

An alternative approach would be to treat the numerical exercise as just one contribution to the debate, to be balanced against other less quantifiable, but no less important issues. In any given time and place, a particular policy will be positive in some of its impacts and negative in others. Decision-makers will always need to consult, identify trade-offs, and agree priorities: such discussions are the stuff of politics, which in the end should be served, and not ruled, by economics.

# LIVING OFF THE LAND

The smoky, cold hut in the mountainous interior of Viet Nam is crammed with men and women from the indigenous H'moung people, dressed in traditional black and indigo leggings and smocks. There is barely a trace of the modern world: no plastic, no calendars or photos on the walls. The women, sporting cylindrical black felt hats and large silver hoop earrings, do not speak Vietnamese. The topic also is traditional: how to use straw (and more memorably, rubbing alcohol) to keep their most prized assets, buffalo, warm and fed in winter to reduce the risk of sickness.

This sanctuary of tradition is under siege. The richest houses in the village already boast a motorbike or a television set and, a few kilometres away, the local town is filling with the more intrepid type of tourist. These visitors will bring income, buying artefacts and food, helping the H'moung to diversify their livelihoods and so reduce their vulnerability to crop failure or a sick buffalo. But the tourists' presence will also dilute, if not destroy, the very 'purity' that drew them here. Do the H'moung care? Not yet, apparently. 'Farming is hard. My dream for my kids is education and a skilled job – I want them to get out', says one man. 'Even if they leave the village and I am alone – I want them to study Vietnamese, English, or French, not H'moung.'

The fast-evolving rural world entails both opportunities and threats for its inhabitants. Change is uneven, and often faster in areas that are more connected to markets, but few areas escape change altogether. Rural isolation is being eroded by the spread of roads, literacy, and communications. Farming communities are becoming increasingly familiar with the urban world, whether from radio, television, or the stories of returning migrants. Increased ease of movement is blurring the boundary between rural and urban, as family members move between the two worlds, combining jobs and production into complex family livelihood strategies.

Members of farming families work as labourers on neighbouring farms, gather wild produce, raise or catch fish, produce crafts and other goods, or offer services such as carpentry or midwifery. In some of the world's more arid areas, some 100–200 million largely nomadic people also live from herding livestock (the challenges facing pastoralists are discussed in Part 4). Almost everywhere, farmers' children leave the farm and head for the cities, sending back money to help their parents survive.

Small wonder people are leaving. Rural households are not only income-poor: literacy rates and life expectancy are consistently below national averages, and school drop-out and infant mortality rates are higher. Poor households in rural areas are particularly vulnerable to shocks, due to the vicissitudes of farming and the absence of buffer mechanisms such as access to credit or insurance. When things go wrong, farmers and farm workers are usually on their own. As if this were not enough, in vast tracts of southern and eastern Africa, the scourge of HIV and AIDS has wiped out the working-age generation and its accumulated knowledge, leaving increasing numbers of child-headed households and fallow land. In Burkina Faso, a study of two villages found that HIV and AIDS had reduced income from agriculture by 25–50 per cent.[19]

For the past two decades, aid donors and governments have effectively withdrawn from the countryside. Aid to agriculture dropped from 11.4 per cent of all aid in 1983–84 to 3.4 per cent in 2004–05.[20] Between 1980 and 2004, spending on agriculture as a share of total government expenditure fell in Africa (from 6.4 per cent to 5 per cent), in Asia (14.8 per cent to 7.4 per cent), and in Latin America (8 per cent to 2.7 per cent).[21] Under 'structural adjustment programmes' (SAPs), a radical free-market approach largely imposed on indebted countries by aid donors, the IMF, and the World Bank, many governments broke up state marketing boards and curtailed investment in extension services to farmers, public research, rural infrastructure, and credit provision.[22]

Though abandoned by governments and by millions of residents, half of the world's six billion people still live in the countryside. Rural areas still account for the majority of people living in absolute poverty and for half of the world's undernourished people. Despite urbanisation, around 50 per cent of people living in poverty will still be in the countryside in 2040.[23]

Despite diversification, agriculture remains at the heart of rural life in developing countries. Two-and-a-half billion people live in households involved in agriculture, over half of them either landless or on farms of less than two hectares. One in five works as an agricultural labourer, a proportion that is rising in most regions.[24]

The history of countries as disparate as the USA, Taiwan, and Costa Rica shows that agriculture can enable people to work their way out of poverty. Moreover, improving farm output is a critical first step for national economic take-off. Citing agriculture's 'special powers,' the World Bank concludes that it is at least twice as effective at reducing poverty as growth in other sectors.[25] Growth in smallholder agriculture is particularly effective, especially in countries with a fair distribution of land (see Figure 3.2).[26]

Agricultural growth generates higher incomes for farmers, including smallholders, and more jobs as labour demand rises, pushing up wage rates. The rural economy as a whole then picks up, as more prosperous small farmers and labourers increase demand for goods and services. Greater numbers of rural jobs and increased incomes generally lead to improved nutrition, better health, and increased investment in education, while increased local tax revenues allow local governments to respond to demands for better infrastructure, such as roads, power supplies, and communications. Agricultural growth also reduces food prices for poor people, whether urban or rural.

The contribution of small farms to growth usually dwindles as an economy takes off. As wages rise and the use of technology increases, the commercial advantage shifts to larger farms, while the centre of gravity of the economy as a whole normally shifts to largely urban manufacturing and services, which suck in labour from the countryside.

## FIGURE 3.2: MORE EQUAL INITIAL LAND DISTRIBUTIONS GO TOGETHER WITH HIGHER ECONOMIC GROWTH

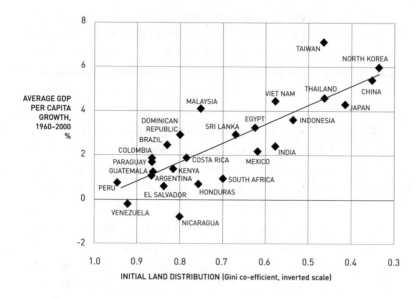

Source: World Bank, *World Development Report 2006*

Beyond its role as a springboard for economic growth, small-scale agriculture also acts as a vital social safety net, employing millions of people who would have minimal prospects of finding decent work in the cities, and providing a social security system of last resort for those unable to survive in the city in times of economic crisis. During Indonesia's financial crash of 1998, agriculture absorbed an extraordinary 4.5 million people in a mass out-migration from the cities, as migrants headed back to their old villages after losing their jobs in factories and on building sites.[27]

Agricultural growth reduces poverty most effectively when small farmers capture a fair share of the benefits. That in turn requires strengthening their power in markets, reinvigorating the role of the state, and ensuring that all the rural poor, male and female, indigenous and non-indigenous, have a voice in these processes.

New trends in agriculture have transformed rural people's lives and livelihoods and have reawakened the interest of governments and aid donors. The rising global demand for food, the advent of supermarkets and contract farming, and a new wave of technological change may hasten the out-migration of small farmers. But these factors could also augur well for agricultural growth and rural livelihoods, if states and citizens can harness them for fighting poverty and inequality. The next section examines how a combination of active citizens and effective states could again make agriculture a source of widespread prosperity.

## ALL CHANGE ON THE FARM

Tourists arriving to see the extraordinary wildlife parks around Kenya's Lake Naivasha pass serried ranks of greenhouses and fields devoted to producing flowers and high-value crops such as green beans and peas for European consumers. The plains around the Colombian capital of Bogotá churn out millions of roses for Valentine's Day bouquets. Indigenous peasant farmers in the Guatemalan highlands grow snowpeas (mangetout) and raspberries for the USA. The coastlines of developing countries everywhere are dotted with fish farms – prawns in Bangladesh, Ecuador, or Indonesia; salmon in Chile.

Driven by booming demand, improvements in refrigeration, and falling transport costs, fresh and processed fruits and vegetables, fish, nuts, spices, and flowers now account for over half of all farm exports from developing countries: about $106bn in 2003–04, overtaking traditional bulk commodities such as coffee, tea, or rice.[28] Even in domestic markets in poor countries, urbanisation and new generations of middle-class consumers are creating booming markets for poultry and vegetables. Whether small farmers can benefit from this 'new agriculture' is a critical question for their future survival, and is linked to the changes in the way that food is bought and sold, both in the North and the South.

Transnational companies have expanded their operations in developing countries to achieve vertical integration of their operations and to appropriate a larger share of value along the production chain. Small producers increasingly deal directly with such large corporations, whether to buy fertiliser or seeds, or to sell their produce or their labour, a negotiation characterised by the enormous imbalance in their relative power – millions of isolated small producers versus a handful of corporate giants. Just four companies account for 45 per cent of all coffee-roasting activities.[29] In cocoa, four companies control 40 per cent of the grinding industry, [30] and similar stories can be told for other food sectors. Six companies now control 80 per cent of global pesticide sales,[31] down from 12 firms in 1994.[32]

Some transnational corporations have stepped belatedly into roles vacated by the state under structural adjustment programmes, albeit with a very different approach. Global seed and fertiliser giants now provide small-scale farmers with inputs, finance, and extension services. Such services are sometimes part of production agreements that also include a guaranteed price, a practice known as 'contract farming'. The impact on small farmers of such arrangements depends on the nature of the contract – there are examples of both 'good' and 'bad' contract farming. When it works well, it combines the best of both small and large farm systems – the higher productivity per hectare of small farms and the access to capital, markets, and technology enjoyed by larger players.[33]

However, contract farming can also involve extortionate interest or extraction of profits, and may push smallholders towards the mono-cropping favoured by the companies. The arrangement shifts control away from women, who still do much of the work but no longer receive the money because contracts are usually signed by men. Most seriously, under contract farming, poor farmers must bear all the risk inherent in their trade. If crops fail it is the farmers, not the companies, who take the hit, and contract farmers can easily get into serious debt as a result.[34]

A study of contract farming in Thailand found that farmers' incomes fluctuated wildly.[35] Farmers had to take on bank loans that took five to ten years to pay off, while companies signed contracts only year-to-year. Some farmers were left without a buyer for more than six months, with no notice or compensation. The average debt of households involved in contract farming was more than ten times the national average for farming households, making it almost impossible for the farmers to quit. They often never received a copy of the contract binding them, and sometimes did not even have the opportunity to read it. The study concluded that the farmers are *de facto* employees, but the company takes no responsibility for social security, sick leave, paid leave, or severance pay.

The typical tourist image of colourful, chaotic street markets and warrens of small shops is a stereotype that is quickly going out of date, thanks to the rapid spread of supermarkets in developing countries. In response to urbanisation, the rise of a consuming middle class, and more liberalised investment rules, locally and internationally owned supermarkets now buy the lion's share of farm production in many countries, creating a demand for intermediate- to high-quality products in countries that traditionally exported such goods.

The first wave of supermarkets hit developing countries in the early 1990s, appearing in major cities in the richer countries of East Asia (outside China), Central Europe, and Latin America. By 2000, they accounted for 50–60 per cent of retail sales, close to their share in the USA or France. They soon expanded to smaller and poorer countries in Central America, the Andes, and Southern and then Eastern Africa. Their take-off in Asia is now registering even faster growth than in Latin America. According to China's Ministry of Commerce, 70,000 supermarkets opened in rural areas of the country in 2005.[36] The phenomenon is now beginning to be seen in South Asia and West Africa.

The implications for small farmers are profound. Supermarkets source the majority of their products locally, and the volumes traded are significant. In Latin America, the value of local food purchased by supermarkets is 2.5 times higher than the region's exports to the rest of the world.[37] Domestic markets are central to the livelihoods of small farmers, and supermarkets could potentially expand farmers' sales. But unless they can meet the supermarkets' demanding quality and quantity requirements, farmers risk being consigned to the least profitable backwaters of the domestic economy, just as they are currently at the global level.

The rise of food processors and fast food chains in developing countries poses similar challenges. Citing problems of scale and quality, branches of McDonalds and Pizza Hut in Ecuador prefer to import potatoes for French fries, even though the Andes is the original home of the potato. Similar problems have dogged the spread of tourism. Caribbean smallholders have watched in frustration as hotels import burgers, vegetables, and fruit from the USA, while they have to eke a living from low-priced and volatile commodity markets such as the one for bananas. In St Lucia, local producers have come up with a brand name, 'Farm Fresh – St Lucia's Best', to build the profile of local suppliers, but they need training and technical support to meet the quality and quantity standards required by the tourist trade.

New corporate buyers could potentially help to revitalise small-scale agriculture. Such an outcome will only occur, however, if farmers organise to increase their ability to negotiate a fair deal, and if they receive the support they desperately need to raise the quality and quantity of their output.

---

## BOX 3.1
## FISHERIES: MANAGING A FINITE RESOURCE

For millions of poor people in rural areas, fishing is a source of livelihood, income, and food. Fish provides at least 20 per cent of the protein consumption of 2.6 billion people (almost half the global population),[38] and fishing directly or indirectly employs almost 500 million people across the developing world. Despite the fact that the world's fisheries generate approximately $120bn per year, 95 per cent of the labour force survives on $2 per day or less.[39] Developing countries account for 50 per cent of the total volume of traded fish, representing the single biggest food item in developing-country exports.[40]

The international trading system in fish suffers from many of the same problems as agriculture: developing-country governments are being pressured to open their markets to cheap imports, with devastating impacts on local fishers, while Northern governments persist in heavily subsidising their fishing industries, which fish with little regard for the health of coastal ecosystems.[41] About half the world's fish catch is taken by small-scale fishers and the other half by large-scale corporate fishing fleets, but small-scale fisheries generate 20 times more jobs.[42]

In most developing countries, fisheries management is weak and overfishing and conflicts between small-scale fishers and commercial fleets abound. Over the past 40 years, standing fish stocks in South-East Asia have been reduced to less then a quarter of their former levels, prompting governments in many countries to try to manage the resource through licences and permits, rather than seek ever larger catches.[43]

The Philippines, home to between one and two million fishers, is piloting an alternative approach known as community-based coastal resource management (CB-CRM), whereby fishing communities are responsible for restoring ecosystems, patrolling fisheries, and monitoring impact. CB-CRM builds on a long tradition of organisation at both local and national levels. Started by the Filipino association Kilusang Mangingisda, which is now a nationwide movement with approximately 400,000 members, the CB-CRM approach has spread across South-East Asia.

With numbers and organisation came influence, and in 1996 the Philippines government revised the fisheries law, establishing municipal jurisdiction over fishing grounds and creating municipal councils where government agencies and representatives of fishing communities now discuss and agree on local fisheries management provisions.[44] Local fishers have seen a halt in the decline of their catches, and in some cases even a recovery, though overfishing remains a problem.

Source: L. van Mulekom (2007) 'Reflections on Community Based Coastal Resources Management (CB-CRM) in the Philippines and SE Asia', Oxfam International internal paper.

## GREEN REVOLUTION REDUX

Modernising and improving on largely traditional techniques for ploughing, sowing, and harvesting is a mainstay of development practice, and certainly part of the answer to the plight of small farmers and to the rising global demand for food. Some observers place enormous hopes in the technological revolution under way in the laboratories of universities and global corporations, trusting in a repeat of the phenomenal increase in agricultural productivity in Asia in the 1960s and 1970s known as the 'Green Revolution'.

The Green Revolution stemmed from two parallel initiatives. Better known is the widespread adoption of new rice and wheat varieties, combined with the use of chemical fertiliser in largely irrigated environments. But equally important was state investment in roads, irrigation, and other infrastructure and institutions to ensure stable prices for farmers. Together, these initiatives spurred significant success in reducing rural poverty, although many farmers went heavily into debt as they had to invest in fertilisers and pesticides, and there were serious knock-on effects on the environment.

Recently, a number of major donors, led by the Gates and Rockefeller Foundations, have set up the Alliance for a Green Revolution in Africa (AGRA), hoping to repeat the Asian experience.[45] They will face a drastically different terrain to their predecessors half a century ago. The first Green Revolution relied on strong civil-service institutions, functioning credit markets, a predominance of rice and wheat production, dense rural populations that made it cost-effective to provide technical assistance and other services, and abundant water for irrigation. Africa, in contrast, has weak or non-existent agricultural support institutions, insufficient water, and a profusion of staple food crops.[46] Moreover, the network of state-funded research that made the Green Revolution possible has largely been supplanted by private corporate R&D.

It is unlikely that any technological magic bullet will address all these issues. Even more challenging is the fact that Asia's achievement was driven by drastically increasing the use of fossil fuels, irrigation, chemical fertilisers, and pesticides, all of which exacted an environmental cost which is now coming home to roost. Modern agriculture has bequeathed a world of exhausted and eroded topsoil, scarce water, irrigation-induced salinisation, water systems polluted by pesticide and fertiliser run-off, and reduced biodiversity. Not to mention global warming: agriculture and forestry produce an estimated one-third of all greenhouse gases.[47]

In these conditions, incorporating small farmers into current commercial agriculture practices hardly appears to be a sustainable option. All agriculture will have to adapt to growing environmental constraints. Technological innovation will undoubtedly play a large role in such adaptation, and small farmers will have to organise and cultivate state support if they are to overcome their relative technological exclusion. If they do not, they risk being driven out of farming altogether.

Recent and incipient waves of technological change pose additional threats and opportunities. For example, nanotechnology (the manipulation of matter on the scale of atoms or molecules) could produce a petroleum-based, stain-resistant substitute for cotton, which would have cataclysmic implications for the ten million small farmers in West Africa who grow cotton for a living.[48] On the other hand, the University of Stavanger, Norway, has developed a nanoporous membrane that can prevent water loss from soil and regulate soil temperature in the face of extreme weather.[49]

Biotechnology, and in particular the introduction of genetically modified seeds for crops such as maize, canola, soybean, and cotton, has attracted the most controversy. Supporters of GM technology claim it will create seeds geared to poor people's needs. 'Golden Rice', a GM variety engineered to remedy the vitamin A deficiency that afflicts hundreds of thousands of children with blindness, is perhaps the best-known example. GM also promises crops appropriate for difficult geographies and climates, for example drought-resistant varieties that could play a role in adapting to climate change.

These optimistic claims are disputed, not least because such warm words are not matched by deeds: the vast majority of GM crops have been genetically engineered to meet the needs of large-scale farms, for instance in reducing herbicide or insectide use and minimising the need for labour. The only major exception to date is insect-resistant Bt cotton, grown by some nine million small farmers in China and India.[50] Although transgenic maize is being grown in South Africa and the Philippines, there is no serious investment in the five most important semi-arid tropical crops – sorghum, pearl millet, pigeon pea, chickpea, and groundnut – which are grown mainly by small farmers.

An alternative route to technological adaptation could be through sustainable agriculture (see Box 3.2). Attempting to marry the best of old and new farming technologies, the sustainable approach seeks to integrate natural biological and ecological processes, minimise the use of non-renewable inputs, and make productive use of farmers' knowledge and skills and their capacity to work together. The most comprehensive survey to date puts the number of farmers involved in transitions towards sustainable agriculture at 12.6 million, between them farming over 1m hectares – 3 per cent of the total cultivated area in developing countries. These farms show a mean increase in yields of 79 per cent, contravening the widespread supposition that sustainable agriculture necessarily sacrifices high yields. Over half of the projects involving integrated pest management have reduced pesticide use *and* increased yields.[51]

Sustainable agriculture may be more compatible with climate change and other environmental constraints than a new Green Revolution. For example, maintaining organic soil cover to minimise erosion, a practice known as 'zero tillage', which has been hailed by the World Bank as 'one of agriculture's major success stories in the past two decades'[52] also sequesters significant amounts of carbon. Carbon constraints, whether through higher prices or government regulation, may work to the benefit of sustainable agriculture and small farmers relative to industrial and large-scale agriculture, which tend to be more avid carbon users.

To date, sustainable agriculture has received relatively little backing from governments, but political pressure from organised farmers and their allies could turn that around. That said, many sustainable practices rely on highly specific knowledge of local ecosystems that it is hard to replicate.

## THE BIOFUEL BOOM

Farmers everywhere try to cash in when demand for a particular product rises, whether through shifts in consumption patterns (such as the transition to meat-based diets in Asia) or technological change. The latest boom commodity, biofuels, uses plant-based 'biomass' to generate energy, for example replacing oil-based fuels in transport or electricity generation. Driven by a combination of rising oil prices, fears over energy security, technological innovation, and concern over climate change, farmers the world over are now growing crops to be made into fuel. The main crops grown for biofuels are sugar, grain, palm oil, and wood.

The impact of such fuels on carbon emissions and the ecosystem is highly disputed (especially in the case of maize-based ethanol).

BOX 3.2
## A BEGINNER'S GUIDE TO SUSTAINABLE AGRICULTURE

Key principles are to:

- Integrate natural biological and ecological processes such as soil regeneration, predation, and parasitism into food production;
- Minimise the use of those non-renewable inputs that cause harm to the environment or to the health of farmers and consumers;
- Make productive use of the knowledge and skills of farmers;
- Work together to solve common problems in areas such as pest, watershed, irrigation, forest, and credit management.

Defining practices and technologies include:

**Integrated pest management**, which uses ecosystem resilience and diversity for pest, disease, and weed control;

**Integrated nutrient management**, which seeks to fix nitrogen within farm systems rather than import nutrients, and to reduce nutrient loss through erosion control;

**Conservation tillage**, which reduces the amount of tillage, sometimes to zero, so that soil can be conserved and available moisture can be used more efficiently;

**Agroforestry**, which incorporates multi-functional trees into agricultural systems and collective management of nearby forest resources;

**Aquaculture**, which incorporates fish, shrimp, and other aquatic resources into farm systems, to increase protein production;

**Water harvesting**, which allows for irrigated cultivation of abandoned and degraded lands owing to better rainwater retention;

**Livestock integration**, which incorporates livestock into farming, including the use of zero-grazing cut-and-carry systems.

Source: J. Pretty (2006) 'Agroecological Approaches To Agricultural Development', background paper for World Development Report 2008, World Bank.

The jury is also still out on whether the biofuel boom, and the scramble for land it has triggered, will benefit small farmers and other poor people or generate sustained growth.[53] Biofuel plantations for maize or sugar create jobs, but working conditions are often horrific, wages are low, and the plantations can squeeze out small farmers. The chair of the UN Permanent Forum on Indigenous Issues recently warned that 60 million indigenous people worldwide face eviction from their land to make way for biofuel plantations.

In the case of palm oil, small farmers account for a significant proportion of total production in Indonesia and Malaysia, where 80 per cent of the world's palm oil is grown, and could stand to benefit from the boom. However, many of Indonesia's 4.5 million small producers are heavily indebted to the companies that buy their crop, and have little power to negotiate decent prices. As with any other commodity boom, the extent to which small producers can exercise power in the new market will help to determine whether biofuels exacerbate exclusion and inequality in the countryside, or whether they will provide new pathways out of poverty for small farmers.

Moving arable land out of food production and into biofuels will push up food prices: good news for farmers, but bad for poor consumers, especially if it leads to global food shortages, as some fear. By early 2008, after several years in which demand outpaced supply, global food stocks had fallen to their lowest level in 20 years.[54] The final irony is that some companies are deforesting land in order to plant palm oil, thus aggravating the global warming which motivated the biofuel boom in the first place.

An extraordinary amount is being asked of agriculture. The World Bank estimates that to meet projected demand (based on a combination of rising population and changing dietary preferences), global cereal production will have to increase by nearly 50 per cent and meat production by 85 per cent between 2000 and 2030. In addition, the burgeoning demand for biofuels and animal feeds cuts into the production of staple foods.[55] Not only must yields rise (there is little spare land, and the remaining forests must be conserved), but they must do so sufficiently rapidly and cleanly to compensate for other negative trends, such as climate change, salinisation, and deteriorating soil fertility.

At the same time, productivity must be increased in a way that benefits poor people and reduces inequality. Technology will have to be governed in a very different way if it is to help achieve these objectives, with a much higher degree of state regulation and direct involvement in R&D, backed up by an enhanced voice for farmers and other citizens' groups in how technologies are developed and used. The current situation, dominated by large corporations, with farmers as mere consumers of technological change, skews agriculture towards a chemical- and capital-intensive model that is likely to bypass small producers and ratchet up inequality and environmental damage in the countryside.

Whether and how agriculture rises to these challenges will depend in large part on how poor people in rural areas organise to make themselves heard, and on the willingness and ability of the state to pursue a pro-poor development path. The next section explores this essential combination of active citizens and effective states.

## POWER IN MARKETS

A hundred rice farmers, men and women, are gathered in the shade of a giant mango tree in the village of Ruwayo, in central Nigeria. The sound of women cracking peanuts into tubs provides a backdrop to a rambling conversation about the life of the small farmer in Nigeria. 'We used to feel the government support in the old days, in the 1980s', says one woman. 'They gave us fertilisers, we could hire tractors.' Now banks will not lend money to farmers without collateral, while money-lenders charge eye-watering interest rates. The local farmers' organisation set up a savings and loan scheme, but their problems do not end with credit. Farmers must take the prices offered by visiting buyers because they have no transportation of their own. If they rent a truck, the police demand bribes at every roadblock on the way into town.

For many of the poorest farming communities, the way forward lies not through high-tech innovation, but through improved organi-sation to enhance their market power. Small farmers lack power in markets precisely because they are small, poor, and unorganised. This makes it harder for them to obtain information on markets and prices, or credit to invest in improvements, or simply to survive between harvests. They have little bargaining power because they lack transport or storage facilities, and are unable to offer a steady supply of produce. They are price-takers, not price-makers.

At a political level, the voices of small farmers are often drowned out by better-organised and resourced groups of large farmers, agribusinesses, and city-dwellers. Moreover, women farmers face prejudice on the part of lenders, agricultural extension workers, and farmers' organisations. Remoteness from a city or town, with their markets full of hungry consumers, is a major obstacle, because small farmers lack the clout to get governments to build roads or other transport links.

Organisation is central to meeting such challenges. In Holeta in the central highlands of Ethiopia, for example, where in 2002 most families lived on less than $1 a day, local farmers were efficient producers of millet, but the price they commanded was barely enough to cover their production costs. So the community established a 'cereal bank' into which producers 'deposit' their harvest and from which they draw corresponding payments. Today, they enjoy a reliable store of grain all year round, sell into the market when the price is high, and no longer need to purchase seed.

People living in rural areas have long organised in a range of different ways: trade unions, co-operatives, funeral societies, mutual health insurance groups, self-help groups, and savings and credit groups. Since the 1980s, the number of independent producer organisations (POs) has mushroomed.[56] Between 1982 and 2002 the number of villages with a PO rose from 21 per cent to 91 per cent in Burkina Faso.[57] Between 1990 and 2005, the number of co-operatives increased from 29,000 to 50,000 in Nigeria.[58] Over a longer period (1966 to 1998) in India the total number of co-operative societies increased from 346,000 to 488,000, involving 65 per cent of all rural households.[59]

In previous decades, the reputation of POs in many countries was tarnished by government-sponsored top-down 'co-operatives' that did little for their members. Even today, in Ethiopia rural co-operatives are largely controlled by party officials, while in Ghana, they must pass a six-month probationary period that is often extended before they can formally register. As a consequence, many POs remain as unregistered, informal organisations, which limits their legal safeguards and their ability to raise loans.[60]

As a new generation of bottom-up POs takes root, that legacy of suspicion is being overcome. In the northern Albanian village of Kiri, where villagers gather wild mountain herbs to sell for cash, the legacy of forced collectivisation under communism made people initially reluctant to form a co-operative. So they set up a Herb Association which helped them improve the quality of their product, find new buyers, and increase household incomes by 40 per cent. Oxfam has seen farmers, governments, and aid donors embrace such initiatives in countries as diverse as Mali, Honduras, and India. A significant pro-portion of new POs are commercially oriented and concentrated in high-value product markets, often for export. Relatively few operate successfully in domestic staple food markets, where prices are too low and transactions too small to cover the costs of organisation, both in finance and time.[61]

---

## BOX 3.3
## THE SWEET TASTE OF SUCCESS IN COLOMBIA

In 2002, a group of private sugar mills applied for a licence to build a large *panela* mill in the impoverished Patía region of northern Colombia. *Panela* is a brown sugarloaf made from sugarcane, which is used as a low-cost, nutritious sweetener. The step up from small, family-run units to industrial production promised to create jobs and improve cost and quality for con-sumers. Just the sort of investment to pull people out of poverty, economists said, as the urban market was largely untapped.

The impoverished farmers who made their meagre living from *panela* did not see it that way, fearing they would be pushed out of even an expanded market. Some Rural Development Ministry officials concurred, adding that a single factory could manipulate prices to both farmers and consumers. Moreover, when the initial tax breaks ran out, the factory might close down, leaving every-one worse off.

The small producers formed an informal association and launched a campaign to persuade the government to reject the planned mill. *Panela* production is the main source of income for the rural population, they argued, and an industrial mill would provide jobs for only a handful of the hundreds of poor farmers and their families who might lose their livelihoods. Furthermore, the profits would accrue to owners who never showed their faces in Patía.

The campaign succeeded in blocking the project – fortunately without violence. The investors shrugged their shoulders and took their money elsewhere, but the experience had changed the farmers. They had discovered not only that many more people were willing to buy their *panela*, but also that they could make more money by selling directly to wholesalers. Most importantly, they had discovered the power of organisation.

Flushed with victory, in 2004 a group of them established their own trading organisation, which after initial difficulties was able to raise the price paid to producers by over 40 per cent. The association plans to further increase producers' income by tapping the more lucrative organic market.

The *panela* producers' experience exemplifies the challenge and promise of achieving economic development in a way that enhances, rather than undermines, small farmers' power in markets and the need for farmers to organise if they are to influence the structure and rules governing the markets in which they operate.

*Source*: C. Penrose-Buckley (2007) *Producer Organisations: A Guide to Developing Collective Rural Enterprises,* Oxford: Oxfam GB.

Marketing is the core activity of most POs, whether they are full-blown co-operatives or looser associations. In addition, POs help farmers obtain cheaper credit and negotiate better prices for inputs such as fertilisers and seeds. Some POs arrange or acquire processing facilities and transport to markets (especially important in remote areas), and provide the kind of training and technical assistance needed to move into higher-value products and to guarantee the higher-quality standards needed to break into more lucrative markets.

- The National Smallholder Farmers' Association of Malawi (NASFAM) was built from the bottom up and currently has almost 5,000 clubs, with 96,000 farmer members. The association markets members' products, such as tobacco, cotton, groundnuts (peanuts), and rice, negotiates better deals for transport and fertiliser, and arranges loans for its members with major national banks.[62]

- In a remote rural area in south-western Uganda, one farmers' association successfully negotiated a contract to provide high-quality Irish potatoes to the Kampala outlet of Nandos, the South African-owned fast food chain. To meet the required volumes, frequency of supply, and quality, the farmers invested in learning technical, organisational, and management skills; the contract provided them with the security to make these investments.[63]

- In Bolivia, the National Association of Quinoa Producers (ANAPQUI) brings together about 5,000 growers of quinoa, a traditional, highly nutritious Andean grain, which enjoys a small but growing export market. The association pays a fixed price, agreed in advance, organises technical assistance, and runs a processing plant for its members. Many quinoa farmers have expanded their farms and some have mechanised their production, thanks to the greater incomes and security they now enjoy, which have also allowed more families to keep their children in school.[64]

Beyond these immediate benefits, the strength in numbers and exchange of experience within POs can build people's self-confidence. POs often become engaged in political action, since their economic success can depend on changing the rules or practices that govern markets, which only states can enforce. These can be as sophisticated as demanding legislation to establish floor prices or competition laws, or as simple as building roads. Where a government is committed to agriculture, POs play a vital role in ensuring that policies reflect the needs of small farmers, and not just of the usually well-organised large farm lobby.

Oxfam's experience suggests that POs work best when they focus on a single role, such as marketing or negotiating better prices, at least to begin with. More ambitious plans, such as owning and operating processing plants, often fail. Focusing on relatively high-value products, such as dried fruit or cotton, seems to work better than concentrating on staple foods. Building on small, pre-existing groups where mutual trust is already established works better than creating large organisations from scratch. Member-driven organisations last longer than top-down ones, while keeping the group independent of political parties and focused on its core business is essential.[65]

POs are not without difficulties. The costs of setting up the organisation, training members, and establishing an efficient administration often have to be raised from outside, either from sympathetic NGOs or the private sector.[66] Members have to invest time in group meetings and activities on top of their daily toil in the fields. When groups become larger, it takes considerable time and effort to manage decision-making in a way that respects all members' interests.

The focus on high-value cash crops frequently discriminates against women, and reinforces male dominance of POs' leadership. It also means that POs tend not to address the needs of the poorest and most vulnerable of small farmers, since high-value crops entail risks that the poorest cannot afford. Women's organisations, such as India's Self Employed Women's Association or Nicaragua's Rural Co-operative Women's Federation, have stepped in, setting up women-only groups among milk producers, salt farmers, gum collectors, and livestock and fruit producers.[67]

Producer organisations frequently face violence at the hands of those with vested interests, be they landowners jealously guarding their property and privileges, or middlemen reluctant to surrender their control over buying or transport. Many governments are not neutral actors in pursuit of the public interest, but rather act on behalf of economically powerful elites. POs may be derailed by violence or party politics, or stifled by red tape – typically, the complexities of legal registration.[69] However, they are an important expression of active citizenship, and can play a vital role in improving the effectiveness of state agricultural policies.

BOX 3.4
## NICHE SOLUTIONS: FAIRTRADE AND ORGANICS

The booming market for organic and fairly traded products offers small farmers the chance to grow and sell higher-value products which are more labour-intensive, thus creating more jobs. Fairtrade products carry the FAIRTRADE Mark, which guarantees that the market chain for the product is certified by the Fairtrade Labelling Organization (FLO) to fulfil international social, economic, and environmental standards. A minimum price is paid to the producer in advance, plus an additional premium that must be spent on community development.

Although the Fairtrade market is growing fast, it remains relatively small. Global sales were estimated at €1.6bn ($2.32bn) in 2006, up 42 per cent on the 2005 figure.[68] Such figures still constitute a tiny fraction (about a hundredth of 1 per cent) of global trade, however: fair trade is neither a panacea, nor a substitute for wider reform of international trading systems, discussed in Part 5.

While organics constitute a larger market, small-scale producers are sometimes excluded by the costs of certification and the demanding standards involved. Moreover, unlike Fairtrade, which is specifically designed for small farmers, large farms have clambered on board the organics bandwagon, threatening to squeeze out small farmers in the same way as with non-organic, high-value crops.

# THE ROLE OF THE STATE

No matter how successful a producer organisation may be, citizen action alone will not meet the challenge of rural development. It also takes an effective state. While governments in numerous countries have recently revived their role in agricultural policy, for two decades both state intervention and agriculture itself were deeply unfashionable with aid donors and governments alike.

Hostility to state intervention in agriculture was not without foundation. Many of the state marketing boards dismantled at the behest of the World Bank and the IMF under structural adjustment programmes (SAPs) were indeed corrupt and inefficient, and paid farmers little and late, if at all. Excessive taxation of farmers and price controls on their products funnelled resources away from deprived rural areas towards the cities and industries that leaders judged to be the future of their countries.

Weak as public institutions were, however, they provided some of the essential services that poor farmers needed. In the wake of SAPs, credit, veterinary care, and technical advice virtually disappeared in many countries, and prices fluctuated wildly, both within and between seasons.[70] Cuts in public credit left what the World Bank termed 'huge gaps in financial services, still largely unfilled'.[71] As Joseph Stiglitz once remarked, the 'invisible hand' of the market was invisible because it was simply not there.[72]

Structural adjustment also had profound impacts on the 'unpaid economy' by reducing state investment in services and infrastructure, thus increasing the burden on women in their roles as family care-givers and water-carriers. Farmers in better-connected areas, such as those close to urban markets, benefited from improved prices, while those without market power – either because they had little land or were from largely excluded groups, such as women or indigenous communities – found the deregulated market much less likely to work for them.

Structural adjustment's cure for agricultural stagnation proved worse than the disease. Thankfully, the political and economic tides are now flowing towards an enhanced role for the state and other institutions and away from the market fundamentalism of the 1990s. At the same time, governments and aid donors are re-evaluating the role of agriculture in development, as witnessed by the World Bank's *World Development Report 2008*, the first on agriculture in 25 years.[73] The report advocated what it called a 'new agriculture for develop-ment agenda', involving efforts to increase productivity in the staple foods sector; connect smallholders to rapidly expanding high-value horticulture, poultry, and aquaculture, as well as dairy markets; and generate jobs in the rural non-farm economy.[74]

However, there is a great deal of inertia in politics and, despite the softening of the rhetoric, the default position of promoting deregula-tion and withdrawal of the state remains strong within governments, among recalcitrant aid donors, and especially at the negotiating tables where trade and investment agreements are hammered out. All such accords curb the scope for state intervention in the economy. Trade negotiations must catch up with the new thinking on agriculture and the role of the state, or they will risk binding countries irreversibly into agreements that could undermine their long-term development (see Part 5).

The answer to rural poverty and inequality is not to give up on the state, but to reform and enhance its support for agriculture and small farmers, especially in the early stages of development, as well as to curb the proclivity of governments and large landowners for intervening in ways that undermine poor farmers. Studies of successful agricultural take-offs show that the process of transformation must be 'kick-started' with the assistance of government interventions. In India, for example, subsidies on credit, fertiliser, and seeds were effective, as were extension services such as training in new technologies and techniques, state spending on irrigation and roads, and steps to curb the volatility of prices paid to farmers.[75] By reducing risks to producers, such measures encouraged them to invest in their farms.

Malaysia's transformation from agricultural economy to manufacturing exporter in the space of three decades was built on effective state intervention in agriculture. This pursued twin objectives: to stabilise rice prices and improve the incomes of the country's millions of small rice farmers, and to generate revenues from exports such as rubber and palm oil. For rice, the government provided input subsidies, particularly for fertilisers, and made large investments in irrigation and land development, especially during the early years. It also guaranteed a floor price for producers, in contrast with other countries that squeezed rural producers in order to keep prices low for urban workers. Outputs and yields responded by growing rapidly during the 1970s, reducing poverty and the risk of inter-ethnic conflict, while export taxes helped to fund the country's industrialisation.[76]

In recent years, Malawi has shown what state action can achieve in terms of poverty reduction, if not yet in terms of broader economic take-off. After a series of poor harvests left almost five million Malawians facing food shortages, the government defied pressure from the country's aid donors and introduced subsidies on seeds and fertilisers to pre-empt famine. The results were spectacular, more than doubling the national maize harvest and averting widespread hunger.[77]

Governments also need to address the need of small farmers for secure title to their land, especially for women (who in many cases have never enjoyed independent rights to the land), including through land reform where necessary. (Land rights are discussed more fully in Part 2.)

As noted above, governments need to support research and development to produce the kinds of seeds and other technologies that small farmers need. Despite the much greater importance of agriculture to their societies, developing countries invest only one-ninth of what industrial countries put into agricultural R&D as a share of agricultural GDP (including both public and private sources).[78] Much of that is geared to large-scale export agriculture with limited relevance to small farmers. Seventy per cent of global R&D on agriculture is undertaken by profit-driven transnational corporations.[79]

Yet public sector R&D has clearly worked. The publicly funded Consultative Group on International Agricultural Research (CGIAR), the international network of agricultural research institutes that spearheaded the Green Revolution, has released more than 8,000 improved crop varieties over the past 40 years.

Successful state intervention can benefit consumers too, by enabling farmers to increase productivity, selling cheaper but still making a better living. Between 1980 and 2000, the Green Revolution in Bangladesh meant that the real wholesale price of rice in Dhaka's markets fell from Tk.20 to Tk.11 per kilo. But over the same period, farmers increased yields from around 2 tonnes to 3.4 tonnes per hectare, effectively offsetting the impact of falling prices on their incomes.[80]

Balancing the needs of producers and consumers is one of the core roles of the state in regulating agricultural markets. Drastic changes in food prices, such as the recent surge in prices discussed on page 227, have a complex impact on poverty, depending on the balance of production and consumption in any given household. Many poor farmers are actually net consumers. One study estimates that 70–80 per cent of rural African households do not grow enough to feed themselves all year round, and so rely on the market to cover the short-fall.[81] Rising food prices hurt poor consumers and may not even help poor farmers, when the benefits accrue to processors and traders and are not transmitted down the value chain.

As in the parallel argument for state intervention to nurture infant industries, the role of the state is particularly important at the earliest stages of development, but it should fall away as agriculture takes off and fully functioning markets emerge in the countryside. An economic analysis of the return on investment in India's Green Revolution found that state spending on credit, electricity, and fertiliser yielded net benefits in the early years, but fell away until by the 1990s all were generating a net loss.[82]

However, this exit can be politically difficult, as the longevity of Europe's Common Agricultural Policy and the US farm subsidies demonstrates. In India, one difficult legacy of the successful kick-starting of the Green Revolution is that the state still spends some $9bn a year on subsidies,[83] mainly on fertiliser, electricity, and irrigation, which largely bypass the poorest people in the countryside, whether landless labourers or smallholders. Fertiliser subsidies in particular have become little more than a slush fund for the fertiliser industry, which receives payments directly from government on a cost-plus basis, thus removing any incentive to improve efficiency. Such arrangements create vested interests that prevent the government from redirecting that money towards public goods, such as rural roads or agricultural research, where investment produces far higher social and economic returns.[84]

## THE FUTURE OF SMALL-SCALE FARMING

High commodity prices, growing demand for biofuels, a possible shift to low-carbon agriculture, booming consumer demand in the cities and in the North for year-round supply, and growing markets for organic and Fairtrade products could all work in favour of small farmers in the coming years. Whether they can break into these new and growing markets will depend largely on their ability to organise and upgrade their production.

Domestic and regional markets may offer more potential than Northern export markets, especially in light of the latter's tariff barriers and intimidating array of health and quality standards (although smallholders in Latin America appear to have had some success in riding the globalisation wave).[85] Africa's domestic consumption of food staples, including cereals, roots and tubers, and traditional livestock products produced and consumed mainly by poor people, is estimated at around $50bn a year, more than five times greater than the value of its traditional commodity exports, and this is expected to double by 2015.[86]

However, with urbanisation and the spread of supermarkets, local markets are becoming more like international ones. Small-scale agriculture will have to learn how to meet more exacting quality standards and face intense competition even to sell locally, or else will be left with the lowest-value dregs of the market. The hiding places from globalisation are shrinking, and both state action and producer organisation are essential to equip small farmers to keep up with the pace of technical and commercial change, and to reform the business model that currently excludes them.

The countryside in many developing countries is being rapidly transformed. While change has brought a mixed bag of opportunities and threats for poor farmers, the threats are greater and the opportunities are slimmer than for large farmers and other powerful players. Many of these changes are likely to drive up inequality in the countryside, both between rich and poor, and between women and men. Poor farmers are more vulnerable, more likely to be squeezed out of new, higher-value agriculture, and less likely to benefit from new technologies.

How governments and rural people shape and adapt to change will to a large extent determine the course of global poverty and inequality over the coming decades. Only a concerted effort by a combination of effective, accountable states and active, organised citizens to redistribute power in agricultural markets can arrest growing inequality and rekindle agriculture's ability to trigger national economic take-off and poverty reduction.

In any case, many rural communities will in all likelihood face a future of out-migration and an ageing population. In Peru's Sacred

Valley, as the evening sun lights up the plots of maize and the dusk is redolent with the smells of eucalyptus and herbs, 18-year-old Segundino punctures the beauty of a tourist paradise: 'We grow maize, potatoes, wheat, everything, but I want to finish school and carry on studying. Farming is pure sacrifice. Here in the community it's just work and school. We play the odd game of football, but that's about it. I want to go to the city.' [87]

Segundino's words are echoed by young people in rural communities around the world. Education, newspapers, radio, television, and the Internet, and consumerism more generally, have profoundly altered the way that rural people think about work, farming, and their – and more particularly, their children's – futures. Farming has become, often in little more than a decade, a low-status occupation to be avoided.[88] Governments can slow the drain to overcrowded capitals by investing in provincial cities and revitalising local economies, but they are seldom able to stop it altogether. Where the productivity and welfare of small farmers can be increased through improved irrigation, credit, technology, and organisation, supporting agriculture is synonymous with development.

Where the land is exhausted or inhospitable, and productivity improvements are unlikely, it may be better for governments and aid donors to facilitate a dignified exit. The key is to give people the best range of positive choices: not obliging them to flee to the shanty towns in hunger and despair, but rather enabling them to make a positive decision either to stay on the land, or to seek a better life in the city, because they are equipped with skills, capital, and the self-confidence born of power and voice, and can prosper in either environment.

## HOW CHANGE HAPPENS CASE STUDY
### THE FISHING COMMUNITIES OF TIKAMGARH

Two hundred men and sari-clad women sit clustered under giant shade trees on the banks of a dried-up lake: a small pond choked with lilies is all that remains of what should be a lake teeming with fish, built by kings over 800 years ago, and recently restored by the community. Birdsong and voices pierce the dry heat. The land is parched, but the story is uplifting.

'Previously we covered our faces in public,' laughs one woman. 'Now we talk back, even to our fathers-in-law.' And not just fathers-in-law. The people of Tikamgarh have come on an extraordinary journey, winning unprecedented rights to the fishponds, and transforming their own lives along the way.

Landlords and contractors have traditionally controlled most fish-ponds in the impoverished Bundelkhand region of India. Struggles for the right to fish and to use the fertile land exposed when the ponds dry out during drought have been violent and continuous, but the 45,000 fishing families of the Bundelkhand seem to be gaining the upper hand.

Over the past 20 years, the introduction of new varieties of fish and the practice of stocking ponds with fish fry raised in nurseries have greatly increased yields. Rather than favouring poor people, however, such tech-nological improvements prompted landlords and contractors to seize even the smallest of the region's 1,000 ponds.

Protests led the fisheries minister in the Congress Party government of Madhya Pradesh, who was himself from a fishing community, to push through legislation in 1996 that granted leases to fishers' co-operatives. A wave of organisation in poor fishing communities followed. Vikalp, an NGO led by Om Prakash Rawat (a former State Electricity Board engineer), played a crucial role in helping them to establish co-operatives.

Contractors retaliated by setting up bogus co-operatives of their own and using other tricks to get around the legislation, and when that failed they resorted to violence. In a particularly bloody struggle over Achrumata Pond, fishers fought a pitched battle with thugs hired by land-lords to steal their fish. The thugs won the first round, burning down the villagers' huts, but the victims then turned to other villages for solidarity.

Co-operative leaders and sympathetic outsiders got to know each other on their endless visits to police stations in search of justice in the Achrumata case. Working together, they convinced the police to accept an official complaint, seen as an unprecedented symbolic blow to the landlords. Word spread and other communities also filed formal complaints.

Although the police did no more than accept their complaints, such official recognition galvanised the fishing communities. Six communities marched to Achrumata and fought back. Three people were seriously injured and houses were burned down in the battle, but the landlords were forced to back off. As their self-confidence grew, the communities seized several other ponds. A meeting of some 150 people then decided to launch a campaign to persuade the authorities to enforce the law.

Fishing communities now control over 100 ponds, and 67 communities are now planning to set up a commercial company to market their fish. Their numbers, and the extent to which they had organised, also persuaded local officials to adopt a more sympathetic stance. With Vikalp's advice, the groups are improving the ponds and their organisation, emphasising the empowerment of women in the process.

The success of the people of Tikamgarh depended on factors common to many change processes. Technological shifts triggered changes in behaviour. A series of violent clashes radicalised people. Government took the lead in passing new laws, and the police, under pressure from a popular movement, amazed everyone by enforcing the rule of law.

The communities themselves are the heroes of the story, but they received important support from enlightened political leaders and NGOs. They overcame a powerful opposition and are now building their organisations – a key step in defending their gains.

Unfortunately, the progress achieved by the fishing community of Tikamgarh is being undermined by a drought that has lasted for three years. Up to 75 per cent of the local workforce has been forced to migrate in search of paid work until the rains return to fill the ponds. 'I don't know why it's raining less – God must want us to migrate,' laments one old man. The skills and organisation gained, however, remain and will be essential as the communities seek to adapt to the changing climate.

*Source:* author visit, October 2006.

CASE STUDY

# THE CHANGING WORLD OF WORK

Asha, aged 13, is one of 2,000 rag-pickers in the city of Nashik in India, an important religious centre on the Godavari River, 185km north of Mumbai. Asha has been rag-picking for around six years. Like other young rag-pickers, she heads out to go rag-picking as soon as she gets up, working solidly for around four hours every morning. In the afternoon, from 12pm to 5pm, she goes to school, where she is in eighth grade. After school, she comes home to help her mother around the house and care for her two younger sisters and her younger brother. 'My life is rag-picking, school, and household chores,' she says. 'I don't have any friends or any entertainment.'[89]

In many developing countries, rubbish recyclers epitomise the struggle to survive. Moving like wraiths through the fumes and smoke of burning rubbish heaps on the fringes of the city, such as Manila's evocatively named (but deeply unpleasant) 'smoky mountain', they are mostly women and children from the most marginalised groups. From the city dump, rubbish bins in residential streets, or vacant land, rag-pickers collect tin, paper, plastic, bones, copper, metal, or glass, which they then sell to scrap merchants for cash. Beatings, rapes, dog attacks, harassment, injuries, illness, and abuse are a daily reality, and exploitation at the hands of the buyers is common.

Urban residents, particularly those living in poverty like Asha, rely primarily upon wage labour or self-employment to survive. In rural areas too, growing numbers of families rely on paid work, either because they are landless, or to supplement farm earnings. Work can be degrading, a desperate scrabble for survival, with people enduring dangers, exhaustion, and hardship to keep hunger at bay. However, decent work can be central to an individual's identity and sense of well-being. Good-quality jobs enhance the quality of life by guaranteeing rights and freedoms and equipping individuals to exercise those rights, as well as paying a decent wage.

## MORE JOBS, MORE JOBLESS

In 2005, close to 2.85 billion people aged 15 and older worked for money – nearly half the population of the planet. The agricultural sector employs the largest labour force in the world, 1.3 billion people, a third of whom work as plantation workers or day labourers; more than half of them are women.[90] As noted earlier, people are leaving agriculture in droves, but contrary to previous centuries when workers moved out of agriculture into industry, overall industrial employment is also falling. The slack is being taken up by the service sector – a vast spectrum of jobs covering everything from maids to street-sellers to modern banks.[91]

Not all those who want work can find it: open unemployment in the world was about 190 million in 2007.[92] An additional 310 million people are under-employed, working for only a few hours a week.[93] In all, close to one billion new jobs will be needed in the next decade, more than double what the economy will produce at current rates.

Youth account for a quarter of the world's working-age population, but almost half of its unemployed. Across all countries, the unemployment rate is two to three times higher for young people than for adults, and worldwide one in seven young people has no job. The particular tragedy of youth unemployment is that, like child malnutrition, it leads to life-long harm because it means foregoing the accumulation of on-the-job skills and an employment history that would send positive signals to future employers. Besides the personal cost involved, youth unemployment has clear costs to society in terms of wasted talent, and the likelihood that disenchanted young people will turn to crime and violence.

The nature of work has evolved rapidly in recent decades, notably through the mass entry of women into the paid workforce, the continued growth of the so-called 'informal economy', government drives to deregulate and 'flexibilise' labour markets, and the expansion of global supply chains and investment. As in the world of smallholder agriculture, these changes present both opportunities and threats for poor people, who need power in markets (in this case labour markets), effective organisations, a responsible private sector, and an effective, accountable state, if they are to reap the benefits.

## WOMEN AT WORK

Millions of women have found jobs on the bottom rung of the globalisation ladder, working in garment factories or in the 'new agriculture', growing fruit, vegetables, and flowers for export. These new jobs are in many ways very positive for women, both as individuals and collectively, not least because they challenge assumptions about what they can contribute to families – and, ultimately, to wider society.

In boom areas such as the clothing industry, women's new jobs have brought them tangible benefits. In 1982 the government of Bangladesh began to promote export-oriented manufacturing; within two years, the garment industry took off. By 2004, an estimated two million people worked in the garment factories.[94] Most of the workforce consists of young women, many of whom have migrated from desperately poor rural areas. The wages earned by these women are exceptionally low by international standards, and barely above the national poverty line. Yet their daily wage rates are around twice as high as those paid for agricultural labourers, and higher than could be earned on construction sites.[95]

Paid employment has improved many women's bargaining power within the family, especially with husbands, fathers, and brothers. A 1990 survey of more than 30 Bangladeshi garment factories found that two out of three women had some control over their earnings. According to one woman, 'In my mother's time…women had to tolerate more suffering because they did not have the means to become independent. They are better off now, they know about the world, they have been given education, they can work and stand on their own feet. They have more freedom.'[96]

150

Many married women workers interviewed in 2003 said that they now take decisions with their husbands on family matters, and 13 per cent said that their husbands now shared some of the housework, especially shopping and cooking – a small but significant shift. 'The garment sector has brought a silent revolution for women in our society,' says Shirin Akter of Karmojibi Nari, an NGO supporting women workers.[97]

However, all too often, jobs in the proliferating garment factories and fruit farms have exacted a heavy toll in the form of excessive hours, workplace abuse, and long-term damage to women's health. Fruit and flower pickers and packers from Colombia, Chile, the USA, and South Africa commonly report headaches, respiratory problems, and eye pain from handling pesticides. Garment factory workers from Bangladesh to Morocco commonly suffer headaches, coughing, vomiting, fever, and physical exhaustion. Poor ventilation in lint-filled rooms can lead to debilitating respiratory diseases. Hired in jobs that demand highly dexterous and repetitive movements, many women suffer joint injuries and back, leg, and shoulder pain.[98]

Paid jobs are also largely in addition to women's previous burden of unpaid work. A study in Ghana showed that women were doing 30–46 hours of unpaid caring work a week, while men in the same categories did an average of eight to 11 hours a week of unpaid work.[99] These statistics may even underestimate the degree of 'time poverty' experienced by women, since the time use studies on which they are based often fail to capture women's 'multi-tasking' between a variety of roles.[100]

Boxed in by long working hours and unreasonably high production targets, many women are unable to care for their children, and so move their daughters into their own previous roles, cutting short their education. Exhausted women stop participating in social organisations, depriving the broader community of their leadership, energy, and creativity. Angela, sewing garments in a Kenyan factory, expresses frustration at her isolation from the wider community: 'It is not possible to do anything else. There is no time to take care of your own children, visit people, do business, or go to college. Even going to church has become a problem …We are somehow isolated.' [101]

## NOBODY'S FORMAL ANY MORE

'In La Paz, everyone works, but no-one has a job,' jokes one Bolivian government official. According to the International Labour Organization (ILO), formal, recognised non-agricultural employment is in the minority across the developing world, varying from 45 per cent of the working population in Asia to a mere 30 per cent in sub-Saharan Africa.[102] In many countries, the so-called 'informal economy' has mushroomed in recent decades, driven by a combination of technological shifts, globalisation, and government policy. In Malawi, only one in every 250 people has a formal job in the private sector.[103]

During Latin America's recession in the 1980s and the adjustment of the 1990s, the informal economy acted as a gigantic sponge, soaking up those who had been sacked, or who were entering the workforce for the first time. As Latin America's streets became clogged with vendors desperately seeking customers, incomes plummeted. In La Paz, where 60 per cent of the workforce is now in the informal economy, there is one street trader for every three families, and there are just not enough buyers to go round.[104]

In part, the informal economy flourishes because of the 'barriers to entry' for formal business. In Angola, starting a new business requires 13 different procedures and 124 days, and costs almost 500 per cent of the average yearly income. By contrast, in the USA the same process requires just five procedures, five days, and 0.7 per cent of the average income of an American. Surveys of self-employed workers and 'micro-enterprises' show that they often prefer the informal sector as it offers more autonomy and flexibility. The picture is different, however, for waged workers in the informal economy, who usually hanker after a formal job with a contract and benefits.[105]

Even when workers have an employer, work has become more precarious; increasing numbers of people are employed on a temporary and casual basis, often without clear employee status. Their jobs are characterised by low or unstable wages, few if any benefits, little access to social protection programmes, lack of coverage by labour legislation, and little or no respect for the internationally recognised rights to freedom of association and collective bargaining.[106]

Recent estimates suggest that 60 per cent or more of women workers in the developing world are in informal employment of this nature, ranging from a low of 43 per cent in northern Africa to as high as 84 per cent in sub-Saharan Africa.[107] It is precisely these jobs that are worst paid and least protected. Worldwide, women earn on average two-thirds of a male wage.[108] Other groups who experience some of the worst wages and working conditions include the world's estimated 191 million migrant workers and 211 million working children between the ages of five and 14 years.[109]

Development thinkers and the ILO used to view the informal economy as an outdated relic of under-development destined to be replaced by regular paid jobs. But informality has become an integral part of modern globalised business practices, leading the ILO in 2002 to revise its definition of the informal economy to include all jobs lacking secure contracts, worker benefits, or social protection, thereby recognising that informal workers' rights are a priority to be addressed.[110]

The informal economy also poses a broader challenge to development, as it weakens the social contract between citizen and state. Finding a job there might be perfectly rational from an individual's perspective, but governments have an interest in expanding the net of the formal economy to broaden the tax base, encourage firms to expand (for example, by gaining access to bank credit), and extend the state's ability to regulate the quality of employment. Building the combination of active citizens and effective states is much harder in an informalised economy.

## BEND UNTIL YOU BREAK

The boundary between formal and informal economies has been blurred by a combination of pressures that have transformed the nature of regular work. Traditional permanent, waged jobs accompanied by benefits such as health insurance and retirement pensions are being replaced by a new age of insecurity in the workplace. The drivers of change are both technological and political. Improvements in communications and other technologies have allowed firms to drive down costs by parcelling out their production chains across continents.

Fordist mass production, with its giant factories, regular jobs, and workplace trade unions has given way to smaller factories pursuing low-inventory, 'just in time' production methods. These require a flexible workforce and make it harder for trade unions to organise across continents and multiple workplaces.

Deregulation of the labour market is often described as enhancing 'flexibility'. Occasionally, flexibility benefits workers, such as when it means greater entitlements to family leave or flexible working hours, but largely it is a euphemism for driving down entitlements and job security.[111] Typical 'flexibilisation' measures include the introduction of temporary contracts, little or no recognition of labour rights such as freedom of association or collective bargaining, part-time working (which limits access to standard benefits such as holiday pay and pensions), piece-rate payments, and making it easier for employers to hire and fire staff.

Women predominate in many of the categories of jobs and workers targeted for flexibilisation or ignored altogether by labour law: domestic workers, home workers, agricultural workers, undocumented workers, and workers in export-processing zones. In the case of domestic workers, a review of the labour legislation in 60 countries revealed that nine exclude domestic workers from their labour code, while 19 refer to them in a 'specific' chapter, which often means that they are afforded a lower degree of protection than other categories of workers.[112]

Flexibility often includes loosening minimum wage requirements and ending sector-wide collective bargaining. As well as introducing or scrapping legislation, governments have undermined labour rights by failing to update labour laws to match the changing nature of work, and by turning a blind eye to the violation of existing labour codes. As a result:

- In Chile, 75 per cent of women in the agricultural sector are hired on temporary contracts to pick fruit, and put in more than 60 hours a week during the season – but one in three still earns below the minimum wage.
- Fewer than half of the women employed in Bangladesh's textile and garment export sector have a contract, and the

vast majority get no maternity or health coverage – but 80 per cent fear dismissal if they complain.

- In China's Guangdong province, one of the world's fastest-growing industrial areas, young women face 150 hours of overtime each month in the garment factories. They have little option but to comply, given that 60 per cent have no written contract and 90 per cent have no access to social insurance, should they be fired.[113]

## DOING BUSINESS THE WORLD BANK WAY

The International Monetary Fund (IMF) and the World Bank have been among the most determined proponents of 'flexibilisation'. In 2002, the World Bank recommended 'eliminating labour-related rigidities' in Mexico, including 'the current system of severance payments; collective bargaining and industry-binding contracts… restrictions to temporary, fixed-term, and apprenticeship contracts'. In 2001, the IMF 'viewed favourably certain aspects of the [Chilean government's] proposal (such as reducing restrictions on work schedules and allowing part-time contracts… )'. However, it 'expressed concern over other elements (such as allowing collective negotiations at the inter-firm level…) which would reduce labour market flexibility'.[114]

Since 2003, the most important source of pressure from the Bank has been the labour section of its annual *Doing Business* publication. The labour market flexibility indicators of this section are often used in World Bank and IMF country-level strategy documents to force countries to do away with various kinds of workers' protection. For example, a recent World Bank Economic Memorandum to Colombia demanded that the government make hiring and firing decisions more flexible in order to improve its *Doing Business* indicators, even though it is uncertain whether this will have a positive economic impact. The World Bank also made compliance a condition for loans to Colombia.

The 2008 edition of *Doing Business* declared the Marshall Islands to be the world's 'Best Performer' for 'ease of employing workers', displacing the previous champion, Palau. What the Marshall Islands and Palau have in common is that they are tiny Pacific island nations that have no labour code and are not members of the ILO.[115]

Infringing workers' rights and limiting their compensation is increasingly common in developed countries as well. For a short time in history, thanks largely to a vocal trade union movement, a few privileged workers won the right to be compensated for most of the costs of maintaining the labour force and of caring for past and future workers: health care, a monthly salary (paying for rest time at weekends), compensation for injury and old age, and paid leave for illness, maternity/paternity, breast-feeding, funerals, religious events, and holidays. In some cases, employers and the state also paid for training/retraining, job search, or removal costs when workers were transferred or economic restructuring took place. In both developed and developing countries, that era now risks being consigned to history, degrading the quality of work and the lives of workers.

Flexible labour policies entail costs to society in terms of the health and education of future generations of workers, and even in the quality and reliability of production. Without a stable income or access to social protection, workers, particularly women workers, are trapped in poverty and are vulnerable to shocks. When in addition the state cuts back social spending, the accumulated hidden costs (ill health, lack of training opportunities, short working life spans, and so on) become overwhelming. The result: greater inequality.

A study of women factory workers in Lesotho, for example, found that long and inflexible work hours, between ten and 12 hours a day during the week and up to ten hours a day at weekends, constituted a major obstacle to mothers caring for their children.[116] During periods when hours were even longer, women reported never seeing their children awake. They were allowed no time off to care for, or get medical care for their children, and their wages were docked when they did. Some women therefore avoided both pre-natal and post-natal clinics, putting their own health at risk as well as that of their children.

For any single country, the flexible labour policies encouraged by international financial institutions may seem necessary to stay competitive with other cheap and 'flexible' countries. But the advice to 'flexibilise' has been given simultaneously to many developing countries, setting national and provincial governments to bid against each other, so reducing the gains from investment for them all.

Cheap labour may produce a short-term boost to a company's profits, but it is a poor development strategy. Since jobs are the key source of income for poor people, low wages drive up inequality and undermine social cohesion; underpaid workers consume less, and so reduce the domestic market for goods and services that is vital for many firms. Impoverished families are unable to spend as much on health and education, undermining the prospects and productivity of future generations. In addition, an economy whose competitive edge derives from low wages is always vulnerable to competition from even lower-wage rivals entering the same markets.

In sectors such as food, clothing, and electronics, global supply chains are driving the push for flexible labour practices. Retail giants have responded to cut-throat competition by pushing risks and costs down the supply chain, as shown in Figure 3.3, and evading their corporate social responsibility.

Oxfam's study of 11 garment factories in Tangiers found evidence of the pressure on suppliers. Together the factories employ more than 6,500 women, producing shirts, trousers, dresses, skirts, and children's clothing for several of the largest Spanish retailers. All the factories reported falling prices, on average around 30 per cent over three years. 'Prices fall every year … a pair of trousers worth €3.30 ($3.90) three years ago is now worth €2 ($2.40),' said one factory manager. 'They always want higher-quality garments, the price goes down due to competition, and you're in no position to argue.' In the previous three years, lead times had fallen from 14 days to five or seven days, some of the shortest in the industry.[117]

At the sharp end of this frantic drive for cost-cutting are the weakest actors in the supply chain – casual workers. Employees interviewed in Bangladesh's proliferating garment factories work a seven-day week, often putting in 15 hours a day or more. In a busy month, workers carry on through the night before snatching a couple of hours' sleep on the factory floor. If a worker puts in over 100 hours overtime a month on top of her normal 63-hour week, she gets a bonus, which brings her monthly earnings to barely $60.[118]

A similar situation applies on export farms. According to one South African apple farmer, 'We employ people as we need them, but you need to break their expectation of having a permanent position, so you hire for two to three weeks and then you let them off for a few weeks, and then you hire them again.' [119]

## TRADE UNIONS CHALLENGED

In the filthy casualty ward of a Bangladeshi hospital, two doctors are bent over a prone figure in the light of a single bulb. The woman on the bed is Minara, a sewing machine operator at one of Bangladesh's 2,700 garment factories, whose workers have just joined a Bangladeshi garment workers' union. She was rushed to hospital an hour ago with deep cuts to her neck, face, and hands after a razor attack by two *mastaans*, thugs hired by the factory owner. Her sister is semi-hysterical, weeping that Minara will now be scarred, and will be thrown out by her husband. [120]

Once the standard recourse for workers in their struggle to claim their rights, trade unions have suffered serious setbacks since the 1980s. Approximately 90 per cent of the world labour force is unorganised, and union membership is declining in direct proportion to the growth of the informal economy. [121] Unions have struggled to reach out to people working within homes, or unprotected by contracts. Workers in the informal economy are not united by the same type of job, or even the same employer. They are determined to hang on to even meagre jobs, and may not share common interests with formally employed workers.

Even in the formal economy, the task of trade unions has been made a good deal harder by changes to labour legislation in recent decades, including the ban on union organisation in many export-processing zones. Worker organisations continue to face repression and violence; union leaders around the world confront harassment, rape, and death. Two countries in every five have serious or severe restrictions on the core right to freedom of association. [122]

Within trade unions, the view among many male workers that women are temporary, secondary, or less valuable workers, 'helping out' their male partners, has hampered the ability of unions to

## FIGURE 3.3: SUPPLY CHAIN PRESSURES
## CREATE PRECARIOUS EMPLOYMENT

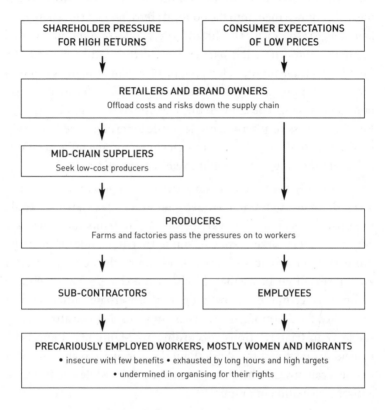

Source: Oxfam International (2004) 'Trading Away Our Rights'.

respond to the changing nature of the workforce. Women are under-represented in union leadership, issues of importance to female workers are often sidelined, and young women in particular may find the typically bureaucratic and procedural style of trade unions off-putting. Research suggests that the reliance of whole families on women's wages, coupled with cultural expectations of women's roles, means that women are often reluctant to risk family livelihoods by embarking on union activity, although when they decide to do so, they can be extremely tenacious.

Many unions have also wrestled with their political role, in particular their links to progressive political parties. Ever since they began to form, the focus of trade unions on the rights of poor workers has inevitably drawn them into the political arena, pressing for changes to labour legislation such as health and safety codes or minimum wages. Many left and centre-left parties around the world were initially founded by trade unions. However, involvement in politics can be a serious drain on resources, and electoral victories by sympathetic political parties can be a mixed blessing. In South Africa, Brazil, and Bolivia, progressive governments desperate for experienced leadership have turned to the trade union movement, skimming off generations of leaders and dragging unions into electoral politics.

Historically, the benefits of an active trade union movement have accrued not just to union members, but to society as a whole. Trade unions have been at the heart of the social democratic contract between state, workers, and business that has underpinned the prosperity and stability of welfare states around the world. They are a vital means of ensuring that the chaos and change that inevitably accompany economic growth do not exacerbate suffering and inequality. Furthermore, investors are more likely to be attracted by stable industrial relations. According to Mamphela Ramphele, managing director at the World Bank, 'Co-ordination among social partners can promote better investment climates while also fostering a fairer distribution of output.'[123]

As the traditional model of organising a stable workforce on a single site becomes less and less relevant, new approaches have emerged. In South Africa, the Women on Farms Project supports workers demanding a minimum daily wage on farms that grow table grapes and other fruits for export. Previously, the women had no organisation – hardly surprising, given their relative isolation and the seasonal nature of their work. Less than 5 per cent of farm workers in South Africa are unionised, and the overwhelming majority of these are permanent workers and hence male. Sikhula Sonke ('We Grow Together'), a women-led trade union formed to defend the rights of seasonal workers, especially women, has a membership of close to 4,000 women farm workers and is engaged in education, women's leadership development, and advocacy. Already, at a local level, the union has won victories over protective clothing, access to toilets in the fields, equal pay for equal work, maternity leave, and respect for minimum daily wages.[124]

Even the rag-pickers of Nashik in India are organising. A local NGO, Lokvikas Samajik Sanstha (LVSS), is supporting the rag-pickers to form a union and gain access to health care, legal support, health insurance, ration cards, education, vocational training, and recreational facilities, and is encouraging them to open bank accounts to save money for emergencies. The rag-pickers have also persuaded Nashik Municipal Council to issue them with photo identity cards, which identify them as legitimate waste collectors, give them access to free medical treatment, help reduce harassment and abuse, and increase personal dignity. The women have even taken over the official role of municipal rubbish collection in some residential areas, which has provided them with increased job security, income, and safety, and the residents with a better service.

There have been other victories for workers' rights in recent years. In 2003, after a 15-year struggle, domestic workers in South Africa were finally brought under the Unemployment Insurance Act covering employed workers, while in Ghana in the same year, the New Labour Act allowed temporary and casual workers to benefit from collective agreements, access to the same medical services as permanent workers, and equal pay for work of equal value.[125]

Given the rise in women's employment and entrenched attitudes in the labour movement, women's organisations such as India's Self Employed Women's Association (SEWA) have also come to play an essential role, capitalising on their experience in popular communications, community organising, and their links with academics and international networks. In Nicaragua, the María Elena Cuadra Movement of Employed and Unemployed Women (MEC), established in 1994, works through community-based rather than workplace-based groups, with 2,000 volunteers reaching out to women in work and at home. MEC helped to win the country's first National Health and Safety Law in 2007, as well as increased site inspections in export-processing zone factories to ensure compliance with health and safety legislation, and human rights training for mid-level private sector managers.[126]

## BOX 3.5
## INDIA'S WOMEN ORGANISE

The Self Employed Women's Association (SEWA), established in 1972, is a union of low-income working women who earn their livelihoods by running small businesses, doing sub-contracting work, or selling their labour. It is the first trade union of workers in the informal economy, not only in India but in the world. With over 950,000 members in 2006, SEWA is also the largest trade union in India.

SEWA groups its membership into four broad occupational categories:

1. hawkers and vendors, who sell a range of products including vegetables, fruit, and used clothing from baskets, push carts, or small shops;

2. home-based producers, who stitch garments, make patchwork quilts, roll hand-made cigarettes (*bidis*) or incense sticks, prepare snack foods, recycle scrap metal, process agricultural products, produce pottery, or make craft items;

3. manual labourers and service providers, who sell their labour (as cart-pullers, porters, or construction workers), or who sell services (such as wastepaper picking, laundry services, or domestic services); and

4. rural producers, including small farmers, milk producers, animal rearers, nursery raisers/tenders, salt farmers, and gum collectors.

SEWA pursues a mix of what it calls 'struggle' and 'development' – that is, unionising activities to improve pay and working conditions – and investments to provide services and promote alternative economic opportunities. Over the years, it has built a network of institutions in both rural and urban areas:

- SEWA Union (the primary organisation to which all members belong and which provides overall governance);

- SEWA Bank (which provides financial services, including savings and credit);

- Gujarat Mahila Cooperative Federation (which is responsible for organising and supporting SEWA's membership in several types of co-operative);

- Gujarat Mahila Housing SEWA Trust (which provides housing services);

- SEWA Social Security (which provides health and child care and insurance services);

- SEWA Marketing (which provides product development and marketing services);

- SEWA Academy (which is responsible for research, training, and communication).

Source: SEWA , 2008 (www.sewa.org).

## GOVERNMENT AND PRIVATE SECTOR CHALLENGED

When governments fail to uphold core labour rights, it is often for political reasons, not economic ones. Faced with powerful business elites who fear trade union activity, governments frequently are unable to resist pressure to use repression rather than foster negotiations. The low political priority accorded such rights means that government labour inspectors are poorly funded, often ineffective, and sometimes corrupt, taking bribes in exchange for turning a blind eye to abuse. Labour legislation is often outdated and discriminatory, providing governments with a poor tool for promoting rights.

What is more, in the absence of effective regulation and enforcement, individual companies find it hard to forego the competitive advantage they gain through violating rights, even when it undercuts the long-term stability needed for sustained growth. The global free-for-all fostered by deregulation and flexibilisation erodes the will of those companies that do wish to respect rights.

A combination of effective states and active citizenship is needed to meet these challenges. Strong, independent trade unions with political clout can balance the overbearing influence that business associations often wield. That allows governments sufficient autonomy to ensure that the legislative framework and state policy encourage rather than discourage respect for rights. Properly funding and equipping labour inspectorates to enforce the law, and ensuring that labour legislation keeps up with the changing workplace, are two essential steps. In Central America, for example, women workers' organisations have criticised occupational health and safety laws based on risks in construction and agriculture – traditionally men's jobs – that fail to recognise conditions such as repetitive strain injuries, which are common to women's jobs in factories and households. Labour legislation may also discriminate against women where only workers in full-time, permanent employment gain access to employment benefits.

The private sector, too, must rise to the challenge of social responsibility. Industries that are physically constrained from moving their capital around, that are making longer-term investments due to other factors such as market size, or that depend on good community relations are most likely to champion more responsible practices. Supermarkets, for example, seeking a 'licence to operate' in large developing countries may be more amenable to pressure to respect freedom of association or collective bargaining (even mighty Wal-Mart backed down over the Chinese government's insistence that it recognise trade unions in its 60 Chinese supermarkets[127]).

Many global supply chain practices result in precarious conditions for workers – and these are precisely the ones considered by businesses to provide an edge in highly competitive markets. In the words of one South African fruit marketing agent, 'Margins are so tight, we've got to survive and thus cut and restructure labour. You can't turn a packhouse on and off, you can't turn tractors on and off, you can't turn trees on and off, but you can turn people on and off.'[128] Oxfam's research has documented pressures and incentives for company buyers to boost sales and profit margins, ignoring unethical practices and even abuses of labour standards.[129] Ethical purchasing managers struggle against common beliefs that promoting decent jobs and labour rights is uncompetitive, and can end up being sidelined, especially in a business downturn.

To change such practices will require a co-ordinated effort across the globe. Activists have galvanised consumer pressure in wealthy countries to get some big brands to move. Driven by public outcry over poor labour conditions in some supply chains, 'multi-stakeholder initiatives' such as the Ethical Trading Initiative have brought together supermarkets and clothes retailers, among others, with trade unions and NGOs to seek ways to protect labour standards in their supply chains.[130] They have identified and piloted corporate purchasing practices that respect 'decent work', freedom of association, and the role of trade unions. Activities include experimenting with different ways of commissioning independent 'social audits' of suppliers and finding ways to promote labour standards among smallholders and home workers. Some institutional investors such as pension funds, who see the risk to corporate reputations and share prices from bad labour practices, have also weighed in.

Many firms are finding that promoting decent work can be good for business. In the Dominican Republic, Costa Rica, Mauritius, and the Philippines, employers have found that low wages and poor working conditions are associated with employee dissatisfaction, whereas higher wages, better working conditions, and more job flexibility help to attract and retain a more contented and better-trained workforce.[131] The 'demonstration effect' of seeing a rival factory gain an edge through promoting better practices can be far more effective in convincing business leaders to follow suit than any number of research papers or campaigns.

---

## BOX 3.6

### CAN TRADE AGREEMENTS PROMOTE LABOUR RIGHTS?

Labour provisions appear in almost all US and EU bilateral and regional free trade agreements, but parties merely commit to uphold domestic labour laws, irrespective of their quality or current levels of enforcement. There is no requirement for ILO standards to be incorporated into domestic law and no enforceable obligations are placed on foreign investors. The US–Jordan Free Trade Agreement, for example, requires only that parties 'strive to ensure' that domestic laws are consistent with 'internationally recognised labour rights'. The agreement has had little effect on working conditions in Jordan, which are atrocious, especially for immigrant workers.[132]

One trade agreement that seems to have improved labour standards is the US–Cambodian Textile Agreement, under which improved access to the US market is conditional on the enforcement of internationally recognised labour rights. Independent monitoring by the ILO prevents the labour clause from being hijacked for protectionist purposes. By 2007, 300 garment factories had joined the ILO project.[133] Wages, working conditions, and respect for workers' rights have improved measurably and foreign investors have benefited from higher productivity and quality and lower rates of accidents, staff turnover, and absenteeism.[134]

In the North American Free Trade Agreement (NAFTA), one of the oldest and best-known of the modern generation of regional trade agreements, the supposed remedy for labour rights violations has proved a paper tiger. After more than a decade, none of the 28 labour standards complaints submitted under the NAFTA side agreement on labour rights has advanced beyond the second step of a seven-step process.[135]

Moreover, many developing-country governments question the underlying purpose of labour rights clauses in trade agreements, suspecting that they owe more to protectionism and a desire to safeguard jobs in the North than to genuine concerns to promote labour rights in the South.

## THE FUTURE OF WORK

Creating jobs, in sufficient number and of sufficient quality, lies at the heart of the challenge of development. For people living in poverty, a decent job is the best guarantee of transforming their lot. Workers must enjoy basic rights if work and the income it brings are to free people from poverty and contribute to national development. The struggle to ensure respect for such rights is far from easy and, in many ways, it is getting harder. The spread of democracy, active citizenship, and literacy in developing countries gives some grounds for optimism, but a dark shadow is cast by the evolution of the economy: away from mass production towards informal jobs and global supply chains, both of which are characterised by a race to the bottom in wages and conditions.

The situation of women workers in global industries is a battle-ground between competing visions of economic development, with consequences for all workers and for the fight against inequality and poverty. One vision recognises caring work as a vital component of economies and affirms the responsibilities of the state and employers to contribute 'employment benefits' and taxes as investments in maintaining a healthy, trained, and productive workforce. The opposing vision ignores the caring economy and treats as 'savings' and 'efficiency' company or government policies to shed the costs of workers' health, leave time, incapacity, or old age.

Although the latter vision ignores the costs of maintaining a healthy society, these do not go away. They shift to workers, with women paying the highest price through their unpaid caring labour and their low wages. Women are ground down by long hours, low wages, and anxiety, and such 'indecent work' fails even to guarantee sufficient food on the table.

For years, ILO conventions and the welfare state promoted shared responsibility for such costs, divided between the state, the private sector, and the worker. Replacing welfare state policies (and trade union aspirations) based on rights with an exclusive emphasis on responsibilities (for example, the responsibility of workers to provide their own support for unpaid caring costs) undermines both workers' lives and the capacity of growth to generate decent jobs, transform lives, and galvanise economies.

To ensure that hard-won labour rights are not swept away, but are extended to women and others in the new economy, will require innovative and dynamic organisation, backed by effective and accountable states. It is a huge test for the labour movement, the women's movement, and enlightened business leaders. Globally, organisations such as the UN and the ILO can play an influential role, as can consumers and retailers. At the very least, the outside world must help, not hinder, the struggle for workers' basic rights.

# PRIVATE SECTOR, PUBLIC INTEREST

As poor men and women seek to feed their families and build better lives, they grapple with a range of risks and opportunities, their strategies constantly evolving to cope with change. In this effort, the market is the sea in which they swim, and the main denizens of that sea are private sector companies.

The private sector spans all private, for-profit businesses, from giant transnational corporations to backstreet workshops and market stalls. In the formal economy, private firms enjoy both rights (for example, limited liability in the case of financial collapse) and responsibilities (to obey laws, for example on working conditions and taxation). How companies balance their rights and responsibilities – that is, whether they have long-term or short-term mindsets, respect labour rights, consider their impact on local communities, or manage their environmental footprint – is determined by the actions of states and citizens, and the will of their owners, managers, and staff.

Private firms directly influence the lives of poor people in six main ways: they provide products and services; generate income and investment; create jobs; develop skills through training and experience; transfer and develop technology; and establish physical and institutional infrastructure. Firms also exert indirect influence, for example through their impact on the environment, or in lobbying for changes to government rules and practices.

In recent years, harnessing the dynamism of the private sector has triggered extraordinary development in a number of countries, especially in Asia. However, in the absence of an effective state and active citizens, especially trade unions, the private sector can also exploit workers, undermine democracy, and despoil the environment.

## SMALL BUSINESS

The power and profile of large transnational corporations (TNCs) leads many NGOs, including Oxfam, to engage them at the international level in an effort to change their policies and practices. Yet on the ground, the development efforts of governments and NGOs alike more often focus on small and medium-sized enterprises (SMEs), which are much more present in the lives of poor people.[136]

SMEs create many more jobs and have more local linkages than TNCs. They employ poor and marginalised people who might otherwise struggle to find jobs in large modern companies, and act as a safety net by soaking up labour in times of crisis. They are incubators of entrepreneurial skills and social mobility, especially for women entering business for the first time. However, small businesses are also responsible for some of the worst abuse of workers' rights, including forced and child labour.

As economies grow, small and medium-sized businesses tend to move out of the informal economy, acquiring legal status, becoming liable for taxes and benefits, and paying wages in a more regular fashion. Not only do they become more formal, they also become more important to the economy as a whole: formally registered SMEs employing up to 250 people account for just 16 per cent of GDP in low-income countries, but this rises to 39 per cent in medium-income countries and 51 per cent in high-income countries. The variation between countries is huge: while less than 5.5 per cent of the formal workforce is employed in SMEs in Azerbaijan, Belarus, and Ukraine, the share rises to more than 80 per cent in Chile, Greece, and Thailand.[137]

Because SMEs can be either exploitative sweatshops or seedbeds of innovation and entrepreneurship, there is little agreement on their contribution to development. Some see them as a distraction from the general business of promoting the private sector, whether big or small;

others see them as something close to a job-creating, growth-promoting panacea; still others worry about their frequently harsh employment practices and hostility to trade unions.

The UN reports that 'SMEs are marginal in the domestic ecosystem. Many operate outside the formal legal system, contributing to widespread informality and low productivity. They lack access to financing and long-term capital, the base that companies are built on.'[138] Egypt's Minister of Investment, Mahmoud Mohieldin, observes that SMEs find it harder to access credit than either large companies (which can borrow from the banks) or individuals, who can turn to a plethora of microfinance providers.[139]

Yet with appropriate government support, SMEs can drive the economy. SMEs played a central role in Taiwan's spectacular growth, built on exports that rose a hundredfold between 1965 and 1987. When labour costs rose in the 1980s, the government actively pushed SMEs to upgrade into ever higher-technology products such as computers, particularly for export. It regulated foreign investment to encourage technology transfer to Taiwanese companies. Over the years, many SMEs became successful exporters, while their linkages to the domestic economy spread the benefits internally. Unlike neighbouring China, SMEs enabled Taiwan to grow rapidly without driving up inequality. In 2006, almost 98 per cent of its approximately 1.3 million enterprises were classified as SMEs; they realised 30 per cent of total sales and employed 77 per cent of the workforce.[140]

States can create the kind of operating conditions that all businesses need, whether large or small, for example by ensuring reliable energy supplies and decent transportation and communications systems. They can avoid getting in the way: excessive regulation can be particularly toxic for SMEs that cannot afford lawyers, and often drives them out of the formal economy altogether, depriving the state of taxes and employees of legal protection. States can also help SMEs develop their businesses with training and support where private suppliers do not exist, particularly in remote areas. Where SMEs lack financial services, governments can act to ensure access to credit.

More broadly, governments can foster technological upgrading, local linkages (both to large firms and to other SMEs), and 'clustering' of SMEs from a particular sector in the same location – such as

Southern Brazil's shoe industry or Bangalore's software cluster. For their part, SMEs need to strengthen their industry associations, so that their voice is not drowned out by the well-organised lobbyists of large domestic companies and TNCs, whose interests are not always compatible with those of small companies. SMEs have also been wrongly left out of the debates on corporate social responsibility. Just as with large firms, there are both good and bad SMEs, and pressure is needed to push firms towards responsible social and environmental practices.

## LARGE FIRMS

Large companies, whether under national or foreign ownership, also play a crucial role in economic development and in the lives of poor people. Although they tend to be more capital-intensive than SMEs, and so create relatively fewer jobs, they have a wider role in that they control complex production and distribution chains, and introduce technology that is then picked up by smaller firms.

Oxfam's analysis of Unilever's 'poverty footprint' in Indonesia showed that, overall, the firm's operations generate about 300,000 full-time equivalent (FTE) jobs. Strikingly, more than half of these jobs are in Unilever's 'downstream' distribution and retail chain, with only about one-third 'upstream' in the part that makes inputs for the company's products. The value added within the value chain is even more dispersed than the benefits of employment within the chain, with Unilever itself accounting for only $212m of the estimated total of $633m in added value from its operations.[141]

Large firms are typically better connected with decision-makers, and use that influence to ensure that state policies serve their interests by giving them tax breaks and other incentives, guaranteeing them high profits, minimising competition, or ensuring privileged access to state spending.

In recent years, global companies have entered low-income consumer markets, epitomised by banks selling microfinance services or companies selling shampoo and other goods in individual sachets rather than by the bottle. Deploying vast advertising and sales campaigns to promote their brands, such TNCs have displaced large local producers and SMEs. Brands are a crucial asset for major corporations in their quest for consumer allegiance, and represent a serious new obstacle for smaller businesses obliged to compete with the bigger players.

While large foreign companies account for a minority of overall investment and employment, their clout is increasing, both in terms of investment volume and the introduction of new technology or management practices that domestically owned companies then follow. Driven by waves of privatisation, deregulation, and the growth of global production chains, the past 15 years have seen levels of foreign direct investment (FDI) to developing countries increase rapidly – from $43bn in 1990 to $316bn in 2006.[142]

Although it is often pointed out that FDI has flowed mainly to the big economies, this largely reflects their greater economic power and larger populations. Five countries – Brazil, China, India, Mexico, and the Russian Federation – accounted for 46 per cent of net FDI inflows in 2005, but this compared with a 55 per cent share of developing-country population and 63 per cent of their GDP.[143]

South–South investment is rising faster than North–South flows, as firms in China, India, South Africa, and the East Asian tigers go multinational. Compared with their developed-country counterparts, southern TNCs are more likely to be state-owned and many are based in the primary sector (oil, gas, mining) or resource-based manufacturing such as iron, steel, and cement.[144] Malaysian and South African investors contributed almost a third of the foreign exchange raised by privatisation efforts in the poorest countries between 1989 and 1998. All the major players in the African telecommunications sector are from other developing countries; these companies have been able to use their operating experience in their home markets to cope with the particular risks of doing business in poor countries.[145]

## TABLE 3.1: SOUTHERN TRANSNATIONAL CORPORATIONS

| Country of origin | Number of firms in the top 50 |
|---|---|
| Hong Kong | 10 |
| China | 7 |
| Taiwan | 7 |
| Singapore | 6 |
| South Africa | 5 |
| South Korea | 4 |
| Brazil | 3 |
| Mexico | 3 |
| Malaysia | 3 |
| Venezuela | 1 |
| India | 1 |

| The top ten Southern TNCs | | Foreign assets ($bn, 2005) | Country of origin |
|---|---|---|---|
| Hutchison Whampoa | Diversified | $61bn | Hong Kong/China |
| Petronas | Petroleum | $26bn | Malaysia |
| Cemex | Cement | $22bn | Mexico |
| Singtel | Telecoms | $18bn | Singapore |
| Samsung | Electronics | $17bn | South Korea |
| LG | Electronics | $17bn | South Korea |
| Jardine Matheson | Diversified | $16bn | Hong Kong |
| CITIC Group | Diversified | $16bn | China |
| Hyundai | Motor vehicles | $13bn | South Korea |
| Formosa Plastic Group | Chemicals | $13bn | Taiwan |

*Source*: UNCTAD, World Investment Report 2007

While China's growing investment in Africa is best known in the extractive industries, where it has been portrayed as leading a new 'scramble for Africa', in fact Chinese firms are taking on a significant number of construction and infrastructure projects that have been avoided as too risky by European or US firms. In Sierra Leone in 2005, within two years of the end of a bloody civil war, China was already investing $270m in hotel construction and tourism.[146]

Southern-based companies have good experience in producing and marketing low-cost products, giving them an advantage in accessing low-income consumer markets. Chinese electronics companies such as TCL make $50 colour television sets in India and Viet Nam.[147]

When India's Tata Motors launched its 'people's car' in 2008 it followed in the footsteps of the Volkswagen Beetle or the Model T Ford, promising to bring cars to new generations of consumers by exporting $2,500-Nanos to the rest of the developing world.[148] Developing-country TNCs are more likely to use 'intermediate' technologies that are more labour-intensive, and so create more jobs.[149] However, the poor performance of Southern TNCs regarding social and environmental responsibility is a cause for concern, and may be due to the absence of strong government or civil society scrutiny at home.

Developing-country governments face dilemmas in balancing support for FDI and for home-grown firms. If foreign investment were identical to the domestic variety in its economic, social, and environmental impacts, there would be no reason for governments to prefer one over the other, but in fact they behave very differently. Each has its merits. Domestic investors are 'stickier': less likely to leave the country, they reinvest more of their profits, and are more likely to keep their higher-value activities, such as R&D and design, at home. This means that there may be developmental reasons for preferring domestic investment, even when a foreign investor's record on corporate responsibility is excellent. For their part, foreign companies can contribute cutting-edge technology, jobs, and tax revenue to a poor economy. They have better access to international markets and sources of credit, often have a better record on wages, labour rights, and the environment, and can influence how domestic companies operate.[150]

These differences may be becoming less significant with time – for example, as domestic businesses move more quickly into liberalised global financial markets, or as TNCs recognise the need to 'become indigenous' in order to understand their customers better and succeed with bottom-of-the-pyramid approaches.[151] But governments still have to weigh up the costs and benefits to determine what combination is most likely to lead to overall development.

Developing countries face five main challenges in harnessing foreign investment for development:

**Linkages**: Foreign companies tend to be less willing to buy inputs from local suppliers, often preferring to source from their own country or parent company (see the Zambia example on page 177). Especially in the case of export industries, this can mean that TNCs' operations come to resemble enclave economies, providing few benefits to the rest of the economy beyond a limited number of jobs. Mexican-produced inputs to the *maquila* belt of 'last touch' assembly factories on the US border accounted for just 3.1 per cent of total value in 2000.[152] Without such linkages, high headline figures for exports are largely cancelled out by the high imports required: the difference, or value added, is much less impressive. The absence of linkages also extends to revenue: many transnational corporations have proved adept at avoiding taxes through tricks such as transfer pricing (see Part 5).

**Technology transfer**: Joint ventures with foreign companies have helped successful developing countries such as Taiwan to absorb and adapt technologies that would otherwise have taken them years to develop. In general, 'spillovers' of technology occur more often where companies have some degree of local ownership.[153] These days, however, proliferating trade and investment agreements restrict the ability of governments to insist on technology transfer, while stronger inter-national patenting rules protect companies that insist on keeping cutting-edge technology to themselves. In light of global warming, encouraging such transfers will be particularly important in helping countries to move rapidly to a low-carbon growth model.

**Profit remittances**: Governments need to maximise investment, while corporations expect to be able to use their profits as they see fit. That may involve reinvestment locally, but often it means sending profits back to the home country. Profit remittances from developing countries rocketed tenfold from $17bn in 1990 to $169bn in 2005, twice the global flow of aid. This represents a serious capital outflow, cutting into the potential developmental impact of FDI.[154]

**Employment**: FDI tends to use capital-intensive technology that generates few jobs. According to the UN, some 70,000 TNCs generate 53 million jobs around the world, but this represents just 2 per cent of the global labour force.[155]

**Race to the bottom**: As poorer countries such as China and Viet Nam have climbed aboard the globalisation bandwagon, the pressure on governments to introduce incentives to attract investment has intensified into a 'race to the bottom'. Governments desperate for foreign capital and technology are going to enormous lengths to outbid their rivals. This includes privatisation of state-owned companies, perks such as tax exemptions for incoming investors, the easing of restrictions on profit remittances, and the establishment of special export-processing zones where trade unions are banned. Such competition deprives governments of tax income and risks undermining labour rights in those countries that have already made some progress.

Global agreements on a universal floor for corporate taxation, and greater efforts to ensure global recognition of the core labour standards of the ILO, could help to reverse the race to the bottom. In the end, however, the main responsibility lies with individual states. Governments in China, Taiwan, Malaysia, Singapore, and Botswana have proved highly effective in getting a good deal out of foreign investment. In the initial stages of its take-off, Taiwan insisted on foreign investors undertaking joint ventures with local businesses in order to accelerate the rate of technology transfer; Botswana negotiated favourable deals for its diamonds with South Africa's de Beers; while all the East Asian countries improved their bargaining power with investors by spending on infrastructure and on health care and education in order to guarantee a skilled, healthy workforce.

As major actors whose activities affect the lives of poor people, transnational corporations have a duty to behave responsibly. What is known as corporate social responsibility (CSR) has many facets, from allocating a small portion of the profits to charity, to producing products that are of particular benefit to poor people (such as BP developing a fuel-efficient stove),[156] to taking into account the social and environmental impact of a company's core business model (which is what really counts in determining its development impact). CSR is examined at greater length on pages 349–50.

A number of factors are pushing TNCs in the direction of social responsibility. The increasing focus of many corporations on domestic markets in countries such as China and India should encourage them to take a more long-term view, since social and political stability and prosperity hold the key to their future profitability. The growing importance of brand and reputation, both to customers and their ability to employ and retain the best recruits, means that corporate leaders are placing more attention on 'non-financial risk', including public criticism of their social and environmental impacts. The concerns of their main shareholders, such as large pension funds, about the long-term impact of corporate misbehaviour on share value and the wider economy are another motivating factor. In developing countries, an increasingly independent media, together with vocal citizens' groups, means that companies' 'licence to operate' is no longer merely a question of bribing a few government officials.

However, firms are not merely passive followers of external signals. Within any given industry, different firms can choose to follow different strategies, with dramatically different impacts on people living in poverty. Following a financial crisis and devaluation in Indonesia in 1998, Unilever reacted to higher import prices by switching to sourcing locally, whereas other foreign companies in the same consumer goods sector closed down altogether.[157] As a result, Unilever's business decision increased its local linkages, while exiting companies added to rising unemployment levels.

Corporate leadership can be crucial at such 'fork in the road' moments of decision, but important roles are also played by active citizens and local communities where TNCs operate. In Eastern Zambia, the arrival of the South African supermarket chain Shoprite spelled disaster for local farmers. Not only did the supermarket take away many of their customers, it would not buy the farmers' produce, preferring to import higher-quality goods from South Africa. Unrest became widespread as rural incomes plummeted and local businesses saw Shoprite scoop up the best premises in town. Even those employed by the company resented the way that all its senior managers were brought in from South Africa.

Local NGOs and academics got involved, alerting 'Mr Fritz', Shoprite's 'big boss' in the capital, Lusaka, that the local community was threatening to burn down the store unless the company changed its ways. A university professor helped win over the company by setting out a plausible business case for local sourcing, given the unreliability of road transport links to South Africa. Thanks to a series of partnerships backed by Shoprite, farmers were able to raise their standards of production, and the supermarket switched to local suppliers without significant reductions in quality or damage to its profitability. Shoprite is now expanding the scheme to its other stores in Zambia.[158]

A healthy private sector is essential in the fight against poverty and inequality. Private firms, large and small, must be able to turn a profit, but should do so in ways that strengthen national development and benefit poor women and men. Companies can choose to adopt strategies that aim to profit by investing in, rather than by exploiting, their workforce, the environment, or the community.

In the Shoprite example, active citizens used broad mobilisation (backed, admittedly, by the threat of violence) to successfully change corporate policies and practices. Parallel to popular action, effective states must ensure that good companies are not undermined by bad, because in too many situations business pressures undermine good intentions. In developing countries, states can help harness the private sector for development by setting minimum standards for all, and shifting the centre of gravity from 'exploit for profit' to 'invest for profit'. Measures include properly funding labour inspectorates and guaranteeing an enabling environment for businesses, particularly SMEs, through improved access to credit and technology. In the North, governments can use regulation to improve the development impact of TNCs, an issue discussed in Part 5.

# GOING FOR GROWTH

Fifty years ago, Korea was poorer than the Sudan. Its main export was wigs made from human hair. Today it is an industrial leader with a GDP per capita more than nine times greater than that of Sudan.[159] In terms of health, wealth, education, and expectations, the lives of Koreans today bear little resemblance to those of their grandparents. Elsewhere, Taiwan and Viet Nam have achieved the rare feat of combining high-speed growth with one of the fairest distributions of income in the world. China's rise since the late 1980s has delivered the greatest reduction in poverty ever recorded.[160] These extraordinary success stories are historically unprecedented features of the modern era: all 12 cases of countries growing by more than 7 per cent a year over a 25-year period have occurred since the Second World War.[161]

The extent and nature of economic growth is central to development and to the lives of poor people.[162] Put simply, countries that have reduced poverty have invariably had to grow to do so. Properly managed, growth in the market economy creates jobs, increases incomes, and generates tax revenues that effective states can invest in infrastructure, schools, and hospitals. Creating wealth is an inseparable part of reducing poverty.

Inequality determines how far growth benefits poor people: a 1 per cent increase in per capita GDP can reduce income poverty by as much as 4 per cent or as little as 1 per cent.[163] Redistribution of wealth by means of land reform or progressive taxation can leave poor people

179

better off even in a shrinking economy, but in practice redistribution alone has never reduced poverty for more than brief interludes. The substantial reduction in poverty in most OECD countries during the twentieth century came through a combination of long-term economic growth and modest redistribution.[164]

According to the Commission on Growth and Development, in very poor countries growth is the main route to poverty reduction, but as a country develops redistribution becomes more important as a way to reduce poverty.[165] As economies grow worldwide, redistribution therefore should become an increasingly important feature of government policy.

Economic growth is a measure of the increase in the output of goods and services in the monetised part of the economy. Growth may result from an increase in the number of workers or an increase in their productivity (producing more goods and services per worker). The latter can be achieved through better technology, through improving the health and skills of the workforce, discovering and developing new natural resources, and through greater efficiency via 'economies of scale'. Upgrading in this way often requires painful structural change, such as moving out of agriculture into manufacturing or higher-tech companies squeezing out lower-tech ones, a process memorably described by the economist Joseph Schumpeter as the 'creative destruction' at the heart of capitalism.[167]

For neoclassical economists and for many policy makers, growth in the market economy is so important that they often lose sight of the fact that growth is a means to promote human welfare, not an end in itself. But growth is inherently disequalising, since richer people generally find it easier than those living in poverty to take advantage of new opportunities and to protect themselves from shocks. Effective states are essential to containing and reversing this disruption, for example through taxation, spending, credit, and regional policies and investment decisions.

At a global level, growth is an increasingly blunt instrument for reducing poverty. Between 1981 and 2001, world GDP increased by $18,691bn. Of this, only $278bn, or 1.5 per cent, accrued to people living below the $1-a-day poverty line, even though they constituted one in three of the world's population at the start of the period.

Worse still, global growth is becoming less effective at reducing poverty. In the 1990s it took $166 of global economic growth, with all the associated environmental costs, to achieve just $1 of progress in reducing poverty, while in the 1980s this figure was $45.[168] Moreover, by exacerbating climate change and other environmental problems, the $165 that poor people do *not* receive imposes a significant toll on their prospects. This cloud has a silver lining, however, as it shows that even minor improvements in the poverty-reducing efficiency of growth would have a massive impact on the lives of the poorest people.

The links between growth and well-being (rather than income poverty) are not straightforward. Comparisons between regions of the world based on public surveys show a fascinating break point.[169] Below a GDP of about $20,000 per head (roughly the level of Portugal or South Korea), people's estimates of their own life satisfaction rise steadily with income. Above that amount, the graph flatlines: higher national income does not make people feel any happier.[170] In fact, subjective well-being on average has not risen in the USA, Europe, or Japan in the past 40 years, despite sustained growth.[171] In seeking to enhance well-being, there is a powerful argument for redistributing wealth from countries with average incomes above the $20,000 'sufficiency line' to those below it.

## HISTORY CHALLENGES RECEIVED WISDOM

For most developing countries, post-1980 efforts to generate sustained growth have relied on the dramatic shock therapy known as the Washington Consensus. Recommended by the World Bank, the IMF, and others, this called for rapid liberalisation, deregulation, and privatisation of developing-country economies. Any proponent of the Washington Consensus visiting Latin America and China in the mid-1980s would reasonably have concluded that Latin America was bound for prosperity, whereas China was doomed. Latin America at that time was moving into a liberalising overdrive, privatising state firms and opening up to trade. In China, meanwhile, tariffs and non-tariff barriers remained high, and the government showed little appetite for ending its deep involvement in crucial areas of economic management such as the banking system.

Twenty years on, China's take-off is mesmerising policy makers everywhere, while Latin America continues its centuries-old cycle of boom and bust. Sustained growth has reduced the number of Chinese living in poverty from one in three in 1990 to one in ten in 2005.[172] Since Latin America embarked on a massive trade drive, increasing its exports from $96bn in 1981 to $752bn in 2007, the number of poor people (defined as those living on less than $2 a day) actually rose from 136 million to 209 million between 1980 and 2005.[173] Shock therapy turned out to be all shock and precious little therapy.

Advocates of rapid trade liberalisation rely heavily on the 'big numbers' generated by computer models seeking to quantify the benefits accruing from tariff and subsidy reductions, but such models often assume away the problems that dog markets in most developing countries.[174] An increasing number of analysts are turning for evidence and guidance to a different discipline – history, in particular that of economies that have successfully 'taken off' in recent decades.

Harvard economist Dani Rodrik has identified 83 episodes of growth 'take-off' in developing countries since 1950, spread throughout the world.[175] On average, such episodes increased economic output by almost 40 per cent within a few years. Even more significant than the general sense of possibility that such surveys awaken are their radical implications for development policy. Rodrik found that 'the vast majority of growth take-offs are not produced by significant economic reforms, and the vast majority of significant economic reforms do not produce growth take-offs'. Instead, the triggers have often been small reforms aimed at freeing bottlenecks in the economy, defying economic orthodoxy but going with the grain of existing institutions.

In India, for example, following his landslide election victory in 1984, Rajiv Gandhi relaxed industrial regulations and rationalised the tax system, and the economy surged.[176] China reformed its rigidly planned economy incrementally (rather than abandoning planning altogether), underplayed private property rights (relying instead on a mix of state ownership, collective local enterprises, and private ownership), and opened up to the world in a carefully monitored and gradual way (complementing its highly protectionist trade regime with special economic zones). Viet Nam, a fellow socialist country, has followed many of the same principles since the second half of the 1980s (see Box 3.8 on page 187).

Success has required a combination of effective states and political leadership. From the historical record, it appears that there are no shortcuts: the private sector on its own has never achieved growth with equity. Furthermore, effective state intervention appears to be crucial for the development of the private sector itself. All take-off countries gave priority to general economic goals such as macro-economic stability, integration into the world economy, high levels of savings and public and private investment, and rapid diversification, while at the same time striving to maintain social cohesion, solidarity, and political stability.[177]

Successful governments have invested in roads, power supplies, and people. Agricultural take-off has generally been an essential first step on the ladder of economic growth, followed by a move into clothing production, then up the value chain into manufacturing and exporting more complex products such as electronics. When trying to achieve this shift, successful economies in South Korea, Taiwan, Viet Nam, and China developed key sectors behind protective tariff barriers, with a hands-on role for the state in guiding the take-off:

- Governments invested heavily in education and training, ensuring that they had skilled workforces able to produce ever more sophisticated goods.
- Governments led the way in encouraging industry to upgrade from low-tech manufacturing, such as garments, to higher-tech manufactures and high-skilled services.
- Governments forced industries to become competitive, not least by obliging them to compete in export markets. Protection, for example via tariffs, was used frequently but for limited time periods, so that industries knew how long they had to become competitive.
- Governments insisted on letting failures go out of business, whereas unsuccessful ones became 'captured' by industrial lobbies and accumulated white elephant industries dependent on continued state support for their survival.
- Governments decided relatively early on whether they would pursue industrialisation by setting up national leader

183

companies (for example South Korea), or by encouraging foreign companies to import technology and operate directly (for example Malaysia), but in both cases successful governments pursued activist policies, rather than *laissez faire* ones.

- The state used its regulatory powers over investment, access to capital (for example via subsidised loans to preferred industries), a panoply of tax breaks, and other incentives to manage industrial transformation.

As economies developed and became more complex, and industries achieved international competitiveness, the costs and benefits of state intervention in both agriculture and industry shifted, and governments started to reduce their role and to open up the economy – exactly the sequence that rich countries pursued at an earlier stage of their development.[178] Deregulation and liberalisation are thus better seen as the outcomes of successful development, rather than as initial conditions.

---

## BOX 3.7
## A TALE OF TWO TIGERS

The People's Republic of China and Viet Nam have been two outstanding success stories of East Asian development over the past two decades. Both have achieved rapid economic growth and spectacular reductions in poverty, and both are Communist systems in transition, moving from centralised state planning to more market-based structures.[179] But China has seen enormous increases in inequality, while Viet Nam has grown much more equitably. Why?

First, the two countries de-collectivised agriculture in very different ways. During the 1990s Chinese farmers saw a 30 per cent fall in the price of grains and a tripling of agricultural taxes, which left poorer regions in the centre and west of the country to stagnate and stimulated a vast out-migration to urban areas. In Viet Nam, by contrast, the *doi moi* reforms launched in 1986 involved a widespread and largely equitable redistribution of land to private farmers, backed up by significant state support for irrigation schemes, seeds, technological upgrading, and price stabilisation. As a result, Vietnamese agriculture has been an important pillar of the country's take-off.

Second, Viet Nam has been far more successful in redistributing resources to poorer regions and maintaining high levels of public spending in education, health, water, and sanitation. In contrast, China opted for 'fiscal decentralisation', limiting central government transfers to poorer provinces, leading to a widening gulf between dynamic coastal regions with their booming export industries and a largely neglected interior. (This is something the Chinese government has sought to correct through its 'Go West' programme of encouraging investment in infrastructure away from the coast).

Third, Viet Nam's recent history of war and national threat reinforces a strong collective sense of 'national mission', imbuing the country's Communist Party with a sense of national legitimacy.

Enormous challenges await both countries as they seek to build on their achievements. Viet Nam's accession to the WTO in 2006 will constrain the government's ability to use subsidies and other elements of industrial policy to guide the economy and redistribute wealth. The country must also deal with increasing inequality between its ethnic minorities and the Kinh majority, rampant corruption, and the increasing need for political participation. If anything, China faces even more extreme versions of these challenges, and on a grander scale.

Source: P. Chaudhry (2007) 'Why Has Viet Nam Achieved Growth With Relative Equity, and China Hasn't?', internal paper for Oxfam International; Le Quang Binh (2006) 'What Has Made Viet Nam a Poverty-Reduction Success Story?' background paper for Oxfam International.

A developing country's success or failure at achieving growth is increasingly linked to its ability to participate in international trade. Global trade is booming, growing much faster than the world economy as a whole. Global exports of manufactured and agricultural products increased by 15 per cent in 2006, to a value of $11.8 trillion. Trade in services such as banking and tourism rose by 11 per cent, reaching $2.7 trillion.[180]

Not surprisingly, trade is heavily skewed towards the rich and middle-income countries (including better-off developing countries). Today, for every $100 generated by world exports, $97.28 goes to the high- and middle-income countries, and only $2.72 goes to low-income countries, even though they contain nearly 40 per cent of the world's people.[181]

Under the aegis of structural adjustment programme agreements with aid donors or bilateral and regional trade agreements, many developing countries have sought to improve their trade balance and attract investment by reducing border tariffs and import and export quotas and, more widely, by reducing state regulation of trade. Trade liberalisation also includes cutting subsidies or restricting the ability of governments to impose rules on investment, and can cause surges of cheap imports against which small farmers or local labour-intensive manufacturers are unable to compete.[182] As firms have sought to modernise production and recruit more skilled workers, the difference between skilled and unskilled wages has risen.

In its 2006 *World Development Report* on equity, the World Bank concluded that opening up to trade has been associated with rising inequality in earnings in many countries over the past two decades. Trade liberalisation has also cut into one of the few easy ways for poor-country governments to raise revenues.

In agriculture, the success of exporters such as Chile and Botswana gives some credence to the liberalising agenda. However, in countries such as Korea, Malaysia, and Indonesia, smallholder development strategies were underpinned by government use of tariffs to stabilise domestic prices (protecting floor prices for farmers as well as ceiling prices for consumers) and thereby encourage investment. Retaining tariff flexibility is particularly important because other instruments, such as quotas, were largely prohibited in the WTO's 1994 Uruguay Round agreements.[183]

In manufacturing, countries with successful growth records – such as South Korea, Taiwan, Viet Nam, China, and Mauritius – have developed core industries behind protective barriers. Trade barriers were gradually lowered once these sectors started to become internationally competitive. Rich countries are now demanding that developing countries cut tariffs significantly, even though they themselves once used high tariffs to protect their own fledgling industries. When they were at the same level of development as sub-Saharan Africa is today, the USA had an average tariff of 40 per cent, Japan

30 per cent, and EU members 20 per cent, far higher than the levels currently being contemplated in today's trade negotiations.[184]

The lesson of history is that trade liberalisation should be asymmetric: rich countries should liberalise more than poor ones, not as a 'concession' but in recognition of the fact that optimal trade regimes evolve along with national economies. The correct balance between liberalisation and protection will vary between countries, and evolves as a country develops. Effective states have been able to pursue a judicious combination of the two, a task that now however is being complicated by the nature of globalisation and the proliferation of international rules on trade and investment.

## BOX 3.8
## THE DISADVANTAGES OF COMPARATIVE ADVANTAGE

The World Bank and other advocates of trade liberalisation in developing countries draw heavily on economic theories of comparative advantage, which were first advanced in 1817 by David Ricardo in his book *The Principles of Political Economy and Taxation.* Many of today's fervent controversies about globalisation are debates with the ghost of this nineteenth-century English economist.

Using a simple numerical example, Ricardo demonstrated that two countries could arrive at a higher level of wealth by sticking to producing those goods that had a 'comparative advantage' over other alternatives (broadly, those goods that were relatively more efficient), then trading those goods with other countries, rather than trying to produce all goods for themselves. At a time when trade was widely viewed as a zero-sum game, Ricardo's was an idea with revolutionary implications.

Applied crudely, as it often is in current debates on trade liberalisation, the theory is of limited value. What Ricardo created was a static model that encouraged countries with a particular mix of skills and resources to focus on those. But skills and resources are not fixed in time. If they were, the USA would never have moved beyond its comparative advantage in land, and would have remained an agricultural economy. South Korea and Taiwan emerged as major industrial powers because they transformed their comparative advantage. Thirty-five years ago, they were protecting themselves from imports of US steel in order to build up a domestic industry. Today, it is the USA that seeks protection from East Asian exporters. The reason: government policies produced changes in comparative advantage.

## CHINA AND THE FUTURE OF OTHER DEVELOPING COUNTRIES

The much commented-upon rise of China since the late 1980s has precipitated a tectonic shift in the global economy. China is fast becoming the world's factory:

- The city of Shunde in the Pearl River Delta has a single giant factory that produces 40 per cent of the world's microwave ovens.
- Shenzhen makes 70 per cent of the world's photocopiers and 80 per cent of its artificial Christmas trees.
- Three out of every five buttons in the world are made in Qiaotou, a dusty, dirty town in Zhejiang province that also ships more than two million zips a day.

China's unique combination of massive scale, rock-bottom wages, high literacy, highly developed infrastructure, and political control over labour enables it to out-compete most of its industrial rivals. China has driven down the prices of most manufactured goods, to the benefit of consumers the world over, but has undercut other developing-country exporters in the process. With 150 million unemployed workers constituting an effectively infinite reserve army of labour, China can continue to be the world's factory without approaching full employment (at which point wages rise and other competitors can enter the market), leaving few crumbs for other developing countries.

The impact of China may also be refuting the received wisdom that getting out of commodities into industry is the route to development. Booming Chinese demand has reversed the long-term decline in commodity prices and in what economists call the 'terms of trade' between raw materials and manufactured goods, sometimes presented as the number of bags of coffee (or barrels of oil) needed to buy a truck.[185] For the moment, coffee and oil prices are high, and the price of trucks (and Nano cars) is falling. Opinions differ as to whether this is the start of an extended period of high prices that defies the normal rules of boom and bust and long-term trade decline. The recovery in tropical commodities such as coffee has lagged well behind temperate crops such as wheat, and history suggests that the boom is unlikely to endure forever, as high prices encourage new entrants to the market or technology finds new, cheaper substitutes for existing commodities.

If the long-term decline in the terms of the trade goes into reverse, however (at least for commodities that are not easily substituted), then developing countries' growth strategies may come to look very different in future to the standard 'subsistence agriculture to export agriculture to garments and textiles to electronics' sequence followed in the past. The rewards from commodity production will be higher and from industrialisation lower; new technologies and globalisation will allow countries to capitalise on new forms of comparative advantage, such as services involving spoken English, or tourism, or culture; and countries may have to focus on domestic and regional markets, rather than trying to compete with China in global trade.

## SUSTAINABLE GROWTH

Economic growth is an essential way to tackle poverty and inequality, as shown by some of the extraordinary success stories of the modern high-growth era, but the quality of that growth matters as much as the quantity. Figure 3.1 at the beginning of this section introduced a more holistic approach to economics. By applying the analytical elements of that approach, development strategists can seek to manage growth so that it maximises human welfare.

**Reducing income poverty:** Growth does not always raise the incomes of poor people. Growth through technology-driven improvements in productivity has been termed 'jobless growth', because it fails to create more jobs than it destroys. The phenomenon is particularly worrying in that job creation is one of the main ways that growth reduces poverty. In developing countries with rapidly growing populations, new generations of youth are not being incorporated into the world of work. Even in China's booming economy, the rate of technological change is such that, despite astonishing gains in output, the number of formal-sector manufacturing jobs fell from 98 million in 1995 to 83 million in 2002, even faster than the fall in 14 OECD countries (86 million to 79 million).[186]

**Environmental sustainability**: As pursued to date, growth has rarely respected the carrying capacity of the environment. The world consists of 11.5bn hectares of biologically productive space – grassland, cropland, forests, fisheries, and wetlands. There are approximately 6.4 billion people on the planet. So, on average, there are 1.8 hectares of 'environmental space' per person, but by 2003 the average human being required 25 per cent more than that – paid for, in environmental terms, by running down the earth's environmental capital.[187]

**Equity**: Global growth during the 1970s and 1980s did not result in increased inequality, according to a World Bank study, but in the decade that followed the richer members of society came to benefit disproportionately and inequality rose in tandem with economic growth.[188] Not only does inequality limit growth's potential to reduce poverty, it creates a 'highly toxic environment' for growth itself.[189]

**Social sustainability**: Growth has unpredictable repercussions on unpaid labour such as caring, household chores, or raising children. Growth has sparked the massive entry of women into the labour force over the past 20 years, but that has only enhanced women's welfare where it has been accompanied by changes in gender roles or matching state action to ease the burden of unpaid work. Where this has not occurred, women's welfare has been undermined.

**Secure livelihoods**: The disruption that accompanies growth can destabilise the livelihoods of poor people. Pro-growth policies recommended by the World Bank and the IMF often explicitly adopt a 'shock therapy' approach of radical change. Many political leaders put 'flexibility' and 'change' on a pedestal, but instability at the macro level (for example in financial markets) has inflicted a series of deep economic crises on developing countries. At the individual level, instability and shocks, such as losing jobs or assets, or sudden shifts in prices for farmers, can be very costly for people living in poverty. Pursuing well-being may therefore mean eschewing the more destabilising elements of the 'dash for growth'. Many poor people see huge advantages in stability and predictability.[190]

**Rights and citizenship**: Historically, growth generally strengthened active citizenship because greater economic security led to increased demand for rights, often led by new middle classes. However, in recent years, measures to achieve growth have weakened the security of poor people and at times have explicitly undermined rights, for example by outlawing unions in export-processing zones. Such measures limit the capacity of growth to reduce poverty and inequality. An active citizenry is essential to ensure that the benefits of growth are evenly spread.

**Effective states**: Pro-growth strategies in recent decades have viewed the state as part of the problem – an obstacle to the smooth functioning of markets. Because effective states are central both to enable growth to take place and to ensure a fair distribution of its benefits, measures to promote growth must strengthen rather than undermine state effectiveness, for example by increasing its tax take and enhancing governance and state institutions.

There is no single policy path for poor countries to achieve welfare-enhancing growth. Strategies initially driven by ideology, whether state-centric or market-centric, have shown some success, but only to the degree that ideology has taken a back seat to the pragmatic long-term task of building public institutions and citizens' rights. The way forward lies not in policy prescriptions, but in states that are ever more capable of experimenting and learning from their mistakes, and in citizens actively defending their interests. Effective states and active citizens offer the best guarantee that the market can deliver both wealth creation and improved human welfare.

## HOW CHANGE HAPPENS CASE STUDY
## BOTSWANA AND MAURITIUS: TWO AFRICAN
## SUCCESS STORIES

By normal criteria, Botswana ought to be a basket case: it has a small population, is arid and landlocked, and is largely dependent on natural resources (diamonds). At independence in 1966, it had just two secondary schools and 12km of paved road, and relied on the UK for half of its government revenues.

Instead, at least until the onset of the AIDS pandemic, Botswana has been Africa's most enduring success story. Its GDP per capita has risen a hundredfold since independence, making it the world's fastest-growing economy for three decades. All this time, it has been one of sub-Saharan Africa's few enduring non-racial democracies, despite being bordered (and occasionally invaded) by racist regimes in South Africa and the former Rhodesia.

A number of factors have contributed to Botswana's success:

**Positive governance traditions.** The traditional governance systems of the dominant Tswana tribes emerged largely unscathed from the colonial period. These emphasise broad consultation and consensus-building, a system described by the country's leading human rights activist as 'gentle authoritarianism'.

**A hands-on role for the state.** The government set up state-owned companies, nationalised all mineral rights, and has run the economy on the basis of six-year National Development Plans. 'We are a free market economy that does everything by planning,' observes one local academic.

**Lucky timing.** Diamonds were not discovered for several years after independence, by which time institutions were in place to negotiate favourable contracts with diamond giant de Beers and to ensure exemplary management of the millions of dollars that began to flow.

**Lack of a military.** Botswana only acquired an army ten years after independence in response to cross-border raids from Rhodesia, so coups were not a temptation.

**Good use of technical assistance.** With only two secondary schools and 22 university graduates at independence, the government hired enthusiastic young expatriates on long-term contracts, avoiding the two-week 'cookie-cutter' variety that prevailed elsewhere. Many of them ended up taking citizenship and staying.

**Leadership.** The first two presidents, Seretse Khama and Quett Masire, built a sense of nationhood and an effective state bureaucracy.

Despite economic growth, however, the country still faces the problems of all resource-based economies that fail to diversify: unemployment, inequality, and persistent poverty. Twenty per cent of the population live on less than $1 a day. The government is banking on diversifying within natural resources (for example, sorting and polishing diamonds at home, rather than in London) and developing services such as tourism and finance, which should create more jobs. But with a single party in power for the 40 years since independence, some degree of erosion (public dissatisfaction, allegations of corruption) seems inevitable.

The success of Mauritius meanwhile has claimed some impressive academic scalps. In 1961 Nobel Prize-winning economist James Meade saw the economy of the Indian Ocean island as doomed to failure – dependent on a single crop, with a rapidly growing population susceptible to ethnic tensions. 'The outlook for peaceful development is poor,' he concluded.

Yet since independence in 1968, Mauritius has become a highly competitive, inclusive democracy generating growth rates more common to East Asia than to Africa (5.9 per cent a year from 1973–99, compared with the African average of 2.4 per cent). Once reliant on sugarcane, it moved into textiles and garments in a classic process of labour-intensive industrialisation, largely led by local investors, and then diversified further into tourism and financial services.

Improvements in human development have been equally impressive. Not only have all the usual indicators improved – life expectancy, school enrolments, literacy, infant mortality – income inequality has actually fallen substantially since growth took off. Finally, all this has been achieved with rich-country levels of social protection: active trade unions, price controls on socially sensitive items, and generous social security, particularly for elderly people and for civil servants.

CASE STUDY

The main reason for Mauritius' success was its intelligent use of trade as a motor of development. Rather than liberalising the whole economy, the government set up export-processing zones in which duty-free access was granted to imported inputs, along with tax breaks for investors. While the workforce in these zones originally earned 40 per cent less than in the rest of the economy, the wage gap dwindled by the 1990s. Mauritius also benefited from preferential access to European and US markets for its sugar and textiles.

Policy success required an effective state, and Mauritius ranks well above the average African country in terms of its institutions, with less corruption, a tradition of transparency and public participation, and a well-paid and effective civil service. Other success factors include the very ethnic diversity that Meade identified as a curse: the Chinese population brokered the initial investments in garment factories from Hong Kong, while the Indian diaspora turned Mauritius into a major offshore financial centre.

*Sources*: author trip report (July 2007); J. Clark Leith (2005) 'Why Botswana Prospered'; M. Lockwood (2005) *The State They're In*, ITDG Publishing; Acemoglu, Johnson, and Robinson, 'Botswana, an African success story'; Subramanian and Roy (2003) 'Who can explain the Mauritian miracle?' in D. Rodrik *In Search of Prosperity: Analytic Narratives on Economic Growth*, Princeton University Press.

CASE STUDY

# SUSTAINABLE MARKETS

In using markets to tackle poverty and inequality, the priority is first to select the right tool, then start building. Up until now, the tool of choice for understanding and managing markets, a very crude version of neoclassical economics, has not been up to the job, offering only a very approximate understanding of the role of markets in human development. Partly as a result, a period of unprecedented economic growth has excluded large portions of humanity from its benefits, generating a world of burgeoning inequalities and stubborn and extreme poverty.

The urgency of finding a better toolkit springs not just from moral outrage at a system that squanders the chance to end so much needless suffering, but from the evidence that climate change and other environmental constraints may be changing the kind of growth that is possible, if the planet's ecosystem is to remain inhabitable by 6.5 billion people (and rising). The challenge now is to move from 'dirty growth' to 'smart growth', guided by a new economics for the twenty-first century that explicitly seeks the elusive goal of human well-being. We must seek both quantity and quality of growth, if the planet, along with its inhabitants, is to survive.

Many men and women living in poverty experience markets as a volatile and uncontrollable force that dictates the terms of their lives. By organising, citizens can gain some degree of influence and power over the market. When farmers can store grain and sell it in the lean season, or when workers can form a union and oblige an employer to pay decent wages, they increase their bargaining power, so that they are not only price-takers but, to some small degree, price-makers in the marketplace. With the support of effective states, such gains can become more frequent and sustained, as when the legal framework facilitates grassroots organisation, when subsidised credit helps farmers hold off on selling until prices rise, or when labour legislation sets a floor for decent wages and working conditions.

Sustainable growth starts with poor people, where they live, what they do to survive, and with developing policies and institutions that support their struggles. It means recognising that most poor people still live in rural areas, where they flourish or fail through a combination of small-scale agriculture, farm labour, fishing, and newer strategies such as migration or catering to tourists. Build the economy there, and poor people will benefit. It means understanding that a large part of human activity takes place outside the monetary economy, where government action has important impacts. It means acknowledging that the private sector and trade (whether internal or international) are the ultimate drivers of the economy, and it means supporting them with policies, investment, and institutions so that their dynamism will reduce poverty and inequality.

The dirty growth era that followed the end of colonialism in the mid twentieth century delivered important progress in human development for a large portion of humanity. The critical task for this century is to devise a clean growth agenda to achieve sustainable progress for everyone. It will require a combination of effective, accountable states and active citizens, both in civil society and in the private sector, backed by a system of global governance that works for all, not just for a privileged few. The prize is a world without poverty and extreme inequality, living within its environmental means. The price of failure hardly bears thinking about.

# LIVING WITH RISK

It is hard to imagine a more precarious life than that of the Karimojong in northern Uganda. Semi-nomadic herders, or pastoralists, they live within fierce thorn stockades, scattered across a baked dusty plain. Visitors must crawl through tiny gaps to get through the defences, which have been set up against cattle raiders from other pastoralist groups. Nearby, charred hut circles show where an army attack recently burned a number of elderly villagers to death, along with a woman who was in the middle of giving birth. Drought is a constant threat, although today the earth smells hot and damp from the first rains, bringing out a horde of brilliant red beetles.

However, the Karimojong are anything but victims, and constantly seek ways to minimise the risks they face. Sitting on cowhides outside their huts, members of a women's group describe how they set up a communal grain bank, and how they now buy sorghum when it is cheap at harvest time, store it in large wicker and mud granaries, and sell it back to the villagers during the hungry months. 'It's better to work as a group – it gives you strength,' they say. 'In a group you can never be lazy, you get motivated.' The benefits extend to controlling their husbands' alcohol consumption: 'If you have a family granary, it's harder to say no to your husband or son when they come and ask for sorghum to make beer.' Laughing, they add that they still keep a small stock at home just in case their husbands become too insistent.

No one's life is free of risk. One way or another, we all suffer from, and have to cope with, insecurity – over jobs, health, relationships, raising our children. While more affluent individuals and societies can manage some risks and avoid others altogether, poor people and poor countries cannot. As a result, the lives of most poor people are built around coping with risk – and, all too frequently, such risks turn into personal or societal catastrophe.

The majority of such catastrophes can be avoided through a combination of protection (by the state, or the international community) and empowerment of the individuals concerned, a combination known as 'human security'. Ending needless suffering of this kind is both a moral imperative and an act of enlightened self-interest in a world where climate change, conflict, and disease show scant respect for borders. This part of the book argues that guaranteeing human security is possible, if governments, citizens, and the international community all take action.

Vulnerability to sudden 'shocks', the result both of individual or social factors (gender, age, disability, health, class, or caste) and of the relative power of an individual or community to defend their interests, is one of the defining characteristics of poverty. When World Bank researchers interviewed 64,000 poor people in 24 countries as part of its *Voices of the Poor* exercise in 2000, it asked them to reflect on how their most pressing problems had changed over the course of the past decade. In their responses, people particularly mentioned far greater insecurity of livelihood than in the past. The only exception to this was in Viet Nam, where all the groups interviewed said that economic opportunities had increased and that poverty had declined substantially in the 1990s.

Physical insecurity also emerged as a major concern. With only a few exceptions, notably in some isolated communities, poor people reported feeling less secure and more fearful than they did ten years earlier. The researchers concluded that: 'Anxiety emerges as the defining characteristic of insecurity, and the anxiety is based not on one but on many risks and fears: anxiety about jobs, anxiety about not getting paid, anxiety about needing to migrate, anxiety about lack of protection and safety, anxiety about floods and drought, anxiety about shelter, anxiety about falling ill, and anxiety about the future of children and settling them well in marriage.'[1]

Insecurity and risk are not just greater for poor people than for rich, but vary across other faultlines of social and economic inequality. Women and children often face different risks from men because they hold relatively less power in most societies, and so are more vulnerable. For example, they may face domestic violence or have less access to food in 'normal' times and have less access to emergency aid after a disaster. In many countries, women face penury after the death of a husband. Similarly, commonly marginalised groups such as ethnic minorities, elderly people, or disabled and sick people often face greater risks.

The individual risks that poor people face reinforce and exacerbate one other, ratcheting up inequality and exclusion. If a family's main breadwinner falls sick or loses his or her job, the family may have to eat less, weakening its resistance to disease, or sell off prized assets such as goats or cows, rendering it less resilient to further shocks. Studies in Malawi show how the famine of 2001–02 drove desperate women and girls to sell sex to survive, greatly increasing their chances of contracting HIV.[2]

When shocks affect the whole community, help from relatives or neighbours is harder to come by, further undermining resilience. A devastating feedback loop can develop between conflict and 'natural' disasters, which drains individual, community, and national resources, weakens institutions, and heightens risk through displacement, the blocking of aid and recovery assistance, and the destruction of physical and natural assets.

Conflict can turn low rainfall into famine. More than 50 per cent of Africa's food crises can be explained by armed conflict and the consequent displacement of millions of people.[3] In 2003, 13 of the 17 countries with more than 100,000 AIDS orphans were in conflict or on the edge of emergency.[4]

One of the menaces of climate change is its tendency to exacerbate existing sources of risk and vulnerability for poor people. In Kenya and Darfur, for example, drought has heightened conflict over diminishing areas of fertile land or depleted supplies of water. In Zambia, droughts have left people more prone to contracting HIV, since they have forced families to marry off daughters early, often to older men who have had numerous sexual partners. Drought and deprivation also force women and girls into the sex industry and stoke migration to the towns, where HIV is more prevalent. The negative synergy works both ways, with sickness, death, and the need to attend numerous funerals undermining farming families' abilities to adapt their livelihoods to a changing climate.[5]

Short-term disruptions and suffering have long-term consequences. Research shows that, even decades after droughts, wars, and floods, those affected earn and consume less, have fewer qualifications, and get sick more often. Moreover, the ways in which poor people cope with such shocks often trade off short-term survival against the possibility of long-term progress.

This section explores some of the multiple risks in the lives of poor women and men. It examines the everyday risks that poor people face, as well as the shocks that can buffet whole communities and countries, from 'slow onset' disasters such as drought to 'sudden onset' catastrophes such as earthquakes and war. It assesses the changing nature of risks, and sets out ideas for preparing people, mitigating the impact of such risks, and addressing their root causes. It shows that poor people are nearly always more vulnerable, and suggests that reducing their vulnerability is crucial in the fight against poverty and inequality.

## WHO IS VULNERABLE?

'Vulnerability' describes the reduced ability of some communities or households to cope with the events and stresses to which they are exposed. Such stresses can equally well be an 'everyday disaster' such as a death in the family, sickness, a robbery, an eviction, or the loss of a job or a crop, or a major event such as a drought or a conflict that affects the whole community. Both types of event can tip poor families over the edge into a downward spiral of increasing vulnerability and poverty. The risk that a poor individual or household faces can be understood as a simple formula: *risk = hazard x vulnerability*. Risk can be the result either of extreme vulnerability to comparably minor events, or of a massive shock that sweeps even well-defended families before it.

Figure 4.1 shows a sample of the risks that can threaten a poor individual or household, and the key assets with which they can manage and withstand them. The factors are constantly evolving through social, political, and environmental change. For example, urbanisation is placing millions of people in potential death traps. Almost half of the world's largest cities are situated along major earthquake faults or are exposed to tropical cyclone tracks, while many large cities are on coasts where they may be vulnerable to rising sea levels, storms, and possibly tsunamis.[6]

## FIGURE 4.1: HOW VULNERABILITY AFFECTS LIVELIHOODS

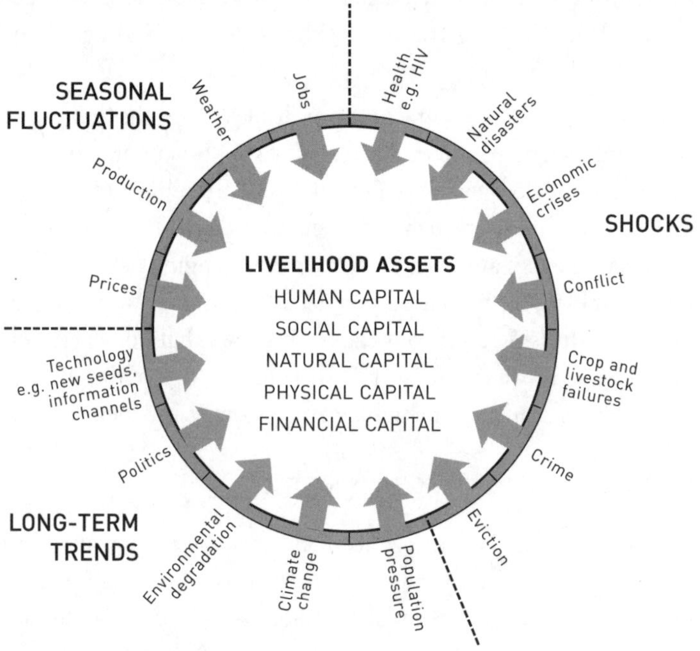

SEASONAL FLUCTUATIONS

Weather · Jobs · Health e.g. HIV · Natural disasters · Production · Economic crises · Prices

SHOCKS

Conflict · Technology e.g. new seeds, information channels · Crop and livestock failures · Politics · Crime · Environmental degradation · Eviction · Climate change · Population pressure

LONG-TERM TRENDS

LIVELIHOOD ASSETS
HUMAN CAPITAL
SOCIAL CAPITAL
NATURAL CAPITAL
PHYSICAL CAPITAL
FINANCIAL CAPITAL

## LIVELIHOOD ASSETS

**Human capital**: skills, knowledge, ability to work, and good health.

**Social capital**: the social resources upon which people draw, including informal networks, either with individuals or wider institutions, such as political or civic bodies; membership of more formalised groups such as churches; and relationships of trust, reciprocity, and exchange.

**Natural capital**: the natural resource stocks on which people can draw, including common resources, land, water, and so on.

**Physical capital**: the basic infrastructure (shelter, transport, irrigation, energy, etc.) and producer goods needed to support livelihoods.

**Financial capital**: savings, wages, remittances, or government transfers such as pensions.

Whether in cities or rural areas, in normal times juggling risk is a large part of what it means to be poor. Families are adept at diversifying their dependence: in rural areas, they send young adults off to work in the city, grow multiple crops in different areas, sell and buy livestock to smooth their income, or collect and sell wild products. In the cities, they hustle a living in the informal economy, working as street vendors, maids, in construction, or recycling rubbish.

If these strategies fail, they resort to more drastic measures that in effect mortgage the future, pulling children out of school, eating fewer meals, or selling off vital assets, even when this reduces future earning power. This happens regularly in 'peace time' but is more widespread when a shock hits a whole community, so that households find it harder to borrow from or support each other or otherwise cope, and local authorities are overwhelmed with the demand for help. At some point, vulnerability can tip over into a downward spiral of hunger, weakness, distress sales, destitution, and even death.

Although vulnerability is conceptually similar to poverty, it focuses more attention on relationships. It provides an X-ray of the power, connections, and exclusion that run through society. When disaster strikes, you find out who your friends are: social ties and relationships with other families and patrons render even very poor households less vulnerable than, for example, wealthier migrant households with no ties in the community or claims on patronage. The most vulnerable people of all are the marginalised groups who constitute the 'chronic poor': ethnic minorities, women heads of households, elderly people, and those who are sick or disabled.

## HUMAN SECURITY

The opposite of vulnerability is security. Broadly speaking, rich and powerful people and communities lead more secure lives. As one resident of Ha Tinh, Viet Nam explains, 'The wealthy can recover losses in one year, but the poor, who have no money, will never recover.'[7] Correcting that disparity is central to tackling poverty and inequality.

To reduce the threat of shocks, individuals and governments must seek to enhance people's security: not the militarised version of security that has dominated public debate in recent years, but a more comprehensive human version, taking the insecure and anxiety-ridden experience of living in poverty as its starting point. Guaranteeing security in this way strengthens poor people's ability to withstand shocks and increases their chances of emerging from poverty, and not falling back.

The human security approach, first put forward in the UN's 1994 *Human Development Report*,[8] unites emergency response and development in a single framework, based on three propositions:

- People vulnerable to shocks are agents of their own destiny, with a series of rights that need to be fulfilled.
- Governments and international bodies are bound to address the full range of risks and vulnerabilities that affect people living in poverty.
- Social, political, and economic stability, generally ignored or downplayed in debates on poverty reduction, equity, and growth, is fundamental for reducing risk.

Like 'sustainable development', many governments have devalued the idea of human security by paying lip service to the concept while ignoring its profound implications. The approach challenges governments and international bodies to build from the bottom up, supporting and complementing citizens' own efforts to reduce their vulnerability and protect themselves from risk, and to provide protection in accordance with international humanitarian and human rights law.

Vulnerable people are far from passive and are constantly seeking ways to prepare for and cope with the daily risks that surround them, including by building assertive organisations that can manage risk directly and press for public policies that reduce risk. Governments can support such empowerment, importantly by ensuring access to health, education, livelihoods, and information, so that more poor women and men have the skills and knowledge required to address risk as active citizens. This theme is explored in more detail in Part 2.

Governments and international bodies must also protect poor and vulnerable people by guaranteeing their rights both in normal times and in times of crisis, for example by ensuring that they are not prey to violence, deprivation, or coercion. They should also act to reduce the likelihood of shocks and to mitigate their impact. Human security thus involves the same two core elements as the fight against poverty: active citizens who organise to assert their rights and effective states that work to fulfil those rights.

The particular vulnerability of children illustrates the importance of a human security approach. Traditionally, children have been largely 'invisible', treated as little more than the property of their parents or guardians. The idea of rights for children, for example not to be beaten, remains contested and uncomfortable for parents both North and South, but the 1989 UN Convention on the Rights of the Child marked a sea change, pressing for improved state protection of children, provision of the essential services needed for children to develop, and for both state and public to acknowledge that children have rights, including the right to be consulted over the decisions that affect their lives.[9]

The primary public responsibility for addressing risk rests at the level of national government, which is the major focus of this section. However, tsunamis, droughts, and conflict show little respect for borders, and many of the most vulnerable communities live in countries where the state is extremely weak, and may well be part of the threat rather than the solution. In such situations, the international community is obliged to act to save lives, be it through development assistance, emergency aid, diplomacy, or international peacekeeping, a role addressed more fully in Part 5. As is true regarding poverty, for issues such as conflict or climate change only simultaneous action at national and international levels will suffice.

Unfortunately, security is not currently conceived this way in most international discussions. Figure 4.2 shows the main causes of death – the ultimate manifestation of insecurity – in the world today. It draws into sharp relief the gulf between the political agenda as established in rich countries, where terrorism is often portrayed as the greatest threat to security, and the reality of the lives of poor people, who face far greater daily insecurity from more mundane but far more lethal threats of disease and 'low-tech' violence.

## FIGURE 4.2: CAUSES OF PREMATURE DEATH WORLDWIDE, CIRCA 2002[10]

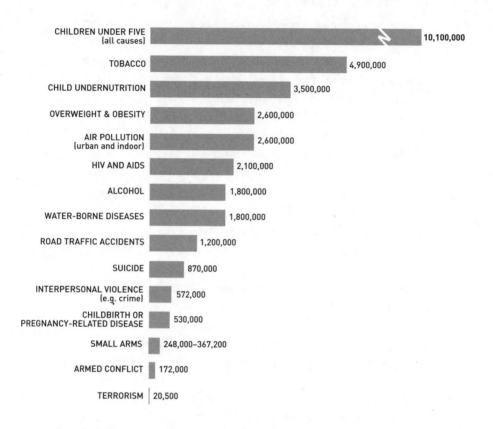

Note: these figures are approximate and often disputed, and in some cases may overlap (for example, some deaths may be double-counted in categories such as child mortality and water-borne diseases). However, they serve to give a sense of relative scale.

# SOCIAL PROTECTION

It may seem surprising that giving pensions to the elderly should help to keep children in school. However, in South Africa and Brazil monthly cheques enable elderly people both to look after themselves and support their grandchildren, conferring dignity in old age and preparing the citizens of tomorrow to play an active and productive role. In the case of South Africa, grandparents have become all the more important since so many parents have succumbed to AIDS.

Pensions are just one example of what is called 'social protection'. Social protection describes all public and private initiatives that:

- Provide income or consumption transfers to poor people;
- Protect vulnerable people against livelihood risks; and
- Enhance the social status and rights of those who are marginalised.

Its overall objective is to reduce the economic and social vulnerability of poor and marginalised groups.[11]

Policies and programmes based upon this approach involve direct resource transfers to poor people, disaster risk reduction (for example, flood protection and crop diversification), and addressing the structural causes of people's vulnerability and marginalisation (for example, legislation on minority rights and anti-discrimination campaigns).

Taken for granted in many developed countries, where welfare states routinely transfer income and support to the most vulnerable (although delivery methods remain controversial), social protection is rapidly gaining support in some of the poorest countries of the world, and challenging many of the assumptions of the aid industry. In 2005, the Ethiopian government introduced a 'productive safety net programme' to support over seven million of its poorest citizens through a combination of public employment schemes and grants to elderly people and expecting and nursing mothers. In Brazil, the *Bolsa Familia* (Family Stipend) scheme provides financial aid to some 11 million poor Brazilian families, on condition that their children attend school and are vaccinated.

Narrowly defined, social protection consists of two components. *Social assistance* transfers resources to vulnerable groups in the form of pensions, child support grants, and so on, while *social insurance* allows individuals and households to protect themselves against risks by pooling resources with others.

However, social protection goes much deeper than this. It tackles head-on a central aspect of poverty, arguing that the state in particular has a duty to seek to reduce vulnerability by guaranteeing the basic rights set out in the Universal Declaration of Human Rights. Such rights constitute a fundamental part of citizenship. Approached in this way, social protection spills over into issues of social services and social equity raised elsewhere in this book – providing decent education, health care, water and sanitation; redistributing land to vulnerable farmers; guaranteeing property rights for women or for squatters in the cities; combating gender-based violence; or guaranteeing labour rights for workers in formal and informal economies alike.

Instead of treating poor people as 'beneficiaries', such a conception of social protection focuses on the rights and voices of poor people themselves, building an enduring constituency and demand for state action, and so promoting the combination of active citizens and effective states that is crucial to development.

When done well, social protection can have an extraordinary impact. In 2007, a combination of child support, disability payments, and pensions was reaching approximately 13 million South Africans, out of a total population of 48 million. Total spending in 2007 amounted to $9bn – 3.4 per cent of GDP.[12] The programme resulted from a combination of high-level political support and an active civil society continually pushing the government to go further.

Emerging from the dark days of apartheid, South Africa's new Constitution promises that 'everyone has the right to have access to social security, including, if they are unable to support themselves and their dependants, appropriate social assistance'.[13] Evaluations show that households that receive social grants are more likely to send young children to school, provide better nutrition for children, and look for work more intensively, extensively, and successfully than do workers in comparable households that do not receive social grants.[14]

As part of its Soviet legacy, Kyrgyzstan has formal systems of social protection which, in principle, cover all its citizens. Kyrgyzstan's social protection system now comprises a social insurance fund from which old age and disability pensions are paid; a health insurance fund, which covers the costs of health treatment for the working population and for children and older people; and a social assistance system, which provides small amounts of cash assistance on a means-tested basis to people living below the poverty line. Although far from perfect, it shows that even a very poor country (in 2005 Kyrgyzstan's annual per capita GDP was $319) can run a social protection system that helps protect the most vulnerable. World Bank analysis suggests that, without the system, the extreme poverty headcount would have increased by 24 per cent, the poverty gap by 42 per cent, and the severity of poverty by 57 per cent. Furthermore, these levels of social protection do not represent an unsustainable drain on public resources: in 2002, they cost 3 per cent of GDP.[15]

Nor is social protection confined to the state alone. A huge amount of such activity takes place 'below the radar' at community level, through family support networks or religious organisations. NGOs such as India's Self Employed Women's Association (SEWA) organise a range of health, maternity benefit, and other insurance and credit schemes for thousands of women in the informal economy, exemplifying how social protection can target gender inequality.[16] International NGOs such as Oxfam are also increasingly introducing elements of social protection into their programmes.

The burgeoning interest in social protection springs both from an improving grasp of the nature of poverty and inequality and from past failure, notably the poor record of the 'safety nets' introduced to soften the impact of structural adjustment programmes and other shocks in the 1980s and 1990s. These typically reached only a portion of their target groups, and could not be introduced fast enough to deal with unexpected crises such as the Asian financial crash of 1998.

At the same time, it became increasingly clear that emergency relief such as food aid, designed to deal with short-term shortfalls in food supply, was obscuring the real nature of chronic (i.e. near-permanent) hunger and vulnerability in many countries. Between 1994 and 2003, for example, an average of five million Ethiopians were declared 'at risk' and in need of emergency assistance every year, and since 1998 the numbers of food aid beneficiaries in Ethiopia have fluctuated between five and 14 million. Hunger is the norm, not an 'emergency'.

The Food and Agriculture Organization of the United Nations (FAO) estimates that chronic hunger lies at the root of 90 per cent of food insecurity worldwide, leaving just 10 per cent attributable to shocks or humanitarian crises.[17] Avoidable deaths associated with malnutrition in six countries in Southern Africa are estimated at between 100,000 and 200,000 every year, compared with the estimated 45,000 who died in the drought-induced hunger of 2001–02.[18] Chronic malnutrition is a far bigger problem than acute malnutrition, and yet it receives far less attention.

A maturing understanding of the nature of poverty, with its growing attention to issues of rights, dignity, and empowerment, and the recognition that inequality and social exclusion are not just damaging in themselves but hold back economic progress, have also played a part in this process. Progressive political leaders in countries such as South Africa and Brazil have seen how popular social protection policies can be, addressing directly the need for the state and others to guarantee basic human rights and to include less active groups, such as elderly or disabled people, who are often sidelined in development policies that focus solely on economic growth.

## CASH TRANSFERS

What do hungry people need? Food would seem to be the obvious answer, but poor people often prefer cash, because it allows them to make their own choices about how best to improve their own situation: what and when to invest and consume. It is also more consistent with a rights-based approach to social protection. Increasingly, cash transfers are supplanting in-kind transfers – for example, cash for work is replacing food-for-work programmes, and school subsidies are starting to displace school feeding programmes.

In response to predictions of acute food insecurity across parts of Southern Africa in 2005–06, Oxfam decided to implement cash transfer programmes as an alternative to emergency food aid in Malawi and Zambia, covering a total of about 20,000 households. Subsequent evaluations showed that neither project encountered any major security problems: the cash was delivered and spent safely.

In both countries, the vast majority of the cash transfers were spent on food, mainly maize. People also made small but sometimes crucial non-food expenditures. In Malawi, the cash enabled people to purchase the subsidised inputs provided through a government agricultural input voucher scheme. In Zambia, where spending on health and education was important, NGOs' efforts complemented the Zambian government's social protection programme, which pays the poorest 10 per cent of communities in one district of Southern Province $6 per person per month, a minimal safety net against the worst forms of deprivation.[19]

In Viet Nam, Oxfam went one step further, deciding to give substantial cash lump sums to some 500 poor households in eight deprived villages, and monitoring how the villagers spent the money. The top six uses were clearing debts (thereby freeing up future income from the burden of debt repayments), buying livestock, repairing and building houses, paying for school fees and books, buying seeds and fertilisers for agriculture, and paying for health care. These results demonstrate how, given the chance, poor people invest in the future, and how varied and unpredictable their needs are: a dozen elderly people opted to spend the money on buying coffins, thereby ensuring that they could live out their days in the knowledge that they would have a dignified funeral.[20] Cash transfers put poor people in the driving seat, spending resources on the things that matter most to them.

Cash transfers have been judged successful in many countries, particularly when made conditional on keeping children vaccinated or in school, as in Brazil's *Bolsa Familia* or Mexico's *Oportunidades* programmes. These have reduced present vulnerability and have also increased school attendance, thereby improving long-term security for the next generation.

Pioneer countries such as South Africa or Kyrgzystan show that social protection can be provided for as little as 3 per cent of GDP. This is serious money, but much of it would be recouped by avoiding emergency spending when things go wrong. In 2005, the UK government's high-level Africa Commission concluded that the costs of pre-emptive social protection are less than the costs of responding after a crisis and argued that, for an annual $5bn–$6bn, 'Five million of the most vulnerable children and another 40 million chronically poor households caring for orphans and other vulnerable children would be supported through community programmes and cash grants, perhaps conditional on school and health clinic attendance. The interlocking cycles of poverty and exclusion trapping millions would be interrupted, preventing the transfer of poverty from parent to child and mitigating the far-reaching impacts of AIDS and conflict.'[21]

Nevertheless, cost is often raised as an objection, not least by the International Monetary Fund in its role as custodian of financial prudence. In 2004, the government of Lesotho introduced a non-contributory pension for all over-70s (against advice from aid donors that it was unaffordable), becoming the fourth country in Southern Africa to do so, after South Africa, Namibia, and Botswana. An additional $5.5bn in aid, as the Africa Commission recommends, would cost less than $5 per person in donor countries, and would equal just three weeks' spending by the US government on the war in Iraq.[22]

Social protection holds the potential to transform the lives of poor people across the world, North and South, and it is evolving rapidly. For aid donors and NGOs, it addresses the divide in their thinking between 'emergencies' and 'development'. Oxfam, like most other aid organisations, deals separately with sudden disasters (where it specialises in delivering food and shelter and in getting water and sanitation working) and with long-term development issues. The two parts of the organisation have different staff, budgets, and mindsets: a can-do engineers' attitude to saving lives in emergencies, contrasting with a more long-term focus on rights, processes, and politics among development types.

However, recognising that vulnerability is chronic, and that, for example, food 'emergencies' in a number of African countries are becoming the norm rather than exceptional events, means rethinking this division. Social protection offers a way to move from an inevitably chaotic emergency response to long-term protection based on the rights of poor people.

If social protection systems are in place before an emergency hits, they also provide a ready-made delivery channel, for example by allowing pensions or child support to be stepped up to help families cope. This can be a huge benefit when delays in creating payment systems can cost lives. However, blurring the boundary between humanitarian relief and long-term development also carries the risk of politicising humanitarian work in the eyes of governments, which sometimes prove more willing to countenance outsiders providing food aid for the hungry than supporting the organisations of poor people demanding land so that they can reduce their long-term vulnerability.

Joining up humanitarian relief and long-term development work is far easier to advocate than to actually do, but the renowned Bangladeshi NGO BRAC (Bangladesh Rural Advancement Committee) has shown the way. Its Income Generation for Vulnerable Group Development (IGVGD) programme builds the productive capacity of chronically poor households and simultaneously provides them with a protective base. Through collaboration with the World Food Programme and local government, families receive a monthly wheat ration for two years, plus training and credit provision by BRAC. Micro-credit has helped to set up income-generating activities, such as poultry, live-stock, and silkworm farming. IGVGD targets in particular widowed or abandoned female heads of household, households owning less than 0.5 acres of land, and those earning less than Tk.300 ($4.40) per month.

Standard bearers for social protection, such as Brazil and South Africa, are now showing increasing interest in moving from targeted interventions such as pensions or child support grants to establishing a national 'basic income guarantee' for all citizens, an idea that has long been debated as a means of addressing poverty in developed countries but has never been implemented (see Box 4.1).

---

BOX 4.1

## THE BASIC INCOME GUARANTEE: THE NEXT BIG IDEA?

*Too many of our people live in gruelling, demeaning, dehumanising poverty. We are sitting on a powder keg... We should discuss as a nation whether a basic income grant is not really a viable way forward. We should not be browbeaten by pontificating decrees from on high. We cannot, glibly, on full stomachs, speak about handouts to those who often go to bed hungry. It is cynical in the extreme to speak about handouts when people can become very rich at the stroke of a pen.*
ARCHBISHOP DESMOND TUTU, NELSON MANDELA LECTURE, JOHANNESBURG, NOVEMBER 2004

As different social protection programmes have multiplied, interest has grown in a much simpler idea. Why not guarantee all members of society a basic income? Typically, advocates argue for this to be linked to national poverty lines, for example set at 20 per cent of GDP per capita, and made universal, so that all citizens receive it. An income tax would fund the scheme, so that richer people contribute more, potentially helping to reduce inequality.

In Brazil, President Luiz Inácio Lula da Silva in 2004 became the first president to sign a law setting out a universal income guarantee.[23] The Brazilian Parliament subsequently approved a Citizen's Basic Income, to be implemented gradually, starting with the poorest families. The *Bolsa Familia* programme is the first step towards the universal benefit, although it is not yet clear when and how the full programme will be implemented.

In South Africa, the Basic Income Grant Coalition is pushing for a universal grant of between $15 and $20 a month, which would cost about 3 per cent of GDP and would be delivered via smart chips on ID cards that could be used at ATMs or banks. However, the government has not so far approved the idea.

In addition to such national, universal programmes, a global one is possible, but it would have to be designed on different lines. Since a global universal basic income guarantee, even if set only to raise all people above the absolute poverty line of $1 a day, would cost some $300bn a year – several times the global aid budget[24] – it would have to be targeted, and could be based on particular countries, or groups or regions within countries.

One possibility is to design a scheme along the lines of the global education Fast Track Initiative, in which donor countries agree to fund any credible plan presented to them by a developing country. Alternatively, an existing agreement, the Food Aid Convention, could be transformed into a form of global safety-net that would secure predictable funding for national social assistance schemes aimed at alleviating chronic poverty and vulnerability.

*Source: International Journal of Basic Income Research*, www.bepress.com/bis

The growth in social protection has also raised old debates about universalism versus targeting. Is it either more efficient or more equitable to target benefits to identified groups of vulnerable communities or individuals, or is it better to give universal benefits, as was the fashion in developed countries in the 1960s and 1970s?

Targeting is very difficult to implement, especially for cash-strapped and debilitated state machineries, as resources are frequently 'captured' by the more powerful members of a community. In India, data from 5,000 households in 12 villages showed that, although subsidised food schemes were ostensibly focused on the poor, the beneficiaries were mainly middle-income families; the situation for pensions was even worse.[25] A wider World Bank study of 111 social protection projects found that targeting worked in three-quarters of them, but benefited poor people proportionally less in the remaining quarter.[26] In general it seems that targeting categories of easily identified people (elderly people, pregnant women, children) is more successful than means-testing populations to establish who is poor.

While more expensive, giving benefits universally carries other advantages: helping to build a political and social consensus for the benefit (since everyone gains), avoiding the stigma that goes with means-testing, and enhancing cohesion by clearly establishing social protection as a universal right, rather than a form of charity to the deprived. In Malawi, farmers rejected the targeting of subsidised farm inputs on the grounds that they were all poor, and it would be divisive.

Social protection epitomises the human security approach, offering a practical and effective way to reduce chronic vulnerability, tackle poverty and inequality, bridge the gap between 'emergencies' and 'development', and nourish the relationship of rights and responsibilities between citizens and states that lies at the heart of successful development.

## HOW CHANGE HAPPENS CASE STUDY:
## INDIA'S CAMPAIGN FOR A NATIONAL RURAL
## EMPLOYMENT GUARANTEE

For the first time in history, citizens of rural India are now guaranteed a job. Within 15 days of a valid application, the government is legally obliged to provide 100 days of unskilled work per year on public works programmes. Activists, politicians, and academics have hailed the National Rural Employment Guarantee Act (NREGA), passed in August 2005, as vital for improving the lot of rural workers.

The Act was born of drought and rural distress in the state of Rajasthan, where civil society networks denounced the failure of public food distribution and employment programmes to prevent starvation. Activists submitted a petition to the Supreme Court in 2001 on the 'Right to Food', which received favourable interim directives. Encouraged, they drafted a Rajasthan State Employment Guarantee Act in 2003, though this was not implemented.

However, the activists' success in rallying civil society reflected the growth of rights-based approaches in India, favouring a demand-based system over the passive beneficiary employment programmes of the past.

From 2001, Congress Party leaders, including party president Sonia Gandhi, raised the issue in the national party. Congress had been in opposition nationally since 1996, but held power in Rajasthan. In 2003, the party suffered a demoralising loss in the Rajasthan election and in other states, leading most to believe that it had no chance in the 2004 national election.

Luckily for NREGA activists, impending political defeat weakened the resistance of fiscal conservatives in the Congress leadership to a potentially costly employment guarantee, and also gave impetus to those who argued that Congress needed a strong, positive policy programme to revive its fortunes. These factors led to an employment guarantee being included in the 2004 Congress national manifesto.

Although unrelated to its presence in the manifesto, the Congress alliance's surprise victory in the 2004 general election, and its formation of a majority government with the support of two left-wing parties that had achieved unprecedented success, marked a watershed for the proposal. Electoral success reinforced the political arguments for action in the minds of Congress leaders. Taken by surprise at its own victory, the party's leadership needed to rapidly cobble together a policy programme. The employment guarantee policy was not only ready to go, but the presence of the left-wing parties would in any case have made it difficult to remove from the programme.

A newly formed National Advisory Council, chaired by Sonia Gandhi and including influential figures closely associated with the NREGA, such as professor and activist Jean Drèze, activist Aruna Roy, and Congress leader Jairam Ramesh, drew up a draft act based on the civil society draft from Rajasthan.

By the time the National Rural Employment Guarantee Bill was submitted to Parliament in December 2004, however, the Ministry of Finance had introduced a number of clauses to limit the government's potential financial liability, sparking a row with activists and left-wing leaders.

A determined campaign, involving a 50-day march across the country's poorest districts to spread awareness of the concept of the right to employment, sit-in protests, direct contacts with politicians, and public hearings – all of which won substantial media coverage – increased risks for politicians who openly supported the Ministry of Finance restrictions, because they would be seen as 'anti-poor'.

Before the bill was re-submitted to Parliament, Sonia Gandhi intervened to remove two of the Ministry of Finance's demands: that the guarantee of employment could be terminated by administrative decree; and that employment would be restricted to applicants holding Below Poverty Line cards. She was also successful in ensuring that the scheme would be implemented mainly through the *panchayats* (elected village governments) rather than by national bureaucracies, an option preferred by the Ministry of Rural Development.

At the last moment, a 'corruption clause' was inserted, permitting suspension of the scheme should corruption be detected. Activists feared that this would create an incentive not to expose corruption. In addition, despite attempts by activists to secure state minimum wages under the scheme, an amendment permitted wage rates of Rs 60 per day (about $1.50), lower than the national floor wage of Rs 66, but still higher than some state minimums.

Passed unanimously, the final text was a compromise – but one with great potential, thanks to civil society's effective combination of public campaigning and a determined political lobby.

*Sources:* I. MacAuslan (2007) 'India's National Rural Employment Guarantee Act: A Case Study for How Change Happens', paper for Oxfam International; www.righttofoodindia.org; www.nrega.nic.in; N. Dey, J. Drèze, and R. Khera (2006) *Employment Guarantee Act: A Primer*, New Delhi: National Book Trust; C. Gonsalves, P.R. Kumar, and A.R. Srivastava (eds) (2005) 'Right to Food', New Delhi: Human Rights Law Network.

CASE STUDY

# FINANCE AND VULNERABILITY

Saving for a rainy day and borrowing when hard times strike have always been strategies used by people living in poverty to reduce their vulnerability to shocks. In recent years, the failure of financial systems to meet the needs of poor communities in many countries has led to the creation of a new phenomenon, microfinance, which was driven first by civil society organisations and 'social entrepreneurs' and is increasingly being picked up by mainstream financial institutions and the state.

Access to credit is critical to any business, however small, while being able to save and borrow enables poor people to smooth out the sudden peaks and troughs in their income and expenditure that can inflict short-term hardship on a family, such as job loss, sickness, funerals, or weddings. However, conventional financial markets systematically exclude many poor people. Banks rarely have branches where poor people live, they require onerous collateral or deposits, or they will not deal in small loan amounts. Gender or ethnic bias frequently has a large part to play. This financial exclusion was exacerbated by the structural adjustment programmes in the 1980s and 1990s, which shut down or privatised state-owned banks, including so-called 'development banks' which had offered subsidised loans to farmers and others.

Poor people's needs are often tiny in financial terms, but are critical to their well-being. A shoe-shiner who cannot afford to buy his brushes will be forced to rent them at extortionate rates. The same goes for a rickshaw driver without his own rickshaw or a seamstress without her own sewing machine. A family without a secure place to hold savings may store its wealth in much riskier investments such as livestock.

Since the early 1970s a number of non-profit microfinance organisations have stepped into this gap, led by the most famous, Bangladesh's Grameen Bank, whose founder Muhammad Yunus was awarded the Nobel Peace Prize in 2006. The growth of microfinance institutions has been spectacular, with the total number of borrowers rising from 13.5 million in 1997 to 113.3 million in 2004, of whom two-thirds were people living on less than $1 a day. The vast majority of these people are in Asia, where over one-third of poor families have access to microfinance.[27]

Although microfinance is generally equated with micro-credit (small loans), in many cases the availability of well-designed, safe, and accessible savings products for poor people is just as important – if not more so – in reducing poverty. The very poorest people are often unwilling to take the risk of a micro-credit loan, but are keen to save small amounts to reduce future vulnerability. Savings groups of 20 or so individuals provide one effective approach, lending to individual members of the group, with the interest going back to the group fund as well as the savings account of each member. A revolving savings and loan scheme of this type can earn members 20–40 per cent a year on their savings, as well as providing the benefits of a micro-credit scheme to those who take out loans.[28]

Other providers are developing 'micro-insurance' along the lines of micro-credit, charging from as little as 50 cents to insure anything from television sets to burial costs. In India, the largest comprehensive contributory social security scheme for informal economy workers is the Integrated Social Security Programme set up by the Self Employed Women's Association (SEWA) (see Part 3, page 162). SEWA's programme insures more than 100,000 women workers and covers health insurance (including a maternity component), life insurance, and asset insurance.[29]

Micro-insurance providers often forego traditional documentation requirements, sometimes selling life insurance to people who do not know their date of birth. As with micro-credit, micro-insurance is increasingly moving into the mainstream, attracting big players such as the insurance multinational AIG. Insurance markets are saturated in many rich countries and growth prospects are limited, so insurance companies are looking for long-term growth in emerging markets.

More than four out of every five microfinance customers are women, often female heads of households, or elderly women, and usually grouped together into groups of three to six, who collectively guarantee loans. With loans, the result has been astonishingly high repayment rates – Grameen claims that over 98 per cent of its loans are repaid – making microfinance both self-sustaining and profitable. Although typically loans are in the order of $100, some are much smaller: Grameen Bank's interest-free loans for urban beggars average $9, and include credit lines with local shops that allow items to be bought for resale, allowing beggars to upgrade to become street-sellers.

The growing commercial interest in such 'bottom-of-the-pyramid'[30] markets has seen the entrance of a number of large commercial banks, often in partnership with existing microfinance organisations, and this has greatly increased the numbers of poor women with access to credit and savings. The first private multinational microfinance bank is Procredit, founded in 1996 and backed by investment from the International Finance Corporation (IFC), the commercial arm of the World Bank.[31] Procredit has set up banks in 22 countries and has taken over institutions in four others. By 2008 it had 17,000 employees, €4.1bn ($6bn) in assets, and an investment grade rating that allows it to raise money in the German bond market.

Long-established commercial banks, such as Citigroup and Standard Chartered, are also getting in on the act, as are domestic banks such as Indonesia's Bank Rakyat Indonesia (BRI). The much-emulated BRI converted itself in the 1970s from a failing state bank into a microfinance institution and became one of the most profitable banks in the country, with 32 million depositors and three million borrowers. Still 70 per cent state-owned, BRI shows what effective state action can achieve in reducing vulnerability.

Since as many as three billion people worldwide still do not have access to financial services, there is plenty of room for expansion. In Latin America, the entry of commercial banks appears to have freed up microfinance NGOs to go in search of even poorer people, and their average loan sizes have shrunk.[32] New trends in microfinance include exploring the links with remittances sent home by migrants and using new technologies such as ATMs and mobile phones. In 2007, in what was described as a world first, Kenya's biggest mobile operator began allowing subscribers to send cash to other phone users via SMS messaging, obviating the need for a bank account and potentially giving whole new groups of customers access to microfinance providers.[33]

Although Kofi Annan called micro-credit 'one of the success stories of the last decade', and the award of the Nobel Peace Prize to Muhammad Yunus boosted the hype still further, it is far from being a 'magic bullet' for reducing poverty. Loans generally go to the moderately poor, missing out the most deprived individuals and communities, who continue to rely on social protection from the state, such as pensions and work schemes.[34] In addition, most business-related loans go into creating more sellers in an already overcrowded informal sector, with few chances of long-term progress, and do not deal with the underlying structural problems of under-development.[35]

In East Africa, commercial microfinance lending at 2–3 per cent a month still leaves villagers with heavy debts, and risks microfinance banks becoming little more than kinder, gentler loan sharks. The flipside of high repayment ratios is that, however heavy the burden of repayments, women are often too fearful of social opprobrium to default (as loans are generally guaranteed collectively). In other cases, men have forced their wives to apply for loans and then taken the money themselves, showing that simply lending to women may not be enough unless unequal gender relations in the home are also dealt with.

Despite these caveats, the rise of microfinance demonstrates how human security can be enhanced by active citizens, including both grassroots organisations and social enterprises that seek to combine social objectives with a sustainable business model. By solving some of the problems caused by financial exclusion, the rapid expansion and diversification of microfinance has enabled millions of poor people to reduce their vulnerability and to climb out of poverty.

# HUNGER AND FAMINE

Hunger exists in a world of plenty. Worldwide, improvements in yields have run ahead of population growth, meaning that there is enough food to go around.[36] In principle, there is no reason why a single child or adult should go hungry. In fact, the world has a growing number of obese people, currently standing at 400 million, two-thirds of whom live in low- or middle-income countries.[37] Levels of obesity in Mexico, Egypt, and South Africa are on a par with those in the USA, bringing with them soaring rates of diabetes and other 'diseases of plenty'.

Yet one in eight of the world's people go to bed with empty bellies, perhaps the starkest proof of the deep inequality and injustice that blights the global economy, both within and between countries. For the past 15 years, as the global economy has flourished, the number of hungry people has been stuck at around 850 million.[38] The global figure masks improvements in Asia but rising hunger elsewhere, particularly in sub-Saharan Africa.

Famine, where hunger tips over into social breakdown and mass starvation, is less common and less devastating than it once was. Asia and the Soviet Union were home to the twentieth century's worst famines, led by the estimated 30 million people who died in China in 1958 and the nine million dead in the Soviet Union in 1921. By comparison, the worst famine of recent decades, in Ethiopia in 1984, claimed an estimated one million lives.[39]

Nevertheless, the average number of food emergencies (crises that stop short of famine) per year in Africa tripled between 1990–92 and 2000–02.[40] In 2005, sub-Saharan Africa experienced a new wave of food crises.[41] One unfolded quietly and mercilessly in the Sahel for months before it became television news; another threatened Southern Africa; and in early 2006 a third emerged in the Horn of Africa, affecting 11 million people.[42] Many more people are suffering from hunger in Africa's less publicised crises, such as in the Democratic Republic of the Congo (DRC), where 71 per cent of the population is undernourished, and in northern Uganda, where 48 per cent of children are stunted due to chronic malnutrition.[43]

---

## BOX 4.2
## COPING WITH HUNGER IN DARFUR

'[T]o understand the demise of [the town of] Furawiya [in Darfur, Sudan], we must go back to the last humanitarian disaster to strike the area, the drought and famine of 1984–1985. When that famine was drawing to a close, I spoke with a young woman in Furawiya called Amina. The widowed mother of three children, she harvested barely a basketful of millet in September 1984, when the third successive year of drought was devastating crops. Rather than eating her pitiful supply of food, she buried it in her yard, mixing the grains with sand and gravel to stop her hungry children from digging it up and eating it. Then she began an epic eight-month migration, not atypical of the journeys that ordinary Zaghawa rural people make. Amina started by scouring the open wildernesses of the Zaghawa plateau for wild grasses, whose tiny grains can be pounded into flour. Together with her mother (who was, like most older rural women, something of a specialist in wild foods), she spent almost two months living off wild grass and the berries of a small tree, known locally as *mukheit* and to botanists as *boscia senegaliensis*. *Mukheit* is toxic and needs to be soaked in water for three days before it is edible; although it has a sour taste, it contains about a third of the calories of grain.

'Having lived solely on wild foods for eight weeks, and having stored enough provisions for a week's journey, Amina left her eldest daughter in the care of her mother and walked southward. She found work on farms in better-watered areas, collected firewood for sale in towns, and sold a couple of her goats (for a meager return, since the market was flooded with distressed rural people selling animals). She finally made it to a relief camp in June, just before the rains were due, and collected one set of rations. With a couple of kilos of sorghum on her back, Amina and her two other children promptly left the camp and walked home (it took one week), dug up the seed Amina had buried the previous fall, planted it, and watched it grow for another three hungry months (again living off wild foods plus the milk from the herds of camels and goats that the Furawiya residents were bringing back from southern Darfur). Finally she harvested her first post-famine crop, which she was threshing the day I arrived.

'A remarkable story of sheer toughness and survival skill, Amina's story brought home to me just how marginal we outsider agents of relief are to the survival of ordinary Darfurian villagers. We provide little help and even littler understanding. A Zaghawa refugee in Chad today, looking across the border to the small town of Tine, with its gracious mosque, sees not a desert but a land in which she can survive, if only given the chance.'

*Source*: Alex de Waal, 'Tragedy in Darfur, On understanding and ending the horror', http://bostonreview.net/BR29.5/dewaal.html

Undernourishment cripples individuals and society. At its most extreme it kills, with young children and babies often the first to die. More commonly, it weakens people, draining them of the energy that they need to work, and making them more prone to disease. Severe malnutrition in children increases the likelihood of future illness and death, reduces school performance, causes long-term brain damage, and reduces future potential and incomes. The UN calculates that the loss of productivity due to malnutrition costs the developing world between 5 per cent and 10 per cent of its GDP every year.[44]

Somewhere around the middle of the current decade, a major change hit the global food system. After 25 years of steady decline, the price of the main global food crops – rice, wheat, and maize – rocketed. The trigger was a combination of long-term factors, notably the rising use of cereals to feed growing demand for meat in China and other developing countries and the decision by the USA and a number of other rich countries to divert maize and other production into making biofuel (see Part 3, page 131). The US ethanol boom accounted for over half of the net decline in world cereal stocks in 2007.[45]

Rising prices hit poor countries hardest and, within those countries, poor people, who tend to spend a greater share of their income on food. They also, of course, benefit farmers, depending on what proportion of the higher prices reaches them through the value chain.

The timing of the price reversal was particularly harsh, since a combination of structural adjustment, population growth, and trade liberalisation has moved the poorest countries from a situation of being in food surplus in the 1970s to being heavily dependent on food imports.[46] By 2005, Sierra Leone and Haiti were spending 80 per cent and 63 per cent respectively of their available export revenue on food imports.[47] High prices are therefore likely to lead to rising borrowing, risking a new debt crisis, or increased hunger. Already, food prices have been blamed for triggering the crisis in the Sahel countries in 2005, and food riots have broken out in Mexico, Morocco, Uzbekistan, Yemen, Guinea, Mauritania, and Senegal.[48]

At the time of writing, the trend looks set to continue. Barring unforeseen technological breakthroughs, food prices are likely to stay high, greatly increasing the vulnerability of poor countries, and poor people within them.

## CITIZENS AND STATES

Reducing hunger, like mitigating the impact of natural disasters, requires action by the state and self-help by hungry people.[49] The state can intervene to improve livelihoods or head off a crisis, can put in early-warning systems to spot signals such as spiralling food prices and, if necessary, can provide food or other forms of social protection. Poor people themselves are best placed to anticipate problems in feeding their families, and to urge authorities to act.

The Nobel Prize-winning Indian economist Amartya Sen wrote: 'No famine has ever taken place in the history of the world in a functioning democracy.'[50] Sen pointed out that, since achieving independence in 1947, India has not had a single famine, even in the face of severe crop failures. When food production was hit hard during the 1973 drought in Maharashtra, elected politicians responded with public works programmes for five million people and averted a famine. Sen concluded that 'famines are, in fàct, so easy to prevent, that is it is amazing that they are allowed to occur at all'.

Famines may be the fruit of autocracy rather than democracy but, as Sen acknowledges, democracy has a much less impressive record in dealing with endemic hunger and malnutrition. More than 6,000 Indian children die every day because of malnourishment or a lack of basic micronutrients.[51] Beyond the political changes required to narrow the distance between governors and governed, Sen sets out a number of proposals for preventing hunger and famine:

- The focus has to be on the economic power and freedom of individuals and families to buy enough food, not just on ensuring that the country has sufficient food stocks. Government-run temporary job creation schemes (as employed by India) are one of the best ways to help people earn enough to buy food.
- A good deal of the mortality associated with famines actually results from diseases that can be brought under control by decent public health systems.
- A free press and an active political opposition constitute the best early-warning system.
- Since famines seldom affect more than 10 per cent of the population, governments usually have the resources to deal with them.

Sen also points to the importance of economic growth and the diversification of rural incomes. Growth generates jobs and tax revenues, allowing governments to fund social protection and relief schemes, while diversification allows poor families to manage risks by reducing their reliance on any one source of income.

In recent years, there have been promising signs in India of progress at national level, as citizens' campaigns around hunger have changed laws and lives. In 2005, the Indian government passed the National Rural Employment Guarantee Bill. The bill provides 100 days of unskilled manual work for every rural household that wants it, and much of the work itself will help to reduce vulnerability, for example by reforesting land or building irrigation canals to poor and marginalised villages. The bill represents a triumph of public action, and is discussed in more detail in the case study on page 217.

Some African governments are following India's example in funding job and social protection programmes. Governments have also recognised the benefits of involving civil society and international agencies in anticipating and dealing with food emergencies. Vulnerability Assessment Committees (VACs) in Southern Africa, made up of governments, UN agencies, and NGOs, monitor harvests, markets, and incomes to provide early warnings of impending problems. The assessment from the Malawi VAC for the 2005 food crisis resulted in timely donor and government intervention. When hunger strikes, the reflex response in rich countries is often to send food. But as Part 5 explains, food aid often arrives too late, in the wrong form, or stifles the recovery of local agriculture. As noted above, except where markets are not functioning, sending cash for the purchase of locally produced food is a much better option.

People's capabilities can be strengthened during and immediately after food emergencies, for example by supporting seed fairs to encourage the planting of traditional crops best suited to the environment, in order to kick-start local food production. Oxfam has found that giving farmers vouchers to buy seeds at fairs offers them greater choice than simply handing out seed packages. Oxfam held 37 seed fairs in partnership with local organisations in Masvingo and Midlands provinces in Zimbabwe in 2004–05, bringing together producers, seed merchants, extension agents, and local people, who were given vouchers to pay for their own choice of seed.

At each fair, hundreds of local farmers crowded in to see what was on offer. The rich diversity of 21 crops and 51 varieties included groundnuts, sorghum, cowpeas, maize, soybeans, sesame, rice, sunflower, and pearl millet, as well as a range of vegetable seeds, some of which were previously threatened with extinction. Many of these traditional crops are cheaper and more tolerant of marginal conditions than high-yielding varieties. Some 23,000 households benefited directly through buying seeds.

When people are in danger of starving, talk of rights and citizenship may seem like a luxury. Nothing could be further from the truth.

A human security approach, guaranteeing people's rights and building systems of social protection, can reduce their vulnerability when a food crisis hits, and so prevent a hazard turning into a disaster. Poor people and communities who can exercise their rights when food is in short supply are better able to cope and rebuild their lives rapidly once the crisis is over. In all these stages, they need active support from states that are both effective in delivering services and accountable to the needs of their people.

# HIV, AIDS, AND OTHER HEALTH RISKS

Prudence Mabele is a party animal. Scrambling onto the stage at a Johannesburg jazz club, her long dreadlocks carve through the air as she dances. Earlier she'd hustled a table in a crowded restaurant and a free concert ticket for a friend. She never stops networking, but usually directs her boundless energy to more lofty ends. She runs Positive Women's Network, a South African NGO that helps women living with HIV to lead full and active lives. Prudence has been HIV-positive for the past 17 years.

However, Prudence faces an uphill task in a country where an estimated 1,000 people die every day from AIDS, and HIV infection rates are still rising due to a combination of poverty, stigma, migration, illiteracy, and mixed messages from a deeply divided government.

The health of poor people is subject to daily attrition from dirty water, malnourishment, and a lack of basic health services. At the household level, illness can be a 'shock' that sends a family into a spiral of impoverishment. Bouts of sickness, especially in childhood, can have life-long impacts in terms of chronic ill health, stunting, and poor educational performance. The best guarantor of security against such harrowing experiences is a functioning health service – a form of medical social protection, discussed more fully in Part 2. When health shocks occur at the societal level, in the form of a disease epidemic, they can set development efforts back decades. From at least the time of the Black Death, such health shocks frequently take the form of new diseases that lay waste to entire populations.

The latest of these is AIDS, which initially seemed to be bucking the trend, attacking health in the rich countries. But soon the basic link between poor health and inequality reasserted itself, as the human immunodeficiency virus (HIV) spread rapidly across the world, affecting poor and vulnerable people, particularly in sub-Saharan Africa and particularly women. Other new diseases, such as avian influenza or severe acute respiratory syndrome (SARS), many of them 'zoonotic' (originating in animals, then passing to humans) also threaten to trigger an HIV-style pandemic, while long-standing maladies such as tuberculosis, malaria, bilharzia, Chaga's disease, and sleeping sickness continue to take an enormous toll on individuals, families, and societies.

In societies where HIV prevalence is high, every aspect of the struggle against poverty and inequality, from production to organisation to daily relations, has been transformed by HIV and AIDS. Taking action now can prevent millions of deaths in the future, as the example of Brazil shows (see page 235). Given that there is not yet a medical cure for AIDS (although there is treatment that stops short of a cure), reducing poor people's vulnerability involves looking at the social and economic context of their lives to find out what makes them vulnerable, and taking steps to remedy these sources of risk. 'It's not the disease that kills, but the lack of other resources – poverty, dirty water, food', says a nurse at an HIV centre in South Africa.[52]

The stigma attached to HIV and AIDS makes the disease far harder to bear. When people living with AIDS in northern Thailand were surveyed, researchers expected them to say that access to antiretroviral drugs (ARVs) was their main worry but, instead, ending discrimination against HIV-positive people was their number one concern.

The first cases of HIV and AIDS were discovered in 1981 in the USA, the Democratic Republic of the Congo, and East Africa. By 1985 cases were reported in every region of the world. In 25 years the disease has spread to virtually every country, with 65 million people infected with HIV and 25 million deaths from AIDS. In 2005, there were 38.6 million people worldwide living with HIV and AIDS:

4.1 million were newly infected with HIV that year, while 2.8 million people died from AIDS.[53] Dying parents have left more than 15 million orphans struggling to survive.[54] Despite the growing numbers of HIV-positive people in India and elsewhere, sub-Saharan Africa remains the global epicentre of the pandemic. Of the 2.3 million children living with HIV and AIDS globally, two million are African.

Advances in drug treatments have meant that AIDS is no longer a death sentence in rich countries, but the high price of medicines and the lack of effective health services have turned it into a killer of poor people, especially women. By December 2006 the World Health Organization (WHO) estimated that two million people living with HIV or AIDS were receiving treatment in low- and middle-income countries, representing just 28 per cent of the estimated 7.1 million people in need.[55]

Women are more at risk, both due to the physiology of disease transmission and because they are less able to refuse sex or insist on condoms, since discrimination and consequent economic vulnerability drive them into a high level of dependence on men. Their demands for treatment or for technologies that prevent transmission, such as microbicides, are less likely to be heard by the authorities. Part 2 of this book notes that women's lack of property rights allows widows (whether due to AIDS or other causes) to be driven from their land, leaving them destitute and vulnerable. Three in every four HIV-positive Africans are women.[56] Women aged 15–24 are six times more likely to carry the virus than men in the same age group.[57]

Such bare statistics utterly fail to convey the depth of the catastrophe that is unfolding in Africa. Stephen Lewis, the UN's former special envoy for HIV and AIDS in Africa, conjures up an apocalyptic vision:

*The pandemic of HIV/AIDS feels as though it will go on forever. The adult medical wards of the urban hospitals are filled with AIDS-related illnesses, men, women, wasted and dying; aluminium coffins wheeling in and out in Kafkaesque rotation; in the pediatric wards, nurses tenderly removing the bodies of infants; funerals occupying the weekends, cemeteries running out of grave sites; in the villages, hut after hut yields a picture of a mother, usually a young woman, in the final throes of life. No one is untouched.*

*Everyone has a heartbreaking story to tell. Virtually every country in East and Southern Africa is a nation of mourners.*[58]

## CITIZENS AND STATES AGAINST AIDS

Because there is no vaccine for HIV or cure for AIDS, and because HIV spreads through sexual contact, this health shock cannot be effectively mitigated by state action alone. In this way AIDS is not unlike diseases spread by poor hygiene. Stopping it requires changes in people's behaviour. The state must take the lead but all of society needs to become engaged: women to demand their rights; men to resist social pressures to have unsafe sex; groups of people living with HIV to organise systems of self-help and demand services from governments; all to understand how HIV is spread and how it can be prevented. Active, empowered citizens are an essential part of stemming the spread of HIV and AIDS and reducing the devastation it wreaks: their 'agency' cannot be neglected.

The pandemic has thrown up some inspiring examples of grass-roots activism. The experience of perhaps the best known, South Africa's Treatment Action Campaign, is discussed in the case study on page 242. In the Ukraine, what went on to become an award-winning movement began when seven HIV-positive activists met in 1999 and set up the All Ukraine Network of People Living with HIV and AIDS. Its combination of self-help, public education, and high-level lobbying has helped to get HIV and AIDS designated as national health care priorities, trebled the national budget for treatment, and persuaded the government to cancel the results of what are delicately called 'non-transparent tenders' for purchases of ARV drugs. The Network has helped to inspire similar exercises across the countries of the former Soviet Union.

In parallel with citizen action, governments both North and South must deliver protection, whether in the shape of properly funded, effective health services and prevention programmes or trade rules that facilitate (rather than obstruct) the provision of affordable medicines. The pharmaceutical industry, for its part, must understand that access to medicines is a fundamental human right, enshrined in international law, and that this places a particular

234

responsibility on drugs companies.[59] Delivering a social good such as access to medicines through market mechanisms is always going to pose challenges: if pharmaceutical companies do not see themselves as bearing the duty to save lives even when it is not profitable, governments must use their regulatory powers to ensure that treatment is available to all.

The attitudes and initiative of political leaders are crucial. South Africa's President Thabo Mbeki questioned the safety and value of life-saving antiretroviral treatment for HIV and AIDS and even publicly doubted that HIV causes AIDS, setting back the national treatment and prevention effort in the worst-affected country in the world. In contrast, Brazil's Jose Sarney threw the state's weight behind the national HIV and AIDS campaign early on, while Botswana's President Festus Mogae spoke publicly about the threat in an effort to reduce the stigma that deterred people from being tested for HIV: 'We are threatened with extinction. People are dying in chillingly high numbers. It is a crisis of the first magnitude.'[60] Botswana was the first African country to commit itself to providing ARVs to all citizens who required them.

Brazil shows what can be achieved by a combination of citizen action and state support. Its simultaneous programmes of prevention and treatment have halved AIDS deaths and infectious diseases related to HIV and AIDS.[61]

**Strong and effective civil society participation**: A key element in Brazil's success has been its combination of an open attitude to sex and a vibrant tradition of civil society activism. AIDS carries less stigma than in other countries, a factor that was pivotal in increasing the visibility of the problem. Gay-rights groups were the first to speak out publicly, and activist groups remain the keystone to the prevention strategy, distributing millions of free condoms and ensuring a supportive environment for people living with HIV and AIDS. Activists also influence the health budget through vocal lobbying and public demonstrations. The media play an active role, with continual advertising through television stations, radio networks, and print media outlets, promoting safe sex and increasing awareness of the epidemic.

**Effective state action**: In 1986 the government, pressured by activists, established a national programme that guaranteed every AIDS patient state-of-the-art treatment, free of charge. Anti-discrimination laws were passed to protect citizens living with HIV and AIDS. Co-operation agreements between political parties safeguarded these laws and the health budget, providing continuity of the programme despite changes in governments.

Brazil took to the world stage to surmount a huge barrier that keeps poor countries from providing free, universal access to ARVs: their cost, which is kept artificially high by overly strict patent rules. Brazil led the way at the WTO Ministerial meeting in Doha, Qatar, arguing successfully for allowing developing countries to break drug patents for compelling reasons of public health. Brazil had already passed legislation permitting the manufacture of generic versions of patented medicines and now produces eight out of 17 of its AIDS medicines itself, reducing costs by 82 per cent. It also uses the threat of issuing compulsory licences to its generic companies for other patented drugs to bargain down prices.

The Brazilian government has established an impressive network of clinics, built on the existing public health system, and has provided additional training to health workers on helping patients on anti-retroviral treatments to take their medicines correctly. A computerised national system allows authorities to exert rigorous control over the supply and distribution of medicines. This makes it possible for health officials to track each individual case of AIDS in the country, to access medical notes and histories from a bar-coded card held by the patient, and to monitor and update the drug regimen for each case from any of the 111 treatment centres across the country. Other state, private sector, and civil society institutions help out by providing free bus passes to AIDS patients, and have also donated food and baby formula.

## AIDS AND AID

Aid donors have made a belated, but welcome, commitment to assist poor countries in the fight against pandemics by setting up the Global Fund to Fight AIDS, Tuberculosis and Malaria. Proposed by the former UN Secretary-General Kofi Annan in 2001, the Global Fund was quickly embraced by the leaders of the G8. It seeks to strengthen countries' health systems and pays for medicines, diagnostic kits, and other medical equipment. This unique international public–private collaboration, dedicated to attracting and disbursing funds to fight the three diseases, is discussed in more detail in Part 5.

AIDS is unlikely to remain the only major pandemic of our lifetimes. Already, tuberculosis is a neglected disease that killed 1.6 million people in 2005, 195,000 of them people living with HIV.[62] With the advent of multi-drug-resistant TB, tackling the disease has become harder than it was 60 years ago. Avian flu, which emerged in South-East Asia in 2003, is currently the most likely candidate to join it. As of January 2008, 353 cases had been reported worldwide, with 227 deaths,[63] and if the rapidly mutating virus acquires the ability to pass directly from human to human, statistical analyses project a death count of 62 million, based on the 1918 influenza pandemic. Ninety-six per cent of deaths are forecast to be in the developing world.[64]

Viruses respect no borders, and tackling pandemics requires co-ordinated international action. In health, this has achieved some spectacular successes, such as the eradication of smallpox and the control of the SARS outbreak of 2003 (see Box 4.3).

---

## BOX 4.3

## SARS: WHAT GLOBAL COLLABORATION CAN ACHIEVE

There is a startling contrast between the prompt and effective global response to severe acute respiratory syndrome (SARS), and the years of neglect over HIV and AIDS. The World Health Organization's Global Alert Response system is a surveillance system that continually tracks the outbreak of emerging potential health epidemics around the world. SARS was one such threat, first identified on 12 March 2003.

Unprecedented global collaboration was the key to the containment of this deadly new disease. Initially, international and national teams on the ground provided information on it, which was quickly disseminated globally, allowing rapid identification of imported cases and thus the containment of the outbreak. WHO went onto something approaching a war footing, receiving daily updates on the situation in countries with outbreaks and demanding the immediate reporting of cases detected in all other countries. Operational teams provided

24-hour advice to countries on SARS surveillance, preparedness, and response measures.

As a direct result of this global collaboration, the cause of SARS was identified and the disease was rapidly isolated and treated. By the beginning of July 2003, just four months after the first case was identified, the human-to-human transmission of SARS appeared to have been broken everywhere in the world. Although some 800 people had died, a global pandemic had been contained.

*Source:* World Health Organization (2003) 'The Operational Response to SARS', www.who.int/csr/sars/goarn2003_4_16/en/print.html

## CHRONIC VULNERABILITY AND HEALTH

Poor health is both a disaster in itself and has damaging knock-on effects. It reduces people's earnings potential, often forcing them into debt, increases the burden on other family members, including children, and transmits deprivation down the generations. The sudden illness of a family member is one of the most common reasons why a family tips over the edge into a cycle of poverty and debt. Chronic illnesses such as HIV constitute a continuing drain on the household, increasing the workload of women and sometimes pushing them into activities that increase the risk of further illness, whether through sex work or the physical toll of excessive hours working in unsafe or unhygienic conditions.

Because of their socialised role as caregivers, women are most active in struggles for better health care. Women are also more likely to contract diseases such as malaria, TB, and HIV.[65] They are usually the last in the family to access health care, especially if it has to be paid for – a sign both of their lack of economic power and of prevalent attitudes towards women in many cultures.

There is no starker condemnation of the failure to guarantee women's right to health than the lack of progress in reducing 'maternal mortality' – the anodyne term for women who die in pregnancy or childbirth. Worldwide, over 500,000 women die each year from pregnancy-related causes – one woman every minute – but that figure conceals extreme inequalities. A woman's risk of dying ranges from one in seven in Niger to one in 47,600 in Ireland.[66] In 2004, WHO estimated that sub-Saharan Africa, between 2001 and 2010, would see 2.5 million maternal deaths, 49 million maternal disabilities, and 7.5 million related child deaths. Children who have lost their mothers are up to ten times more likely to die prematurely than those who have not.[67]

Maternal mortality reflects ethnic as well as economic inequalities. In Mexico, the risk of dying of causes related to pregnancy, childbirth, or postpartum is three times higher in indigenous communities than in the rest of the country.[68]

The struggle against ill health, ignorance, and poverty starts in the womb. A quarter of children in the developing world have a birth weight below the critical minimum of 2.5kg because their mothers are undernourished.[69] Evidence from countries where girls are taken out of school and married off in their early teens shows the link between early motherhood and babies who are more likely to be underweight and have a lower chance of survival.[70] Malnourished children are more likely to fall ill, less likely to perform well in school, and so less likely to earn a decent income in adulthood.

The failure to bring down maternal mortality rates contrasts with solid progress in other areas where state capacity is clearly improving, such as improvements in access to water and sanitation. The rapid scale-up in global immunisation since 2001 has also reduced the death toll, saving an estimated half-a-million lives.[71] As a result, in terms of life expectancy poor countries are catching up with rich ones.

The record on providing health services to poor people around the world is one of some success in targeted interventions, against a background of disintegrating systems and increasing inequality. Most health-care services are provided by national systems that have been underfunded for decades. Global efforts to boost health-care coverage have provided essential support, but founder on this legacy of neglect.

For example, immunisation coverage has greatly increased since WHO launched its Expanded Programme on Immunisation in 1974. In 2006, global coverage for DTP3 (three doses of the diphtheria –tetanus–pertussis combination vaccine) was 79 per cent – up from 20 per cent in 1980.[72] Unfortunately this was done in a way that did not provide the necessary investment in underlying health services.

Therefore when donors lost interest and their funding for vaccine programmes decreased, there was a collapse of many vaccination programmes and a falling vaccination rate in the following years. Currently, private philanthropy and government-led public–private partnerships (PPPs) are reinvigorating vaccination programmes, but their sustainability requires massive and long-term investment in public health services, something that many donors have yet to accept.

People with less political clout, such as those living in remote locations, urban slums, and border areas, as well as indigenous groups and displaced populations, are most likely to miss out on vaccination – an indicator of their lack of access to other essential health services. An estimated 2.1 million people around the world died in 2002 of diseases preventable by widely used vaccines. This toll included 1.4 million children under the age of five.[73]

On top of continuing epidemics of preventable diseases such as chest infections, malaria, and TB, and of treatable ones such as AIDS, the wealthier developing countries now also face a rise of 'first world' ailments such as heart disease, diabetes, and cancer, creating a 'triple burden' of old, new, and chronic disease that threatens to overwhelm underfunded health services. More than half of the world's new cases of diabetes are in India and China. Half of global cancer deaths are in developing countries, including (due to late diagnosis and lack of treatment) 95 per cent of deaths from cervical cancer.[74] Since these afflictions usually strike wealthier urban populations who enjoy greater political clout, providing treatment for them may drain resources away from tackling the health risks facing poor people, through preventive strategies and long-term investments in health systems.

An additional global problem is the extraordinarily unequal geographic distribution of health spending and health workers. The Americas, with 10 per cent of the global burden of disease, have 37 per cent of the world's health workers and absorb more than 50 per cent of the world's health financing. Africa, on the other hand, has 24 per cent of the disease burden but only 3 per cent of health workers, and commands less than 1 per cent of world health expenditure. Moreover, Africa's attempts to increase provision are constantly undermined by the exodus of its nurses and doctors in search of higher wages in richer countries.[75] The African Union estimates that low-income countries subsidise high-income countries to the tune of $500m every year through the loss of their health workers.[76]

A human security approach to reducing vulnerability to ill health requires action to empower poor people and communities, enabling them where possible to prevent ill health striking, to cope with it if they are unsuccessful, and to recover as quickly as possible thereafter. Communities must be given much greater say in how services are delivered.

Human security also requires effective state protection, in the shape of a health system that provides universal access. Tackling inequality means a shift to primary and rural health care and making services work for women, by promoting and retaining female staff and supporting women as users of health-care services. Solving the work-force crisis will require governments to pay decent salaries, recruit more staff, and invest in decent health planning systems. They must also invigorate the public service ethos, which has taken a battering from the anti-state message of governments and aid donors alike in recent decades. Governments need to invest in free primary care, abolishing any remaining user fees, and to focus on preventive rather than purely curative services (health professionals the world over share the same desire for the latest high-tech toys, when money is often much more effectively spent on basic health education). Rich countries can help by not luring away qualified nurses and doctors, a point discussed in Part 5.

People will always fall ill, but whether sickness destroys lives is largely determined by social, political, and economic conditions. HIV, while still a personal trauma, is no longer a death sentence in rich countries. In poor ones, however, health shocks such as HIV all too often are a cataclysmic addition to the daily toll of ill health, which weakens and undermines poor people, communities, and countries in their struggle for development. The chances of enjoying good health are unforgivably skewed between rich and poor people and countries. Sickness and poverty feed off each other, and the best way to address them involves bringing together states and citizens, backed by the resources and global collaboration of the international community.

## HOW CHANGE HAPPENS CASE STUDY:
## SOUTH AFRICA'S TREATMENT ACTION CAMPAIGN (TAC)

When nearly three dozen international pharmaceutical corporations sued in 2001 to overturn a South African law allowing the importation of cheaper generic medicines, an upsurge of activism gave them such a public battering that they were forced to drop the case. At the heart of the protests was the Treatment Action Campaign (TAC), an organisation of HIV-positive people in South Africa, a country with one of the highest prevalence rates in the world. Close to 20 per cent of its population carry the virus.

Formed on International AIDS Day in 1998, TAC's 15,000 members are a fair cross-section of South Africa's people: 80 per cent of them are unemployed, 70 per cent are women, 70 per cent are in the 14–24 age group, and 90 per cent are black. But TAC's clout is far greater than its numbers or demographics suggest.

After it had forced the companies to climb down and then drastically cut the prices of antiretroviral (ARV) medicines, TAC took on the ANC government. Despite the court victory, some in the government, in particular the President, Thabo Mbeki, continued to question the link between HIV and AIDS. Confusing political statements, combined with slow delivery on the ground, undermined what appeared to be good plans to distribute ARVs to public health clinics.

While post-apartheid democracy made violent repression unlikely, TAC's campaign to change government policy was still long and difficult. TAC used legal challenges regularly and to great effect, winning a series of court victories on access to treatment based on the 1994 Constitution, which enshrined the human right to health care. Official participatory structures of the post-apartheid order, such as district health committees, offered TAC opportunities to build public support.

However, South Africa's majority rule also produced what is in effect a one-party state, in which criticism of the ANC is easily portrayed as an attack on democracy. Whatever their private views, few influential voices were willing to publicly disagree with government policy. TAC was obliged to go beyond the courts and use confrontational tactics. Its members broke patent rules by importing cheaper Brazilian generic medicines in 2002 and held repeated loud and angry demonstrations.

TAC was astute in building broad alliances both within and out-side government, and at local, national, and international levels. The campaign showed a remarkable tolerance for difference, even working with the Catholic Church despite disagreement over the use of condoms. By not denouncing the ANC govern-ment (unlike many other social movements), TAC managed to find and cultivate allies within the party who eventually became instrumental in changing government policy.

Since its campaign did not threaten major political or economic interests (other than the foreign drug companies), it was probably more suited to an insider–outsider-type strategy than issues such as land reform or the fall of apartheid itself. As an organisation of HIV-positive people, TAC also empowered its members to become their own most effective advocates, running 'treatment literacy' campaigns that provided the basis for both self-help and social mobilisation.

Despite TAC's enormous success in influencing public opinion, President Mbeki remained defiant, giving full support to Health Minister Manto Tshabalala-Msimang, who had earned the nickname 'Dr. Beetroot' for her repeated assertions that garlic, beetroot, and better nutrition offered better prospects for treating AIDS than ARVs.

Only in 2006, when the battle over who would succeed Mbeki began in earnest, did the façade of party unity begin to crack. Mbeki's position on HIV and AIDS became a lightning rod in the leadership contest. TAC's protests at the 16th International AIDS Conference in Toronto in August that year helped escalate the international public humiliation of the ANC at the hands of UN officials and the media.

By late 2006, a change of policy on ARVs was essential for the ANC leadership to regain its authority. As it looked for a face-saving exit, the Health Minister's (non HIV-related) sickness and temporary departure from office allowed the government to back down with good grace, finally acknowledging the scale of the problem and agreeing to do more, working with civil society and restructuring the South African National Aids Council.

Deputy Health Minister Nozizwe Madlala-Routledge, a sharp critic of the government's policies, acknowledged the role that TAC played. 'Activism', she said, 'did change policy and force

CASE STUDY

government to alter course – partly by strengthening different voices in government.' And one study concluded: 'The AIDS campaign, which has been far more concerned to use the instruments offered by constitutional democracy than any other attempt to win change in post-apartheid South Africa, has also been far more successful than its counterparts in winning change.'

*Sources:* Steven Friedman (undated), 'The Extraordinary "Ordinary": The Campaign for Comprehensive AIDS treatment in South Africa'; author interview with Mark Heywood, TAC, July 2007.

CASE STUDY

# THE RISK OF NATURAL DISASTER

January 2001 was a bad month for earthquakes, with major tremors striking in India, El Salvador, and the north-west USA around Seattle. On the face of it, nothing could more resemble 'acts of God' than earthquakes, which in ages past were seen as instruments of divine wrath. However, the human impact was anything but preordained. These three earthquakes were of similar orders of magnitude, but killed 20,000 people in India, 600 in El Salvador, and none in Seattle. Even allowing for geological differences, the explanation for such a huge disparity lay not in nature, but in poverty and power. Nature is neutral, but disasters discriminate. In India, poor enforcement of building codes added to the toll, as high-rise buildings collapsed. In El Salvador, mudslides swept away the shanty homes of families who had fled rural poverty and who had nowhere else to live but the steep, deforested slopes of ravines.

Like other sources of vulnerability, disasters shine a spotlight on inequality. Rich countries and communities have resources and systems that can cope (much of Europe and North America have a natural disaster that strikes every year – it is called winter). Poor countries and communities lack the resources to cope with shocks. The hazard may be natural but the risk (*hazard x vulnerability*) is generated by social, economic, and political inequality and injustice. Far more attention needs to be paid to reducing the vulnerability aspect of risk by redistributing voice and power to poor people,

245

whether in the process of preparing for disasters, or in the subsequent response and recovery process. Such an effort must combine empowering poor people and communities to become active protagonists in preparing for, and coping with disasters, with building effective and accountable state machineries for disaster management.

Disasters strike in many forms, but (with the exception of the 2004 Indian Ocean tsunami) the most deadly is drought and subsequent famine, which accounted for nearly half of all disaster-related deaths in 1994–2003. Floods, earthquakes, and hurricanes and other 'windstorms' accounted for the majority of the remainder.

Every day, almost 200 people die as a result of a disaster, but the number of deaths has halved over the past 30 years, thanks to a combination of more effective early-warning systems and better disaster preparedness at the community level.[77] However, the total number of people *affected* by disasters is rising, and almost doubled between 1990 and 1999. Clearly, while public capacity to prevent deaths is improving, the vulnerability of people living in poverty remains, and is exacerbated by issues such as increasing population in vulnerable areas and the deterioration of the environment, including climate change.[78]

At a national level, poor countries and weak governments are less able to protect vulnerable people. On average, the number of people affected by disasters in developing countries is 150 times higher than in rich countries, whereas the population is only five times greater. The corresponding economic losses are 20 times larger, when expressed as a percentage of respective gross national products. In 2002, over a third of all 'natural disasters' occurred in Africa, constituting one of the region's largest obstacles to reducing poverty, conflict, and food insecurity.[79] Poor people in wealthy countries also suffer when their governments fail to invest in disaster preparedness or to maintain essential infrastructure, as became evident in the USA in the wake of Hurricane Katrina in 2005.

Within all countries, marginalised people and communities are more likely to be hurt than the powerful, with factors such as age, gender, disability, political affiliation, or ethnicity weighing heavily. Disasters also have a disproportionate effect on women. In the wake of a disaster, women tend to have less access to health, social, and information services than men, and therefore are less able to deal with further stresses.

However, women also possess skills and knowledge that are vital to ensuring a successful recovery. In January 2001 more than 20,000 people died and thousands went missing in the north-west Indian state of Gujarat, after the worst earthquake in over 50 years. Oxfam saw at first hand how the work of one of its partners, the Self-Employed Women's Assocation (SEWA) was faster, better targeted, more efficient, and better linked to longer-term development than that of others – arguably because of SEWA's membership structure and because it worked with (and was more accountable to) poor women. In particular, SEWA put much greater emphasis on the importance of income in sustaining women's livelihoods after a shock, developing insurance schemes and other ways to reduce women's vulnerability.[80]

Vulnerability is also partly about where poor people are obliged to live, whether on the islands of the highly hazard-prone Ganges delta in Bangladesh, in refugee camps or squatter settlements awash with small arms and a culture of impunity in Sierra Leone and Liberia (in the 1990s), or on the steep slopes of Central America vulnerable to drought, flooding, and landslides. Around urban centres, poor people are often forced to build on high-risk land, without building codes or infrastructure and at risk from flooding, mudslides, or earthquakes.

The nature of 'development' itself can add to vulnerability, when it ignores the voices and needs of poor people. In Afghanistan, the new Shiberghan highway linking Faisabad to Mazar-e-Sharif – completed in the winter of 2005 and supposed to be one of the best roads in the country – is an ecological nightmare for local farmers as it blocks natural drainage, increasing the risk of floods and threatening to wash away their crops and mud homes.[81]

Preservation of the natural ecosystem saves lives. The Maldives islands suffered less from the 2004 Asian tsunami than other countries because their up-market tourism industry had preserved the virgin mangroves and coral reefs surrounding the coastline.[82] Coral reefs act as a natural breakwater and mangroves are a natural shock absorber.[83] In the Indian state of Tamil Nadu, the villages of Pichavaram and Muthupet, which have dense mangroves, suffered few casualties and minimal economic damage, whereas Sri Lanka paid the price for its depleted protective layer.[84]

247

In regions prone to disasters, a downward spiral comes into play, as one event drives poor people further into poverty and places them even more at risk to future shocks. In part due to climate change, the total number of natural disasters has quadrupled in the past two decades – most of them floods, cyclones, and storms.[85] Small- and medium-scale disasters are occurring more frequently than the kind of large-scale disaster that hits the headlines. As the gap between such events shortens, even if each is fairly small, poor people and communities find it harder to recover before the next blow hits, pushing them into a downward spiral of destitution and further vulnerability from which they struggle to recover.[86]

---

## BOX 4.4:
## THE ASIAN TSUNAMI OF 2004

The greatest natural disaster of recent times took place on 26 December 2004, when a massive earthquake off the west coast of northern Sumatra led to movement along a 1,200km section of the sea floor, generating a series of tsunamis that killed people in 14 countries around the Indian Ocean. Indonesia, Sri Lanka, the Maldives, India, and Thailand were the hardest hit. Over 227,000 people lost their lives and some 1.7 million were displaced. A massive, media-fuelled global response resulted, producing an estimated $13.5bn in international aid, including $5.5bn from the public in developed countries.

An in-depth evaluation of the relief effort identified a number of areas of good practice by aid agencies, including the widespread use of cash grants to those affected, rapid rebuilding of houses and schools, and greater use of complaints mechanisms and consultation with affected families than in previous disasters. Pointing out that, 'Disaster response was mostly conducted by the affected people themselves', the evaluation team concluded that, 'The international response was most effective when enabling, facilitating and supporting [local people and national institutions], and when accountable to them.'

However, the evaluation found that this was often not the case. Aid agencies under pressure to spend money visibly opted for high-profile flagship projects, rather than painstaking collaboration

248

with local organisations. National governments were mistakenly written off as 'failed states' and ignored. Aid was often supply-driven, rather than in response to the expressed needs of the affected communities. Because aid was often distributed to those who were more articulate or powerful, such as fishermen wanting replacement boats, rather than marginalised women and poor communities, it ended up reinforcing inequalities in society.

More broadly, the evaluation highlighted the irrationality of a media-driven global system that raised over $7,000 per person affected by the tsunami, but only $3 per person affected by that year's floods in Bangladesh.

It concluded by driving home the human security message of empowerment plus protection, arguing that, for all the successes of the response, 'A regulatory system is needed to oblige agencies to put the affected population at the centre of measures of agency effectiveness', and called for 'a fundamental reorientation from supplying aid to supporting and facilitating communities' own relief and recovery priorities.'

*Source:* J. Telford, J. Cosgrave, and R. Houghton (2006) 'Joint Evaluation of the International Response to the Indian Ocean Tsunami: Synthesis Report', London: Tsunami Evaluation Coalition.

## REDUCING RISK

Previously we just reacted. We'd work together, but now we plan before the flood happens. It's meant that, for example, we didn't have to leave this place this year. Before the flood came every family had dried food and a portable oven stored. Cattle were moved and placed in a safe place. When we saw that the tube well was going under water we started to store water in pots. We don't have to wait for outside help.

HAWA PARVIN, VILLAGE DISASTER PREPAREDNESS COMMITTEE, KURIGRAM DISTRICT, BANGLADESH, 2004[87]

With disasters, an ounce of prevention is worth a pound of cure. Mozambique's response to a potentially lethal combination of floods and a cyclone in 2007 showed what good national leadership and planning can achieve, even in one of the world's poorest countries.

The key to success lay in the government's prior preparations. In October 2006, it adopted a 'Master Plan' for dealing with Mozambique's vulnerability to natural disasters, covering issues ranging from the need for re-forestation and the development of a national irrigation system to the development of crops that can survive prolonged droughts. The Master Plan also argued that Mozambique needs to reduce its dependence on agriculture as the main source of livelihood in rural areas through, for example, the development of its tourist industry, while setting out a clear strategy for emergency management.

The plan notes that many people have grown up in conditions of war and disaster, where 'begging has become almost a way of life'. It argues that the 're-establishment of self-esteem, self-confidence and dignity' are a basic precondition for 'combating extreme poverty and reducing the country's vulnerability to natural disasters'. For this reason, the government is determined to avoid 'running to international donors without first exhausting national capacities'.

The strategy was first tested by the floods of 2007. It was an impressive debut, as the government succeeded in evacuating everyone from the flooded areas without loss of life. Emergency preparedness measures undoubtedly reduced the number of deaths and injuries caused by the cyclone that struck around the same time. People whose homes were destroyed were moved to temporary accommodation centres and provided with food, some health care, and basic social services. A subsequent evaluation concluded that, without this assistance, there would have been deaths and widespread suffering, and that 'the real needs for emergency relief were largely met' by the operation.[88] Throughout this exercise, the government of Mozambique made a deliberate decision not to issue an emergency appeal for international assistance, demonstrating the impact an effective state can have in dealing with risk and vulnerability.

A comprehensive human security approach to reducing the risks posed by natural disasters should include ongoing 'mitigation' efforts. Planning systems, building codes, and environmental regulations, for example, can limit damage. Early-warning systems and public education programmes are also key: if villagers in Sri Lanka had known that the sudden retreat of the sea was the precursor to a tsunami, they would have fled to higher ground, rather than rush to collect the fish left flapping on the suddenly exposed sea floor. More broadly, risk reduction overlaps with social protection schemes, which can reduce vulnerability to shocks and can also be rapidly expanded after a shock to allow communities to recover as quickly as possible.

Poor communities and civil society organisations can also take pre-emptive action to greatly reduce vulnerability. The fruits of such 'community disaster preparedness' were seen in April 2007, when flash floods and mudslides due to heavy rains and snowmelts swept across large areas of northern Afghanistan. Unlike many devastated communities, the village of Dari-Souf Payan in Samangan suffered only a single casualty and limited damage to property.

The seeds of preparedness had been planted less than six months earlier in a South–South exchange of ideas. In January 2007, the Bangladeshi NGO BRAC (Bangladesh Rural Advancement Committee) had initiated a community-based disaster risk reduction programme (CBDRR) in the village. BRAC trained a total of 30 facilitators from the community (20 women and ten men) to work with groups of 50 families each, establishing Village Disaster Management Units with separate committees for women and men, in keeping with cultural norms and to ensure that women's concerns were voiced.

In April, when the heavy rains commenced, committee members went to each house to discuss the impending floods and the need to move to higher ground. After the floods, with BRAC's support, the committees mobilised the community to dig out the irrigation channels, to enable floodwaters to drain away and life to return to normal as soon as possible.[89]

Cuba is perhaps the most renowned exponent of community-based disaster preparedness, as a neighbourhood representative from the Cuban Women's Federation in Havana explains

> *I am responsible for this part of the neighbourhood. If a hurricane hits, I know that inside one multi-family unit is an old woman in a wheelchair, who is going to need help to leave. I have 11 single mothers on second and third floors of apartment buildings with children under two, who will need more support to evacuate and special needs in the shelters. I have two pregnant women, one on that block and one on this one, who will need special attention.* [90]

---

BOX 4.5:
## CUBA VS KATRINA, LESSONS IN DISASTER RISK REDUCTION

Two months after Hurricane Katrina inundated New Orleans in 2005, killing around 1,300 people, Hurricane Wilma, at one point the strongest hurricane ever recorded, struck Cuba. The sea swept 1km inland and flooded the capital Havana, yet there were no deaths or even injuries in the city. Nationwide, 640,000 people were evacuated and only one life was lost. The six major hurricanes that rolled over Cuba between 1996 and 2002 claimed only 16 lives.

What did this poor developing country, subject to a long-standing economic embargo by the USA, do that the wealthy superpower next door failed to? Both countries have 'tangible assets', including a well-organised civil defence capability, efficient early-warning system, well-equipped rescue teams, and emergency stockpiles and other resources. But 'intangible assets' present in Cuba and apparently lacking in the USA proved to be just as important. The oil in the Cuban civil defence machine that enables it to function properly includes effective local leadership, community mobilisation, a strong sense of solidarity, and a population that is both well educated and trained in disaster response.

Cuba has developed a 'culture of safety,' which centralises decision-making in a crisis but decentralises implementation. Many ordinary people play important roles in disaster preparedness and response. Frequent and repeated use of the system has built high levels of trust between communities and civil defence officials.

'Any child in school can give you an explanation – how you prepare, what you do. Students know what to do, they know the phases [the four emergency phases: information, alert, alarm, and recovery], what to do in each phase...how to gather things in the house and put them away...shut off the water and electricity. All students, workers, and small farmers get this training', explains José Castro of the civil defence unit in Cienfuegos.

Once a year, at the end of May, the entire country participates in a training exercise in risk reduction, including a full day of simulation exercises, and another identifying vulnerable residents, cutting down branches that might fall on houses, checking reservoir walls or dams, cleaning wells, identifying places to evacuate animals, and so forth.

*Source:* Oxfam America (2003) 'Cuba – Weathering the Storm: Lessons in Risk Reduction from Cuba.'
www.oxfamamerica.org/newsandpublications/publications/research_reports/art7111.html

Disaster risk reduction not only reduces suffering and saves lives, it can also limit the economic damage. During the 1998 floods in Bangladesh, for example, the value of cattle saved by a four-acre flood shelter exceeded the construction cost of the shelter by a factor of 17. Reconstruction costs for a new deep-water port in Dominica after it was hit by Hurricane David in 1979 were equivalent to 40 per cent of the original investment, compared with the 12 per cent extra that it would have cost to build the original port to a standard that could resist such a hurricane.[91]

In both economic and humanitarian terms, it may be a no-brainer, but reducing risks *before* a disaster is uphill work politically, as UN Secretary-General Kofi Annan recognised in 1999: 'Building a culture of prevention is not easy. While the costs of prevention have to be paid in the present, their benefits lie in a distant future. Moreover, the benefits are not tangible; they are the disasters that did not happen.'[92] Governments often find it easier to raise money internationally when disaster has already struck, and television coverage is raising money in donor countries.

The key to overcoming such political obstacles is a combination of political leadership, pressure from an informed civil society, and a shift in the international aid system towards prevention. Following the 2004 tsunami, the international community came together to try and create this shift, adopting a ten-year blueprint for disaster risk reduction known as the Hyogo Framework, which to date has been signed on to by 160 countries.

The Framework sets out the responsibilities of states and international organisations in creating a robust disaster risk reduction system and marks a great step forward, both in recognising the leading role of national governments and in moving from the traditionally disaster-driven international response to a more comprehensive approach to reducing risk and building human security. The Hyogo Framework's key message is that disaster reduction should be made a central part of the overall development agenda. Only time will tell whether Hyogo makes a real difference, or whether it merely adds to the shelves full of worthy but ultimately ineffectual international declarations. Much will depend on sustained international scrutiny and pressure for change.

## MAKING DISASTER RESPONSE ACCOUNTABLE

Placing more emphasis on 'downward accountability' to the beneficiaries of emergency relief drastically changes the way in which aid organisations respond to an emergency. A culture of consultation and listening, treating people as citizens and holders of rights rather than mere recipients of charity, leads to better aid. When an earthquake struck the Indonesian city of Yogyakarta in 2006, Oxfam's initial consultations with the residents came up with the surprising result that the most urgent need was for plastic sandals: Yogyakarta is a modern city, with lots of concrete and glass. People forced to flee their homes in an earthquake in the middle of the night often did so without their shoes, leaving them to wander streets strewn with broken glass. The team found a supplier and within hours was handing out flip-flops.

By asking survivors of the 2004 tsunami in Aceh one simple question – 'Do you prefer/traditionally use squat latrines or pour flush latrines?' – Oxfam was able to get its response right from the outset. Unfortunately, others failed to ask and as a result built thousands of unpopular squat latrines, which remain unused all over the island.

Responsiveness and accountability must be joined in any rights-based approach to emergencies. This requires a number of practical mechanisms, including:

- Ensuring the appropriate level of participation by affected communities in all aspects of an aid agency's response, from initial assessment to final evaluation;
- Providing information relevant to communities' needs in order that they may claim their rights under international humanitarian law;

- Providing a means for communities to voice both positive feedback and criticism to those providing humanitarian assistance, and to receive appropriate redress;
- Documenting efforts to ensure accountability, and making records available for public scrutiny.

Establishing a complaints mechanism in its Malawi food crisis response programme in 2005–06 allowed Oxfam to discover and rectify crimes being committed by 'middlemen' in the programme, who were stealing food that should have been going to beneficiaries. The beneficiaries probably would not have had the courage, or known how, to contact Oxfam and the police had they not been involved in discussions in the first days of the programme about their rights and how best to make complaints.

Achieving this kind of accountability involves both learning how to do it (bearing in mind that it is it is far from easy to achieve in the middle of a humanitarian catastrophe) and establishing a system for assessing and reporting back on progress, so that organisations can see how well they are doing and generate the pressure to improve.

There are various ways in which the effort to improve downward accountability could evolve further. One option is to focus on setting standards and indicators for best practice, as the Sphere initiative has set quality standards for humanitarian assistance more generally. A system of peer review, with published results, could improve levels of transparency and speed up efforts to spread best practice among NGOs. Eventually, it may become necessary to opt for a system of certification by independent auditors. This might help to assuage those critics of NGOs who argue that self-regulation is not enough in an age when the public has moved from a 'trust me' to a 'show me' culture; however, there are concerns that such formal Northern accounting and auditing models could increase costs and exclude nascent Southern aid agencies that could otherwise become important players in the future.

The very word 'disaster' comes from the Latin for 'ill-starred', but it is inequality and injustice that determine who is at risk from disaster, not the stars. And by hitting poor and marginal groups hardest, disasters ratchet up inequality within and between countries.

In enhancing human security, the stereotype of pale-skinned 'angels of mercy' rushing to the rescue of hapless, suffering people is thankfully ever less accurate. The reality is very different: human security stems from poor communities coping with risk through their own efforts, supported by effective, accountable states. Most natural disasters are largely predictable, and damage can be minimised by efficient organisation, sound risk analysis, and planning and investment in reducing risk. The key is to enable populations to prepare for disasters before they occur, to cope with them once they strike, and to rebuild as soon as possible thereafter.

# CLIMATE CHANGE

We have a word for it – it's chivala. It means the warming of the earth. And of course people see that changes have come, but they don't really link them to the global issue. People hear about things on the radio, and they have knowledge of El Niño, but they don't understand how these things are linked up.

THOMAS BWANALI, SHIRE HIGHLANDS MILK PRODUCERS, MALAWI, JUNE 2007

Every time there is a major 'weather event', be it drought in Africa or Australia, floods in Europe or Bangladesh, or a hurricane in New Orleans or Grenada, lobbyists and media alike immediately launch into a speculative debate about whether climate change is its 'cause'. Weather systems are so complex, and climate models so new, that specific events can still seldom be pinned on a single cause. However, the fact that the global climate is changing – with enormous ramifications – is beyond doubt. The temperature of the Earth is increasing: so far, every year in the new millennium has ranked among the ten warmest years since records began in 1850, while 2005 tied with 1998 as the hottest year on record.[93]

Climate change has been the subject of decades of global scientific study. Set up in 1988, the Intergovernmental Panel on Climate Change (IPCC) brings together hundreds of the world's top scientists to periodically assess all relevant, published climate-related research from around the world. Its 2007 report reflected a firm consensus, higher confidence, and more robust findings, based on the availability of more up-to-date studies covering a wider area compared with previous reports. It concluded that human-induced climate change is now 'unequivocal', is already well under way, and is occurring faster than expected.[94]

The IPCC's grim global prognosis includes more erratic and severe weather patterns and further rises in sea levels. Low-lying island states such as Kiribati, the Maldives, and Tuvalu could disappear altogether, while countries such as Viet Nam and Egypt face devastation along their coasts: a one-metre rise in sea levels (an estimate by the World Bank of the possible impact of climate change) would flood the homes of 10 per cent of their populations, inundating major cities, and prompting massive refugee crises. The World Bank study concluded, 'Within this century, hundreds of millions of people are likely to be displaced by sea level rise; accompanying economic and ecological damage will be severe for many. The world has not previously faced a crisis on this scale.'[95]

The IPCC's 2007 Assessment Report concluded that, without urgent action to curb greenhouse gas emissions, the world's average surface temperature is likely to increase by between 2°C and 4.5°C by the year 2100, with a 'best estimate' of 3°C.[96] A growing body of scientific evidence supports the conclusion that warming beyond 2°C constitutes a 'dangerous' level of climate change.[97] In many countries, poor communities are already facing dangerous impacts. While any estimate of the casualties inflicted by climate change is necessarily approximate, WHO suggests that the warming and precipitation trends attributable to man-made climate change over the past 30 years already claim more than 150,000 lives a year – most of them in poor countries.[98]

The deep injustice of climate change is that those with the least historical responsibility stand to suffer most from its predicted consequences. Many of the citizens of developing countries in equatorial regions, who have historically produced very low levels of greenhouse gases per capita, will be hardest hit. This is due to the severity of the predicted environmental changes in these countries and to the countries' lack of resources to cope with them.

Poor countries will be hardest hit through a combination of droughts, falling agricultural yields, more severe hurricanes, flooding, and storm surges. They will likewise face increased threats to health, for example from water stress leading to diarrhoea and cholera or the spread of malaria-carrying mosquitoes to new areas as temperatures rise. The increased frequency of such incidents will leave communities with far less time between shocks in which to rebuild their assets and resilience.

Within these communities, women will be particularly adversely affected. Women's roles in rural households – providing food, fuel, water, and care – depend heavily on natural resources being reliably available. When droughts, floods, or unpredictable rainfall make resources scarce, women may be forced to spend more time caring for malnourished children or walking to collect water and fuel. Women's relative lack of access to assets and credit leaves them more dependent on nature for a living, with all its increasing uncertainties.

When women and men are pushed into extreme measures to cope with severe weather events, the consequences can be devastating. In parts of Southern Africa, for example, researchers have found that during a drought the rate of new HIV infections rises. Why this correlation? Because if crops fail, many men migrate to urban areas to find work as labourers and when they return months later, some bring back the virus with them. Likewise, parents may marry off their daughters at a younger age to men who have had several wives or partners, in order to obtain cash from the dowry and to have fewer family members to feed. And some women, left in the village to cope with a failed harvest, resort to selling sex in exchange for money or food for their children, because they have no other asset to cash in.[99]

Across continents, climate change is set to exacerbate the conditions that force people to cope in such extreme ways. Tropical and sub-tropical countries (primarily in sub-Saharan Africa and South Asia), where poor people have few alternatives to farming or pastoralism, will become hotter, drier, and more drought-prone, or wetter with more intense rainfall and flood risks. The IPCC concludes that in some African countries rain-fed agricultural yields could fall by as much as 50 per cent as early as 2020, seriously threatening food security.[100]

In Africa's large river basins, total available water has already decreased by 40–60 per cent.[101] If current trends continue, climate models predict that by 2050 much of sub-Saharan Africa will be significantly drier, with 10 per cent less rainfall in the interior and water loss exacerbated by higher evaporation rates. In South-East Asia, climate change is predicted to affect the Indian monsoon, where a 10 per cent fluctuation in average rainfall can cause either severe drought or flooding.[102]

The increased energy in the climate system is likely to increase the frequency and magnitude of flooding in many regions. More intense downpours will also affect the capture of water by the soil as infiltration rates decline, more water runs off, and soil erosion increases. Increased temperatures and declines in snowfall are expected to accelerate the retreat of glaciers, substantially reducing the volume of meltwater on which many higher-latitude countries depend. In Peru, for example, glacier coverage has fallen by 25 per cent in the past 30 years, while in China virtually all glaciers have shown substantial melting.

Overall, it is estimated that these changes will increase the number of people suffering water resource stress by half a billion by 2020, with enormous implications for food security and health. WHO estimates that by 2000 climate change was already responsible for approximately 2.4 per cent of diarrhoea cases worldwide and 6 per cent of malaria cases in some middle-income countries.[103] Such rates are set to rise further as climate conditions worsen.

Declines in food and water security could result in substantial numbers of environmental refugees and internally displaced persons. The UN warns that, without action now, there could be over 150 million environmental refugees by 2050, due to the likely effects of global warming.[104] Such a scale of migration is likely to increase conflict, within and between countries, and induce global social and economic instability.

BOX 4.6:
## CLIMATE CHANGE, WATER, AND CONFLICT IN CENTRAL ASIA

Climate change is worsening the difficulties faced by the former Soviet states of central Asia, where cotton farming and deforestation have already undermined the ecosystem. Like its neighbours, Tajikistan lives by water-intensive cotton farming, which is based on a dilapidated and hopelessly inefficient irrigation system. A civil war further damaged infrastructure, and nearly a quarter of the population uses irrigation channels – contaminated by farm chemicals – as their main source of drinking water. Far downstream, the Aral Sea continues to shrink, exposing the fertiliser and pesticide dust washed into it in years past, creating a toxic wasteland for people living on its shores.

Bad as things already are, climate change could precipitate a 'tipping point'. Tajikistan's glaciers, the source of most of the water in the Aral Sea Basin, have shrunk by 35 per cent in the past 50 years, and what is left will shrink even faster as temperatures rise.

In mountain valleys, the rapid melting of ice increases the risk of floods and landslides. Downstream, it is likely to increase competition for water. Regional water-sharing systems once closely woven together by Soviet design have unravelled and must now be managed by five fractious and poverty-stricken new countries, each of which wants more water for national development, and all while the overall supply is dwindling – a sure recipe for future tension.

## BUILDING RESILIENCE TO CLIMATE CHANGE

There are two broad routes to reducing people's vulnerability to harm: reduce the extent of the hazard that they face, or reduce the risk of that hazard harming them. In the case of climate change, urgent action is essential on both fronts. The hazards of climate change are floods, droughts, hurricanes, erratic rainfall, and rising sea levels, the result of human-induced global warming. Those hazards have to be tackled at their source: global emissions must peak by 2015 and then fall by at least 80 per cent of 1990 levels by 2050, in order to prevent global warming exceeding the high-danger point of 2°C (see Part 5).

However, even if greenhouse gases are rapidly brought under control, the delayed effects of emissions already released mean that rising sea levels, droughts, floods, hurricanes, and rainfall variability will become more severe at least until 2030.[105] In the jargon, tackling climate change cannot focus only on 'mitigation' (reducing emissions), but must also give priority to 'adaptation' (building people's resilience to climate impacts). Adaptation is now essential, and communities need substantial national and international support to do it successfully.

Human communities have of course adapted to natural climate variability for millennia by growing diverse crops, using irrigation to manage scarce water, or carefully selecting seeds for the coming season. Still, some of the poorest communities today cannot cope even with this natural variability and are severely set back by natural droughts or floods, taking months or years to re-establish their livelihoods. Human-induced climate change will further exacerbate this stress because the speed, scale, and intensity of the severe weather events it causes will push many communities beyond the bounds of their experience. They will be forced to find ways of coping with environmental change on a scale not seen since the last Ice Age: rainy seasons that do not arrive, rivers that dry up, arable lands that turn to desert, forests and plant species that disappear forever.

In some parts of the world, just how the climate will change is inherently uncertain. In West Africa, for example, it is hotly debated whether rainfall will decrease and cause drought, or increase and cause flash floods, or stay the same on average but become far more unreliable, making farmers' planting decisions much riskier. Where change is this unpredictable, people must prepare themselves by acquiring information, resources, infrastructure, influence, and opportunities to diversify their livelihoods. Long-term development is one of the most important routes to building the adaptive capacity of an individual, community, or country.

Development and disaster preparedness may be essential for building resilience to climate change, but climate change in turn forces a rethink of development and disaster planning. It is no good investing in hydroelectric power plants if the river's flow is falling by 10 per cent each year. Likewise, there is little point in pouring resources into rain-fed agriculture if the rain is about to stop falling. Effective climate adaptation deliberately integrates better awareness of future climate impacts into current planning and actions, whether these are oriented towards minimising risk or maximising opportunity.

Where changes in the climate are becoming clear, some communities are already taking action. A study in four villages in South Africa and Mozambique facing increasing droughts and floods and more erratic rainfall confirms that poor people are already finding ways to adapt, by:

- **Building social institutions**: Communities set up numerous associations, communal food projects, co-operatives, and women's groups to share risk and confront threats together.
- **Diversifying livelihoods**: Communities sought to move into new areas of activity, such as fishing, vegetables, or construction, while some entered the more commercial end of farming, by introducing irrigation and selling rather than consuming their produce.
- **Looking beyond the village**: For example, by building links with nearby towns, sending more male migrants off to work in towns and commercial agriculture, or by building complementary links with other farming areas.[106]

At the same time, there are clear limits to how successfully poor communities can adapt if they do not have wider support. Many people lack viable opportunities to diversify their livelihoods or have no money to pay for the technologies they need, such as irrigation systems or insecticide-treated bed nets. Most have very little access to reliable climate information that would help them to plan more effectively, or have no means of learning how other communities in a similar situation have adapted. Research among subsistence farmers in Zimbabwe found that nearly half of those interviewed said that they would want to adjust their farming according to long-term forecasts, but their lack of cash and credit would prevent them from doing so.[107] Likewise, a study by ActionAid of climate change in African cities found that the ability of urban slum dwellers to adapt to increased flooding was weak, because they could not easily organise as a community and so were less able to take the collective action needed to build resilience.[108]

## ADAPTATION REQUIRES CITIZENS AND STATES

Glacial melt in the Himalayas is causing more frequent and more severe flooding in the plains below, where millions of people live. The scale of flooding in 2000 certainly came as a shock to riverside communities in India's West Bengal. 'There was an announcement over a loudspeaker, warning us that there would be a severe flood,' recalls Dipali Biswas, a resident of Nadia district. 'But we were still not aware just how severe it would be. When I saw the water rise above the roof of my house, I was stunned.'

Since then, the local NGO Sreema Mahila Samity (SMS) has initiated community-based disaster planning, supporting women as leaders in their communities to set up village task forces, plan and practise disaster response, learn to build quick-assembly boats and flood shelters, raise the foundations of their houses, and establish flood-proof communal grain banks. Dipali is a member of her village's Early Warning Task Force. 'These days, we can hear about floods in many ways,' she explains, 'from the village committee, from a telephone number that we can call to get the latest information, from the TV and radio, and of course from observing the river ourselves. During the flood season, we never miss a radio or TV weather report.'[109]

Dipali's village is as ready as it can be for the floods that climate change will undoubtedly make worse, and the active citizenship of her community has been essential for that preparedness. But all their preparation will succeed only if the local government provides accurate and timely flood warnings, and that in turn depends on the national government investing in India's meteorological infrastructure. In short, active citizens can only succeed in adapting to climate change if they have the support of effective states.

All countries need to assess their vulnerability to climate change, identify adaptation options and plan responses to protect their populations from impacts. Poor countries, especially, need to make this a priority as part of their development strategies. In addition to promoting community risk reduction initiatives and integrating climate risk into development plans, governance at local, regional, and national levels must be strengthened; information systems to accurately forecast and monitor climate impacts must be established; technologies must be developed or adapted for changing local conditions; and infrastructure and ecosystems such as forests must be protected.

In planning and implementing climate adaptation, local and national governments must ensure that adaptation initiatives give priority to those people most vulnerable to climate risks. That means taking account of the different impacts of climate change on women and men, and likewise understanding the impacts on and needs of indigenous communities. Rural women and indigenous communities generally face more climate risks because of their intense dependence on natural resources. However, their knowledge of biodiversity and the options for managing it in times of stress will be essential for spurring innovative approaches, and so their involvement must lie at the heart of successful plans to adapt.

On Nicaragua's Atlantic Coast, the traditional authorities of the Miskitu Indians are trying to remedy some of the damage already caused by climate change. The community's long-standing equilibrium with the forest was based on its ability to forecast the weather and so know when to plant crops, but that predictability has gone. 'The summer now is winter. April used to be summer, but it rained all month. Now, in May (winter) it doesn't rain. We listen to the thunder, we see the lightning that should let us know the rain is coming, but it is not', says Marciano Washington, a farmer on the bank of Coco River. 'We can't depend on nature any more. We don't know when to plant our crops.' The traditional indigenous authorities, along with a local NGO, Christian Medical Action (CMA), are introducing an early-warning system to monitor rainfall and river levels, in order to provide that information in a format useful for the community's way of life.

Effective state action on adaptation may also call for a reconsideration of wider economic policies, such as land ownership and use. Economic reforms in Viet Nam, for example, have seen public mangrove forests along the coast replaced by private shrimp farms, which have brought income to some but at the same time have curtailed poor people's livelihood options and destroyed vital natural buffers against storm surges. The increasing income inequalities that have resulted from this have also undermined the solidarity that previously helped to ensure the communal maintenance of dykes, thus exposing coastal villages to climate-related rises in sea levels.[110] In the absence of publicly planned adaptation based on broad consultation, private responses will occur instead and these may well exacerbate the wider community's vulnerability to climate change.

Appropriate technologies – new and old – will also be needed for poor farmers to adapt to climate change, and will require significant national and international agricultural research into drought- or flood-tolerant varieties of seeds. Social organisation and local land policy will also be essential if poor farmers are to succeed in using new seeds. In Mozambique, where climate change is expected to bring both drought and floods, groups of villagers have experimented with drought-resistant varieties of rice, maize, cassava, and sweet potato. By working in groups, combining poor and better-off households and involving both female and male farmers, the villagers were able to share the risks of new practices and learn for themselves through trial, error, and experimentation. These informal associations have started, with some success, to lobby local authorities responsible for land allocation so that farmers obtain parcels of land in several different locations. This diversification of seeds and soil strengthens their resilience to either more drought or more floods.

Climate change is the biggest threat to long-term poverty reduction – and yet reducing poverty is essential in equipping poor people to deal with unavoidable climate impacts. As the evidence of climate change accumulates, the necessity for urgent action to tackle it becomes undeniable. Climate change is not a linear or reversible process, but it appears to have a number of unpredictable 'tipping points' that, once passed, could have catastrophic and irreversible consequences. It is in no country's long-term interest to wait until millions of people are tipped over the edge into climate disaster.

As the Stern Report confirmed in 2006,[111] mitigation – rapid cuts in emissions to avoid catastrophic climate change – is essential and urgent. However, time is not on the side of the 'indecision-makers' who for years have stalled and delayed international agreement to act. Unless global emissions begin to decline by 2015, there is little chance of avoiding catastrophic climate change beyond 2°C – with devastating

266

consequences for people living in poverty and appalling implications for the stability of global society and its economy. Urgency and leadership are thus central to taking action, while there is still time. Action by citizens in both North and South, allied to business sectors with a longer-term progressive vision, will be crucial to make sure that such leadership is successful. This is examined in detail in Part 5.

For poor people, climate impacts are already outpacing their ability to cope, and for them adaptation is unavoidable. But they need significant support to do it on the scale and with the speed of innovation and learning that is needed to cope with rapid and unprecedented change. Overall, making climate adaptation work requires the same kind of community-based approaches, backed by committed government policies, that work for other development issues: building human security through a combination of active, capable citizens and an effective, accountable state.

# LIVING ON THE EDGE:
## AFRICA'S PASTORALISTS

Foreign visitors to the Kenyan capital of Nairobi are used to seeing, amid the traffic jams and smog, the distinctively tall, red-cloaked forms of Maasai herdsmen on a visit to the city. The Maasai are the most internationally recognisable of the world's 100–200 million pastoralists – mobile livestock herders living in arid and semi-arid areas that constitute some of the harshest and remotest places on earth.[112]

In such hostile conditions, it is hardly surprising that pastoralists are subject to higher levels of risk and vulnerability than people living in areas where farming is a viable option. Rain is scarce, infrastructure is almost unknown (or at best dilapidated), and guns abound due to poor security. Nevertheless, there is a considerable body of evidence that pastoral livelihoods are in fact well-designed risk management and adaptation strategies.[113] Several studies have even found that economically, pastoralism compares favourably with commercial ranching.[114]

Pastoralists are not only an important and sizeable group in themselves, but their livelihood epitomises the links between poverty, risk, and vulnerability. Pastoralists are experts at risk management, showing extraordinary resilience, but all too often their efforts are undermined by the prejudice and incomprehension of governments and society at large. Pastoralists are also at the sharp end of climate change, and could provide valuable lessons in how to cope with a drier, hotter planet.

Pastoralism in the arid and semi-arid regions of Africa evolved in response to long-term climate change. When the Sahara entered a period of prolonged desiccation some 7,000 years ago, mobile live-stock herding – pastoralism – enabled people to adapt to an increasingly arid and unpredictable environment.[115] 'Shocks' such as drought are not rare events but part of the natural order, and the reason why pastoral communities live the way that they do.

Pastoralists have highly effective coping strategies to make them resilient to such risks. They integrate livestock husbandry with other activities such as farming and the extraction of minerals, dry-land timber, and forest products such as honey and gum. They co-exist with the wild animals so vital to tourism, and provide important 'environmental services' such as protecting dry-land forests and water catchments and maintaining wildlife dispersal zones outside of national parks.[116] In the Shinyanga region of Tanzania, Sukuma agro-pastoralists who own more than two million cattle in the region have, with support, reforested an estimated 250,000 hectares of once degraded land.[117]

Mobility is at the core of pastoral life, and is crucial to managing risk in harsh and unpredictable environments. By moving their cattle, goats, and sheep and negotiating the sharing and maintenance of scarce pasture and water, communities survive off large areas of range-land that lack permanent water sources. However, while pastoralists have shown their durability, they remain socially and politically margin-alised and have experienced increasing disruption, vulnerability, and suffering in recent years. Despite the increasing frequency of drought, the gravity of the current situation for pastoralist communities stems more from years of neglect and misunderstanding by central govern-ments than from the unpredictability of rainfall.

Government action in pastoral areas has often been hostile, overtly or otherwise, guided by a paradigm of rangeland management imported from the very different environmental conditions of North America. Officials and 'experts' believed that pastoralism was irrational and outdated, that land should be individually, not communally owned, that pastoralists should be settled, and that 'development' would follow. They saw pastoralism as environmentally damaging, backward, and unproductive.

Like Australia's aborigines, or Canada's Inuit, pastoralists were subject to deliberate attempts to undermine their lifestyle and culture. According to a recent Human Rights Watch report, the government of Uganda continues to flout the rights of pastoral communities through 'unlawful killings, torture and ill-treatment, arbitrary detention, and theft and destruction of property'.[118]

## PASTORALISTS AS CITIZENS

Making up a small proportion of the national population in any given country, and living in remote areas, pastoralists often lack the power and space to organise themselves effectively. Pastoral voices are not heard; local associations are often weak and frequently are co-opted by powerful elites. However, pastoralists are getting organised. Laws or charters have been passed in several countries that formally recognise pastoralism and provide a better institutional framework for the management of rangelands.[119] Many of these laws recognise the importance of mobility to the pastoral system – Mali's pastoral charter devotes a whole chapter to it.

An example from Senegal in 2005 illustrates some of the important faultlines in debates over pastoralism and shows what can be achieved through mobilisation. The country's President Wade announced on radio that he was going to sell off 3,000 hectares of the 'Doli ranch' for peanut production. This area was a key dry-season grazing area and drought refuge which, although called a ranch, was actually under the control of resident livestock herders. Following failed meetings between the prime minister and livestock producers, the president issued a decree in November 2003 transferring ownership of 44,000 hectares of the area.

Pastoralist groups responded by organising what turned out to be a very effective media campaign. They warned people living in the capital Dakar that, if the government went ahead, they would boycott all livestock markets. They also criticised the underlying rationale behind the land transfer (namely that pastoral production was out-moded and inefficient) and official attitudes towards the livestock production sector in general. The government subsequently withdrew its plans, providing pastoralists with a victory in what has become known as *'l'affaire du ranche de Doli'*.[120]

While specific campaigns will not necessarily change attitudes toward pastoralism, they illustrate the power of collective action. In East Africa, the UN Office for the Co-ordination of Humanitarian Affairs has been working to develop pastoralists' voice in Ethiopia and elsewhere. Gatherings have been organised for pastoralist representatives from across the globe to provide a space for them to share their experiences and ideas, and to engage with government and donor representatives on their own terms.

At community level, local associations help to reduce vulnerability by providing vitally important veterinary drugs and managing and improving scarce water resources. As they have gained recognition, the associations have engaged with government, advocating for better services and budgets and a greater role in conflict management. In West Africa, membership-based pastoral associations, including AREN and the sub-regional network Bilitaal, have many thousands of subscribing members, combining representative legitimacy with political clout and a degree of economic autonomy.

## FORWARD-LOOKING TRADITIONALISTS

Pastoralism, with its strong emphasis on family and clan loyalties, and on common, rather than individual, ownership of land and forests, throws down a profound challenge to many of the assumptions that underlie 'modern' governance. Whether such visions can co-exist is a test of the ability of governments and societies to recognise and encourage pluralism, rather than uniformity.

Despite widespread stereotypes that pastoralists are static and backward, pastoralists themselves recognise the need to change and adapt. As they are experienced opportunists, used to exploiting every millimetre of rainfall, their adaptability should come as no surprise. In 2007, pastoralist leaders from across Africa wrote: 'The outside world is changing rapidly, altering production methods and exchange systems, affecting the very fabric of all societies. Bearing this in mind and the fact that pastoralists are fully capable of adjustment, we are not concerned with protecting pastoralists from these changes. This would be impossible in any case. Our concern lies with the strengthening of the pastoralists' ability to adapt as well as with the broadening of their choices and opportunities.' [121]

A positive future would see those pastoralists who are active in mobile livestock production being able to combine the best of past traditions with modern technologies, such as solar-powered radios for education or satellite phones to check on market prices or outbreaks of disease.[122] Many households would also have a settled base where children would live for part of their schooling and where elderly family members would stay. Indeed, pastoralists could be among the best placed people to adapt to climate change, since they have been adapting to climate variability for millennia.[123]

In the end, though, the ability to call on the support and resources of government to assist pastoralists to respond and adapt to climate change is likely to be fundamental to their ability to cope. Many former pastoralists would move to the towns and cities, enabling families to reduce their vulnerability by diversifying their livelihoods: the point is that such migration would be a positive choice, rather than a desperate flight from drought, hunger, and violence.

This vision cannot be achieved without real changes in the relationship between pastoralists and their governments. The reasons why pastoralism is in crisis lie in the action and responses of duty-bearers, not flaws in the livelihood itself which, like any production system, needs to be understood and nurtured. To achieve genuine human security, pastoralists need the right and capacity to decide their own destinies. They also need governments to support them when times are hard.

# VIOLENCE AND CONFLICT

Humanity will not enjoy security without development, it will not enjoy development without security, and it will not enjoy either without respect for human rights.

FORMER UN SECRETARY-GENERAL KOFI ANNAN[124]

The gunmen have taken people's land, their houses, their sons, and forced their daughters to marry them. This is the nation's blood.

WOMAN, MAZAR-E-SHARIF, AFGHANISTAN[125] ·

Half a dozen black vultures darken the sky in Ursula's drawing of her old house in the Colombian countryside. 'That's maize, an apple tree – we had all sorts of fruit', she explains. 'That's a garden. That's a *golero*, a bird that eats the dead. There were lots of *goleros* where we lived.' A toothy nine-year-old, she wears red stud earrings, an array of cheap plastic bangles, and traces of varnish on her nails. Her dark Indian features grow solemn as she explains why she had to leave her farm.

*We saw everything when they shot my papa. Everything.*
*They made us go outside when they got there at 6am. When my*
*mother tried to go back in, they said, 'Get out or we'll shoot you'.*
*My brother tried to escape and they shot him, then my Dad went*
*crazy and attacked them with a machete and they shot him too.*

*My mother only cried a month or two after they buried him.*
*She was pregnant with my little sister. She said she was going to*

273

*come out all sick, but she was fat and big. She's five now and she's*
*nearly as big as me! Lots of mothers in my barrio lose their babies.*

Ursula thinks it was the guerrillas who killed her father, but she is not sure. In Colombia, death could come at the hands of the army, the police, drug gangs, paramilitary death squads, common criminals, guerrilla fighters, or street gangs. Colombia's murder rate is one of the highest in the world, more than nine times that of the USA.

The threat of violence is commonplace for people living in poverty. In their homes, women often face the threat of violence at the hands of husbands and fathers, which is often condoned by society; violence against children is even more widely accepted. The notion that children are individuals with rights, enshrined in international law since 1989 under the UN Convention on the Rights of the Child, has still to permeate many communities, leaving children the most invisible, powerless, and excluded members of society, at the mercy of parents, step-parents, and older siblings.

Outside the home, the threat of violence is also ever present, especially for women and for young men, and is often symptomatic of the lack of an effective state. Deadly violent crime is closely associated with poverty and inequality. Every country with a high annual rate of homicide (more than ten murders per 100,000 people) is either a middle- or low-income country, while most wealthy countries have lower homicide rates than the global average. The US murder rate, of 5.7 per 100,000 in 2006,[126] is a fraction of that for sub-Saharan Africa at 17–20 per 100,000. Latin America and the Caribbean, although now almost free from armed conflicts, is the world's most unequal region and has the world's highest murder rate at 25 per 100,000, rising to 61 in Colombia, where endemic violence and a 50-year-old conflict create an archetypal vicious circle.[127]

## VIOLENCE AGAINST WOMEN

Violence and the threat of violence constrain the hopes and choices of women. They sap women's energy, compromise their physical and mental health, and erode their self-esteem. The damage carries a cumulative cost to society, since abused and injured women are less able to work, care for their children, or become active citizens.

Throughout history, societies across the world have condoned violence to enforce inequality between men and women, and oblige women to conform to expectations of childbearing and child rearing and household work. It is terrifyingly widespread – enough to make women who have not experienced it personally sufficiently scared not to take risks of their own. The UN estimates that at least one in three women has been physically or sexually abused at some point in her life.[128]

The traditional view of marriage as a contract through which male-led families purchase a woman's body and her labour power remains current in many places. Far from being a haven in a heartless world, in most settings home remains the place where a woman is most at risk of violence. In parts of Africa, South Asia, and Latin America, wives are still routinely beaten to 'correct a fault', an act that many women and men view as normal. In one survey, over three-quarters of Ugandan women agreed with at least one justification for wife-beating, while in Nigeria's Zamfara state the Sharia Penal Code permits a man to beat his wife, as long as he does not cause her to be hospitalised.[129] In both developing and industrialised countries, a man's right to have sex with his wife whenever and however he wants has only very recently been questioned.

Pervasive violence outside the home also severely restricts women's participation in public life. Simply to attend an evening meeting, never mind speaking out publicly or running for office, entails risks that are too often prohibitive. While violence of this kind does not discriminate between rich and poor, wealthy women can at least reduce the risk by paying for transport or security guards.

Over the past three decades, the international women's movement has made great strides in lobbying states to criminalise violence against women. Domestic violence laws have entered the statute books and the 1979 Convention on the Elimination of All Forms of Discrimination Against Women (CEDAW) is supposed to hold states to account. Rape during conflict is now recognised as a war crime and can, in principle, be prosecuted as such. While very significant, these laws often fail to protect women. The attitudes of public officials may be quite hostile, women may lack the education or money to understand or pay for the law, and many women, particularly in rural

275

areas or among religious minorities, find that 'customary' or 'religious' law overrules civil law in cases of domestic violence.

In a number of countries, women's legal organisations visit remote areas to raise awareness that violence against women is a crime and to provide legal aid to poor women. Yet even then, women must brave the disapproval of their families or communities for blowing the whistle on these practices. Widespread changes in attitudes and beliefs that condone violence are critical.

In South Asia, the 'We Can' campaign is supporting a model of change focused on attitudes and beliefs. We Can's campaign to end violence against women works through people-to-people contact and a massive network of over 1,800 civil society organisations in Bangladesh, Sri Lanka, India, Nepal, Pakistan, and Afghanistan.[130] Individual 'change makers' sign up to the campaign, promising to change themselves and to influence their family, friends, and neighbours on the need to end domestic violence and change attitudes towards women. They are armed with some basic materials, including resources suitable for those unable to read, such as posters addressing everyday forms of violent discrimination.

In a process reminiscent of viral marketing, those they 'convert' become change makers themselves. So far, just over one million people have signed on. The campaign's target is five million change makers who will each, in turn, reach at least ten others – which the alliance hopes will be enough to achieve a critical mass that can transform power relations in the home and attitudes towards domestic violence across South Asia. Surprisingly, 40 per cent of the change makers are men, an affirmation of the campaign's premise that real change is possible, and perhaps that men too find their traditional gender roles oppressive.

Such deep transformation in entrenched beliefs is neither easy nor rapid, and not everyone supports the changes – some men boycott the meetings and criticise the women's assertiveness. But the men and women involved report enormous improvements in their family lives and a spillover effect in other areas: men's groups have started savings schemes, for example, and the number of girls going to school has risen.

The success of innovative approaches like the We Can campaign suggests that the state alone cannot solve the attitudes and beliefs side of the development equation. Activism can be a potent force for changing community social institutions that perpetuate violence against women.

## WAR

Beyond such 'social violence' lies another, more cataclysmic shock – war. The modern era is bloody on an unprecedented scale. Nearly three times as many people (110 million) were killed in conflict in the twentieth century as in the previous four centuries combined.[131] In this century there is now a 'rump' of more than 30 protracted conflicts, most of them civil wars, which have evaded attempts at resolution.[132] They grind on alongside this decade's new conflicts in Iraq, Darfur, and elsewhere. In addition, inter-communal violence, from Gujarat in India to Karamoja in Uganda, takes many lives. In 2002 and 2003 'one-sided violence', including the deliberate slaughter of civilians, was as common as armed conflict between two or more armed groups.[133] Political violence today is concentrated in developing countries where violence is as deeply entrenched as poverty and inequality.

Conflict has driven some 33 million people from their homes, 12 million of them refugees and asylum seekers, the rest internally displaced.[134] This represents a four-fold increase since the early 1970s. Flight disrupts lives for generations, but the experience varies enormously. Some people, as in Lebanon in August 2006, flee to neighbouring towns or villages for a period of weeks. Others, as in northern Sri Lanka, have fled and returned many times over the course of 20 years. Still others, such as Somalis in Kenya, have been warehoused in refugee camps for up to 15 years.

The end of the Cold War helped bring down the curtain on a number of wars and allowed major returns of refugees in Angola, Mozambique, Cambodia, Central America, and Afghanistan. At the same time, new conflicts erupted in the former Soviet republics, the Balkans, the Middle East, West Africa, the Democratic Republic of the Congo, across the Great Lakes region, and in the Horn of Africa.

Today, though the US-led wars in Afghanistan and Iraq and the Russian war in Chechnya may appear to buck the trend, poverty and greed, not geopolitics, are the common denominators in the world's wars, and domestic politics remains the crucial factor in how such conflicts play out. From 1945 to 1989, just over a third of the world's conflicts were in low-income developing countries; since then it has been more than half.[135] By 2000, some 100,000 Africans a year were being killed in wars, more than in the rest of the world's conflicts combined.[136] Countries with the lowest GDP per capita are now almost four times more likely to suffer conflicts than those with per capita GDP of $5,000 or above.[137]

Conflict is contagious, as war-torn countries drag down their neighbours with a combination of refugees, economic collapse, illegal cross-border arms trading, and violence that spills across borders, as has happened between the countries of Central and East Africa in recent years. By one calculation, the average civil war costs a country and its neighbours a phenomenal $64bn.[138]

In a devastating downward cycle, conflict destroys national economies, deepens poverty, and sows the seeds of further violence. Most of the world's poorest countries (22 out of 32) and most of the countries failing to reduce child mortality (30 out of 52) have been at war at one time or another since 1990.[139] According to one study by the International Rescue Committee, infant mortality in western DRC was only marginally worse than in the rest of sub-Saharan Africa in 2002; in the war-torn east of the country, it was twice as high.[140]

Conflict both feeds and is fed by inequality. Civil wars are generally more likely to erupt in countries that have severe and growing inequalities between ethnic or regional groups, such as those prevailing between the Hutu and Tutsi peoples prior to the Rwandan genocide of 1994. Violent crime is generally more likely where there are deep gaps between individuals, as in Latin America. In many places, both types of inequality co-exist, with devastating consequences. In turn, conflict drives up inequality because it particularly harms the weakest and most vulnerable members of society – marginalised groups such as ethnic or religious minorities, or vulnerable groups within the rest of society, such as elderly or disabled people, or children.

In the cruel calculus of war, civilians rarely remain untouched, especially if they are already poor and vulnerable. Combatants, be they insurgents or governments, routinely view civilians as potential sources of enemy support and therefore legitimate targets, no matter that international law insists on respect for civilian neutrality. Even when not deliberately targeting civilians, governments at war often restrict human rights and mechanisms of democratic accountability, thus undermining incentives to win popular support rather than coerce it through fear.

Conflict affects men, women, and children differently. In the massacres in Rwanda in 1994, or in Srebrenica, Bosnia in 1995, the majority of victims were men. Elsewhere, women and girls have borne the brunt. Of approximately 21 million internally displaced people in the world, 70–80 per cent are women and children.[141] The 2005 UN *Human Development Report* estimated that two million of the three million deaths directly related to violent conflict since 1990 were deaths of children.[142]

During armed conflict, violence against women takes on a new and even more sinister dimension when armies use mass rape and sexual enslavement as weapons of war. This sophisticated strategy kills and scars women, and inflicts deep psychological wounds on entire communities. The intent is to destroy social cohesion by impregnating women so that they bear the children of the enemy. The women who survive this act of warfare, broken and traumatised, are commonly stigmatised and rejected by their own families and communities.

In 2005, the UN reported that one region of the DRC suffered 25,000 such attacks a year.[143] In Sierra Leone, a 2002 study found that more than half the women in the country had been sexually attacked during the war that ended that year.[144] Mass rape in war has also been documented in Peru, Cambodia, Uganda, Liberia, and Somalia.[145] In Darfur, the threat of sexual violence against women is most prevalent when women leave villages or camps to collect firewood. They must choose between the threat of rape and feeding their families. (In response, Oxfam has piloted the use of fuel-efficient stoves to reduce the need to collect firewood.)

Even in democracies, the violence that one group inflicts on another is often rooted in the idea that the victims are 'the other' –

inferior on the grounds of social, ethnic, or religious difference, and therefore without the rights that the perpetrators claim for themselves. In the Moluccan islands of Indonesia in 1999 a dispute between a Muslim youth and a Christian bus-driver in Ambon city rapidly escalated into fighting that displaced 400,000 people, many of them for years. Periodic communal violence along religious lines has plagued India ever since independence.

Such prejudice can be manipulated for political gain anywhere in the world – in Colombia to legitimise the murder of civilians allegedly collaborating with guerrillas, in Darfur to set 'Arabs' against 'Africans', in Iraq to stoke conflicts between Shia and Sunni communities, and in the Western media to deny basic rights to those branded 'terrorists'. However, such divisions can be turned around through efforts by governments and the communities concerned. Since 1994, there has been remarkable progress in Rwanda in bridge building between Hutu and Tutsi communities. Similar efforts elsewhere, such as between Palestinians and Israelis, may not yet have reduced conflict, but are certainly part of any long-term solution.

In practice, there is no neat dividing line between war and peace. The self-reinforcing cycle of poverty and violence makes it particularly difficult for poor countries to escape from conflict, even after 'peace' has been officially signed. Although the DRC has supposedly been at peace since 2002, violence has continued, even after successful elections in 2006, and 2007 saw an upsurge of attacks on civilians, including mass displacements and reports of widespread sexual violence. This is far from unique: 40 per cent of countries collapse into war within five years of signing peace deals.[146] Even when all-out conflict is avoided, armed violence is a genie that is extraordinarily difficult to put back into the bottle, spilling over into domestic and sexual violence and violent crime, especially when there are no viable new livelihoods for the young men who previously lived from war. El Salvador and Guatemala, for example, ended civil wars in the 1990s, only to see a proliferation of gangs, kidnap rings, and other forms of violent crime, often involving demobilised soldiers and police.

Wars and other complex emergencies represent the failure of political leaders to resolve social and economic problems. Their failure is in part due to the inability of national governments, particularly in poor countries, to provide effective, accountable state institutions such as the rule of law, or control of national borders. This is not just about the state's *capacity* to provide these services; it is also about political leaders' *choice* as to whether or not they will do so. In many places, like southern Sudan, it is a combination of both; the region's embryonic structures are still being built up, but that does not explain away the continued failure of the Sudan People's Liberation Army to uphold the rights of children – according to recent reports some SPLA elements continue to recruit or conscript child soldiers and there are allegations of other violations of the rights of children.

In conflicts around the world, the state's security services can abuse human rights just as much as their non-state enemies – and that applies to some developed states, such as Israel, as well as developing ones. A strong state is essential, but by itself is not enough to guarantee that civilians are protected from the worst horrors of war.

Conflict both undermines states and is more likely in situations where the state is already weak or non-existent. The UK's Department for International Development (DFID) lists 46 such 'fragile states'; 35 of these were in conflict in the 1990s. On DFID's estimate, these states account for one-third of people living on less than $1 a day.[147]

Domestic factors tend to outweigh external ones in most crises, but international factors often exacerbate local problems. When global economics and politics marginalise large swathes of the world, some societies are stretched to breaking point. Climate change is already aggravating the process. According to one study in 2007, 102 countries will face an increased risk of violent conflict as climate change exacerbates the 'traditional' risks of inequality and unaccountable governance.[148]

The ready availability of weapons drastically increases the death toll of any given conflict. Arms manufacturers, from both North and South, are flooding developing countries with guns. There is one 'small arm' for every ten people on the planet and a further eight million new weapons are added every year, along with another two bullets per member of the human race.[149]

In many of today's conflicts, war has become an economically lucrative business, which political and military elites want to keep going for as long as they can. This is the 'political economy of war', a self-serving and self-sustaining system that in many instances has replaced the traditional quest for military victory. In the upper echelons, the war to control territory brings in its train the chance to extract revenue from the population, or from natural resources. At the bottom of the heap, war guarantees young men adrenalin, power, and income, while it destroys the very economy that could offer them peaceful alternative livelihoods.

Ninety-five per cent of hard drug production occurs in countries that are engulfed by civil war, i.e. in areas outside the control of a recognised government.[150] While many local conflicts, as in Darfur, involve fighting over *scarce* resources, the world's deadliest conflicts are more often fuelled by *abundant* resources. Globalisation has increased the opportunities to profit from exporting minerals, oil, and timber from war-torn areas to international markets (and is often linked to the growth in organised international crime).

Resource wealth enriches combatants and allows them to prosecute war; it has provided the continuing motive for fighting in around one-third of wars from 1990 to 2002.[151] The resources vary from country to country and include timber in Cambodia; gems and opiates in Afghanistan; natural gas in Baluchistan; diamonds in Angola, Liberia, and Sierra Leone; oil in Sudan; coca and gold in Colombia; and the lucrative combination of copper, coltan, cobalt, gold, and timber for those who continue to plunder the DRC.

## CITIZENS AND STATES BUILD PEACE

Violence, like other sources of insecurity, requires action on many fronts, but it especially requires efforts to build an effective and accountable state and to empower the individuals and communities most at risk from its depredations – poor people, women, and socially excluded groups such as ethnic and religious minorities.

Faced with a world of threat and vulnerability, poor people are far from being passive victims, although they are often forced to make almost impossible choices in juggling risks. Poor people work to address chronic violence, defuse potential conflicts, resolve them once they strike, and help each other to cope with their impact. Often religious leaders seize the initiative from combatants. In August 2002 in Nigeria's Kaduna state, the epicentre of the country's inter-communal violence where both Muslims and Christians see themselves as economically and politically marginalised, former militants from each community encouraged 20 senior religious leaders to sign a declaration of peace. Since then, these leaders have been credited with helping to restrain violence during state and federal elections, and have intervened in disputes in Kaduna schools, preventing minor arguments from turning into major incidents.[152]

Similarly, Christian church leaders in the DRC province of Maniema led their communities in calling on fighters to demobilise and disarm, helping to ease tensions between the communities and ex-combatants born of numerous instances of abuses during the fighting. Councils of respected community members, both men and women, designed reconciliation processes using traditional ceremonies. Medical and therapeutic help for women who had been raped, and the distribution of seeds and tools to revitalise the local economy, also helped to heal the scars of war.

While communities must act to protect themselves, the primary responsibility for addressing violence and armed conflict and for alleviating the suffering it causes rests with national governments. In a culmination to a decade of discussions, the UN agreed in 2005 that every government had a 'responsibility to protect' its population from genocide, war crimes, crimes against humanity, and ethnic cleansing. That responsibility 'is held, first and foremost, by national authorities', it stressed, before going on to outline the international community's role when states fail to comply (see Part 5).[153]

Governments are more likely to want to fulfil this duty, and to be able to do so, if they are accountable to the victims of conflict. Unlike famine, war has taken place in modern democracies, when irresponsible leaders exploit grievances for political and economic gain, or when the lure of 'simple' solutions overwhelms common sense. Yet democracy and an active citizenry can be an effective antidote to war, since they encourage leaders to find political rather than military answers to differences.[154]

In Colombia, which has been dogged by conflict and human rights abuses for the past 50 years, human rights activists have risked their lives by consistently challenging the government in the courts and the media, and have won some notable victories. The Constitutional

Court, for example, found the government's failure to protect internally displaced people to be unconstitutional – and in response, the government committed more than $2bn to IDPs for the period 2005–10. The state's independent Human Rights Ombudsman's office has set up a groundbreaking early-warning system to investigate allegations of abuses by civil society organisations.

Individual leaders can also make a remarkable difference. Nelson Mandela steered South Africa towards peace without retribution, while on the other side of the coin Jonas Savimbi, the Angolan rebel leader, pursued a relentless war until his death in 2002, after which a peace deal was agreed.

Besides avoiding messages of hate and division, governments need to ensure peaceful livelihoods for those who, without them, are most likely to turn to violence. From Haiti to Sierra Leone, governments have proved better at disarmament and demobilisation than at the third task, reintegration of former fighters into peaceful society. All too easily, demobilised combatants drift into lives of banditry or crime. The reintegration into society of young women involved in conflict as fighters or sex workers is often forgotten by the authorities, and is complicated by the social stigma attached to their wartime activities.

Many conflicts are born of felt grievances and are rooted in long-standing inequalities, and can only be resolved with measures that address the roots of discontent. Societies torn asunder by social, economic, or political exclusion will not achieve peace unless they seek, and find, genuine political solutions. The opposite approach to resolving conflict – seeking outright military victory – may seem superficially attractive, but it is never easy and can condemn a country to protracted pain. When warring parties seek that victory at all costs, ignoring the restraint that international humanitarian law demands, they fuel a cycle of atrocities that makes peace very much more difficult to find.

The conflict between Israel and the Palestinians demonstrates all too clearly how a vicious circle of violence sustains the very fear and hostility that make peace so difficult to achieve. Rooted in Israel's occupation and its treatment of Palestinians, the 60-year conflict is sustained by a cycle of atrocities committed by both sides that, since the start of the second Palestinian uprising in 2000, has cost the lives of over 4,000 Palestinians and 1,000 Israelis, including in total 900 children.[155]

The occupation that lies at the heart of the conflict continues. Nearly half-a-million Israeli settlers have illegally transferred into East Jerusalem and the West Bank. Two-and-a-half million Palestinians living there have been denied access to 40 per cent of the land, 90 per cent of water resources, and 1,600km of roads.[156] The panoply of Israeli restrictions – checkpoints, permits, closures, and the 'Wall' that cuts through the West Bank – destroys Palestinians' lives and livelihoods, and prevents thousands of people from taking their products to market.

Of course, negotiating an end to conflict is never easy, but one of the more encouraging trends of recent years is that most conflicts that are resolved are resolved peacefully. For most of the twentieth century, the most common way of ending wars was through outright victory, often at enormous human cost. Since the end of the Cold War, that seems to have changed. Sadly, most mediation efforts still fail, but between 2000 and 2005, peaceful mediation ended 17 conflicts, whereas only four were concluded by military victory. The empirical evidence that it is worth giving peace a chance is getting stronger.[157]

In preventing and resolving conflict, huge responsibilities also lie with rich-country governments. They share the responsibility to protect civilians, and their own actions often fuel conflicts, for example through their hunger for natural resources, their refusal to receive refugees, their unbridled arms production and exports, or the destabilising impact of the 'war on terror'. These issues are discussed in Part 5.

# SHOCKS AND CHANGE

For better or worse, shocks, whether wars, natural disasters, or economic crises, change history, but most development thinking is essentially gradualist, attempting to promote reform and progress within existing institutions and systems. It therefore ignores the possibility of sudden shifts and struggles to understand the link between social and political upheaval and change. The World Bank, for example, portrays war as 'development in reverse', whereas conflict has unpredictable consequences for development, triggering anything from human catastrophe and state collapse to economic modernisation – for example in Mozambique, where war accelerated a shift from subsistence to waged agriculture.[158]

Moreover, the weeks and months after a conflict ends are a crucial 'moment of opportunity' when, amid the chaos of disarmament, often violent elections, and feuds over political power, new institutions take shape, resources are allocated, and the peacetime order emerges. It is then that previously marginalised voices can make themselves heard – but they are all too often ignored, missing a chance to engage still-emerging political systems in tackling inequality and exclusion.

Disasters are also 'political moments' that can make as well as break movements for change. They highlight corruption and political bias: in Nicaragua, popular outrage at the theft of relief money by the Somoza dictatorship after the earthquake of 1972 was a 'tipping point'

286

in the upsurge of protest that led to the Sandinista Revolution seven years later. The feeble response of the Mexican authorities to the earthquake of 1985 galvanised independent social movements and weakened the stranglehold of the Institutional Revolutionary Party, which had ruled the country since 1929. Catastrophic famines in Bangladesh in 1971 and in Ethiopia in 1985 led respectively to independence and the fall of a dictatorship.

The 2004 Asian tsunami set the stage for a resumption of peace talks between the separatist Free Aceh Movement (Gerakan Aceh Merdeka, or GAM) and the Indonesian government, culminating in the signing of a peace agreement in August 2005 that officially brought a 30-year conflict to an end. The historic peace deal was followed quickly by the release of Acehnese political prisoners, the withdrawal of government troops from the province, the decommissioning of rebel-held weapons, and the establishment of a government authority to oversee the reintegration of ex-combatants and co-ordinate assistance for conflict-affected communities. The following year saw a far-reaching autonomy law, giving the long-neglected province control over its natural resources.

On closer examination, even gradual change often turns out to have been a series of small shifts in which shocks played an important role. Key moments in the steady spread of women's suffrage in Europe, for example, came after wars had redrawn social relations, sending women out into newly independent roles in the workplace.

Heraclitus believed that 'war is the father of all things'. Modern observers might not be so militaristic, but conflict is undoubtedly a major source of political and social upheaval, not all of which is negative, as the creation of the European welfare states following the Second World War demonstrates. War or other disasters hardly constitute a path to change for which reasonable people would advocate, because of the immediate human cost and because the changes that emerge are just as likely to be negative as positive. The point rather is to recognise the potential of shocks to bring about change and to seize the 'moments of opportunity' that arise, to encourage positive changes and to prevent negative ones.

This raises challenging questions for the aid community about how to respond to wars, natural disasters, or political upheavals.

Major changes (both good and bad) that would normally take decades to happen may occur in weeks or months. Should humanitarian and development practitioners respond differently to promote wider systemic change, embrace new approaches to old problems, or encourage shifts in positions and alliances of political actors and movements for change?

Clearly there is a need to re-evaluate the division between a 'humanitarian' approach to shocks (governed by the strictly neutral imperative to save lives) and the 'development' approach to peacetime (driven by the often political support for social change), appreciating how the seeds of vulnerability to shocks are sown through bad peace-time development models, and the role of shocks in triggering long-term change.

## BUILDING REAL SECURITY

All of us, but particularly people living in poverty, experience a bewildering and ever-changing world of risk and vulnerability. New threats such as climate change or HIV join ancestral fears of illness, hunger, poverty, and violence. Still other threats will doubtless appear in coming decades. In this complex and uncertain scene, 'security' is about much more than the absence of war or terrorism. In the lives of vulnerable individuals and communities, security covers a great span of daily anxiety and risk.

Given the high price of inaction on climate change, violence, hunger, and disease, a combination of public pressure and far-sighted leadership is urgently needed, in both North and South. Vulnerable people must be equipped to cope with risk, by strengthening their own capabilities and by building the state's capacity to provide support and protection.

The concept of human security offers an invaluable compass in this task, as well as the seed for a new model of development. At a national level, governments need to understand security as an essential aspect of development that guarantees human dignity. Easing human suffering by addressing the causes of vulnerability and anxiety should be central to economic and social policy making. The growth mono-mania of recent decades is self-defeating (it has not delivered better economic growth) and is insufficient. Governments need to generate sufficient resources to get the job done, in terms of volume and predictability and from both domestic taxation and international aid. They also need to build effective and honest civil services with the skills to manage complex processes, such as social protection, disaster risk reduction, and environmental and social adaptation. Moreover, they need the freedom to make the right decisions, without excessive interference from international financial institutions, aid donors, or vested interests, whether local or global.

Creating the political will to build and then use this capacity wisely is a major challenge. The greatest source of hope lies in the long-term improvements in governance, such as the spread in recent decades of critical media, multi-party democracy, and an active civil society, all of which increase the pressure on governments to work for the benefit of their people. The extent of these changes is assessed in Part 2.

For rich-country governments, corporations, and other bodies to contribute positively to this effort – or at a minimum to do no harm – a shift in mentality is required at both government and corporate level, away from seeking short-term profit and toward the pursuit of the longer-term benefits that accrue from stability and prosperity. Some governments have broadened their conception of the national interest to recognise, first, that security for one state and one group of people depends on the security of others in many parts of the world; and second, that states or intergovernmental bodies such as the European Union, which derive their internal legitimacy from their respect for universal rights, must for their own credibility and coherence act consistently to uphold those rights everywhere in the world. The role of the international community in human security is examined in Part 5.

Progress on building the capacities of people and governments to reduce vulnerability will not come about simply through the jockeying and evolution of political and economic self-interest. Change is a much deeper process, involving ideas and beliefs and our changing understanding of rights and responsibilities, of what is natural, desirable, or acceptable. The vulnerability and anxiety that blights too many lives, especially those of poor people, must become unacceptable in every country, just as slavery or women's exclusion from the vote passed from being 'natural' to 'wrong' in the public mind. In building a new global solidarity with and among poor people, tackling risk and vulnerability must be considered as urgent and necessary a task as ending hunger and poverty.

# WHO RULES THE WORLD?

Global institutions such as the World Bank, the IMF, and the United Nations, transnational corporations, rich-country governments (and even international non-government organisations such as Oxfam) are sometimes viewed as the most powerful and dynamic forces in the fight against poverty and inequality. This book has argued, on the contrary, that the main actors are poor men and women and their national governments – a combination we have called active citizens and effective states.

This is not to deny the power of global institutions. In tackling global poverty and inequality they can, by both action and omission, be either part of the solution or part of the problem. They can foster efforts to build an effective, accountable state and an active citizenry, or they can undermine or even crush them. This part of the book examines those aspects of the international system most relevant to the fight against poverty and inequality, and explores how global institutions can be placed at the service of development.

The web of international institutions, laws, regulations, and agreements collectively known as 'global governance' is constantly growing in range and density. Global governance can help the fight against poverty and inequality in eight main ways:

- Managing the global economy through, for example, rules on trade and investment;

- Co-ordinating the systemically important countries, for example through the Group of Eight (G8), to manage the functioning of international financial markets;
- Redistributing wealth, technology, and knowledge through aid or other mechanisms, such as international taxation;
- Averting environmental or health threats, through agreements such as the Montreal Protocol (on ozone depletion) and the Kyoto Protocol on climate change, or through institutions such as the World Health Organization or UNAIDS;
- Avoiding war and limiting abuses during war by providing a forum for negotiation of differences, and upholding the body of international humanitarian law, such as the Geneva Conventions;
- Preventing powerful countries or corporations from harming weaker and poorer ones. This 'stop doing harm' agenda includes regulating the arms trade, carbon emissions, corruption, and destructive trade policies;
- Providing a safety net for the most vulnerable people when disaster strikes and states are unable or unwilling to cope, as through the relief work of UN agencies or the international community's embrace of the 'responsibility to protect';
- Changing attitudes and beliefs, for example through the Convention on the Elimination of Discrimination Against Women (CEDAW) or the Convention on the Rights of the Child.

Unfortunately, global governance often fails to live up to these high ideals. Whether by using aid for short-term political purposes, waging war rather than averting it, or using regional trade agreements to impose economic straitjackets rather than the freedom to pursue wise development policies, the misguided actions of global institutions and the short-sighted policies of wealthy countries often pose threats to development. The whole project of multilateralism – the nations of the world working in concert to address its many challenges and problems – was dealt a severe setback when the invasion of Iraq bypassed the UN system.

Powerful states are inevitably tempted to bend institutions of global governance, but they do not always succeed. Public pressure can persuade the more enlightened leaders to put building a stable and fair global system ahead of their own short-term self-interest. Moreover, the rule of law through international institutions can become capable of influencing even the most powerful of nations as, for example, when the WTO ruled against US cotton subsidies in 2005 because of the damage they do to producers in other countries.

The global balance of power is shifting rapidly, as the world enters what some have hailed as the 'Asian Century'. A new 'global middle class' of increasingly assertive developing countries, led by China and India, is challenging the dominance of Europe and North America in global institutions, while a range of regional organisations and initiatives such as the African Union or the Shanghai Cooperation Organisation is creating a more varied political geography than the traditional global–national divide.

Global governance systems must adjust, and rapidly, to this new geometry of power, and yet the WTO is frozen, regional trade agreements are proliferating and introducing profoundly unfair trade and investment rules, the G8 is failing to keep its promises on aid, and the threat of climate change dwarfs the pallid attempts at an international response. At the time of writing, a looming financial crisis hangs over the global economy, threatening an even greater test of the ability of global institutions to cope with change and instability. This century, humanity will either sink or learn to swim together.

# THE INTERNATIONAL FINANCIAL SYSTEM

## THE WORLD BANK AND THE INTERNATIONAL MONETARY FUND

In 2005, the World Bank and the International Monetary Fund (IMF) told the government of the impoverished West African nation of Mali that it would have to privatise its energy companies and its major export sector, cotton, if it expected to see any loans or credits. Mali's President Amadou Toumani Touré went to Washington to plead his country's case, but later could only lament: 'People who have never seen cotton come to give us lessons on cotton...No one can respect the conditionalities of certain donors. They are so complicated that they themselves have difficulty getting us to understand them. This is not a partnership. This is a master relating to his student.'[1]

The ensuing liberalisation of the cotton sector left Malian cotton farmers exposed to world cotton markets, where prices are artificially suppressed by massive US and EU subsidies, and they received 20 per cent less for their cotton in 2005 than in the previous year. Combined with unfavourable exchange rates, rising input prices, and late rains in 2007, the result has been devastating, with thousands of farmers running up unpayable debts and some leaving cotton farming altogether. Production in 2007–08 collapsed to half its previous level.[2]

The acronyms of faceless international organisations do not usually start riots, but the three letters IMF provoke explosive reactions.

Throughout the 1980s and 1990s, 'IMF riots' periodically ravaged cities throughout the developing world, leaving hundreds of people dead and wounded and losses of millions of dollars in damaged and looted property. In the South Korean financial crisis of 1998, restaurants offered cut-price 'IMF menus' to the newly unemployed, who protested with placards carrying the eye-catching slogan 'IMF = I'm Fired'.

For much of the past 25 years the IMF and the World Bank have been pursuing nothing less than a radical overhaul of the way that developing countries run their economies. That role has been hugely controversial and, in many eyes, profoundly destructive. Bloodied by failure and a chorus of criticism from both left and right, the institutions stand at a crossroads: confused, divided, and (in the case of the Fund) increasingly ignored by the more powerful developing countries, yet they remain a central cog in the machinery of global governance. This section explores how they got here, and what needs to happen next.

The international financial institutions (IFIs) – chief among them the World Bank and IMF, but also including regional development banks and other institutions – are most influential in the poorest countries, which are largely isolated from other sources of international capital. Better-off middle-income countries can often turn to banks or other sources of capital, but have to resort to the IFIs in the event of a financial crisis. More generally, the IFIs exert enormous influence through their role as gatekeepers of other donor lending and as sources of research and technical assistance, which helps them determine what are considered 'sound' policies in the aid world and in many developing-country governments.

The IMF and the World Bank were born in July 1944 in Bretton Woods, New Hampshire, when the outcome of the Second World War was already evident. The new institutions formed part of an attempt by the victorious powers to prevent a repeat of the global economic collapse of the 1930s, which had sown the seeds of war. While constitutionally part of the UN system, the giant multilateral financial organisations were set up in a radically different manner. While the UN system works largely on a 'one country, one vote' principle (with the notable exception of the Security Council), in general decisions at the IMF and World Bank are taken on the basis of 'one dollar, one vote', guaranteeing the dominance of the USA and other major donors.[3] At US insistence, the organisations were located in Washington, within walking distance of the White House, rather than with the UN in New York.

The Fund and Bank were arguably given the wrong names at birth. The IMF is supposed to lend money like a bank when financial crises threaten, while the World Bank funds projects and government reform programmes to address longer-term development issues. The two institutions were created not to feed global markets but to step in where markets failed, in order to mitigate the harsh effects of global capitalism.[4]

At first, they confined their attentions to rebuilding Europe with loans to Denmark, France, and Holland. As Europe began to recover, they began to look farther afield. The Bank's first loan to a developing country went to Chile in 1948. However, it was the breakdown in the early 1970s of the system of fixed exchange rates, followed by the onset of a global debt crisis in the early 1980s, that catapulted the Fund and Bank to global prominence. Across large swathes of Latin America, Africa, and Asia, governments had run up large debts and then saw interest rates spiral just as the prices of their exports collapsed. Desperate to reschedule their debts and find new sources of capital, they turned to the Fund and the Bank.

In return for loans, the two IFIs demanded far-reaching reforms, disguised by bland euphemisms such as 'stabilisation' and 'structural adjustment'. Acceptance of such policy reforms quickly became a litmus test for countries to access development assistance from donors, turning the Bank and the Fund into the gatekeepers of the global financial system.

Although Nineteenth Street in Washington DC, which separates the two institutions, is a border of fierce institutional rivalry, the Fund and Bank largely shared the same DNA of economic orthodoxy. They both believed that the underlying problems of developing countries sprang largely from a mistaken, state-centred development model that ran out of steam in the 1970s, echoing the anti-state 'Reaganomics' and 'Thatcherism' of the time. The ultimate foe was price inflation; the broad solution was 'less state, more market'. The programme was stabilisation by cutting state spending to reduce inflationary pressures, followed by structural adjustment – a mix of deregulation and liberalisation designed to unleash the 'animal spirits' of the market.

With only minor variations, this recipe – dubbed 'the Washington Consensus' – was implemented across dozens of countries in Latin America and Africa.[5] Home-grown economists and politicians who shared a belief in the diagnosis and the proposed cure led the way, deploying the powerful leverage exercised by the Fund and Bank to push through unpopular reforms.

If structural adjustment were a medicine, it would long ago have been banned due to its adverse side effects. From 1960–80, sub-Saharan Africa's 'failed' statist economic model grew at an annual per capita rate of 1.6 per cent. At the time these figures were seen as scandalously low, but in hindsight they look like a golden age. From 1990–2005, Africa's GDP grew by an annual per capita rate of only 0.5 per cent.[6] In Latin America, the 1980s became known as the 'lost decade' of development. In Russia, 'shock therapy' reduced people's life expectancy by four years from 1990–2000, and incomes plummeted by a third. In China and Viet Nam, however, which rejected the Bank and Fund's policy prescriptions in favour of a more cautious and partial transition to a market economy, incomes increased by 135 per cent and 75 per cent respectively during the same years.[7]

Tellingly, even the man who coined the term 'Washington Consensus' later stressed: 'I never thought of the Washington Consensus as a policy manifesto, for it omitted a number of things that seemed to me important, most notably a concern for income distribution as well as for rapid growth.'[8] And so it proved: rising inequality became one of the most alarming features of stabilisation and structural adjustment.

One of the most ambitious reviews of the impact of these policy reforms on the ground was carried out by a network of NGOs, trade unions, and academics in a dozen countries that had gone through World Bank-funded adjustment programmes. Using a methodology jointly designed with the Bank, the Structural Adjustment Participatory Review Initiative (SAPRI) involved thousands of local organisations participating in national field exercises on four continents, the majority of which were carried out jointly with the Bank and national governments.

Its conclusions, published in April 2002, were damning:[9]

**Trade liberalisation** has led to growing trade deficits, export growth typically based on natural resources and low-skilled labour, and the failure of many local manufacturing firms, particularly innovative small and medium-sized ones that generate a great deal of employment. Transnational corporations have often been the principal beneficiaries.

**Financial sector liberalisation** has directed financing toward large (usually urban) firms, with the largest share of loans going to a few powerful economic agents. Small and medium-sized firms, rural and indigenous producers, and women are largely excluded from borrowing, thereby exacerbating existing inequalities.

**Labour market reforms** have led to fewer regulations concerning labour stability and firing practices, thus facilitating the widespread use of temporary contracts and leaving workers with little recourse when employers choose to cut back their workforce. Labour rights have been affected by restrictions placed on the right to strike and to bargain collectively.

**Privatisation** has earned mixed reviews. Civil society groups drew a distinction between enterprises involved in production (where privatisation sometimes made economic sense) and those delivering basic services, such as water and electricity (where access to affordable, quality services did not improve for the societies as a whole and, in some cases, worsened). In El Salvador, for example, poor consumers saw their bills rise at nearly twice the rate of increases for high-end consumers.

**Agricultural reforms** have generally included the removal of subsidies on agricultural inputs and credit, liberalisation of producer prices, privatisation of state entities involved in marketing and distribution of inputs and produce, liberalisation of trade in agricultural inputs and commodities, and currency devaluation. For example, in the first half of the 1990s the World Bank and the IMF required that the state marketing board in Zambia be abolished, all maize and fertiliser
subsidies removed, and price control ended.[10] Although some reforms of state systems were clearly required, only those producers with previous access to resources and economies of scale have been able to benefit, and markets have often failed to fill the gap left by the retreating state.[11]

When critics raise these issues, the response of the IFIs is usually, 'We have changed; these criticisms are out of date'. Indeed, the way the Bank in particular works and thinks has moved on significantly (the Fund is more resistant to change). In response to criticisms, both internal and external, the Bank pays much more attention to process, working closely with civil society organisations on topics such as social inclusion and accountability that would have cut little ice at the height of the Washington Consensus in the 1980s and early 1990s. Unfortunately, Oxfam's experience has been that this change in attitude to process has not always been matched by changes in policy advice to governments. In particular, in the case of economic conditionality, while there has been a reduction in the number of prior actions and triggers attached to World Bank lending that specify economic policy reforms, conditions still routinely push specific economic policies. That experience has been borne out by the findings of numerous external evaluations, suggesting that the barriers to change are not just intellectual but political and institutional, and that deeper reform of the IFIs is urgently needed.

In response to increasing evidence of the failure of adjustment to deliver growth and poverty reduction, and to the widespread public condemnation generated by the Jubilee 2000 campaign, in September 1999 the Fund and the Bank announced that poverty reduction would be placed at the heart of their policy design. They agreed that 'nationally-owned participatory poverty reduction strategies should provide the basis of all their concessional lending and debt relief'. In time, lending by both institutions would be based on Poverty Reduction Strategy Papers (PRSPs), drawn up by country authorities for submission to the Bank and Fund Boards. The IMF duly renamed its Enhanced Structural Adjustment Facility as the new, more wholesome-sounding, Poverty Reduction and Growth Facility (PRGF).

The Bank and, to a lesser extent, the Fund publicly acknowledge that imposing a string of economic policy conditions on governments does not work. The Bank in particular has promised to greatly reduce the number of conditions it imposes, base them on assessments of their likely impact on poverty, and support only those that enjoy government 'ownership'. Practice has fallen far short of official policy, however. Undertaking impact assessments to check what the effect will be on the poorest people, before any major reform is recommended, is now official policy for both the Bank and the Fund – but too often this analysis does not happen, or does not really influence the policy that the IFIs finally recommend or attach as a condition to a loan.[12]

While some progress has been made in reducing the overly specific and often damaging conditions attached to Bank loans, in the case of PRSPs civil society organisations are consulted when it comes to 'soft' items concerning public spending but are often not invited when the subject turns to broader economic policy issues. For the first draft of Armenia's PRSP, for instance, a group of young economists from the Economic Development Research Centre (EDRC), a civil society organisation, worked closely with the ministry of finance to set targets for reducing inequality as well as for increased growth. When the second draft was released in May 2003, these targets had been unceremoniously dropped in favour of figures agreed with the IMF under the PRGF agreement.[13]

An evaluation of the involvement with PRSPs of Oxfam's civil society partners in 33 countries concluded that the design of the agreements was undermining both citizens' organisations and the effort to strengthen institutions such as parliaments and political parties. The report found that 'consultation' was a more appropriate description than 'participation' in almost all cases. Important stakeholders, both powerful ones such as elected politicians and powerless ones such as rural women, had rarely been involved; and donors maintained far too much control over policy content, employing conditionality and 'backstage' negotiation to the detriment of participation processes.[14]

When the World Bank surveyed poor-country government staff in 2005, 50 per cent still felt that 'the Bank introduced elements that were not part of the country programme',[15] and a 2006 study by the Norwegian government of IMF conditionality revealed that 23 out of 40 poor countries still had privatisation and liberalisation conditions attached to their IMF loans.

There has also been some policy reform over the road at the IMF. In 2007, the Fund announced that it would be less conservative in its policy advice to low-income countries and would accept that they needed to spend in order to grow. However, while the Bank and the

Fund now both acknowledge the crucial role of essential services such as health, education, water, and sanitation, the IMF refuses to rule out completely the imposition of limits on total government spending on wages, such as for new teachers and nurses, far beyond the requirements of macroeconomic stability.[16] Economist Joseph Stiglitz argues that the Bank and Fund are still prey to a 'fixation on single low digit inflation.'[17] In July 2007, the Fund's executive board agreed that wage bill ceilings would 'be used only in exceptional cases,' but it has failed to specify what such circumstances would be and it remains to be seen whether this new policy will be respected in future negotiations.[18]

Numerous different currents of opinion can be found among the World Bank's staff, some of whom have produced groundbreaking critiques of structural adjustment and insights into the lives of poor people (some of them quoted in this book).[19] The Bank's social development advisers often differ with its economists on the relative importance of empowerment and economic orthodoxy in bringing about development, and debates are often heated. However, a study of the Bank's system for categorising 'effective states' suggests that its liberalising DNA is largely intact. Its CPIA (Country Performance and Institutional Assessment) purports to be an objective indicator of the quality of a country's institutions, and is often used by donors to allocate aid. But to get a high score, a country needs to reduce import tariffs to less than 7 per cent and to have low levels of public debt, as well as labour laws that allow workers to be hired and fired at low cost. Such recipes owe much more to ideology and bias than to any historical evidence of what works for development.

Any visitor to the Bank or Fund will soon realise that their staffs are hardworking and smart, and genuinely committed to promoting growth and poverty reduction in developing countries. So why does the sum of their actions fall so far short of their shared aspirations? Three powerful forces largely determine the intellectual and policy inertia that holds back efforts to learn from the failures of adjustment and to change the way that the Fund and the Bank work:

**The power of their shareholders**: The USA and, to a lesser extent, the other rich countries exert huge influence through their positions on the boards of both organisations, and often use their position to promote their own national interests: for example, liberalisation programmes typically provide improved access for rich-country investors and exporters.

**Their choice of economic frameworks**: There are many other possible responses to sluggish growth and inflation, but the orthodox approach is overwhelmingly dominant, with more heterodox economists facing hostility and criticism.

**The institutional pressures of bureaucracy**: As in any institution, staff concern for career and salary leads to a high level of conformity and conservatism. If you follow the standard recipe and things go wrong, it is the institution's fault; if you try something different and it doesn't work, the buck stops with you.[20]

As the Bank and Fund try to reconcile political pressure, public disenchantment, and the fierce academic debates over their policies, doubts and confusion abound over their future roles. Large developing countries such as the BRIC group of Brazil, Russia, India, and China no longer depend on the Fund for sources of capital (although they engage with the Bank for both loans and policy advice on issues such as climate change). Latin America and East Asia have sought to build regional alternatives. Venezuela and Argentina have proposed a 'Bank of the South', which would initially fund regional infrastructure projects such as oil and gas pipelines, but could take on a more overarching role. And at a meeting of ASEAN+3 finance ministers in Kyoto in 2007, the countries of East Asia agreed to press ahead with an $80bn regional currency swap arrangement that looks remarkably like an Asian Monetary Fund.

While the Bank has proved more agile in finding new roles for itself, for example through its enormous output of research and policy advice, the Fund seems particularly becalmed. George Schultz, treasury secretary under US President Gerald Ford, put it this way: 'If it disappeared tomorrow, I don't think people would miss it very much.'[21] Schultz's statement could perhaps be more usefully rephrased as a question: 'In today's world, if the IFIs did not exist, would it be necessary to create them?' The answer to that is far from clear. Multilateral approaches that manage to avoid excessive control by the major powers provide a source of loans and technical and policy advice that governments find useful. Some parts of the World Bank family, such as the regional development banks, may need to become more prominent. But to remain both relevant and useful, the IFIs must assert their independence from their larger shareholders and place themselves at the service of their customers.

Where effective states are able to insist on sensible policies, rather than succumb to pressures to follow Washington Consensus blueprints, the Fund and Bank could play a positive supporting role:

- The World Bank could strengthen its support for 'global public goods', such as technological advances in health or agriculture, where it should work with UN bodies and other elements of the international system. In these areas, national governments or individual companies may not have sufficient incentives to invest, since the benefits (or harm) accrue to everyone rather than just to their own country or firm. Although the Bank is moving into these areas, to date it has done so in an ad hoc and chaotic fashion, setting up some 70 separate trust funds for work on different issues, with little overall sense of direction or priority.[22]

- The Bank and the Fund could isolate policy advice and research from lending. The institutions' policy advice is hugely influential but is akin to 'tied aid', in that it comes attached to loans and financial dependence.[23] Research and policy advice could be required to stand on their own merits by giving developing-country governments 'technical assistance vouchers' that they could cash in with the most suitable provider, whether the World Bank, another UN body, or a university. Another idea would be to split up the Bank's policy department, move the parts to various developing countries, and require them to compete for business.

- The Fund should concentrate much more on monitoring the national economic policies of those systemically important countries that could threaten global financial stability, even though the developed countries have in recent decades remained sublimely indifferent to IMF criticism.[24]

- To get real reform under way, donor governments should stop making their own aid conditional on countries having a Fund or Bank programme in place. Giving the IFIs such exaggerated influence as 'gatekeepers' is neither warranted by their past performance nor helpful in encouraging policy pluralism and national ownership.

- Donor governments will also have to drive reform of the institutions themselves, starting with their governing bodies. In the concessional lending arm of the World Bank, for example, sub-Saharan African countries represent 27 per cent of all member countries but have only 8 per cent of the votes. Canada and Italy have the same voting shares as China, and Belgium has 50 per cent more votes than Mexico.[25] Moreover, the heads of the Fund and the Bank are still political appointees of, respectively, the EU and the USA. Until a meritocratic appointments system is introduced, it is hard to see why any developing country should turn to the IFIs for advice on good governance. At a staff level, the Bank and Fund also need to improve their grasp of politics and social change, if they are to support country-led processes rather than impose economic blueprints.

The World Bank and the International Monetary Fund stand at a historic crossroads, similar to that which they faced after the collapse of the fixed exchange rate system in the 1970s. How they chart a new course will determine both their future relevance and their contribution (whether positive or negative) to the global effort to tackle poverty and inequality.

## DEBT CRISES

Debt is a key reason why the international financial institutions exert so much leverage over poor countries. In Dickensian Britain, the debtors' prison awaited those who could not meet their personal or business debts. Bankruptcy procedures finally superseded such grim establishments, allowing individuals to clear their debts and rebuild their lives. Countries that default on their foreign borrowing, however, until very recently faced a similar fate: an interminable process of restructuring, dried-up access to credit, and painful squeezes on public spending, with a drastic impact on poor people.

There are at least three different sorts of crisis involving debt, each of which requires a different response. First, in very poor countries the crisis consists mostly of unmanageable debts owed by the national government to creditor governments and to the IFIs (although some of these have come from loans to pay off private creditors). In middle-income 'emerging markets', where private lenders have lent to private borrowers, a mass default can threaten the whole economy, as occurred in several East Asian countries in the late 1990s. And finally, in middle-income countries crises can be due to government borrowing from a mix of private and public creditors, as in Argentina in 2002. The first case is a chronic problem, built up over years and popularly known as a 'debt crisis', while the others are sudden-onset disasters related to capital markets and are known more commonly as 'financial crises'. The former will be discussed here, and the latter addressed later in this section.

Until the mid 1990s, rich countries adopted a standard approach to debt crises in both poor and middle-income countries, based on three principles: first, multilateral debt (i.e. that owed to the IFIs) must always be serviced, while other debts could be rescheduled; second, negotiations must be undertaken on a 'case by case' approach, in which creditors negotiate jointly as a group but borrower countries have to face their creditors alone; and third, structural adjustment conditions are to be part of every rescheduling deal. The core aim of this approach was to keep countries from defaulting. In practice this meant drastic cuts to public spending, which was repeatedly slashed in the middle of economic crises to keep repayments flowing to Western banks and credit institutions.

Debt crises thus produced a perverse flow of resources from poor to rich – a society-wide squeeze familiar to anyone who has ever taken out a bank loan. During the 'lost decade' of the 1980s, Latin America sent the rich world over $500 for every man, woman, and child on the continent, even as growth slumped and poverty grew.[26]

In the face of public protest, and as structural adjustment failed to trigger sufficient growth even to stave off default, creditor governments and the IFIs embarked on a series of debt relief initiatives that grew in coverage as each in turn failed to solve the problem. The international community introduced the Heavily Indebted Poor Countries Debt Reduction Initiative (HIPC for short) in 1996, its Enhanced version (often known as HIPC II) in 1999, and the Multilateral Debt Relief Initiative (MDRI) in 2005; each was more comprehensive than the last.

Active citizens played a large role in obliging governments in both rich and poor countries to move on the debt issue. The Freedom from Debt Coalition in the Philippines and Koalisi Anti Utang in Indonesia both campaigned against 'illegitimate debt'. In May 1998, 70,000 Jubilee 2000 supporters formed a human chain around the G8 summit in Birmingham, UK and – as politicians inside the meeting later confirmed – forced debt onto the summit agenda, which culminated in the Enhanced HIPC programme a year later. Global campaigning by Make Poverty History and the Global Call to Action against Poverty achieved a similar breakthrough at the G8 summit in Scotland in 2005. Each time, governments swore that the latest debt relief initiative would be the last. Luckily, citizens refused to believe them and, when the plight of debtor nations failed to improve, continued to campaign for more.

Naturally, creditors continued to try to set the terms of the negotiations, but effective states proved themselves able to negotiate better terms. Argentina played hardball with the IMF and other creditors after its 2002 crisis, and was thus able to rebuild its economy at record speed.

With HIPC, the creditors began to break new ground by actually writing off debts, rather than simply rescheduling them; by including multilateral, rather than just bilateral, debt; by dividing relief equitably among creditors; and, in the Enhanced HIPC initiative, by basing debt relief on a 'poverty reduction strategy' drawn up by the government in consultation with civil society (see page 301). The most recent incarnation, the MDRI, has gone still further by offering full cancellation of countries' debts to the IFIs incurred up to certain dates, a limited application of the '100 per cent cancellation' that campaigners had long called for and which creditors had long claimed was impossible.

Serious concerns remain about both the HIPC and the MDRI, not least the extent to which they have entrenched the force of, in particular, IMF conditions. Countries must comply with these to get debt relief, which forces them to spend years implementing painful structural adjustment policies in order to access the debt cancellation that was promised to them as a solution to an urgent crisis. This is connected to the fact that the HIPC and the MDRI are designed, implemented, and monitored by the IFIs, with creditors treated as generous benefactors

– rather than those responsible for often irresponsible or self-interested lending that contributed to the crisis in the first place – and debtors as errant children who need to behave.

Nonetheless, debt relief has translated into big money. The total debt relief for the 22 countries that had completed HIPC by mid-2007 is estimated to be worth $70.7bn in today's money, combining agreements with multilateral institutions and bilateral and commercial creditors. Because it directly frees up funds for governments to spend over many years, debt relief is a very efficient form of aid: the additional debt relief agreed in 2005 provided these countries with an estimated $1.3bn of extra funds in 2007 alone.[27]

It should be remembered, however, that debt relief is often dwarfed by the amount that poor countries have already paid on these loans. In 2004, the Nigerian government reported that the country had had original loans of $17bn, had repaid $18bn, and still owed $34bn. Its much-trumpeted 2005 debt-relief deal finally led to significant debt cancellation, but the deal required the country to make a down payment of a further $12bn.[28]

Indebted countries face new threats in the shape of so-called 'vulture funds'. In 1999, as Zambia was trying to negotiate clearance of the debt it owed to Romania, a company called Donegal International, registered in the tax haven of the British Virgin Islands, swooped in and bought up the debt – then valued at around $30m with accrued interest – for a knockdown price of $3.3m. The company then sued Zambia in the UK courts for the full amount of the debt, plus compound interest, demanding a staggering $55m in total. In the end the judge ordered the Zambian government to hand over $15.5m.

So far at least 40 such lawsuits have been launched by vulture funds against highly indebted poor countries, and many of them are still outstanding. The debts known to be subject to litigation amount to $1.9bn. The bad news is that, in many cases, the law is on the side of the vulture funds: $991m has been awarded so far.

A few major corporations have attempted similar legal arm-twisting. In 2003 the Big Food Group, at that time owner of the UK-based Iceland supermarket chain and other companies, sued Guyana for over £12m, only to drop the case after an outcry by UK NGOs.

In December 2002, Nestlé agreed to return a $1.5m settlement to the Ethiopian government to be put towards famine relief, after a campaign by Oxfam and others.[29] These were high-profile brand-name companies worried about their reputation. Vulture funds have no such scruples: although the G8, the IMF, the World Bank, and others have expressed concern, no action has yet been taken.[30]

The way that debt and default have been handled represents a major failure in global governance, needlessly increasing the human suffering that inevitably accompanies economic crises and ratcheting up inequality in their wake. It has shielded banks and Western institutions by imposing further sacrifices on those least able to cope. Twenty-five years of repeated efforts have failed to put an end to debt crises.

Cancelling poor countries' debts, while necessary, will not address the underlying reasons why debts build up unsustainably after each debt-relief exercise. Two sensible proposals would help to change the way that capital flows to poor countries. First, the poorest countries should receive grants, not loans. Second, creditors should share the risk, for example by tying remaining repayments to commodity prices (since a country's ability to repay is linked to its export earnings), by lending at fixed interest rates, or by helping borrowers insure their debt repayments against shocks.

Creditors also need to accept that both parties to a loan – lender as well as borrower – must share responsibility for ensuring that the money is wisely used. In 2006, the Norwegian Development Ministry showed the way when it announced that it would cancel – without conditions – debts being paid by five low- and middle-income countries, on the grounds that they were incurred through Norway's own 'development policy failure'. The Norwegian government concluded it had been at fault for carrying out 'inadequate needs analyses and risk assessments' for export credits extended to Ecuador, Egypt, Jamaica, Peru, and Sierra Leone (the credits were related to Norway's Ship Export Campaign of 1976–80, which sought new markets for its shipbuilding industry).[31]

Norway's Development Minister Erik Solheim explained that, 'By cancelling these debts we want to give rise to an international debate on lender responsibility'. The G8 looked like it might take up his call the following year, when finance ministers announced their support for the development of a 'Charter of Responsible Lending', but nothing concrete has yet been agreed.

Action is also needed on so-called 'odious debt' racked up by corrupt or repressive regimes. Until 2006 Ethiopia, for example, was still repaying debts incurred by the repressive Mengistu regime that was in power from 1974–91, much of which went to finance the suppression of the erstwhile freedom fighters who are now in government. Similarly, the ANC government in South Africa is repaying debts incurred to prop up apartheid, and the Chilean government is paying off debts taken on by the dictator Augusto Pinochet.

A just solution would be to forgive odious debt through some form of international adjudication and, by giving the UN the authority to declare 'credit sanctions' against current regimes, make it clear that debts to these regimes would be considered odious. This would prevent the 'immoral hazard' of banks and governments lending to repressive regimes and thus saddling their peoples with the obligation to repay the loans.

One especially pernicious side effect of successive debt-relief initiatives has been to extend the influence of the IMF and the World Bank. Unless these institutions are substantially reformed, we are unlikely to see the sort of just and inclusive development model that would make debt crises a thing of the past.

## FINANCIAL CRISES

Citizens' confidence is measured every four years with an election. The market measures business confidence every four seconds.

MARCUS FARO DE CASTRO, BRAZILIAN ACADEMIC [32]

In rich and poor countries alike, the ubiquitous glass and steel skyscrapers of the banks and other financial institutions are one of the characteristic landmarks of the new age of globalisation. The rise of global finance has been extraordinary. The breakdown in the early 1970s of the global system of fixed exchange rates established at the Bretton-Woods Conference in 1944 unleashed a world of financial volatility in which huge profits could be made by those who knew how to ride the ever-increasing surges of capital flowing across borders.

By 2007, the average daily global turnover in traditional foreign exchange markets stood at $3.2 trillion, five times the 1989 figure and 90 times the volume of global trade.[33]

This financial tsunami has been driven by a combination of technology and politics. Computerisation and the Internet have turned global financial markets into integrated 24-hour operations, while governments around the world have acted to remove barriers to capital flows. In this they have been urged on by orthodox economists, notably at the IMF and World Bank, who argue that allowing capital to flow freely (known as 'capital account liberalisation') boosts efficiency and growth.

Poor countries undoubtedly need capital to invest, both in the private sector and in public investment such as roads, energy generation, or schools and hospitals. Poor people need access to finance for mortgages, to finance small farms and businesses, or to cover the costs of ill health or other shocks. However, instead of a steady transfer of long-term investment, capital flows have been so short-term, volatile, and huge that in the past decade alone, they have triggered financial meltdowns in Russia, Malaysia, Brazil, South Korea, Thailand, Indonesia, the Philippines, and Argentina. By one calculation, banking and financial crises have wiped 25 per cent off the economic output of developing countries over the past 25 years.[34]

The most recent wave of crises has prompted a rethink in Washington, with some recognition that, while foreign direct investment (FDI) tends to be both stable and productive, the more short-term flows often encouraged by capital market liberalisation are downright damaging. Even before a crisis hits, capital account liberalisation carries some serious risks:

- Investors are prone to 'herding', jointly rushing into (or out of) an economy in such huge numbers that they destabilise it. This was something recognised by the economist J.M. Keynes as long ago as 1941, when he said, 'Loose funds may sweep around the world, disorganising all steady business. Nothing is more certain than that movement of capital funds must be regulated.'[35]

- Sudden inflows can lead to currency appreciation, making the country's exports less competitive.
- The threat of crises forces governments to waste resources amassing huge 'war chests' of international reserves to ward off a run on their currency.
- The constant need to appease the markets can undermine democratic government. Private credit ratings agencies such as Standard and Poor's or Moody's judge the creditworthiness of governments, determining the interest rates at which governments can borrow on financial markets. Their judgement on what financial risk is posed by different economic policies is typically based on a highly orthodox economic analysis that has often been proved to be of limited value (see Part 3) but which exerts a huge influence over policy decisions, such as how much a government feels able to spend or the setting of interest and exchange rates.

When a stampede of capital out of a country triggers a crisis, there is an almost inevitable sequence of events. The government raises interest rates in a vain attempt to lure investors back, but the exchange rate continues to drop, eventually triggering a run on the banks. Credit dries up and business grinds to a halt, job losses mount, and the government turns to the international community for help.

Such help comes at a price: governments are usually required by the IMF or other bodies to cut spending and raise interest rates, exacerbating the recession, and typically end up bailing out the financial sector by taking over its bad debts. Private debt is converted into public debt, so that creditors get paid but the taxpayers get stuck with the bill. As one foreign banker admitted to the *Wall Street Journal* at the time of the Latin American debt crisis of the 1980s, 'We foreign bankers are for the free market system when we are out to make a buck and believe in the state when we're about to lose a buck.' [36]

The impact of these arcane financial manoeuvres on poor people can be devastating. In the 1998–99 financial crisis, Indonesia's economy was cut almost in half (a loss of 45 per cent of GDP). [37] In Argentina, poverty doubled in a single year during the crisis of 2001–02. [38] Since rich people are usually better at protecting their assets (for example, by spiriting their wealth out of the country before a crisis hits), financial crises almost always increase inequality. In the words of Thai economist Pasuk Phongpaichit, 'For the poor, growth may trickle down – but disaster sweeps down like an avalanche.' [39]

There are numerous sensible ways to avoid such disasters. Countries that have maintained capital controls and have been cautious in opening up to capital flows, such as China, Chile, and India, have avoided crises of this kind. Governments raising money on international capital markets could link repayments to growth or commodity prices, so that they can pay more back in good times, less in bad times. The IMF attempted to devise an orderly process for bailing out governments, similar to a company bankruptcy procedure, to replace the chaotic and damaging confusion that usually surrounds a financial crash, only to have its proposals for a 'Sovereign Debt Restructuring Mechanism' blocked by a combination of powerful governments and financial interests, as well as some developing-country governments. [40]

The last point illustrates a serious obstacle to change. Whatever the obvious long-term benefits of managing capital flows to avoid crises, there are profits to be made from volatility. In the middle of the market mayhem of the late 1990s, NatWest bank happily reported that 'currency and interest rate volatility provided significant trading opportunities'. [41] Only firm political leadership can overcome such opposition. Within developing countries, financial sectors wield increasing economic and political clout, and constitute a domestic lobby for liberalisation and against the kind of controls that can bring stability but would cut into their profits.

While the IMF has backed off from its mid 1990s call for capital account liberalisation to become part of its core business, the push for deregulation continues by means of regional trade agreements. In its bilateral trade agreements with Chile and Singapore, the USA insisted on the elimination of widely applauded controls aimed at deterring short-term speculative capital flows and encouraging longer-term investment. [42]

At the time of writing (early 2008), storm clouds are gathering in global capital markets, triggered by the sub-prime mortgage collapse in the USA and the bursting of other 'bubbles' in rich economies. The long, debt-driven boom in the rich world looks increasingly fragile:

the USA is currently racking up huge debts due to large fiscal and trade deficits and is covering them by borrowing some $2bn a day, largely from developing countries running surpluses, notably China.[43] In a highly risky 'mutual hostage arrangement', any major shock or loss of confidence in the US economy or in the dollar could devastate both the USA and China and other Asian economies (which would see their dollar reserves fall in value).

So far, in a warped mirror image of events after the Asian financial crisis of the late 1990s, wealthy companies are snapping up assets in 'fire sales' of distressed companies. But whereas in 1998 it was Northern TNCs buying out companies in Indonesia, South Korea, and other crisis-hit economies, in 2008 it was the 'sovereign wealth funds' of developing-country governments (mainly oil producers and Asian tigers), using their estimated $2.9 trillion in assets to bail out struggling Northern companies on Wall Street and beyond, and in the process gaining significant degrees of ownership and control.[44]

However, beyond this interesting exercise in role reversal, should the feared recession finally break in the North, developing countries are likely to be hurt too. Although in some ways they are less vulnerable – growth in the larger developing countries is primarily in the domestic economy rather than being export-driven, which means that commodity prices are likely to stay high even if the US and European economies slow – many smaller developing countries still depend on exports to (and capital flows from) the USA and Europe. Financial 'contagion' could infect developing-country banks and finance companies. Historically, each new crisis is unpredictable and exposes a new source of instability – and the most vulnerable countries, and the poorest communities within them, are unlikely to escape unscathed.

## TAXATION

A major component of capital flows that cries out for effective regulation is tax evasion and avoidance. Put simply, the developing world is missing out on an estimated $385bn a year (five times the volume of global aid) due to the evasion and avoidance of *existing* taxes. This happens through a number of mechanisms:[45]

- Assets are held offshore in tax havens that guarantee secrecy and so help rich people avoid paying taxes. The notorious US energy company Enron showed how it was done. According to the US Senate report into the company's collapse, Enron's accountants set up a global network of 3,500 companies, 440 of them in the tax haven of the Cayman Islands, and paid no federal income tax at all between 1996 and 1999.[46]
- Corporations are adept at abusing so-called 'transfer pricing', which involves under- or overcharging for trade within different company affiliates in order to minimise tax. One study revealed companies recording internal transactions of television antennas from China priced at $0.04 and Japanese tweezers priced at $4,896.[47] Shell companies are set up in tax havens to further reduce liabilities: roughly half of world trade is believed to pass through tax havens, at least on paper.[48]
- Tax competition forces governments to offer ever greater tax holidays to investors to match those of rival locations.
- Individuals and companies simply do not pay the taxes due.
- Governments are unable to tax an increasing amount of economic activity due to the growth of the informal economy.

Moreover, developing countries are under huge pressure through trade talks and aid conditions to cut what is currently one of their most effective means of raising taxes – trade tariffs.

Taxation lies at the heart of the social contract between citizen and state, and is discussed more fully in Part 2. To make national tax systems work for the poor, governments need to build up their ability to collect taxes and to do so progressively, so that rich people pay more than poor people. But unless international measures are taken to shut down the luxury boltholes used by tax avoiders, poor countries will continue to miss out on the lion's share of the revenue they are due.

Such measures could include rules for greater transparency from corporations: for example, specifying how much tax they pay to each government, rather than a single global aggregate figure across the whole company; improved exchange of information between governments; and an end to secrecy in offshore tax havens. More ambitious would be a global agreement on a minimum level of corporate taxation to reduce the pressure for tax competition, or the creation of a World Tax Authority that could, among other things, help set rules for allocating the profit income of TNCs, assist the international exchange of taxation information, and help to protect national tax regimes from predatory practices such as tax competition.[49]

In 2003, the then President Chirac of France commissioned a high-level study of international taxation as a way to raise money for development. The Landau Commission concluded that a range of international taxes were both feasible and could raise significant sums.[50] They would need to be introduced simultaneously by all major financial centres, to avoid creating a new generation of tax havens, but the Commission did not see this as an insuperable obstacle. Moreover, such flows would be more stable and predictable than aid that has to be negotiated every year or two. The options discussed included:

**Environmental taxes**: these include taxes on carbon, or sectors not currently covered by the Kyoto Protocol, such as maritime and air transport. Environmental taxes have a double benefit of curbing greenhouse gas emissions and raising funds for development. The Climate Change Adaptation Fund discussed on page 410 is an example.

**Taxes on financial transactions**, such as foreign exchange transactions. Sometimes known as a 'Tobin tax'[51], these would impose a very small tax on the huge daily volumes of financial transactions, which would raise significant sums without significantly interfering with the workings of capital markets.

**A surtax on the profits of TNCs** as a 'normal counterpart to the benefits they derive from globalisation'.

**A tax on arms sales**, whether domestic or international.

In July 2006 France went a step further and introduced a small 'solidarity contribution' on airline tickets, the proceeds of which were destined for buying supplies of drugs to treat HIV, malaria, and TB in the poorest countries.

The anarchy and volatility of international finance constitute a major threat to the livelihoods of poor communities, and are a critical missing piece in the architecture of global governance. Bringing some sort of order will require both international efforts and more assertive national policies from developing-country governments to regulate capital flows in the interest of their long-term development. The extraordinary ingenuity of the rich world's 'financial engineers' (amply demonstrated in multiple corporate scandals) should be redirected into coming up with reasonable forms of national and international taxation that can generate funds for development, without doing serious damage to the economy.

Reform must also address the opaque nature of the current international financial architecture, giving citizens and poor-country governments a far greater say in its workings through a combination of transparency and greater democracy in decision-making. To curb the extreme volatility of capital flows will be politically difficult, as volatility has acquired its own constituency in the shape of powerful financial institutions which profit from the daily surges of capital markets. But the alternative is that an increasingly uncontrollable world of international finance will destabilise governments, drive up inequality, and precipitate deeper and more frequent financial crises.

# THE INTERNATIONAL TRADING SYSTEM

## TRADE RULES

At 7.30am every morning, the streets of the Bangladeshi capital of Dhaka light up as a Technicolor tide of young women in vivid saris emerge from the slums en route to the thousands of mouldering factories that line the streets of the city. The women remain there until well into the night, cutting and stitching clothes for export. On the other side of the world, in the southern Brazilian town of Sapiranga, the smell of glue hangs over the streets, emerging from the many shoe factories, ranging from giant modern plants to backstreet workshops, that churn out millions of pairs of shoes for shipment to the malls and high streets of North America and Europe.

Shopping is an exercise in globalisation. Buying food, clothes, shoes, or electronics binds consumers and some of the world's poorest workers into a single global web of trade and investment. International trade has a key role to play in the fight against poverty and inequality, promising benefits to both producers and consumers. It can create jobs and wealth that offer a lifeline to poor families and communities, and provide cheaper goods and services.

However, the system is rife with rigged rules and double standards, which sabotage the potential benefits. Four key obstacles must be addressed for trade to fulfil its potential:

**Barriers**: Trade rules allow rich countries to use tariff and non-tariff barriers to keep developing-country exports out of lucrative markets. The average US tariff for all imports is 1.6 per cent, but this rises to 14–15 per cent for some least developed countries (LDCs) in Asia, such as Bangladesh, Nepal, and Cambodia. As a result, in 2004 the US Treasury collected roughly the same amount in tariff revenue on imports from Bangladesh ($329m) as it did on imports from France ($354m), even though France exports 15 times as much to the USA. In the same year, US aid to Bangladesh was just $74m.[52]

**Subsidies**: Agricultural trade rules allow US and EU agricultural subsidies to drive down world prices and make it impossible for poor producers to compete. The value of subsidies and other support to agriculture in OECD countries now runs at $268bn a year, more than double the value of global aid.[53] Due to massive subsidies and other support, the USA is able to export its cotton and wheat at 35 per cent and 47 per cent respectively of their cost of production. The EU exports sugar and beef at 44 per cent and 47 per cent respectively of their internal cost of production.[54]

**Forced liberalisation**: Trade rules oblige some poor countries to reduce tariffs, removing a key source of government revenue, turning artificially depressed world market prices into local prices, and undermining both farmers' livelihoods and longer-term efforts to industrialise the economy. The World Trade Organization, along with many bilateral and regional trade agreements, seeks to elevate principles of deregulation, liberalisation, and equal treatment between foreign and domestic companies to a status akin to that of human rights, even though they run counter to the historical experience of successful countries. Such agreements tend to erode the 'policy space' needed to upgrade the economy and to build strong national champions in modern industries. For example, limits on foreign investment in key industries, used by (among others) Japan, South Korea, and even the USA during their take-off periods, now fall foul of the WTO's 'national treatment' principle; the widespread use of 'local content requirements' to oblige companies to source from local suppliers violates the WTO's TRIMS (Trade Related Investment Measures) agreement, as would Taiwan's use of export requirements, obliging foreign companies to reach a certain level of exports.[55]

**Patents:** Intellectual property laws restrict developing countries from accessing technology and drive up the cost of all technology-rich products, including life-saving medicines. The trade deal currently proposed between the USA and Colombia, for example, would increase medicine costs by $919m by 2020 – enough to provide health care for 5.2 million people under the public health system. Under the US–Dominican Republic–Central America Free Trade Agreement (DR-CAFTA) the prices that poor farmers pay for agrochemicals are expected to rise several-fold.[56]

While the current international rules for the flow of goods, services, capital, and knowledge create problems such as these, the *lack* of rules in other areas creates further obstacles to development: first, managing the flow of the other factor of production, labour (i.e. people); and second, regulating the behaviour of the most powerful actors in the international economic system, transnational corporations.

International trade is governed by overlapping sets of rules and regulations. Importing companies impose ever more sophisticated standards on quality, safety, and traceability, which would-be exporters must satisfy. Governments impose another layer of health standards. Regional and bilateral trade and investment agreements limit what tariffs a government can charge on imports, what subsidies it can pay its producers and exporters, what obligations it can place on foreign investors, and how it regulates patents. Standing above all these, and to some extent locking them in place, is the World Trade Organization, which oversees 15 agreements signed during the 'Uruguay Round' of global trade talks.[57]

The forerunner of the WTO, the General Agreement on Tariffs and Trade (GATT) was set up after the Second World War, in part to avoid a return to 1930s-style trade wars between the major powers which triggered a traumatic global recession. However, with the upgrading of the GATT into the WTO in 1995 came a number of worrying developments that coincided with, and to some extent came to epitomise, growing public disquiet about the impact of globalisation, as became clear when the WTO's Seattle ministerial meeting in 1999 collapsed amid public protests and clouds of teargas.

Two years later, the WTO sought to recover from the 'battle of Seattle' by launching a set of global trade talks dubbed the Doha

Development Agenda, so named to reflect the mandate they had of redressing some of the injustices of the global trading system. The final statement from the Doha Round included nine separate references to the need to guarantee extra flexibility to developing countries through 'special and differential treatment' and a promise to deal with the tariffs that keep many developing-country exports out of rich-country markets. Working groups were set up to look at some of the most pressing issues facing developing countries, such as Trade, Debt and Finance, and Trade and Technology Transfer, and discussions were mandated on the particular problems facing small economies.

Six years on, the Doha round appears deadlocked. Deadlines have come and gone, and the promises made in 2001 have long since been broken. The rich countries in the WTO have appeared incapable of accommodating the demands of a large number of increasingly assertive developing countries, and this has produced a long and dispiriting stalemate. Throughout the course of the round, Oxfam and others have supported developing-country governments and civil society organisations in focusing attention on the links between trade and development and the need to right the rigged rules and double standards in the system, if globalisation is to work for development.[58]

In agriculture, for example, international trade rules impede the efforts of developing countries to develop their economies and reduce poverty. Rich countries and poor countries support their farmers in different ways. Subsidy superpowers such as the EU and USA support agriculture with large helpings of state aid. Cash-strapped poor countries have to use import tariffs to keep up prices for their farmers and protect themselves from dumping. Rather than favour tariff-dependent developing countries, the trade rules do precisely the opposite. Through a series of carefully crafted loopholes, the WTO Agreement on Agriculture allows rich countries unlimited subsidies, while trying to impose cuts on the use of tariffs by poor and rich countries alike. The rich countries' reluctance to end this double standard lies at the heart of the stalemate in the Doha Round.

Perhaps the most egregious example is the US cotton industry. Taxpayers provide a mere 25,000 US cotton farmers and corporations with annual subsidies of up to $4bn, resulting in overproduction and dumping on world markets that cost ten million poor farmers in West Africa between 8 per cent and 20 per cent of their income.[59]

The WTO's Agreement on Agriculture did, however, close down some of the avenues for Northern subsidies, and developing countries such as Brazil have become increasingly assertive in taking the subsidy superpowers to the WTO court and winning, as in the cases of US cotton subsidies and EU sugar subsidies. According to trade lawyers, a total of some $13bn in rich-country agriculture payments are on the wrong side of the law, and this promises a procession of court cases at the WTO in coming years.[60]

In addition, the Doha negotiations at least introduced some useful ideas for how to adapt agricultural trade rules to meet the needs of poor people, which may eventually be adopted. Vulnerable developing countries won recognition for their right to have extra flexibility to protect 'special products' of particular importance to food security and rural development from premature liberalisation. Regrettably, rich countries and large developing-country exporters launched a concerted attempt to water down these exemptions by restricting the criteria and permitted number of products.[61]

The rise of China and other leading developing countries is changing the dynamics of international trade negotiations. Where once the USA and the EU used to negotiate between themselves and then present the rest of the world with a *fait accompli*, the WTO is increasingly multipolar, with India and Brazil at the heart of negotiations, alongside larger groupings such as the G90 alliance of smaller economies. This geopolitical shift holds out the prospect of fairer trade rules, but only if the USA and the EU can be persuaded to put long-term development at the heart of trade negotiations – something which currently looks a long way off.

While most public attention has focused on the WTO, there has been a proliferation of bilateral and regional accords, which are in many cases even more damaging. Around 26 developing countries have now signed 'free trade agreements' (FTAs) with rich countries, and more than 100 are engaged in negotiations. An average of two bilateral investment treaties are signed every week. Virtually no country, however poor, has been left out.

As of early 2008, 15 Caribbean countries had just concluded FTA negotiations with the EU and these were due to go for signing. Another 20 countries in Africa and the Pacific had initialled partial FTAs with a view to concluding full agreements by the end of 2008. Of the total 35 countries that had initialled FTAs with Europe, nine were least developed countries. This sets a new precedent, as prior to these agreements no LDC had entered an FTA with an industrialised country.

Rich countries are using these bilateral and regional accords to win concessions that they are unable to obtain at the WTO, where developing countries can band together and hold out for more favourable rules. The USA and EU are pushing through rules on intellectual property that reduce poor people's access to life-saving medicines, increase the prices of seeds and other farming inputs beyond the reach of small farmers, and make it harder for developing-country companies to access new technology, an issue explained in detail below.

Free trade agreements have also been used to challenge local government decisions, as in the infamous case of Metalclad in Mexico. When Mexican state and local officials used their authority over land use regulation to stop the US multinational from operating a hazardous waste disposal facility on top of an aquifer that provided drinking water to a town in the state of San Luis Potosi, Metalclad brought a suit against Mexico under NAFTA's Chapter 11 on investment, claiming that its property rights had been violated. A NAFTA tribunal, meeting in secret as is the custom in international arbitration, agreed that Metalclad's rights had indeed been violated and ordered the Mexican national government to pay $16m in damages.[62]

New trading powers such as India and China are also pursuing regional agreements and may duplicate many of the rigged rules and double standards that abound in North–South deals, since the outcomes of trade negotiations reflect the balance of power between the negotiating parties more than their geographic location. Accords between countries of similar weight can be fairer, as (at least in theory) can the WTO, where developing countries at least enjoy safety in numbers, although their interests often diverge. Negotiations between countries of vastly disparate power – the USA and Peru, for example – risk becoming neo-colonial impositions.

Most alarming among the EU's bilateral and regional negotiations are the Economic Partnership Agreements (EPAs) with former colonies in Africa, the Caribbean, and the Pacific. In these David-and-Goliath talks, the EU claims not to have any 'offensive interests', but its behaviour to date suggests that its default position is to make traditional 'eye for an eye' demands for concessions, irrespective of their impact on development.

Going beyond the provisions negotiated at a multilateral level, these agreements impose far-reaching, hard-to-reverse rules that systematically dismantle national policies designed to promote development. The overall effect of such rule changes is to undermine the development of effective states. They strip developing countries of the capacity to effectively govern their economies, robbing them of the tools they need to gain a favourable foothold in global markets, and transfer power from governments to largely unaccountable multinational firms.

Although developing-country governments have proved themselves to be increasingly assertive at the WTO and in some regional and bilateral agreements, the balance of power in international trade negotiations remains tipped heavily in favour of rich countries and large, politically influential corporations. Furthermore, within developing countries, trade policy is often the exclusive province of large exporters, while small businesses, trade unions, NGOs, women's groups, and indigenous peoples have very few mechanisms for participation, and their rights and needs are largely ignored.

Trade rules have proved largely immune to the progress achieved in recent years in recognising the importance to development of rights and equality, evidenced in areas such as aid, conflict, and debt relief. Instead, rich-country trade negotiators continue to pay lip service to development, while arguing that 'political realities' oblige them to get as much as they can and give as little as possible in return. Recalcitrant business lobbies are likely to urge them to defend perceived victories, no matter what the developmental cost. One US negotiator at the WTO memorably summed up this attitude when he reminded delegates that the US Congress needed to see 'blood on the floor' in the form of painful concessions from poor countries before it was likely to agree to do anything itself in what had been packaged as the 'Doha Development Round'.[63]

These kinds of attitudes, and the developing countries' refusal to cave in, have paralysed the Doha Round. On one level, this is better than accepting a 'bad deal' and the multilateral trading system continues to function, however unfairly. But storm clouds are gathering over the global economy, fuelling protectionist sentiments in the North, and that system is more fragile than it would be were the round to be functioning smoothly and fairly. All it takes is for one major power to openly defy a ruling by the WTO to precipitate a crisis of authority and legitimacy in the institution, with serious consequences for the multilateral system. Rich countries have both a moral duty and a long-term self-interest in ensuring that this does not happen.

Shifting governments to the long-term vision that underpinned, for example, the USA's willingness to give unilateral market access to its defeated opponents after the Second World War will not be easy. The strong economies need to offer more and demand less, rather than push the weak into further disadvantage. Developed countries ought to cut subsidies and open up their markets, while allowing developing countries more 'policy space', not less, so that they may find the right trade and investment policies among the wide range that have led to economic take-off in different countries.[64]

Official trade rules are often less important in determining the effectiveness of trade for development than the trade 'realities' of the system: access to finance; technology; or the nature of the chain of buyers and sellers for a particular product. These are discussed in Part 3. More equitable global institutions and fairer rules for trade will not deliver development on their own, but they hold out hope of at least reining in the rapacious behaviour of the most powerful corporations and countries, allowing poor countries and citizens to harness trade for their long-term development.

## INTELLECTUAL PROPERTY

The global governance of 'intellectual property' (IP) such as patents, copyrights, and trademarks constitutes one of the most glaring examples of the rigged rules and double standards that bedevil the international trade system. While powerful governments seek ever greater liberalis-ation of trade and capital markets, they are using their negotiating clout to force the global system towards increasing levels of 'knowledge protectionism' in the shape of IP rules that close down the flow of knowledge and technology. IP negotiations lure the corporate lobbyists out of the shadows, revealing their extraordinary access and influence over the US and EU governments, among others (see page 328).

The underlying principles of IP protection are simple. New inventions are often costly to develop, and if rival firms were allowed immediately to copy and market new inventions, the incentives for companies to invest in R&D would be few. IP laws provide companies with a temporary monopoly during which they can charge high prices to recoup their investment.

The task of maintaining a balance between society's interest in creating incentives for innovation on the one hand, and promoting the widespread dispersion of inventions on the other has been fraught ever since the Venetians first introduced patents at the end of the fifteenth century. Corporations find it far easier to make a profit from monopoly than from innovation, and so have invariably argued for strengthened IP rules, often to the detriment of wider society. At an international level, rich countries have consistently used IP to preserve their technological edge and 'kick away the ladder' from potential competitors.

Ironically, even in the rich countries the proliferation of patents threatens to undermine their purported aim. In many fields, firms seeking to innovate must navigate through a 'patent thicket' protecting existing technologies that they want to incorporate into a new design. In stampedes such as the patent applications on hundreds of thousands of gene sequences for fragments of human DNA, the hard slog of innovation has given way to a Klondike-style gold rush of 'patent mining' as an easy source of profits.

The role of technology in development follows a fairly standard path, described by one UN report as 'a developed, innovating "North" and a developing, imitating "South"'.[65] All countries initially grow by imitating and adapting existing technologies. As they approach the global 'technological frontier', they move into innovation. One of the reasons why countries such as China or India, which are in 'catch-up' mode, grow so much faster than the industrialised countries is that adapting existing technologies is much easier than creating new ones.

Historically, IP legislation has followed development: as countries have grown richer, and as they evolve from imitation to innovation, they have introduced more stringent IP laws. Chemical substances remained unpatentable until 1967 in West Germany, 1968 in the Nordic countries, 1976 in Japan, 1978 in Switzerland, and 1992 in Spain, by which time these countries' chemical industries had established themselves.[66] This pattern has been broken over the past 20 years by a combination of new institutions such as the WTO and regional trade agreements and an extraordinarily aggressive campaign by large corporations and their home-country governments.

Global IP legislation also imposes a growing financial burden on poor countries, through the costs of introducing largely irrelevant or unsuitable IP laws to comply with the WTO and through the drain of spiralling royalties to the owners of patents – almost always rich-world TNCs. In 2005, developing countries paid out a net $17bn in royalty and licence fees, largely to companies in the industrialised nations. The USA was the big winner from the system, earning a net $33bn, considerably more than its overseas aid budget.[67]

The spread of potentially damaging 'one size fits all' international IP rules took off in the 1980s, when a number of pharmaceutical and other companies scored the spectacular coup of persuading the US delegation to include them in the Uruguay Round negotiations that led to the creation of the WTO. Industry lobbyists overwhelmed opposition from the secretariat of the GATT (which hosted the talks) to adding IP to the agenda. The agreement on Trade-Related Aspects of Intellectual Property Rights (TRIPS) introduced a global IP system, including a minimum patent protection period of 20 years, along with protection for industrial designs, trademarks, copyrights, and other IP rights. Unlike several other WTO agreements, the TRIPS rules applied even to the poorest developing countries, although they were given longer deadlines for implementation.

Nowhere have TRIPS been more controversial than in the drugs industry. Each year more than ten million people in developing countries perish from infectious and parasitic diseases, most of which could be treated with existing drugs.[68] Although there are other important factors behind the death toll, such as dilapidated health services, high drug prices are a key barrier to saving lives.

The vast majority of people in developing countries have to buy their own medicines. For example, in India over three-quarters of all spending on health services is out of pocket, of which 75 per cent is spent on medicines.[69] People in the developing world are thus acutely vulnerable to high prices.

Pharmaceutical giants spend considerable amounts of money trying to delay the introduction of off-patent generic versions of medicines for as long as possible, and TRIPS rules are a vital part of their armoury in this effort. The gap between the prices of patented and generic medicines is large, for a variety of reasons: R&D costs are high, relative to other industries, and the costs of copying a medicine are usually very low; companies pursue very different business models, with producers of patented medicines investing massively in advertising, absorbing the cost in high prices, while generics concentrate on high volume and low costs. As long as they can retain a monopoly, pharmaceutical companies know that desperate people will pay whatever they can for the medicines that can keep them alive: it is the epitome of a sellers' market.

Prior to the creation of the WTO, some 50 developing countries either excluded medicines from eligibility for product patents, or provided shorter periods of protection and other safeguards.[70] Thanks to flexible IP regimes, India became known as the 'pharmacy of the developing world', manufacturing most of the world's generic medicines and exporting them to poorer developing countries. Since 2001, for example, competition among Indian generics producers has driven down the cost of first-line antiretroviral medicines from $10,000 per patient per year to the current level of less than $100 per patient per year.

Although the poorest countries have a grace period until 2016, most of them do not have manufacturing capacity and therefore have no means of producing generic medicines for their populations. The damage is most severe in the case of 'new diseases' such as HIV and AIDS, and other diseases with rising incidences such as cancer and asthma, which require new generations of drugs, all of which are under patent. In fact, access to these medicines has already been curtailed because the world's major producers of generic, low-cost medicines were obliged to implement the TRIPS agreement by 2005.

The TRIPS agreement allowed some flexibility for developing countries to override patent rules to protect public health, but this promptly degenerated into a legal battleground as rich corporations and countries turned to the courts in an effort to restrict them from doing so. In 2001, a group of 39 of the world's largest pharmaceutical companies took the South African government to court over the terms of its 1997 Medicines Act. At that time around 4.5 million people in South Africa were infected with the HIV virus, but the vast majority of them did not have access to effective treatment, in part due to the extremely high prices of ARVs. Other problems included the highly unequal health infrastructure inherited from the apartheid period, lack of finance, and lack of political will in some sections of the government to tackle HIV and AIDS.

The companies decided to pursue legal proceedings despite the devastation caused by South Africa's public health crisis, sparking international condemnation. They argued that the Medicines Act, which allowed 'parallel imports' (imports of cheaper patented medicines), breached the TRIPS agreement, when in fact TRIPS is neutral on this issue. Citizen campaigns (spearheaded by the Treatment Action Campaign and including a global campaign by Oxfam and MSF) and public uproar became such a serious threat to the drug companies' reputations that they dropped the lawsuit.

The case also helped to galvanise the passage of the Doha Declaration on TRIPS and Public Health, agreed upon by all WTO members prior to the start of a new round of global trade negotiations in November 2001. The Doha Declaration unequivocally recognised that the TRIPS agreement 'can and should be interpreted and im-plemented in a manner supportive of WTO members' right to protect public health, and in particular, to promote access to medicines for all'. The legal clarity of the Doha Declaration, combined with the bad publicity from the episode, motivated some drug companies to stop opposing the import or local production of generic antiretroviral medicines, and to offer some of their ARVs and other medicines at lower or 'no-profit' prices in sub-Saharan Africa. Yet such ad hoc initiatives have mostly been limited to a few high-profile diseases (in addition to HIV and AIDS, TB and malaria), and even for those diseases have fallen short.

Prices for some key medicines, including first-line ARVs, have fallen sharply in recent years. But newer antiretroviral medicines, needed because they are more effective or to overcome toxicity or resistance to first-line medicines, are often ten times more expensive. In addition, developing countries face an increasing burden of non-communicable disease – according to WHO, over 80 per cent of deaths from non-communicable diseases today occur in developing countries. New medicines to treat cancer, heart disease, and diabetes, patented aggressively by the industry, are priced out of reach of poor people.

The pharmaceutical industry continues to aggressively seek to enforce patents and to charge high prices for medicines in low- and middle-income countries across Asia and Latin America, keeping medicines unaffordable for millions of poor people. When countries recently tried to use TRIPS safeguards, it again jumped all over them, even returning to the aggressive legal tactics that had earned it such a black eye a few years previously. Novartis and Pfizer became embroiled in legal disputes in India and the Philippines respectively, while Thailand's decision to issue a compulsory licence for its second-line HIV medicine Kaletra prompted Abbott Pharmaceuticals to de-register seven new medicines from the Thai market. Abbott was charging patients nearly $2,200 per year for the drug.[71]

Rich countries are also working to render the public health safeguards in TRIPS meaningless by including more stringent patent rules in bilateral agreements. The US–Jordan FTA, signed in 2000, required Jordan to agree rules on so-called 'data exclusivity', which block the registration and marketing approval of generic medicines for five or more years, even when no patent exists. Data exclusivity has delayed generic competition for 79 per cent of medicines launched by 21 multinational pharmaceutical companies between 2002 and mid-2006 that otherwise would have been available in an inexpensive, generic form.

Partly as a result of such TRIPS-plus rules, medicine prices in Jordan have increased drastically, threatening the financial sustainability of government public health programmes. Stricter levels of intellectual property protection have conferred few benefits with respect to FDI, domestic R&D, or accelerated introduction of new medicines.

A second concern over the potential negative impacts of IP rules is so-called 'bio-piracy' – the theft and patenting of traditional knowledge from developing countries. One of the most notorious examples occurred in 1995, when two researchers from the University of Mississippi Medical Center were granted a US patent for using turmeric to heal wounds, an art that has been practised in India for thousands of years. To get the patent repealed, the claim had to be backed by written evidence – an ancient Sanskrit text.[72]

Similar patent disputes have broken out over attempts by US firms to patent basmati rice (a tasty variety perfected over generations by Indian farmers), *ayahuasca* (an Amazon rainforest plant sacred to Colombia's indigenous peoples), the neem tree (an Indian plant traditionally used to produce medicines and pesticides), and extracts of black pepper.[73] In 2005, the Peruvian government accused Japanese scientists of trying to patent the extract of *camu-camu*, a pale orange fruit found in the Amazon that has the highest concentration of vitamin C of any known plant, 60 times greater than lemon juice.[74]

Besides excluding communities from the profits of products based on the traditional knowledge that they have developed, bio-piracy is emblematic of a wider problem: the transfer of knowledge from the public to the private domain, which puts profit before innovation or human welfare.

There is no shortage of ideas as to how to restore IP rules to their proper place in the global system. These include:

- Within TRIPS, recognise that different levels of development require different kinds of IP rules, including much easier recourse to safeguards and flexibilities such as compulsory licensing and parallel imports of life-saving drugs and technologies, and much greater commitment to technology transfer.

- More radically, remove IP from the WTO altogether, scrapping TRIPS, and return the issue to a reformed version of the UN's World Intellectual Property Organization (WIPO). WIPO has been criticised for 'sending missionaries to convert the uncivilized economies of the South'[75] to the merits of strict IP rules, but since 2004 a group of developing countries led by Argentina and Brazil have successfully introduced a development agenda for WIPO.

- Establish international guidelines on the balance between public interest and incentives for innovation, and give priority to ensuring that knowledge and innovation is placed at the service of development, perhaps through an 'International Convention on Access to Knowledge'. Examples of approaches based on access to knowledge include the open source movement that generated the Linux computer operating system and the user-generated free online encyclopedia, Wikipedia.
- Explore alternative ways of encouraging research and development into pressing issues (health, climate change). These could include increasing public funding and 'advance market commitments', whereby aid donors promise to purchase large quantities of a yet-to-be-invented medicine or vaccine for particular health problems at a negotiated price. A suggestion by Joseph Stiglitz is to offer a large prize for the invention of a drug, on the proviso that it is not placed under patent and can go straight to generic production.

The current system of global rules on knowledge is a severe and growing obstacle to development. It drives up inequality, creating a world of technological haves and have-nots, stifles innovation even in the North, and in the worst cases constitutes little more than what economists call 'rent seeking'. The obstacles to changing it are not intellectual – there are any number of good reform proposals – but political. Those corporate leaders with a longer-term understanding of the need to tackle inequality and poverty must rein in their lobbyists, while politicians in both North and South must show leadership and curb the kinds of backdoor political influence that allow short-term corporate self-interest to stop knowledge flowing in the global economy.

Such changes require active, informed citizens, as the case of South Africa's Treatment Action Campaign shows (see page 242). They also require effective states, able to stand up to pressures in trade negotiations or in their own courts in the interests of tackling poverty and inequality. Developing-country governments, backed by public pressure at home and internationally, have become increasingly assertive in defending their citizens' right to health and knowledge. It is vital that they are allowed and encouraged to do so.

## MIGRATION[76]

Migration is the oldest action against poverty. It selects those who most
want help. It is good for the country to which they go; it helps break the
equilibrium of poverty in the country from which they come. What is
the perversity in the human soul that causes people to resist so obvious
a good?

J.K. GALBRAITH, *THE NATURE OF MASS POVERTY*, 1979

While the international community expends huge efforts constructing
a system to manage international flows of capital, goods, and services,
there are no effective global rules for the flow of the other 'factor of
production' – labour. This constitutes a vacuum at the heart of global
governance. Only one developed country (Belgium) has ratified the
1990 International Convention on the Protection of the Rights of All
Migrant Workers and Members of their Families, which came into
force in 2003 and aims to guarantee the rights of migrant workers; all
the other signatories are countries of origin, not destination.[77]

When an Oxfam researcher approached groups of youths on the
beaches of Senegal, waiting to take their chances in risky boats to the
Canary Islands and thence to Spain, they gave a simple but powerful
reason for why they were about to risk their lives: 'Because it is close,
and there is work.' Nothing determines an individual's life chances
more than where he or she is born, and migration is the most straightforward way to change those chances for the better.

Throughout history, migration has been one of the most effective
responses to poverty. Between 1846 and 1924, 48 million Europeans
left the Old World and scattered around the globe. In the UK,
Portugal, and Italy, a third of the population abandoned their native
lands.[78] In relative terms, these numbers are some five times higher
than current levels of migration, even allowing for 'illegal' migrants.
What is new is the desire to prevent such movement: our great-grand-
parents faced far fewer obstacles than today's would-be migrants.
Passports did not assume their modern form until after the First
World War: not a single person was refused entry to Britain in the
nineteenth century.[79]

Migrants face an ever-expanding array of barriers, both legal and
physical. Where First and Third Worlds meet, on the US–Mexican

border, or at Melilla, a small Spanish enclave in the north of Morocco, borders are studded with watchtowers, fences topped with barbed wire, and police equipped with planes, helicopters, boats, radar, thermal imaging equipment, and electronic detectors.

However, the migrants keep coming. The economic and social forces driving immigration are irresistible and growing. Greatest of them all is the wage gap between rich and poor countries. Even allowing for differences in the cost of living, wage levels in high-income countries are approximately five times higher than those of low-income countries for similar jobs, and the gap is growing as inequality between countries rises inexorably.[80] Demographic differences add to the pressure to migrate: migrants are usually young, and youth unemployment is high in developing countries, while the ageing populations of rich countries demand ever more workers, especially in low-skilled jobs such as home health aides, caretakers, fast food workers, or drivers.

With the exception of the political barriers imposed by Northern governments, migration is getting easier. Transport costs are falling, access to information means that migration is no longer a leap into the unknown, and improved communications mean that migrants can stay in touch with their families and countries by phone, Internet, and home television channels on cable.

Currently, the number of people living legally outside their country of birth is estimated at 192 million, or 3 per cent of the world population. The total number of migrants is as much as one-and-a-half times greater.[81] This includes South–North migration and increasing South–South movements, such as the thousands of Bangladeshis working in the Gulf states or the many Filipino women who work as domestic servants in Hong Kong and the Middle East. South–South migration is now nearly as great as South–North, largely between countries with common borders.[82] Both can involve trafficking, sexual abuse, and violations of labour rights, such as the widespread abuse of Burmese migrants in Thailand.

Migrants send vast sums back home. Recorded remittances to developing countries were expected to reach $240bn in 2007, eight times the 1990 level.[83] Flows through informal channels could add another $100bn to that figure.[84] By comparison, global aid flows in

2005, even when inflated by debt relief to Iraq, came to $107bn. Moreover, remittance flows are steadier and more reliable than either FDI or aid.

Remittances, flowing to poor families across the developing world, are typically spent on basic needs, including education and health care. They allow families and communities to cope better with the risks that afflict those living in poverty, whether at an individual level, when a family member falls ill or a crop fails, or at a community level – diaspora communities are usually the first to react when a monsoon or an earthquake hits. When Ecuador suffered an economic crisis in the late 1990s, thousands of people left the country, many for Spain, and remittances rapidly expanded to 10 per cent of GDP – a vital lifeline for a country in crisis.[85] Remittances from migrants are also critical in helping people survive drawn-out crises like those in North Korea, Myanmar, and Zimbabwe.[86]

These cash injections have a tangible impact: children from households where a family member has migrated are more likely to attend school, stay in school for longer, and progress through school significantly faster than their peers in non-migrant households. The positive educational impact is particularly strong for girls. In Pakistan, for example, girls' enrolment rates increase from 35 per cent to 54 per cent if they live in a migrant household.[87] The World Bank estimates that remittances have reduced poverty by 11 percentage points in Uganda, six in Bangladesh, and five in Ghana.[88]

Not only does migration ease unemployment in the migrant's country of origin, it can increase the flow of capital into the country, encourage foreign trade and investment via burgeoning diaspora communities, and stimulate technology transfer and tourism, as well as aid. More intangibly, migration boosts the inflow of new ideas. See Box 5.1.

---

## BOX 5.1
## MIGRANTS MAKE A DIFFERENCE

Zacatecas is a Mexican state with a history of migration to the USA that goes back over 100 years. For the past 15 years, Zacatecan migrants have been forming 'clubs' in the USA to send remittances to finance social infrastructure projects back home. One of the first clubs was formed by migrants from Jomulquillo, a farming village in an area of Zacatecas that was depopulated as a result of successive droughts in the 1970s. 'Fourteen years ago we were having a party', remembers Antonio Rodriguez, a 53-year-old chef who has been living in Los Angeles since the late 1970s. 'We said to ourselves, we have good clothes and cars and at home they have nothing – and we decided we had to do something about it.'

The Jomulquillo club has since raised thousands of dollars through social events, raffles, and collections. It has financed a metal bridge to span the village stream, while drainage, sewers, and running water have been installed. The school has been refurbished, a dance hall built, and a paved road now links Jomulquillo with Jerez, the nearest market town. 'The old people couldn't believe it', says Mr Rodriguez. 'We felt very good about the work we did there.' By the end of 2005, migrant groups and governments had invested $230m in a total of more than 5,000 small-scale projects across Zacatecas.

Sudanese migrants in Qatar have performed similar socially conscious miracles of generosity in their home communities. Perhaps the most spectacular remittance-funded project is the international airport in the Indian state of Kerala, opened in 1994 and funded by some of the four million workers, mainly in the Gulf states, who were fed up with the delays and hassle with grasping customs officials at Delhi airport and who wanted a direct route home.

*Source*: Financial Times, 31 August 2007 and 29 August 2007

For poor people, migration inevitably brings costs as well as benefits, including the personal cost of leaving home and country, and the higher risk of abuse in the workplace, especially when the migrant is in the country illegally and lacks recourse to the law.

Women make up just over half of all migrants. They face greater risks and threats than men, but they also have the chance to gain economic independence. Women whose partners migrate are also more independent, typically much more likely to open their own bank accounts, register land or housing in their own names, or look for their own sources of income. Women migrants tend to send more money back to their families (Bangladeshi women send home an average of 72 per cent of their salaries) and, when at the receiving end, tend to spend more of it on health and education.[89]

Concerns surround the 'brain drain' of key workers such as doctors and nurses: at least 12 per cent of Indian doctors work in the UK, and Jamaica and Grenada have to train five doctors for every one that stays.[90] Teachers and nurses have a right to migrate, like anyone else, but people in poor countries also have a right to expect professionals trained with public money to stay and work in their home country for a number of years after graduation.

Most public debate on migration is over the costs and benefits to the recipient country, rather than to the country of origin. Here there is a gulf between evidence and public perception, and between economics and politics. Studies suggest that, without immigration, the Spanish economy would have stagnated over the past five years, and in 2005 immigrants paid in €5bn more in taxes than they received in services:[91] they are most definitely not the parasites of popular prejudice. Spain's experience is widely shared. Numerous economic studies show that migrants add to the demand for goods and services, introduce new ideas and skills, and do not drain social service spending. Instead, they are among the most dynamic members of society and are unlikely to live on welfare when they could be earning more by working. Studies in the UK, Australia, and elsewhere show significant net payments to the state from migrants.[92]

Yet popular sentiment in some recipient countries is increasingly anti-immigrant and constitutes the main barrier to making migration work for development. US academic Lant Pritchett has identified a number of 'framing' assumptions that influence the debate on migration: that it is morally legitimate to discriminate on the basis of nationality; that development is about countries, not individuals; that our responsibility towards others varies with geographical proximity.[93]

This raises the thorny question of whether there is a 'right to migrate'. The UN Declaration of Human Rights states only that 'everyone has the right to freedom of movement and residence within the borders of each State' (so there is a right to internal migration) and that 'everyone has the right to leave any country, including his own, and to return to his country' (so there is a right to emigrate but no obligation on any country to admit the migrant, excluding asylum cases, which are covered elsewhere). More recently the UN's Special Rapporteur on the right to food has argued that the right of asylum should be expanded to include people fleeing from hunger and famine, which would certainly include some of those currently classified as 'economic migrants'.[94] In general however, there is little comfort to migrants from international human rights law: they are on their own.

Stopping migration is both wrong and impossible. But for the foreseeable future, arguing for a return to a world of completely free movement of people is a forlorn task. An approach with more prospect of success would be to ask, 'What are the policies toward migration that would be most beneficial to the world's currently poor people (nearly all of whom reside in poor countries) and yet are (or could be) still politically acceptable in rich countries?' [95] Such an approach would rule out two common proposals: select migrants based on a combination of qualifications and wealth, or agree rules through the WTO. The first approach would prevent most poor people from migrating, while any agreement in the WTO is likely to be extremely weak and ineffective. Bilateral agreements provide more prospect of success.

Improving the contribution of migration to development requires action at a global level, as well as by governments, backed up by public pressure, both North and South. In the long term, the flow of people deserves as much attention as that of capital or goods, perhaps through a World Migration Organisation, which would replace the largely toothless International Organization for Migration.[96] In Europe a Common Migration Policy could help by rescuing the issue from the point-scoring and xenophobia of national politics, where political leaders live in fear of being branded 'soft on migration'.

Increasing the proportion of migrants who migrate legally is vital to guaranteeing their rights and safety, and all governments should sign and ratify the 1990 International Convention on the Protection of the Rights of All Migrant Workers and Members of their Families, and ensure that migrant workers enjoy the same rights as nationals. In 1998, Italy showed the way with the 'Testo Unico' law, which guaranteed medical assistance and labour rights regardless of citizenship status, and a range of measures to protect migrants from violence and sexual trafficking.[97] In part thanks to pressure from organisations of migrant workers and their allies, Hong Kong has some of the most enlightened policies in this area, including a range of migrant workers' unions and 'mobile ambassadors' based at the airport, who provide arriving migrants with information on government policies, contact information for NGOs working with migrant labourers, and government training courses on issues such as labour rights.[98]

In the North, active citizens have a vital role to play in pushing the case for better migration rules and combating the worst abuses. Migrants themselves are leading the way: in 2007, 158 immigrant advocacy groups from around the USA launched a nationwide boycott of Western Union, the largest US money-transfer company, accusing it of charging exorbitant fees while failing to adequately reinvest in immigrant communities.[99]

Internationally, the main objective should be to increase flows of new temporary migrants, who then return to their countries of origin. Circular migration eases fears in recipient countries and maximises the benefits to home countries, as returning migrants bring home new skills, ideas, and cash. Surveys show that would-be migrants much prefer the idea of temporary migration to a permanent move, were both options to be made legal.[100]

One possibility would be to pay a portion of a migrant's social security or pension payments into a 'return fund', similar to a standard pension scheme, which would become available only upon his or her return. This would ensure that workers arrive back home with a sizeable pool of resources to invest. There could be penalties for home governments whose nationals failed to comply with return requirements.

For example, quotas for sending countries could be reduced in proportion to the numbers of migrants who failed to return, thus increasing incentives for them to create a hospitable economic and political climate at home to encourage their nationals to return.

Developed-country governments can minimise the risks of brain drain by addressing the causes of the workforce crisis in their own public services and avoiding cherry-picking the skilled workers that developing countries so desperately need. Ethical codes of practice for recruiting countries have been tried, with some success. For example, the UK's ethical recruitment code has halted the increase in recruitment of overseas nurses in the National Health Service, although most private agencies do not apply it. Rich governments could also reimburse developing-country governments for the cost of training new health and education workers.

Lobbying by migrant worker organisations has helped to convince developing-country governments to act to maximise the benefits of migration. Both the Philippines and Sri Lanka require workers leaving the country to register with the government. Departing migrant workers must pay a fee for registration and provide the details of their employment, including the name of the employer and the country to which they are migrating. In return, the government tracks employers, and those who violate employee contracts or exploit migrant workers in any other way are blacklisted. As an additional incentive for registration, the government of Sri Lanka provides departing workers with life insurance, scholarships for children, airport assistance, interest-free loans to help with migration costs, and other benefits.[101]

Increasing the quantity and quality of migration is one of the most effective ways to tackle global poverty and inequality. It would correct one of the fundamental injustices of globalisation: the fact that capital and goods can largely flow free of hindrance, but people cannot. However, it remains largely a Cinderella issue in the development debate, one that politicians and lobbyists avoid for fear of nationalist backlash. In the years to come, migration will only increase. For anyone concerned with development, ensuring that it contributes as much as possible to human welfare is an urgent and critical task.

# GLOBAL BUSINESS

International rules and treaties governing trade, migration, and other economic matters are made among states, and guide the policies and practices of national governments. The gaping hole in global govern-ance – the elephant in the room – is the lack of rules for global business, the transnational corporations (TNCs) that exercise a central role in growth and development as generators of jobs, tax revenues, technology, and consumer goods, yet are subject to the disciplines of international treaties only if national governments choose to make them so.

The positive contribution of businesses to development through wealth creation, innovation, and technological transfers is often undermined by a deeply unjust structure of global governance that accords them vast privileges and powers but few responsibilities. Corporations must be subject to effective regulation by states as part of a renewed social contract geared to generating sustainable growth with redistribution.

Many companies have made progress, especially on environmental issues, but also increasingly on social issues (see Box 5.2). These are often the biggest firms which have the resources and capacities to address problems and which risk their 'licence to operate' if they do not meet public expectations. Public reporting among a handful of companies has improved dramatically, and for many so has performance.

---

## BOX 5.2

### EARNING A 'LICENCE TO OPERATE'

At both national and international levels, civil society organisations such as trade unions, consumer movements, and NGOs can play a useful role in harnessing the benefits of foreign direct investment. In south-eastern Madagascar, the mining company Rio Tinto is currently developing an ilmenite mine, the raw material for the production of titanium dioxide pigment, mainly used in paint production. The company was once notorious for ignoring the health and safety of its workers and the surrounding communities, leaving environmental and social disaster in its wake.

Motivated by a combination of pressures, including judicial rulings in Australia, concern over the damage to its reputation caused by a bad press, and NGO campaigns, the CEO of the Australian half of the company championed an effort to rebuild its 'social licence to operate' from local communities and governments. Over 20 years, the company conducted preparatory research and trust building with local communities and NGOs before moving forward with the project.

Initially sceptical NGOs have been won over by Rio Tinto's change of approach (the Worldwide Fund for Nature and Conservation International among them). The transformation was also encouraged by pressure from investors, and by partnerships with experienced NGOs which helped Rio Tinto to address the project's social and environmental impacts.

Some general lessons emerge from this and other experiences of changing corporate behaviour:

- The company recognised there was a business case for sustainable development.
- Communities, consumers, and NGOs put initial pressure on the company.
- NGOs acted as an important bridge for the company to work with local communities.
- Government regulation forced strategic change.
- There was buy-in and leadership for change at the top of the company.

*Sources*: Oxfam, based on published sources and telephone interviews with protagonists.

Regrettably, there are still many companies whose operations abroad fall well short of the legal standards of their home countries. The problem with voluntary standards in these situations is precisely that they are voluntary, leaving enforcement to the companies themselves and allowing 'free-riders' to ignore such standards, and so gain a cost advantage over their more scrupulous rivals. Voluntary standards are important but they cannot replace the need for international standards that prevent the abuse of power by large TNCs operating in developing countries.

In business, as in politics, size matters. In 2007, Wal-Mart's sales came to $345bn, more than the GDP of all 49 least developed countries put together, or of major economies such as Saudi Arabia, Poland, or Indonesia. All told, the universe of TNCs now spans some 77,000 parent companies with over 770,000 foreign affiliates. In 2005, these foreign affiliates generated an estimated $4.5 trillion in value added, employed some 62 million workers, and exported goods and services valued at more than $4 trillion.[102]

The growth of TNCs has been driven by changes in business, technology, and politics. Improved communications and falling transport costs have allowed firms to spread production and management chains across countries in order to maximise profitability; meanwhile structural adjustment and liberalisation programmes worldwide have removed tariff and investment restrictions and have privatised numerous state-owned industries, often putting them into the hands of TNCs. As a result, FDI in developing countries is growing at some 10 per cent a year. In 2006 it reached $368bn, more than three times the annual volume of aid.[103]

While global governance is weak or non-existent when it comes to regulating corporate behaviour, it often imposes rules on governments that benefit companies, and these sometimes damage development prospects. TNCs have persistently and successfully lobbied for changes in national policies and in the rules of international trade and investment. In layer upon layer of bilateral, regional, and global agreements, developing-country governments have surrendered the right to regulate foreign investment in their own national interests. Investors have increasingly sought to use these provisions not just against expropriation by government, but against any government policy that affects their profitability.

Corporations have always tried to influence governments, but with increasing size has come increasing clout. The strong-arm tactics of the pharmaceutical industry to prevent developing-country governments from overriding patents in order to save lives are notorious. In the USA, pharmaceutical companies spent $759m to influence 1,400 Congressional bills between 1998 and 2004, and they employ 3,000 lobbyists.[104] Most of these focus on domestic legislation, but lobbyists also play a key role in shaping the US negotiating position at the WTO and elsewhere.

In the Uruguay Round of negotiations that led to the creation of the WTO in 1995, the pharmaceutical lobby steamrollered through an agreement on intellectual property whose implications were unclear to many of those involved. Only after it came into effect did developing countries realise the extent to which they had signed up to a major extension of corporate monopolies and high-priced drugs that would amount to a death sentence for thousands of sick and dying people.

Corporate lobbyists from the financial sector also spotted an opportunity to use WTO rules to prise open new markets through a 'General Agreement on Trade in Services' (GATS). David Hartridge, Director of the WTO Services Division, later acknowledged that 'without the enormous pressure generated by the American financial services sector, particularly companies like American Express and Citicorp, there would have been no services agreement.' [105]

On some issues, companies use their influence to press for positive change. In the Netherlands, ABN AMRO went to the Dutch parliament with Oxfam Novib to argue for stronger Dutch regulations on cluster bombs. In the UK, institutional investors such as Insight have lobbied the British government to improve its handling of the OECD guidelines on multinational enterprises.[106] Climate change, in particular (as explained below), has seen its share of both progressive and damaging corporate lobbying.

Using their clout to promote their private interests at the expense of the public good is only one of the worrying aspects of corporate activity that Oxfam has found in its work with transnationals in such disparate fields as coffee, mining, and garments. Other issues that point to the need for better governance of corporate behaviour include:

- **Commodity value chains**: Since the days of the East India Company, monopolies and cartels have allowed large corporations to manipulate markets. In recent years, a small number of TNCs have come to dominate the 'value chains' of products such as coffee, tea, grains, fruit, and vegetables. The six largest chocolate manufacturers account for 50 per cent of world sales. Just three global companies control 80 per cent of the soybean crushing market in Europe and more than 70 per cent in the USA.[107] Such market concentration ratchets up global inequality, depriving poor countries and producers of many of the potential benefits of trade.

TNCs have used their increased market power to claim an ever larger slice of the cake. In the early 1990s earnings by coffee-producing countries were some $10bn–$12bn and the value of retail sales of coffee, largely in industrialised countries, about $30bn. Now the value of retail sales exceeds $70bn, but coffee-producing countries only receive $5.5bn.[108] Such control can prevent poor countries from breaking into the more profitable 'value added' parts of the commodity chain, for example processing coffee or making chocolate, rather than simply exporting the raw materials.

- **Labour rights**: In sectors as diverse as food, clothing, and electronics, retailers have responded to cut-throat competition by pushing risks and costs down the supply chain, with devastating effects on the men and (mainly) women in far-flung countries who produce the goods. Oxfam's research on 11 independent, small- to medium-sized garment factories in Tangiers that produce clothes for Spanish retailers found intense work schedules to meet demands for quick turnarounds, often compounded by abuses such as forced overtime, denial of even elementary rights such as being able to use the toilet, and short-cuts that endanger health and safety (see page 157).

One study shows that in developing countries TNCs themselves are generally less likely to kill, injure, or abuse local workers and populations than domestic companies.[109] However, the incapacity or unwillingness of TNCs to assume responsibility for the conditions under which their suppliers produce the goods that they sell constitutes an obstacle in the fight against poverty and inequality.

- **Oil, gas, and mining**: In countries such as Sierra Leone, Angola, and the DRC, violent warlords have used revenues from the mines owned or linked to both national companies and to TNCs to buy arms and pay off their supporters, fighting 'resource wars' that exact a devastating human toll. More broadly, TNCs have done little to stem the corruption that is common in the extractive industries, thus undermining political stability and long-term development. This issue is discussed in Part 2 (see page 89).

- **Corruption**: World Bank figures suggest that $1 trillion in bribes is paid annually by international companies to secure lucrative deals. In 2004, the World Bank estimated that over 60 per cent of multinational corporations paid undocumented bribes in non-OECD countries to procure contracts.[110] The export credit agencies of rich-country governments, which insure large companies to trade and invest in developing countries, can be complicit in corruption, most directly by including 'commissions' that hide bribes in the overall sum underwritten, and most notoriously in the arms trade, which accounts for 50 per cent of the bribes paid worldwide between 1994 and 1999, according to the American Chamber of Commerce.[111]

There are several promising developments in this field, provided Northern governments are willing to back them. The OECD Convention on the Bribery of Foreign Officials in International Business Transactions (the OECD Anti-Bribery Convention) makes it a criminal offence for a representative from a business operating from any OECD country to bribe a government official anywhere in the world. In contrast with the civil penalties imposed before the Convention was introduced, company directors and managers may now face jail terms if they engage in active corruption. While countries such as the USA, France, Germany, and Italy have enforced anti-bribery laws, since the Convention took effect few significant prosecutions have occurred in Japan, Canada, or Australia. The UK government drew widespread condemnation in 2007 when it suspended investigations into a lucrative arms deal between British Aerospace and Saudi Arabia, citing national security considerations.[112]

Most countries lag behind the USA in holding their companies to account; the 1977 Foreign Corrupt Practices Act has led to numerous prosecutions. For example, in 2006 the US Securities and Exchange Commission (SEC) alleged that Brazilian and South Korean subsidiaries of the Tyco conglomerate had repeatedly made illegal payments to government officials in those countries in exchange for business. The SEC action was settled with $50m in penalties.[113]

The International Chamber of Commerce and Transparency International have each developed a voluntary code of conduct against bribery, and the UK government has encouraged companies to adopt similar voluntary codes for arms production and commerce. The UN Convention Against Corruption (UNCAC) came into force in 2005; it was signed by 140 countries, of which 80 have ratified the Convention. UNCAC covers both developed and developing countries, and requires state action on public and private corruption, on both bribe-givers and bribe-takers. It also promotes international co-operation (for example, joint investigation, extradition, legal and technical assistance, information sharing); provides for asset recovery (for example, returning millions of dollars stolen and stashed in Northern banks); and provides protection to whistle-blowers.

Finally, the international effort to track down and seize the financial accounts of suspected terrorist organisations gives the lie to previous claims that regulation is politically impossible. Northern governments could prevent banks and offshore tax havens from accepting the proceeds of corruption. This is a civic responsibility of the large private companies involved, and is in the interests of ensuring long-term prosperity by promoting stable, democratic countries around the world.

The governance of TNCs must address both responsible and irresponsible firms, not least to ensure that the latter cannot gain an unfair advantage by abusing employees, communities, or the environment, in the process undermining the contribution to development of foreign trade and investment. As well as restoring the role of the state in effectively regulating and managing foreign investment and trade in the national interest (see Part 3), a number of steps are needed at a global level.

**Responsibility:** The first step is for TNCs to accept responsibility for people whose lives they affect, and not just for their direct employees, who are often few in number. After initial denial, most major garment brands today accept some responsibility for the labour conditions in their suppliers' factories.

Recognition of corporate social responsibility (CSR) is now spreading to some of the rapidly growing domestic companies in developing-country giants: a 2008 survey by the *Economist* magazine found CSR thinking established in Brazil and India and growing in importance in China; however, it was little in evidence in the other 'BRIC' country, Russia.[114] In Hong Kong, Oxfam is in regular dialogue with clothing companies that have regionalised and now run garment factories in Cambodia and other countries in the region. In Indonesia, Unilever conducted groundbreaking research with Oxfam to understand its 'poverty footprint', exploring its impact on small farmers, suppliers, and distributors, as well as employees.[115]

**Transparency**: For firms to be accountable, they must first provide information on issues such as their social and environmental policies and impacts. Nike broke new ground in 2004 when it published a list of its supplier factories worldwide. There are numerous initiatives to codify how data should be collected and reported. The Global Reporting Initiative, in particular, has become increasingly sophisticated and is now commonly used by leading companies across various industries.[116] The general principle of transparency should also be extended to corporate lobby activities at both national and international levels.

**Monitoring and verification**: If companies are to be transparent, they must have something worth reporting. In many cases, corporations are only now learning how to gather relevant social and environmental data (it took one major European garment retailer two years just to establish where its clothes were being made), and there is a clear need to develop robust systems for doing so. Learning from peers and other experts is crucial. The Ethical Trading Initiative brings together companies (mainly from the supermarket and garments sectors), trade unions, and NGOs to promote, monitor, and independently verify labour rights throughout global supply chains.[117]

**Legal reporting requirements**: Efforts to improve corporate performance (and curb abuses) can be greatly helped by home-country governments passing legal requirements on companies to monitor the impact of their activities and to publish reports of their findings. In the UK, changes in the law requiring companies to publish their assessments of so-called 'non-financial risks' have galvanised efforts by long-term investors such as pensions funds to ensure that the companies in which they invest are not risking reputational damage, or endangering their long-term survival, by cutting corners on social and environmental issues.

**Competition law**: Given the increasing control of numerous markets by handfuls of global corporations, there is a strong argument for some form of global competition authority. Although in theory such an authority could be housed in the WTO, many developing countries argue that the agenda there is more likely to be driven by TNCs' desire for improved market access than by a concern to improve development outcomes. As a result, competition was dropped from the Doha agenda in 2004. A separate global competition authority, perhaps housed within the UN system, is more likely to command trust.

**Liability**: When companies commit serious abuses, such as the notorious 1984 gas leak at the Union Carbide plant in Bhopal, India that killed an estimated 20,000 people and left a further 100,000 with lifelong damage, should they be liable to prosecution in the country where the abuse takes place, or in a court in their home country? Other countries could follow the example set by the US Alien Tort Claims Act and allow victims to sue in a company's home country (this is particularly important in cases where the rule of law is weak). Alternatively, judgements made in foreign courts could be enforced by courts in rich countries by, for example, collecting damages.

---

### BOX 5.3
### CORPORATE RESPONSIBILITY OR ACCOUNTABILITY? VOLUNTARY SCHEMES VS REGULATION

Most businesses argue for corporate responsibility, achieved by self-regulation through voluntary initiatives. Civil society organisations, on the other hand, tend to demand corporate accountability, in particular to those stakeholders whose lives are directly affected: people displaced by mining, women denied proper working conditions in sweatshops, farmers denied a living wage by the prices given for their produce.

Voluntary initiatives range from TNC public relations-based promises to behave well, through peer review, to so-called 'multi-stakeholder' initiatives involving corporations and other relevant groups in jointly developing guidelines, monitoring performance, and dealing with problems, which can be very effective. Some of these are intergovernmental, such as the

UN Global Compact, while others are independent, such as the Ethical Trading Initiative.

The more effective initiatives are those that involve a range of stakeholders, independent forms of monitoring, and verification of corporations' claims and performance, and in addition are clearly linked to international standards such as the conventions of the International Labour Organization or UN human rights law. For example, a number of large firms have joined the Business Leaders Initiative on Human Rights chaired by the former UN Human Rights Commissioner Mary Robinson, to pilot the implementation of UN human rights law (including ILO conventions) across their organisations, and have involved human rights NGOs in their implementation.

Corporate responsibility initiatives are more effective when they are driven by a company's board and CEO – not just by the corporate social responsibility department – and when they lead to changes in the core business model rather than remaining an 'ethical add-on'. So, for example, retailers need to take into account the impact that ordering rapid turnaround times on large volumes of clothing or other goods has on hours and working conditions at the end of the supply chain, while drugs companies need to adopt different pricing strategies for rich and poor countries as a standard, rather than an occasional concession to public or government pressure.

Voluntary initiatives play an important role in encouraging businesses to engage properly in corporate responsibility. For example, the UN Global Compact has been extraordinarily successful in encouraging large numbers of businesses in developing countries to embrace CSR, as a first step on the way to lifting standards. The voluntary nature of this has been critical, as has the UN convening role.

Voluntary initiatives can also end up influencing legal frameworks, for example when leading companies lobby governments to pass rules that require laggard companies to report, thereby preventing them from gaining an unfair competitive advantage. In the UK, the Ethical Trading Initiative successfully lobbied the government to introduce controls on so-called 'gang masters' organising migrant labour in British farms and packing houses, and to enforce minimum labour standards.

That said, there is still a pressing need to address the lack of global governance relating to businesses working in developing countries, where the regulatory framework and/or the capacity to enforce it is weak. There should be no double standards in the way that businesses operate at home and abroad.

*Sources*: www.unglobalcompact.org; for a dauntingly comprehensive guide to global business and human rights, see: www.business-humanrights.org/Home.

The UN, for one, thinks that the days of corporate impunity are coming to an end, with the UN Special Representative on CSR issues arguing that, 'Corporations are increasingly recognized as "participants" at the international level, with the capacity to bear some rights and duties under international law.'[118]

Scrapping bad laws could help as much as passing good ones, and two prime candidates for the dustbin are the WTO agreements on TRIPS and TRIMS (Trade-Related Investment Measures), both of which severely curb the ability of developing countries to use industrial policy effectively. An agreement to set a floor on global corporate taxation would also ensure that poor countries avoid a regulatory 'race to the bottom', instead receiving a decent tax revenue with which to fund public services and infrastructure.

The key test for efforts to improve the impact of TNCs in developing countries is whether they strengthen or undermine efforts to build active citizenship and effective states. Wherever possible, TNCs should be regulated by strong national governments, accountable to their citizens.

The best initiatives already do this: supply chain initiatives based on ILO Core Conventions strengthen labour rights and the voice of trade unions in often hostile settings. The Extractive Industries Transparency Initiative (EITI) supports improved governance in resource-rich countries through the verification and full publication of company payments and government revenues from oil, gas, and mining, providing the information that civil society watchdogs need to monitor what their governments are doing with the income from natural resources.[119] Companies involved in the Ethical Trading Initiative have lobbied governments such as that of Bangladesh to improve the quality of their labour inspectorates.

The drivers of such changes have included not just workers, campaigners, and NGOs but also institutional investors concerned about the long-term viability of their investments. So-called 'shareholder advocacy' has become an important factor in pressing for improvements both in individual companies and more broadly. In the USA, a shareholder resolution that won an unprecedented 92 per cent of the vote persuaded the gold-mining giant Newmont to set up an independent global review committee to scrutinise 'the company's policies and practices relating to existing and potential opposition from local communities'.[120]

Such successes remain the exception. The long hard slog of citizen activism and government regulation is essential to harness the benefits and curb the threats of globalised business.

Globalisation is leading to ever-expanding trade in goods, services, knowledge, and people. These flows are always subject to rules of some kind – even free markets need rules, and the global system is far from a free market. But rules emerge from negotiations and politics: they are the outcome of power struggles, more than an exercise in logic or the maximisation of human happiness. In such struggles the powerful, be they corporations or governments, are much more likely to impose solutions that benefit themselves, often at the expense of the weak.

Rewriting the rigged rules of international trade is central to making global governance work for development. The system needs more rules in some areas, such as taxation or migration, and fewer rules in others, such as intellectual property. Rewriting the rules will need a combination of active citizens, North and South, and assertive, effective governments able to correct the imbalances of power that dog global negotiations. If that revision of global trade rules can be achieved, the power of globalisation to deliver sustainable growth with equity can be realised.

# THE INTERNATIONAL AID SYSTEM

A few years ago, vacancies for nursing posts in Malawi were running at over 60 per cent, and large swathes of the country had no doctors at all. Low pay and poor working conditions were driving staff away at an alarming rate, to work for NGOs, private hospitals, or in other sectors altogether – or even to migrate overseas.

This seemingly intractable crisis, familiar to most developing countries and some rich ones as well, was transformed by a judicious influx of aid. With 90 per cent funding from the UK and the Global Fund to Fight AIDS, Malaria and Tuberculosis, Malawi's Ministry of Health increased salaries by 50 per cent for 5,400 front-line health workers, recruited 700 new health staff, expanded and improved training schools, and plugged critical gaps with expatriate volunteers.

'In 2003, resignations of nurses were at one or even two a week. It was shocking', said Dr Damison Kathyola, director of Kamuzu Central Hospital in the Malawian capital Lilongwe. 'Since we introduced incentives, we've somehow stemmed it to one or two a month.'[121] Aid from rich countries to poor ones can relieve poverty and suffering, fund the clean water and millions of teachers and health workers that poor countries need, and provide an injection of capital and know-how to help kick-start economic growth. Aid's most tangible successes have been in health, where vaccinations have eradicated smallpox and have saved 7.5 million lives from 1999–2005 simply by halving deaths from measles.[122]

More broadly, many of today's successful countries began their take-off with an influx of aid, such as the US Marshall Plan that transformed post-war Europe, the aid that funded the initial take-off of Botswana, Taiwan, and South Korea, and the transformation of Spain and Ireland by EU structural funds.

Aid can redistribute wealth from rich regions, countries, and people to poor ones, fight deprivation and invest in global public goods, such as disease control and environmental protection. However, aid cannot achieve such progress on its own. Well-designed aid programmes complement and support national and community development efforts, strengthening both effective states and active citizens. In contrast, poorly designed aid competes with states and citizens or even undermines them.

Overseas development assistance (ODA), as aid is officially called, is a relatively recent phenomenon, one born out of decolonisation and reconstruction after the Second World War. Its birth is often linked to the inaugural address of US President Harry Truman in 1949, in which he announced that 'For the first time in history, humanity possesses the knowledge and skill to relieve the suffering of ...the half of the people of the world living in conditions approaching misery.' The war years and their immediate aftermath saw the creation of many of the organisations that still dominate the international aid scene today, including the UN, the World Bank, and the IMF, and international NGOs.

Aid inspires passion. Zealous advocates see aid as one of the great causes of modern times and argue that a 'big push' can lead to the 'end of poverty', in the title of the book by perhaps its most prominent advocate, Jeffrey Sachs. Equally passionate sceptics point out that President Truman's words of 1949 could just as easily reflect the state of the world 60 years later. If $2.3 trillion in aid since 1950 has had so little impact, they argue, surely aid doesn't work? [123] Eminent economists on both sides swap contradictory numbers and conclusions (see Table 5.2 on page 359). Others see aid as being driven primarily by self-interest and foreign policy, arguing that the allocation of aid based on Cold War alliances (however grisly the regime) has now morphed into aid based on support for the 'war on terror', which has little to do with development need.

## TABLE 5.1: THE MILLENNIUM DEVELOPMENT GOALS

| GOAL | KEY TARGET |
| --- | --- |
| 1 ERADICATE EXTREME POVERTY AND HUNGER | Halve the proportion of people living on less than $1 a day by 2015.<br><br>Halve the proportion of people who suffer from hunger by 2015. |
| 2 ACHIEVE UNIVERSAL PRIMARY EDUCATION | Ensure that all children complete a full course of primary schooling by 2015. |
| 3 PROMOTE GENDER EQUALITY AND EMPOWER WOMEN | Eliminate gender disparity in primary and secondary education by 2005, and in all levels of education by 2015. |
| 4 REDUCE CHILD MORTALITY | Reduce the mortality rate of children under five by two-thirds by 2015. |
| 5 IMPROVE MATERNAL HEALTH | Reduce by three-quarters the ratio of women dying in childbirth by 2015. |
| 6 COMBAT HIV/AIDS, MALARIA AND OTHER DISEASES | Halt and begin to reverse the incidence of HIV/AIDS and other major diseases by 2015. |
| 7 ENSURE ENVIRONMENTAL SUSTAINABILITY | Halve by 2015 the proportion of people without access to safe drinking water and basic sanitation. |
| 8 DEVELOP A GLOBAL PARTNER-SHIP FOR DEVELOPMENT | Develop a non-discriminatory and rules-based trading system, provide more generous aid and deal comprehensively with the debt problem. |

Even aid's supporters disagree about whether it should be viewed as a sensible and generous gesture of solidarity to rebalance the extreme inequalities in the global distribution of income, or as a matter of justice: minimal reparations for problems caused by the rich countries through colonialism, imperialism, and today's unfair trade and finance regimes.

Whatever the motives, the purpose of the international aid system became much clearer as, throughout the 1990s, a series of UN summits set globally agreed objectives on poor people's access to wealth, water, education, and health, as well as the essential steps needed to achieve them, all culminating in the Millennium Development Goals, which were agreed at a special summit in 2000 (see Table 5.1). These provided unprecedented levels of international agreement, strengthening the arguments for increasing aid and focusing it on fighting poverty. Mass global movements, including Jubilee 2000 and the Global Call to Action against Poverty (GCAP), raised the political profile of development issues and increased the political rewards for taking them seriously. The AIDS crisis prompted growing public concern, which was reflected in new bilateral funding and the establishment of large dedicated funds both in the USA and globally.

## INTERNATIONAL NGOS

Although they constitute only a minor part of the overall aid system in terms of their financial clout, international non-government organisations (INGOs) such as Oxfam are among the more recognisable voices in the development debate.[124] Most INGOs have their head offices in the rich, developed countries and raise their money there from the public and from governments. They work in partnership with increasingly influential Southern-based NGOs specialising in advocacy (such as Third World Network and Focus on the Global South) or in programming on the ground (such as BRAC and SEWA).

Like official development assistance, INGOs are a relatively recent phenomenon. Oxfam, for example, was founded in 1942. Working primarily with funds donated by the general public, INGOs can be distinguished from government aid agencies in three key ways: they are relatively independent from the geopolitical interests of states; they offer ordinary citizens (particularly in the North) an opportunity to take part in efforts to fight poverty and inequality as supporters, volunteers, or contributors; and they often engage more effectively than governments with citizens in the developing world who are excluded from existing institutional structures.[125]

It is noteworthy that the major INGOs are based in the same countries that won the Second World War and which came to dominate the institutions of global governance: the USA, Britain, and France. A second tier is made up of INGOs based in other former colonial powers (the Netherlands, Belgium, Italy, Germany, Spain, Japan), with a smattering from rich countries with less historical baggage in the developing world (Canada, Australia, New Zealand).

The major agencies underwent a huge expansion in the 1980s, when they began attracting government funding and when the public began to donate massively in response to humanitarian disasters, most notably the Ethiopian famine early in that decade. With growth came scale, professionalism, co-ordination, and an increasing diversification of activities.

Total government support to INGOs concerned with development issues totalled an estimated $379m in 2003, a tiny fraction of overall aid, but nearly three times the amount given a decade earlier. Meanwhile, national NGOs operating in their own territories received some four times that amount.[126] Total revenues from all sources, including public donations, to development NGOs are estimated at about $12bn a year, just over one-tenth of the volume of official government aid.[127]

## THE QUANTITY OF AID

In a reflection of the geopolitical motivation for much aid, volumes declined precipitously when the Cold War ended, falling to a low of $58bn in 2000. However, the millennium marked an apparent turn-around, with global aid reaching $107bn in 2005, and promises that it would increase even further.[128] Renewed faith in aid is due partly to careful advocacy at the UN and among publics in donor countries, and partly to new concerns about failed states and their relationship to terrorism. However, some dubious accounting practices have inflated the figures. Debt cancellation for Iraq, which was clearly driven more by geopolitical than by developmental concerns, single-handedly boosted the aid figure by $12.2bn in 2005.[129] Moreover, total aid fell back to $104bn in 2006 (again inflated by Iraq)[130] and, barring miracles, was set to fall further in 2007, leaving a mountain to climb to meet the promises made at the Gleneagles Summit in Scotland in 2005.

The heightened international focus on security post-9/11 has also played a part in increased aid volumes, particularly to Iraq and Afghanistan. As Richard N. Haass, President George W. Bush's Director of Policy Planning Staff, put it within months of the 9/11 attacks: 'In the conduct of the global campaign against terrorism... our tool kit must also include effective foreign assistance.' [131]

In 2005, rich countries pledged to increase their aid by a further $50bn by 2010, with half of this going to Africa. European governments made the lion's share of these promises, setting themselves an aid target of 0.51 per cent of their gross national income by 2010, on the way to reaching 0.7 per cent of GNI by 2015 (see page 381 for the background to the 2005 breakthrough).

If that schedule is kept to, foreign aid from traditional donor governments would be two-thirds European by 2010, and the European Commission would be a bigger donor than the World Bank. However, by early 2008, the promises of 2005 were starting to look very fragile. Aid from G8 nations to poor countries actually *fell* in 2006 for the first time since 1997. Based on the actual trend since 2005, the G8 would miss the target of a $50bn increase by fully $30bn. The price of this broken promise? UNAIDS and the WHO say that it would cost five million lives, providing the money were put to vital health interventions for women, children, and people living with HIV and AIDS.[132]

The past decade has also seen the entrance of new donor countries, including China, India, Brazil, South Africa, Russia, Venezuela, and Saudi Arabia, which are now a significant part of the aid picture. China is estimated to be providing some $1.5–$2bn a year in aid, about half of which goes to Africa. It is popular with African governments, as Senegal's President Abdoulaye Wade explained during one tense exchange with the EU: 'If I want to do five kilometres of road with the World Bank, or one of the international financial institutions, it takes at least five years. One year of discussions. One year of back and forth. One year of I don't know what. With the Chinese it is a few days and I say yes or no, they send a team, and we sign.' [133]

Besides new national donors, 'philanthropreneurs' such as the Bill & Melinda Gates Foundation have also joined the big league. The scale of international private philanthropy is difficult to measure, but estimates range from $10bn–$25bn annually.[134] While they are not on the same scale, INGOs are also raising and spending much more than ever before.

Politically, the rise of new donors enhances the bargaining power of poor countries and thus their ability to avoid damaging conditions. At the same time it undercuts the often overstated clout of donors to pressure for human rights and governance reforms. In addition, as will be explored below, it vastly complicates the picture regarding aid accountability.

## TABLE 5.2: THREE GRAND NARRATIVES ON AID: SACHS, EASTERLY, AND COLLIER COMPARED

| The aid optimist: Jeffrey Sachs (*The End of Poverty*) | The aid pessimist: William Easterly (*White Man's Burden*) | Paul Collier (*The Bottom Billion*) |
|---|---|---|
| **Core argument: diagnosis** | | |
| An aid optimist: extreme poverty can be eradicated within a generation. Poverty trap: poverty itself leads to under-investment in basic services, which depletes poor people's capital stock and leads to deeper poverty. Hostile geography: remote, landlocked, or mountainous countries face huge additional obstacles. | An aid pessimist: aid has failed because it is planned from the top down, without account-ability structures and without feedback from the people served. It creates perverse incen-tives (e.g. promotion based on how much money you manage to disburse) that have little to do with development or poverty reduction. In contrast with top-down 'Planners', bottom-up 'Searchers' find out what local people want, and supply it using market mechanisms. Searchers nimbly adapt to local conditions, and keep the customer satisfied. They understand incentives and accountability. | Four 'traps' keep a billion people excluded from global prosperity: The Conflict Trap; The Natural Resources Trap (too much rather than too little); Being Landlocked with Bad Neighbours; Bad Governance. Collier analyses four instruments to deal with these: Aid Security (i.e. military intervention) International laws and charters Trade policy. |

| The aid optimist: Jeffrey Sachs (*The End of Poverty*) | The aid pessimist: William Easterly (*White Man's Burden*) | Paul Collier (*The Bottom Billion*) |
| --- | --- | --- |
| **Core argument: solutions** | | |
| Massive though affordable injection of aid by rich countries. | There is no 'big idea', but some principles: | Focus on the most difficult environments. |
| Target basic services (agriculture, education, health, water and sanitation, communication, and transport) to unlock the poverty trap. | Make aid agents individually accountable. | Accept more risk, and a higher rate of failure. |
| | Let those agents search for what works. | Be flexible, seize reform opportunities at an early stage. |
| Then poor people will be able to save, invest, and prosper on their own. | Evaluate, based on feedback from the intended beneficiaries and scientific testing. | |
| Sachs' work has led to the creation of the 'Millennium Villages Project', which seeks to put these ideas into practice through integrated rural development projects in selected villages across Africa. | Reward success and penalise failure. | |

| The aid optimist:<br>Jeffrey Sachs<br>(*The End of Poverty*) | The aid pessimist:<br>William Easterly<br>(*White Man's Burden*) | Paul Collier<br>(*The Bottom Billion*) |
|---|---|---|

### Strengths

| | | |
|---|---|---|
| A powerful piece of aid advocacy that counteracts the unwarranted pessimism often surrounding the aid debate. | Suspicious of the 'It's up to us' view that sees aid as a way for the rich countries to single-handedly end poverty in poor ones. | On aid, positioned somewhere between Sachs and Easterly, but leaning towards Easterly on aid scepticism. |
| Sachs himself is an extraordinary ambassador: fervent, inspiring, hyperactive, and tireless. | Stresses the need for donors to be made accountable to aid recipients. | Good discussion of when and when not to give aid and whether to do so in the form of finance or technical assistance. |
| Advocates repair of the aid machinery: | Identifies the importance of incentive systems in determining the behaviour of aid and government officials. | Strongest on the links between conflict and development, including the case for military intervention in cases such as Sierra Leone, and the need to be much more |
| National poverty strategies developed by recipient governments identifying investments and financial needs to meet the MDGs. | Rightly dismisses top-down structural adjustment, shock therapy, and conditionality (Easterly was a World Bank insider). | creative about seizing moments of post-conflict reconstruction to help countries escape from poverty. |
| Co-ordination among donors to meet financial needs. | The detail of his argument, in contrast with the overall message (and the title), argues for 'better aid' rather than 'no aid', and sets out some good ideas for how to achieve it. | Also very convincing on the special problems (and limited solutions) of Africa's landlocked countries. |
| Grants, not loans. | | |
| Long-term, predictable aid. | | |
| Decentralisation of investment decisions. | | |
| Emphasises basic technologies and interventions that have worked in a variety of contexts. | Has a strong sense of the indigenous creativity in developing countries that can trigger development. | |
| Tackles head-on some of the anti-aid arguments on corruption, past failure, authoritarian governments, and culture. | Good complement to Sachs in advocating services and technologies beyond the basics. | |

| The aid optimist:<br>Jeffrey Sachs<br>(*The End of Poverty*) | The aid pessimist:<br>William Easterly<br>(*White Man's Burden*) | Paul Collier<br>(*The Bottom Billion*) |
|---|---|---|

### Weaknesses

Massive aid is necessary but may not be sufficient: Sachs assumes that breaking the poverty trap alone will unleash economic growth. Interventions are limited to agriculture, basic social services, and basic rural infrastructure.

Underplays the importance of politics and power in development:

Weak on institutions: Strong institutions (especially public institutions) are needed to translate national strategies into effective investments on the ground.

Weak on citizenship: Active citizenship is needed to set priorities for decentralised investments targeting the poorest people and to hold local and national institutions accountable.

Sachs' big push is similar to the integrated rural development programmes of the 1970s, which failed due to lack of government support, manipulation by local elites, and low levels of participation (although Sachs addresses this last point by stressing the importance of participation in project design).

Undermines support for massive increase in aid budgets that is necessary to provide basic social services and meet the MDGs.

Underplays the importance of politics and power in development:

Ignores the role of the state in creating the market conditions in which 'Searchers' can flourish.

Market solutions will not work for people whose wealth and income are too low to register as 'market demand'.

Ignores the central role of planning in development success stories such as China, Viet Nam, South Korea, or Botswana.

Does not give a chance to donors to apply lessons learned and plan aid with more accountability and recipient ownership.

Stronger on critique than on proposition.

Overall the diagnosis is much more compelling than the conclusions (except on post-conflict reconstruction).

Blind spots on inequality, sustainability and climate change, and rights.

Largely ignores political science, history, and other disciplines in favour of almost exclusive reliance on the mathematical wizardry of 'econometrics' to establish links and causation between variables such as aid and conflict. Applicability of this kind of econometric analysis is disputed.

The dramatis personae are made up almost entirely of benevolent economists and heroic finance ministers, faced with incompetent or corrupt governments and civil servants trying to thwart them. No recognition of the role of political parties, trade unions, or active citizenship of any sort.

An orthodox liberaliser on trade and investment, with little time for NGO concerns about negative impacts of premature liberalisation.

*Sources*: J. Sachs (2005) *The End of Poverty: How We Can Make it Happen in Our Lifetime*, Penguin; www.millenniumvillages.org; W. Easterly (2006) *White Man's Burden: Why the West's Efforts to Aid the Rest Have Done So Much Ill and So Little Good*, Penguin; P. Collier (2007) *The Bottom Billion: Why the Poorest Countries are Failing and What Can Be Done About It*, Oxford University Press.

## THE QUALITY OF AID

Good aid can transform lives; bad aid undermines development. Aid donors have always been motivated by a mixture of altruism, hubris, and self-interest. Sadly, when it comes to determining the priorities and methods of aid spending, dedicated and knowledgeable aid practitioners are too often overruled by the dictates of domestic politics or geopolitical calculations. An analysis of President Bush's budget request for fiscal year 2008 showed that the largest recipients of US aid were Israel and Egypt (which between them absorb one out of every four US aid dollars), and concluded 'the lion's share of US foreign aid still goes to ten countries, the majority of which are geo-political allies in the "global war on terror" or the war on drugs'.[135] A high proportion of aid is tied to purchases of goods or services in the donor country, with aid programmes designed according to commercial self-interest rather than need. Aid can also fall prey to the short attention span of politicians and their publics, who prefer projects that can show 'results' in a year or two to those that make a long-term contribution.

Aid allocation is often distorted by geopolitical interest. A recent study showed that when a developing country becomes a non-permanent member of the UN Security Council, its aid from the USA increases on average by 60 per cent.[136] In Europe's case, cultural ties (for example a shared language) and post-colonial guilt are also factors, with a disproportionate amount of aid going to former colonies. Other problems include Byzantine procedures, the policy changes that donors demand as conditions for giving aid, waste caused by tied aid and an over-reliance on technical assistance, and overlapping and un-co-ordinated approaches that undermine state structures. These reduce the effectiveness of aid and can handicap the effort to build active citizenship and effective states.

The delivery of aid is extraordinarily complex and cumbersome. Developing countries with limited numbers of trained officials must grapple with a proliferation of international 'financing mechanisms', including 90 global health funds set up to address specific diseases or problems. Uganda has over 40 donors delivering aid in-country. Government of Uganda figures show that it had to deal with 684 different aid instruments and associated agreements between 2003/04 and 2006/07, for aid coming into the central budget alone. The island of St. Vincent (population 117,000) was asked to monitor 191 different indicators on HIV and AIDS.[137]

In 2006 some Malian civil servants spent over 100 days managing donor missions (a telling expression) from just two of the country's donors, the World Bank and the IMF – that is one in every three working days. A senior official from the Ministry of Finance in Mali noted, 'They usually come three to four times a year and stay for more than one week, visiting up to ten ministries at a time when here. Our hands are completely tied.'[138] A survey of 14 countries by the OECD and the World Bank showed an average of 200 donor missions per year, three-quarters of these by a handful of donors (the 'chronic travellers'). Cambodia and Viet Nam each received 400 missions, Nicaragua 289, Bolivia 270, and Bangladesh 250.[139]

Most aid is still given on a short-term basis (one to three years)[140] and its volume tends to fluctuate, undermining the ability of developing-country officials to undertake long-term planning and investment. A recent study by the IMF, for example, revealed that aid flows are more volatile than fiscal revenues, and the higher the aid dependency of a country, the more the volume fluctuates. Worryingly, the study showed that aid volatility has increased in recent years.[141] Unable to count on steady revenue, developing-country governments hesitate to invest in recurrent costs, such as the salaries of public sector workers, which are a crucial step in providing essential services such as health care, education, social protection, and water and sanitation.

Donors continue to force developing countries to give back a considerable part of their aid money by making them purchase inappropriate and expensive goods and services from the donor country. The OECD estimates that such 'tied aid' raises costs by between 15 and 30 per cent.[142] In 2001, OECD members agreed to untie all their bilateral aid to least developed countries (LDCs), except for food aid and technical assistance. However, as of 2006, only the UK, Sweden, Ireland, Luxembourg, and the Netherlands were abiding by this agreement, with all other donors falling far short. The USA was the worst culprit, with 70 per cent of its bilateral aid to LDCs remaining tied.[143]

The professionalisation of the aid field over the past 30 years has led to improved levels of monitoring, evaluation, reflection, and planning. The same process, however, has also skewed budgets toward spending on technical assistance. The high-priced consultants who propose, monitor, and evaluate aid programmes now pocket 20 cents of every aid dollar.[144] A study of technical assistance in Mozambique found that rich countries were spending $350m per year on 3,500 technical experts, while the entire wage bill for Mozambique's 100,000 public sector workers was just $74m.[145] While technical assistance may be helpful, for example in enabling governments to learn from the experiences of others, donors ought to place developing countries in control of technical assistance funds, so that they can decide whether to hire local or other consultants to undertake work that fits their own needs and priorities.

Even when well-intentioned, the long shopping lists of 'conditions' attached by donors undermines the essential task of building institutions and policies rooted in local economic and social structures – the path followed by all of today's successful economies. Of course, taxpayers in rich countries – and citizens of poor countries – are entitled to expect aid to be used to promote development and to be clearly accounted for. However, many donors undermine quality by imposing their own preferred economic policy reforms. 'Conditionality' often obliges poor countries to implement policies based on dogma and ideology, rather than on evidence – for example, privatisation and liberalisation which, as discussed in Part 3, have a poor track record in triggering growth or reducing poverty.

Donor hubris can also erode state institutions. One insider account of Ghana's attempt to adopt new policies after the 2000 election of an energetic new president highlights the corrosive impact on institutions of aid dependence. Aid donor staff were ideologically hostile to the president's proposals to promote industry, and distrusted the abilities of government staff to design such a programme. They insisted that the government use 'technical assistance' to design its flagship industrial policy and, desperate for resources, the government agreed. Soon the Ministry for Private Sector Development had more foreign consultants than civil servants. With policy backgrounds rooted in the international aid industry, the consultants themselves were sceptical of many of the government's ideas. Instead of aid backing a genuine effort to build an effective state, it bogged the government down in a debilitating wrangle with donors, sucking the energy out of its development plans.[146]

One innovative approach undertaken by donor and recipient governments to address the poor quality of much aid is the Education for All (EFA) initiative, which since 2000 has helped well over 20 million children who would never have received an education to enrol in school. Under the EFA compact, poor-country governments promised to draw up realistic long-term education sector plans and to increase their own investment in primary education. Donors in turn promised to work together so that, as the World Bank's Development Committee put it, 'No countries seriously committed to education for all will be thwarted in their achievement of this goal by a lack of resources.' Not only have some 30 developing countries had their plans endorsed and funded but, egged on by citizen campaigns, governments in 70 countries are spending more on education as a proportion of total government expenditure.[147]

Traditional donors grouped in the OECD's Development Advisory Committee (DAC) have also acknowledged the need to improve quality. The Paris Declaration on Aid Effectiveness of 2005 laid out a set of principles to be implemented by both donors and recipients over the following five years.[148] Developing countries agreed to give priority to the fight against poverty, promising to produce national poverty plans with the participation of their citizens and national legislatures. They also agreed to create more transparent and accountable management systems for public finances, in order to ensure that resources go where they are intended.

Rich countries in turn agreed not only to provide more aid, but also to align their aid around developing-country priorities and systems, in recognition of the fact that recipient-country ownership over the development process is an essential prerequisite for successful development. They also agreed to cut the high administrative burden by working in a more co-ordinated fashion, for example by organising joint visits and reporting.

While the Paris principles are generally positive, they address efficiency more than effectiveness, and civil society organisations have pointed out that the principles appear to be divorced from values such as justice, human rights, gender equality, democracy, or even the reduction of poverty. What is more, the Paris Declaration covers a shrinking proportion of the global aid pie, since it does not apply to new donors or to private foundations.

Like windfalls from oil revenue, large inflows of aid risk undermining the social contract between state and citizenry. Aid-dependent governments often respond more to the interests and desires of donors than to those of their citizens. One cross-country study found a 'robust statistical relationship between high aid levels in Africa and deteriorations in governance', arguing that 'political elites have little incentive to change a situation in which large amounts of aid provide exceptional resources for patronage and many fringe benefits'. [149]

This pitfall can be avoided in part if donors also fund civil society and parliamentary watchdogs that hold government to account. While the volume of aid to such accountability mechanisms is likely to be dwarfed by flows to the state, it can help to make states responsive and can be crucial for the active citizen side of the development equation. In the longer term, using aid to fund education and adult literacy programmes can strengthen citizens' movements and spread notions of rights that can compensate for the potential damage to the social contract.

Some economists, along with the IMF, argue that large aid inflows cause economic problems in recipient countries, such as rising inflation, appreciation of the exchange rate, and knock-on effects that undermine economic competitiveness – a syndrome known as 'Dutch disease'. [150] The fear of Dutch disease, however, seems to be far greater than the reality. A recent survey of aid in seven countries found little evidence that large scale-ups in aid had actually caused Dutch disease, partly because developing-country governments were already used to dealing with the manifold effects of volatile and unpredictable aid. [151]

One way to minimise the dangers of aid dependence might be to impose time limits on aid, as the USA did with European recipients of the Marshall Plan and with its aid to South Korea and Taiwan in the 1960s. In a manner analogous to the temporary protection of infant industries, time-limited aid would provide both resources and incentives to build up alternative revenue streams through taxation or economic diversification by the time the deadline arrived – another task that aid can support. Such an approach would be politically difficult in practice, but some form of exit strategy is essential for both donors and recipients.

As Uganda's President Yoweri Museveni told a conference in Washington DC in 2005: 'I have made revenue collection a frontline institution because it is the one which can emancipate us from begging, from disturbing friends…if we can get about 22 percent of GDP [double the current rate] we should not need to disturb anybody by asking for aid….instead of coming here to bother you, give me this, give me this, I shall come here to greet you, to trade with you.' [152]

The best kind of aid strengthens responsive state structures. In Botswana, which for many decades has been Africa's economic success story, the government took control of aid immediately after independence and made sure that it was integrated into its own national budgeting and planning procedures. Though heavily dependent on aid (even in 1973, when its economic take-off was well under way, aid funded 45 per cent of total government expenditure), Botswana refused donor proposals that did not fit its own priorities and insisted on tailoring donor activities to the government's way of doing things.[153]

By contrast, when donors fund myriad small projects, or set up parallel systems with NGOs or other service providers, they are more likely to undermine the state than strengthen it. Qualified staff leave government for better-paid jobs in the aid world, and government planners struggle to implement coherent national development plans that pull together different and often competing players.

Part of the answer to better aid lies in providing governments with core funding, known as general budget support (GBS), or with funding earmarked for a particular sector such as agriculture or health (known as sector-wide approaches, or SWAPs). In 2004 only $2bn of the $79bn global aid budget was in GBS form, although the amount was rising fast.[154] Rather than insisting that aid be spent on 'flagged' projects, where visiting development ministers can hold their photo opportunities, GBS or SWAPs enable governments to spend it on strategic recurring costs such as teachers' and health workers' salaries.

A rigorous evaluation of the impact of GBS in seven countries found that it boosted funding to basic public services in health and education, and reduced the transaction costs of multiple meetings, donor visits, and reporting requirements.[155] More importantly, GBS can strengthen the institutional capacity of governments to deliver on reduced poverty and inequality. However, it places particular demands on donors, who have to make credible long-term commitments. Project funding can be switched on and off, with only limited impact on overall stability. Not so with GBS, since if aid for salaries and other 'recurrent costs' is withdrawn, governments have to find the money themselves, with the risk of running up excessive deficits.[156]

Debt cancellation under the World Bank's Heavily Indebted Poor Countries (HIPC) initiative is effectively a massive experiment in budget support, under which governments must reallocate the money that they no longer have to pay as debt service to poverty reduction plans. Social spending has risen significantly in HIPC countries and, as savings are guaranteed over many years, debt relief has been used to finance recurrent costs, as has happened in Burkina Faso, where thousands of new teachers have been hired.

## CORRUPT OR FRAGILE STATES

Concerns about aid quality can seem Utopian when many of the world's poorest states are either fragile or bent on pillaging their own populations. For aid donors, corrupt and fragile states constitute an intractable headache (although this does not approach the migraine faced by their citizens). Such states tend to be among the most in need of assistance, yet the mechanisms for effective delivery tend to be weak and prone to diversion. The gut reaction of politicians to deny aid to such regimes, unfortunately, often exacerbates the problem.

In the final years of Daniel Arap Moi's three-decade reign in Kenya, for example, donors cut off aid due to pervasive corruption. A new government was elected in 2003 on a platform of fighting corruption and introducing free primary education, and aid was duly reinstated. Soon, 1.6 million children saw the inside of a classroom for the very first time. The government covered most of the cost of free schooling, with substantial support from aid. But it failed to follow through on its initial steps to fight corruption and even reinstated two corrupt ministers, one of them as minister of education. In such a situation should donors cut aid, even if doing so would once more exclude children from school?

Withholding aid has proven to be a blunt instrument for addressing corruption. Like attempts to force change by attaching conditions to loans, or offering technical solutions (legal reform, training, and the like), cutting off aid frequently ignores the political foundations of the problem, which ensure that corruption will persist as long as someone finds it useful and profitable.

Corruption, discussed in more detail in Part 2, is as much a symptom of poverty as a cause, and its prevalence often dwindles as a country develops. Despite the rhetoric emanating of late from the World Bank, corruption will not make or break the long-term struggle to build effective governing institutions. Aid can play a role in reducing 'corruption for need' by raising the low public sector wages that force teachers, health workers, and civil servants to demand payments from poor people for services that ought to be free. Donor governments can do much to counter 'corruption for greed' by punishing corporations that offer bribes and closing tax havens where ill-gotten gains can be safely hidden.

In the case of fragile states, where governments abuse or neglect their citizens and corruption is rife, Simon Maxwell of the Overseas Development Institute, a London-based think-tank, identifies six possible approaches for donors:[157]

- Engage in dialogue, whether bilateral or multilateral (for example, via the African Union);
- Bypass government altogether (for example, by setting up refugee camps or funding civil society);
- Reward governments for progress either on poverty or on fulfilling conditions agreed between donors and recipients;
- Invest in state capacity by training civil servants or police;
- Invest in non-state capacity by funding human rights organisations or the media;
- Take over the reins of government, either through a peacekeeping force or a full-scale invasion.

There is another option: walk away. The US Millennium Challenge Account, for example, practises 'selectivity,' by which aid goes to governments that can demonstrate effective, democratic governance or progress in reducing poverty. Where imposing conditions on governments in exchange for aid failed, selectivity would reward achievement rather than promises. Of course, walking away may leave poor people in the lurch, and oblige more expensive interventions later on. The model for the selectivity-based allocation of aid is the 'poor but virtuous' country, where extensive poverty coincides with a well-intentioned and legitimate government. Unfortunately, few such countries exist. For all its superficial appeal, selectivity is unlikely to be of much help to the poorest communities.

Selectivity highlights a paradox: aid tends to work best in countries that need it least. This dilemma has no easy answers, but some general principles should apply. First, aid must not undermine the state, for example by setting up long-term parallel systems to deliver services that drain staff from an already enfeebled state system. On the contrary, the aim must be to build an effective and accountable state. Second, humility is in order. Donors alone cannot 'solve' the problem of nation-building; they can merely support or undermine indigenous efforts. Nation-building is a long-term exercise ill-suited to the short concentration spans of rich-country politicians. Finally, if walking away exacerbates human suffering, then aid donors should do so only if they are certain that the long-term benefits outweigh the immediate costs.

## INGOS AND AID QUALITY

INGOs are relatively free from the pull of domestic politics that distorts the aid efforts of governments, and the ethos of altruism runs wide and deep within them. However, altruism can at times become a mask for hubris and is not always sufficient to keep self-interest at bay. Having grown in size and profile, INGOs can at times exaggerate their own importance or delude themselves into believing that they alone are privy to the answers to development's riddles.

The autonomy of INGOs is restricted by the high dependence of some on funding from Northern governments, primarily as implementing agents for official aid and emergency relief programmes.[158] That dependence is likely to rise if governments stick to their 2005 promises to increase aid volumes, leading INGOs to become further enmeshed with the foreign policy aims of rich countries.

As INGOs have grown in size and influence, their thinking and practice have evolved. The charity ethos that predominated in the

1950s and 1960s was replaced by self-help mantras in the 1970s and 1980s (captured in the slogan 'Give a man a fish and he eats for a day, teach a man to fish and he eats for life'). Since the mid1990s, a 'rights-based approach' has steadily gained ground among many INGOs and some government donors. The shift to a rights-based approach has placed civil and political rights and economic, social, and cultural rights centre-stage. Also growing in weight are concerns for the environment (suppose pollution kills the fish?) and sustainability (suppose the man catches all the fish?).[159]

The practice of INGOs has also expanded beyond community-level development and relief work. In recognition of the impact of wider social and political processes on their work, beginning in the late 1970s, INGOs took up the task of building solidarity with struggles against oppression in Southern Africa and Central America. The developing-country debt crisis and IMF structural adjustment programmes in the 1980s and 1990s then moved INGOs to devote increasing resources to public education, campaigns, and lobbying, aiming to influence the behaviour of governments, corporations, and other institutions that affect the lives of poor people.

Today, INGOs are far more than providers of finance (their budgets are dwarfed by those of government donors). Rather, they act as catalysts, brokering relationships between social movements, governments, and the private sector, raising public awareness directly or through the media, and as lobbyists, putting co-ordinated pressure on international organisations such as the World Bank or the WTO. Southern-based INGOs are increasingly influential in this work.

From the mid 1990s onwards, the largest development NGOs began to formalise their relationships into federations and confederations, such as Oxfam International. They recognised that the collapse of Communism, the new drive for globalisation, and powerful new communications media made a global response to suffering and poverty both necessary and feasible. No longer just loose collections of national NGOs bearing the same name, these INGOs are now transnational organisations responding globally on issues such as aid, debt relief, the roles of the UN, the IMF, and World Bank, the arms trade, climate change, and international trade rules.

The growth in INGO advocacy has helped to challenge the Washington Consensus policies of liberalisation and deregulation espoused by the World Bank and major aid donors since the 1980s. However, INGOs have proved more adept at criticising existing policies and practices than articulating a convincing and comprehensive alternative paradigm. One reason for this may be that NGOs' promotion of active citizenship, which has undoubtedly helped push issues of rights and participation up the political agenda, has not been matched by a clear view of the role of the state in development or of how best to create (rather than merely distribute) wealth.

As they have grown, INGOs have been subject to scrutiny and criticism. Although some critiques are motivated by political differences, many of them pinpoint issues that deserve urgent attention, and have given rise to profound (not to say interminable) soul-searching.

**Efficiency:** The same critique of government aid made earlier can apply to INGOs. Their aid at times suffers from delays, underfunding, lack of co-ordination, or inappropriateness, and imposes excessive demands on local partners. While in part a result of the increasing dependence of INGOs on government funding (which imposes its own delays and demands), these faults also result from the breadth of the development agenda. They can best be remedied by greater transparency and more effective mechanisms of accountability.

**Respect for the role of the state:** Some INGOs provide basic services such as health care and education in developing countries, particularly in situations where the state is unable to deliver them. Such efforts can never achieve the required scale or scope, and may compete with the building of an effective state. Even in Bangladesh, which has some of the largest and most influential NGOs anywhere in the world, total combined NGO services reach only about 18 per cent of the population.[160] In the long run, the aim must be to strengthen government systems to ensure that poor people have access to essential services.

**Short-termism and service delivery:** The cult of 'results-based management' imposed by government funders can bias the activity of INGOs and their local partners towards short-term, measurable results and away from efforts to promote longer-term change and respect for rights. It is easier to measure how many clinics or school places have been created than the extent to which attitudes to women's rights have changed. Similarly, the large chunks of government aid money on offer can turn NGOs into mere 'ladles in the global soup kitchen', focused on service provision.[161] Much of the new aid money is for relief and emergency work, which reinforces the bias toward service delivery, rather than social change. Some NGO insiders have gone so far as to say that 'We need to bury the aid paradigm in order to liberate ourselves to achieve the impact we say we want'[162] – something that is unlikely to happen while official aid budgets are on the rise.

**Caution and compromise**: Whether through the conscious desire to curry favour, a greater understanding of the constraints on Northern decision-makers, or the more subtle influences exerted by regular contact with government and the desire to be seen as 'sensible inter-locutors', INGOs often adopt more conciliatory attitudes towards governments than their grassroots partners and allies. Dependence on government funding, or fear of being denied permission to operate, can lead to self-censorship and a narrowing of permissible debate. In some cases, donor influence is stark, as with US government funding for HIV and AIDS that requires programmes to promote abstinence rather than condom use.

**Accuracy**: Under pressure to keep donations flowing so as to maintain far-flung networks of offices, staff, and in some cases warehouses of supplies, INGOs sometimes move too quickly to cry wolf, as occurred in Southern Africa in 2004 when food supplies were thin and some agencies claimed that famine was imminent. The same pressure that tempts INGOs to overstate crises, combined with their can-do ethos, may also cause them to be less than forthright about the limits of their ability to cope with the aftermath of catastrophes, thus raising unrealistic expectations.

## ACCOUNTABILITY

After quality, the second key challenge facing the international aid system, including INGOs, is accountability, and the two are intimately linked. One of aid's most withering critics, William Easterly, who crossed over after 16 years in the World Bank, ridicules top-down 'Planners' as modern-day Soviet commissars, out of touch, inept, and self-serving. He contrasts them with bottom-up 'Searchers', who are open to new ideas and opportunities, nimble, and driven by consumers (in this case poor people), not dogma:

*In foreign aid, Planners announce good intentions but don't motivate anyone to carry them out; Searchers find things that work and get some reward. Planners raise expectations but take no responsibility for meeting them; Searchers accept responsibility for their actions. Planners determine what to supply; Searchers find out what is in demand. Planners apply global blueprints; Searchers adapt to local conditions. Planners at the Top lack knowledge of the Bottom; Searchers find out what the reality is at the Bottom. Planners never hear whether the Planned got what they needed; Searchers find out if the customer is satisfied. Will Gordon Brown be held accountable if the new wave of aid still does not get 12-cent medicines to children with malaria? Indeed, the two key elements that make searches work, and the absence of which is fatal to plans, are feedback and accountability.*[163]*

Easterly is onto something: the absence of accountability lies at the heart of the problem; effective aid has to be tailored to local cultures, politics, and institutions and must avoid the curse of blueprints designed in Washington, Brussels, or London. Many of the problem areas discussed above arise precisely from this mistaken top-down Planners' approach. But Easterly's proposed cure – a naïve faith in markets – conveniently ignores the realities of powerlessness and marginalisation in the lives of many poor women and men, and the vital importance of building an effective, accountable state.

There is a fundamental inequality about the way that international aid works. Recipients are accountable to donors, and they must file hundreds of reports and host dozens of 'donor missions' to prove it. Accountability rarely operates in the opposite direction. Some poor countries make the attempt – Afghanistan, for example, decided in 2002 to set the ground rules for donor engagement in its reconstruction[164] – but most have neither leverage nor recourse to sanctions against donors if advice is poor or if projects are damaging. A new architecture is needed that makes donors accountable to recipients.

Part of the answer ought to lie in a good-faith implementation of the Paris Declaration, but the Paris commitments are themselves weak in some areas, lacking specific targets on issues such as reducing tied aid, counting debt relief as aid, or moving to long-term aid. Aid donors should accept that developing-country governments must remain in the driver's seat, working with civil society, the private sector, political parties, and other domestic actors to devise policies that fit national needs.

Without a change in mindset on the part of donors, however, Paris-style co-ordination between aid providers could actually increase their ability to speak to recipient governments with a single voice, undermining 'nationally owned' strategies that donors do not like. Donors should also welcome, rather than fight, assertive governments such as Ghana, Botswana, or Afghanistan which insist on aid on their own terms.

For their part, INGOs regularly criticise companies and governments both North and South for their lack of responsiveness to people living in poverty, but many NGOs are less formally accountable to their supporters than governments are to their electorates, or companies to their shareholders.

INGOs have responded by improving their transparency (for example, publishing their financial statements and policies), agreeing codes of good practice on issues such as humanitarian relief work, adopting membership structures, and instituting peer reviews and regular consultation with a range of 'stakeholders', including partner organisations in developing countries.[165] In most countries, INGOs are accountable by law to the host government (which can lead to tensions when states resent NGO activities). They are also subject to rigorous reporting requirements to their official funders. In 2006, 11 of the major INGOs from the human rights, development, environment, and consumer sectors created the INGO Charter of Accountability to set a standard for their members and to give stakeholders greater confidence.[166]

While activists from developing countries appreciate the support that their organisations receive from INGOs, they often complain that INGOs are domineering, using their resources and skills to hog the limelight, impose their own agendas, and lure talented staff away with the promise of higher salaries. In the long term, this dynamic could well undermine the effort to build active citizenship in developing countries, and is particularly significant in light of the growth of increasingly sophisticated Southern NGOs, which are challenging the traditional roles of their Northern counterparts as intermediaries between Northern funders and poor communities and as 'builders of capacity' of grassroots organisations.

In these bouts of North–South arm wrestling, developing-country governments are often in a stronger position than they realise, since donor staff are under huge pressure to disburse money. 'Weapons of the weak', such as passive resistance or agreeing to one thing and doing another, can often pay better dividends than a stand-up fight. As one Rwandan official wryly observed, 'When dealing with donors, you have to deal with them as you would milking a cow. Treat them nicely and more milk flows than you would have expected; treat them badly and they kick over the bucket.' [167]

Empowering aid recipients would be an attempt to make aid more like a competitive market and less like a monopoly (in that sense the Paris Declaration is, if anything, making aid more monopolistic, albeit with benign intent). Creating such a marketplace would go with the trend towards an ever greater proliferation of aid providers – new donors, vertical funds, philanthropreneurs, Western governments, and multilateral and regional institutions. However, at the moment aid is a market where the consumers (developing-country governments) find it very hard to exert choice precisely because they have no power.

One idea might be to allocate the overall global aid budget to recipient countries, which could then decide which aid agencies to use. A successful voucher system would depend on a healthy level of competition so that the 'consumer' would have clout. Harvard economist Dani Rodrik half-jokingly proposed breaking up the World Bank's policy advice arm into separate competing bodies, based in different developing countries. [168] They would then be forced to provide the advice that developing countries actually want and are prepared to spend their aid revenues on, turning the current relationship on its head by 'putting the first last'. [169]

Alternatively, aid could be reconceived as transfer payments, like those made by central governments to provincial ones, to be spent within agreed guidelines but in the way that the recipient government chooses (GBS comes close to this vision). Either of these options would bring the aid system more into line with the overall purpose of redistributing global wealth from rich to poor regions, countries, and people.

Even stopping short of such seismic shifts, the global aid system could be run much more accountably. For all their faults, the WTO and the UN provide forums where rich and poor countries meet to try to manage their overall trade and political relationships. No such forum exists for aid. The UN's Economic and Social Council (ECOSOC) could become one, or alternatively the rich countries' invitation-only club, the OECD, could expand the inclusion of poor countries in its influential Development Assistance Committee (DAC) and embrace new donors such as China and the Gates Foundation, which currently operate without even the minimal peer review offered by the DAC.

The voice of aid recipients could be strengthened by creating an international Ombudsman who would investigate complaints of abuse or broken promises. Or recipients could band together, turning the tables by regularly compiling and publishing their own appraisals of the quality of aid from the various providers. There is nothing like coming last in a league table to shame politicians and civil servants into action.

Alternatively, aid could take a leaf out of the oil industry's book, and introduce an 'Aid Transparency Initiative' in which both donors and recipients would publish their aid agreements so that civil society organisations, parliaments, and others find it easier to track where the money goes and hold them to account if it fails to benefit poor people and communities.

## MAKING AID WORK

This book argues that the redistribution of the voice, power, assets, and opportunities that constitute development is most likely to occur through a combination of active citizenship and effective states. Aid must be measured against its effectiveness in building the capacities of both state and society to address poverty and inequality.

Despite moves to improve the system, aid remains hampered by politics, arrogance, and self-interest. In the future, a higher proportion of aid-receiving countries are likely to be those with weak states and profound economic and political problems. At the same time, the proliferation of donors will complicate the already slow-moving efforts to harmonise donor activities around the Paris Declaration.

Much of the force for change will have to come from outside the cosy aid world, building on the progress already made by developing-country governments, spurred on by civil society organisations demanding greater accountability and effectiveness, supported by NGOs both North and South, and perhaps by the more far-sighted private sector leaders who see both the human and commercial case for building prosperity in the South.

In a fast-evolving world, how can INGOs best contribute to building accountable citizenship and effective states? In 2000, when aid budgets appeared to be in terminal decline and 9/11 had yet to transform global politics, a number of NGO-watchers met to discuss 'NGOs beyond aid'.[170] They suggested that non-government development agencies 'adopt a fourth, value-based position between state, market and civil society....In this the NGO role is one of multi-sector negotiation, as well as of promoting and exacting compliance of duty holders to deliver people's rights.'

Unpicking the jargon, the gathering suggested that NGOs should aim to be:

- Supporters of poor people and their organisations, helping them to build the skills and organisational capacity needed to demand their rights and feed their families;
- Negotiators and trusted mediators, whether bringing together rival groups to prevent tension turning into conflict, or getting small farmers into a room with supermarket buyers to thrash out the practicalities of selling into a global market;
- Respected watchdogs of the behaviour of powerful governments and corporations, including themselves;
- Acknowledged innovators in the public interest, in areas such as health, education, water, and sanitation, with a constant eye on seeing their own small efforts adopted by governments or other bigger players.

At a global level, they suggested that INGOs should mobilise the public and pressure for international action to address problems that national governments alone are unable to solve, notably where the formal machinery of global institutions is inadequate. (Oxfam's work on debt, aid, trade and, increasingly, on climate change seeks to address some of these gaps in global governance.)

A decade on, this position looks prescient, although it should be complemented by a growing role in facilitating exchanges of ideas from South to South, from South to North, and vice versa – recognising that many issues such as inequality, exclusion, environmental sustainability, or accountability are common to all countries irrespective of latitude or longitude. Though the proposals are in need of a healthy dose of humility, these roles would steer INGOs away from becoming simply non-profit service providers. Above all, INGOs must keep their eyes firmly on the developmental prize of supporting (and never presuming to replace) active citizens and effective states.

Aid is not a panacea for development, and aid alone will not 'make poverty history'. It can help or hinder developing countries on the road to building active citizens and effective states, but it cannot substitute for the national development process. As one former Eritrean finance minister reflected at the time of the historic Gleneagles G8 summit of 2005:

> By many measures, it's been a great year for Africa, with debt relief, awareness-raising concerts and G-8 leaders pledging more aid. I'm gratified the world has turned so much attention to my continent. At the same time, a voice inside me wants to shout: 'Wait. This is not the way real development happens!' …
> We continue to ignore the stark lesson that externally imposed development models haven't gotten us far. The only way forward is for Africa to drive its own bus and for the driver and passengers to be in full agreement about where they're going. That said, we do need help filling up the tank. [171]

Putting aside delusions of omnipotence and omniscience is a vital first step in making aid work for poor people. The rich countries' first priority should be to ensure that they 'do no harm'. They must move from a paternalistic, post-colonial mindset to relationships based on mutual respect between people facing many problems in common. They must give aid in ways that build government capacity and help build accountability to citizens, rather than fuel conflict or corruption or undermine state development. They must keep the promises made in the heady days of 2005 and help 'fill the tank' by delivering more and better aid. The rest is up to the peoples and governments of the developing world.

## HOW CHANGE HAPPENS:
## THE 2005 GLENEAGLES AGREEMENTS

At their annual summit in 2005, the leaders of the Group of Eight (G8) countries promised a dramatic turnaround in the rich world's willingness to fund development. They agreed to increase global aid levels by around $50bn per year by 2010 and to write off the debts of up to 50 of the world's poorest countries. Though critics derided the commitments as inadequate, and collective backsliding subsequently removed much of their lustre, the promises at Gleneagles constituted a marked departure from past practice. If nothing else, leaders would pay a political price for reneging on their pledges. How did such a commitment come about?

The months leading up to the Gleneagles Summit in Scotland saw an unprecedented combination of government and civil society activism. The British host government, keen to ensure that the event would be perceived as a success, championed development funding from the start, setting up a high level 'Commission for Africa' in 2004 which included several African heads of government and musician/activist Bob Geldof, and which produced a well-argued and costed plan for how the extra aid should be spent.

Civil society groups, meanwhile, campaigned in 70 countries across the globe, including all the G8 nations, as part of the Global Call to Action Against Poverty, a campaign known in the UK and a number of other countries as 'Make Poverty History'. Nelson Mandela added his considerable moral weight when G8 finance ministers met in February. Then celebrities Geldof, Bono, and others organised a series of 'Live 8' concerts in most G8 countries the week before the summit, which were watched by two billion people. The campaign culminated in a march of 225,000 people in Edinburgh to deliver a petition that carried an astonishing 38 million signatures.

The combination of public pressure and the UK government's astute manoeuvering of the summit agenda strengthened the hand of pro-aid ministers in G8 governments, weakened the resolve of blockers (USA, Japan, and Italy), and convinced those who could have swung either way (Canada and Germany). The first sign of movement came as early as

CASE STUDY

381

February, when G8 finance ministers outlined a debt cancellation plan. Then in May, EU leaders committed to aid increases that went a long way toward meeting the $50bn target.

Activists both inside government and out benefited from a broader revival of commitment to development, evidenced in the reversal of falling aid levels since 2000 and the endorsement that same year of the UN's Millennium Development Goals. The efforts of African governments to promote a sense of progress – through the New Economic Partnership for African Development, the spread of elections, and the restoration of promising levels of growth – also helped make aid politically palatable. Leaders may also have wanted to rebuild international co-operation after deep divisions over the 2003 invasion of Iraq.

Strong growth in the global economy was a factor, allowing the G8 leaders to concentrate on long-term issues, breaking free of the crisis management mindset of previous summits. And unexpected events too played a critical role. The Asian tsunami six months earlier had prompted an unprecedented display of public generosity, which in several cases had shamed politicians into increasing government humanitarian relief, and demonstrated the level of public interest in development issues. Then on the first full day of the summit, terrorist bombings in London killed more than 50 people, evoking a sentiment of solidarity in which G8 leaders were keen to support the British government.

The upbeat message on aid and debt contrasted sharply with the leaders' inability to achieve significant progress on climate change or the stalled trade talks at the WTO. Generally speaking, leaders find it easier to promise money than to change their own policies: reductions in carbon emissions or righting the rigged rules of global trade cannot be achieved by writing a cheque.

The lesson of 30 years of G8 summits is also that progress is often achieved only through reiteration – the same issue returning year after year to the summit agenda. The 2005 summit marked the fifth successive discussion on Africa, whereas climate change had not figured on the G8 agenda since 1997. The reappearance of climate change on the agenda in the years following Gleneagles may therefore hold out some hope for future progress in the talks on a successor to the Kyoto Protocol.

382

In sum: growing public legitimacy of the issue, leadership by a government willing to champion it, massive public expression of support, annual iteration, a demand restricted to money, and a confluence of unexpected events were the elements that made the Gleneagles Agreements possible.

*Sources*: Oxfam International (2005) 'What Really Happened at the G8 Summit?';
N. Bayne (2007) 'Overcoming evil with good: impressions of the Gleneagles Summit,
6–8 July 2005', in M. Fratianni, J.J. Kirton, and P. Savona (eds.) *Financing Development: The G8 and UN Contribution*, Aldershot, UK: Ashgate.

CASE STUDY

# THE INTERNATIONAL SYSTEM FOR HUMANITARIAN RELIEF AND PEACE

## THE INTERNATIONAL HUMANITARIAN SYSTEM

Most humanitarian relief is provided locally, by neighbours, relatives, and friends and local and national governments. But when wars and other calamities undermine their ability to cope, the professional institutions of the international humanitarian system are often called upon to help. A well-governed and well-run humanitarian system provides a vital safety net in times of crisis, so that vulnerability, whether chronic or short-term, does not turn into a downward spiral of disintegration, rising inequality, and impoverishment. Today, however, the system is in disarray, undermined by political and commercial self-interest and unilateralism (notably over Iraq). Over the coming years, world leaders will have to decide whether they want to create a stronger, fairer multilateral system that builds on welcome progress in a number of areas. This section examines the global system of humanitarian response, and suggests how its failings can be corrected.

The provision of life-saving assistance is as old as recorded history. Religious institutions ran most humanitarian work in the past, and today they remain key mobilisers of solidarity with the victims of war and natural disaster. For example, the Muslim tradition of tithing or alms, known as *zakat,* prescribed in the Koran, to this day delivers direct cash assistance freely and quickly to those most in need.

The past 150 years have seen the emergence of professional institutions specialising in humanitarian relief, some of them based on religious institutions, others governmental and non-governmental. Founded in 1863, the Red Cross movement became a global force at the turn of the twentieth century, when it was joined by the Catholic charity Caritas. After the First World War, the International Federation of the Red Cross and Red Crescent Societies (IFRC) was formed, as was the Save the Children Fund. Oxfam grew out of the Oxford Committee for Famine Relief, set up in 1942 in response to famine in Nazi-occupied Greece, and CARE was founded in response to the refugee crisis that followed the Second World War. Médecins Sans Frontières (MSF) emerged during the Biafra crisis in Nigeria two decades later. Over the past decade, many of these large humanitarian agencies, including Oxfam, have formed international networks of like-minded organisations to expand and improve their global reach.

The UN system, with its numerous specialised agencies, plays a crucial lead role in preparing for and responding to natural disasters, food emergencies, and conflict.[172] Following the end of the Cold War, the UN and NGOs embarked on a major expansion of their capacities, as did the governments of wealthy nations. Today's humanitarian system is a labyrinth of national governments, UN agencies, NGOs, and the Red Cross movement, whose total spending averaged $5.7bn annually between 1999 and 2002. The unprecedented response to the Asian tsunami of December 2004 pushed this up to an estimated $18bn in 2005.[173]

Taken together, these actors form a rudimentary global welfare system that attends almost every war or natural disaster. Despite its success at saving lives, however, the humanitarian system is dogged by a series of organisational and other barriers, which result in delayed responses to crises, underfunding, poor co-ordination, and inefficient and at times downright misguided actions. Most serious for the longer term is the tendency of international humanitarian aid groups to bypass local and national organisations, both civil society and government: this not only fails to build the capacity of local organisations to undertake emergency response, but actually undermines it by luring away qualified staff and monopolising logistical resources. There have, however, been significant improvements in recent years, discussed in greater detail below.

The humanitarian system has a number of failings:

**Allocating funds according to media coverage or politics**: The aid provided by donors is often too little or arrives too late. In Niger in 2005, warnings of food shortages came as early as October 2004, yet only when pictures of suffering children hit the world's television screens eight months later did the international community take action. By that time, three-and-a-half million people were going hungry; many had sold livestock, land, seeds, or tools, or had gone into debt to buy food, rendering themselves even more vulnerable to future crises.

Reliance on this 'CNN effect' distorts the allocation of aid by diverting it away from situations of chronic vulnerability or emergencies that lack dramatic newsreel footage. Although UN flash appeals (for rapid-onset natural disasters or sudden deteriorations in existing humanitarian crises) are put out within days, most of them receive less than 30 per cent of the funds they request in the first month. In many of these crises, time costs lives.

In 2005 the UN estimated that 16 million people were at immediate risk in ten 'neglected emergencies' in Africa alone, which consistently suffered low levels of funding. The reasons varied from a lower media or political profile (for example, the Democratic Republic of the Congo) to the relative number of people affected (for example, floods in Madagascar) to the long duration of the crisis (for example, northern Uganda's 20-year conflict). Even when the UN wins pledges of aid, some countries fail to make good on their promises. A year after the 2003 earthquake in Bam, Iran, only $17m of the $32m pledged had been received.[174]

All too often, aid follows political self-interest rather than need. UN figures for 2006 show that at any one time there is a skewing of aid towards the emergency that happens to be in the political spotlight: the appeal for the Lebanon crisis that year received 123 per cent of funds required, compared with an average of 66 per cent; Burundi received just 45 per cent of what was required.[175] The size of the disparity proves incontrovertibly that humanitarian aid is being directed for reasons other than the humanitarian imperative to deliver aid where it is needed. Although the UN system has its failings – for example, the variable quality of its humanitarian assessments – simply blaming the UN is too easy; it is the donors who are fundamentally responsible for giving some emergencies little or no funding, while others get much more.

**Poor co-ordination:** The explosion in the numbers of humanitarian agencies demonstrates the abiding strength of voluntary action, and this core compassionate impulse is laudable. However, it can complicate the effective delivery of aid. In the days and hours after a natural disaster, or in the 'fog of war', an element of chaos is unavoidable. Urgency can save lives but can also compound the confusion, undermining the impact of the response. The UN's Office for the Co-ordination of Humanitarian Affairs (OCHA) seeks to co-ordinate the work of the many UN and NGO agencies responding to a disaster, but it faces a daunting task. In Aceh, Indonesia following the 2004 Indian Ocean tsunami, OCHA held daily co-ordinating sessions to identify needs, allocate responsibility, and avoid duplication of efforts. But with over 100 agencies around the table, simply running the meeting was a challenge; dozens more simply failed to attend or to acknowledge the UN's co-ordinating role.

These problems, however, should not be exaggerated. Two major evaluations of humanitarian assistance at moments of exceptional crisis (the Rwandan genocide and the Asian tsunami) – a decade apart and spanning the period of greatest growth in the NGO sector – concluded that the failure to effectively co-ordinate many hundreds of agencies did not prevent a relatively small core of major NGOs from providing the bulk of the critical humanitarian assistance effectively.[176]

Besides the myriad non-government agencies that turn up in the wake of a disaster, the sprawling UN system of dozens of different funds, programmes, commissions, and specialised agencies is particularly chaotic and in need of rationalisation and reform.[177] In Viet Nam, there are 11 UN agencies, which between them account for only 2 per cent of aid flows. In Ethiopia there are 17 different UN agencies; in Zanzibar there are 20.[178] Twenty-seven UN agencies claim some degree of responsibility over water and sanitation. The level of fragmentation and the 'turf wars' between competing UN bodies led the UN's exasperated special envoy to Africa on AIDS to lament, 'Nobody is responsible. There is no money, there is no urgency, there is no energy.'[179]

**The wrong kind of aid**: When faced with a distant emergency, members of the general public often give what they have at hand. As a result, donations of used clothing or canned goods that are too expensive to ship, or are simply not needed, can eat up the scarce resources of humanitarian agencies. The clogging of the port of Colombo, Sri Lanka with containers of spontaneously collected and dispatched children's clothes and toys after the tsunami, for example, was so severe that it delayed the location and release of equipment essential for supplying clean water.

Sadly, donor governments often behave in a similar way, disposing of surplus goods that are unsuitable for the crisis in question, or which could be sourced much more economically in or near the area experiencing the disaster. Expired medicines commonly turn up in such donations, but perhaps the most egregious example is in-kind food aid.

Ask members of the public about their picture of humanitarian relief and they will often cite feeding the hungry. Food aid is a precious resource that saves lives where there is a regional shortage of food, as in North Korea today. Worldwide, about 10m tonnes of foodstuffs are provided each year to some 200 million needy people, at an estimated total cost of $2bn.

All too often the root problem is poverty, not production, and hunger occurs even when food is readily available in local markets. Under these circumstances, shipments of surplus grains from the USA and elsewhere can undermine local farmers by flooding the market and driving down prices. Even when food is not available locally at the time of an emergency, food aid takes on average four to six months to arrive, by which time the country concerned may be recovering – and the sudden arrival of cheap food can ruin local farmers just as they are getting back on their feet.[180]

In-kind food aid has become a knee-jerk response to crises, not because food needs to be shipped halfway around the world, but because rich countries need to dispose of their surplus farm production. In fact, the donor group charged with overseeing food aid is housed not at an aid body but at the International Grains Council, a trade body based in London.

Shipping food from donor countries can also be wasteful. With high oil prices, transport can eat up much of the food aid budget –

up to 40 per cent in Canada's case in 2004, which helped to prompt a policy change to allow increased local sourcing.[181] In addition, a third of the global food aid budget is wasted because the USA insists on processing food aid domestically and shipping it via national carriers.[182] An OECD study found that the actual costs of tied food aid transfers were on average approximately 50 per cent higher than local food purchases and 33 per cent more costly than procurement of food in third countries (so-called triangular transactions).[183] An extra $750m a year in aid for poor countries could be released if rich countries, particularly the USA, gave food aid as cash instead of in kind.

Where food is available on local markets, food aid can also be demeaning: evaluations of cash-transfer schemes show that people prefer cash to soup kitchens because cash provides a greater choice over spending priorities and respects their dignity, rather than treating them as passive beneficiaries. When people use the cash to buy agricultural inputs, it also helps to improve livelihoods and boost the local economy (see Part 4).[184]

Three of the four major donors – the EU, Canada, and Australia – have promised to use food aid more judiciously and to increase the proportion they buy in developing countries, rather than source it from home.[185] Largely due to the lobbying of agribusiness and shipping interests, the USA remains defiant and, as the supplier of more than 50 per cent of the world's food aid, continues to distort the world's response to crises.

**Short-term solutions for long-term problems**: As discussed in Part 4, there is increasing recognition that much of the vulnerability experienced by poor people and communities is actually chronic rather than event-driven, and needs to be dealt with through national government social protection systems, supported by international aid, rather than through short-term humanitarian assistance. This blurs the boundaries between 'emergencies' and 'development', but it also more accurately reflects real life for millions of people living on the edge of poverty.

Recognition of these failings has prompted a spate of initiatives in recent years aimed at turning the international humanitarian system into something closer to the co-ordinated response of a modern welfare state. The UN has introduced a 'cluster approach', nominating lead agencies in nine areas of humanitarian action (for example, UNICEF leads on nutrition, water, and sanitation, while UNHCR is in charge of managing camps for people affected by war or disaster).

At the UN 'World Summit' in September 2005, the organisation's 192 member governments promised to improve the timeliness and predictability of humanitarian relief, including upgrading the UN's existing Central Emergency Response Fund (CERF). This would enable the UN system to provide a rapid response and adequately fund 'neglected emergencies', rather than waste precious weeks and months passing the hat round to donors.

In its first year, the CERF committed $259.3m for over 331 projects in 35 countries. This included $182.4m for rapid response and $76.9m for underfunded emergencies. Donors duly upped their pledges to $342m for 2007. CERF funding has undoubtedly saved lives, particularly in underfunded or 'forgotten' emergencies. However, even the CERF suffers from administrative and disbursement delays both at its head-quarters in New York and in the field, since funding is channelled through UN agencies that have done little or nothing to adapt their own procedures – early signs that an overly cumbersome system for disbursing funds might undermine the CERF's effectiveness.[186]

In 2006 a high-level panel appointed by the UN Secretary-General made some further recommendations that could improve its humani-tarian response: UN bodies need to work together as a single entity in any given developing country, with a single boss, budget, and office; funding for UN operations, both to promote development and to react to short-term emergencies, needs to be more predictable and long-term; the UN needs a single, powerful voice on women (it currently has three separate entities); and it needs to pay more attention to environmental and sustainability issues.[187]

For their part, in 2003 donor governments set up the Good Humanitarian Donorship initiative to identify and promulgate best practices. This is based on 23 principles, including increasing the timeliness of aid and providing aid according to need.[188] International NGOs have also set up a series of learning and accountability projects, most sporting the inevitable acronyms. HAP (The Humanitarian Accountability Partnership) looks at downwards accountability to those affected; ALNAP (The Active Learning Network for Accountability and Performance in Humanitarian Action) brings together evaluation and learning across the sector; and the Sphere Project promulgates technical and good practice standards, through a humanitarian charter, a website, and a comprehensive manual for humanitarian workers on the ground.[189] Finally, the Code of Conduct for the International Red Cross and Red Crescent Movement and NGOs in Disaster Relief seeks to maintain high standards of behaviour, along with independence, effectiveness, and impact.[190]

As discussed in Part 4, all these initiatives are characterised by varying degrees of self- and peer review, transparency, and public reporting, but stop short of anything more binding, such as disqualification or legal liability in cases of negligence or abuse. The preface to the NGO Code of Conduct states, 'It is a voluntary code, enforced by the will of those accepting it to maintain the standards laid down in it.' NGOs have thus far been unable to agree on any of the various proposed models of certification or accreditation, let alone issues of legal liability and disqualification. There are numerous reasons behind this, one being that national governments of affected countries ought, arguably, to be the ones making informed choices, rather than being told who it is that (largely) Northern actors see fit to license.

The humanitarian 'community' (some would call it an industry) has for the time being opted to pursue a centralised model of co-ordination and propagation of good practice. As in the case of the increasingly complex and ungovernable international aid system, the system could be treated more like a market than the global equivalent of a state welfare body. Because new NGOs, new donor governments, and private sector businesses are constantly joining in, reporting and transparency may be more effective than trying to co-ordinate the activities of hundreds of different organisations. As one author remarks: 'Less time spent waiting for the new organogram from Geneva, or campaigning for the right resolution to be passed in New York could leave more time for shaping an innovative solution on the ground.'[191]

To 'empower the consumer' in such a market would be even harder than in the case of development aid, since people who have been struck by a disaster are unlikely to shop around for the best provider. The real consumer in such circumstances is likely to be the national government in question, which would screen and choose the international relief organisations best suited to its needs.

For the foreseeable future, millions of poor people and their communities will continue to depend on international help to cope with chronic vulnerability or to get them through disasters that are seldom of their own making. Success in this effort switches off a grinding engine of deepening inequality, suffering, and poverty. Helping people in such situations is a hugely complex and challenging task, combining the immediate need to relieve suffering and prevent deaths with the longer-term effort to rebuild states and enable people to retake control of their own lives. The international system that has grown up around this task has its share of problems, but in recent years there has been notable progress in achieving a fast, co-ordinated response. The prize could not be greater.

## PEACE, WAR, AND THE RESPONSIBILITY TO PROTECT

In Oxfam's long experience of providing relief in conflict zones, it has learned that protection from violence can often be even more urgent than the provision of clean water, food, or shelter. As Part 4 showed, conflict hits poor people and communities the hardest, driving up inequality and making them more vulnerable to other risks such as drought or disease.

International attitudes to such civilian 'collateral damage', often caused by armies that deliberately target unarmed civilians, are changing after a prolonged effort to change attitudes and beliefs about violence. Under international humanitarian law, warring parties have particular obligations to limit harm to civilians and to protect the lives and security of people in their territories, as well as their access to essential services. When states and others are unable or unwilling to fulfil their responsibilities, international law demands that all states must take action.

One of the reasons why the UN was founded was to avert war and limit abuses by combatants. This function was made more explicit in 2005, when world leaders agreed that every government had a 'responsibility to protect' its population from genocide, war crimes, crimes against humanity, and ethnic cleansing. Crucially, it added that the international community had a responsibility to support governments to do this and in extreme cases, with the authority of the UN Security Council, to intervene to do it themselves.[192]

When the UN Security Council authorised a limited military intervention for humanitarian reasons in northern Iraq in 1991, few people realised that it would open up a debate lasting 15 years. That debate was galvanised by the genocide in Rwanda in 1994 – when, even though a small UN peacekeeping force was in the country, the international community was unwilling to act to prevent the massacre of some 800,000 civilians over a period of six weeks. Many African governments concluded that the lack of Western intervention in the wars raging in Liberia or the Democratic Republic of the Congo (DRC) was not a belated recognition of Africa's independence, but rather evidence that Africans simply did not count.

Developing-country governments remained suspicious until the former foreign ministers of Algeria and Australia, Mohamed Sahnoun and Gareth Evans, turned the argument on its head in their landmark 2001 UN report 'Responsibility to Protect'. Rather than arguing the rights and wrongs of Western states intervening, they zeroed in on their responsibility to do so, based on their obligation under international law to uphold the rights of people under threat – and, even more importantly, the prime responsibility of states themselves to protect their own citizens.

They made it clear that states could not just exercise the responsibility to stop war crimes once they had already started. They also had to prevent those crimes, and help prevent the conflicts in which such systematic violence against civilians is all too common. They pointed out that *military* intervention must be the last resort. In the great majority of cases, peaceful measures like diplomacy, including coercive but peaceful means such as asset freezes, travel bans, and suspensions from regional organisations, are more likely to succeed, and at far less cost. Any of these sanctions must be carefully targeted at the political and military leaders responsible for the war crimes that the international community is concerned about, not at a whole population as was the case with the discredited blanket sanctions against Iraq and other countries.

The only problem was that their report came out in the wake of the US-led invasion of Afghanistan, raising fears that were only compounded by the invasion of Iraq in 2003, which the UN failed to prevent. Controversies over US unilateralism made it imperative that any intervention be authorised by the UN. In 2003 and again in 2006 France acted on this lesson, leading the UN-approved EU intervention in the DRC to complement the work of the UN mission there.

The 2005 UN Millennium Summit caught this political wave, placing the issue on the agenda in a way that no government could duck. Moreover, most governments by then had an interest in 'saving multilateralism', which had been seriously damaged by the UN's failure to prevent the Iraq war. Hold-outs India, Pakistan, and Russia agreed, albeit reluctantly, and the UN summit duly endorsed the responsibility to protect and the central role for the UN in authorising any intervention.[193]

The UN made it clear that the use of international force should only be a last and rare resort – like a form of political chemotherapy, it may be a necessary evil to get rid of the cancer of conflict, but it is likely to involve serious side effects in terms of undermining sovereignty and state-building and potentially undermining long-term development. The main responsibility to protect falls on states. At an international level, early and robust 'preventive diplomacy', deploying human rights monitors, sanctions targeted at those in power (not in poverty), and incentives for improved behaviour should be exhausted before force is considered.

Where international interventions have succeeded, they have helped to build peace across four 'pillars': development, reconciliation, building a political framework, and providing security. Action on all four is needed on every level, from local civil society to national governments, and must be sustained for periods that outstretch the often short attention span of the international community.

The UN's blue-helmeted peacekeepers are an increasingly common sight in conflict-torn lands across the world, and have scored significant successes. The UN saw its deployments grow by over 500 per cent from 2000 to 2005, and at the end of 2006 it had over 80,000 peacekeepers in the field, surpassing its previous peak of 77,000 during the Bosnian war.[194] UN peacekeepers have more frequently been mandated to use force, with the organisation moving from being a hapless observer of atrocities in Rwanda or the Balkans to a greater readiness to distinguish between victim and aggressor, and to defend the former. In the past decade several hundred thousand combatants have taken part in UN 'disarmament, demobilisation, and reintegration' (DDR) programmes in 30 countries.[195]

However, the inability of peacekeepers to protect civilians or even in many instances keep the peace shows how much remains to be done. UN peacekeeping is overstretched because the major military powers, while providing valuable cash and equipment, contribute almost no troops; in 2006, no G8 country was among the UN's top ten troop donors.[196] Similarly, the trend towards greater reliance on regional peacekeepers – such as the African Union (AU) in Darfur – who lack sufficient resources for training and equipment, without sufficient Northern support and (until 2008) without being complemented by other troops, looks like an abdication of responsibility, when effective protection requires swift deployment with the advanced equipment that only rich countries possess. Such neglect contrasts sharply with the billions thrown at the much more amorphous 'war on terror'.

One answer could lie in creating a UN standing military force, something the great powers are reluctant to contemplate. Currently, the UN has to approach donors for money and personnel each time it is called upon to intervene in a conflict. Former Secretary-General Kofi Annan likened this to a fire brigade that must first buy a fire engine before it can respond to a conflagration. It took more than a year after peace was agreed in southern Sudan in 2005 for governments to offer sufficient soldiers to the UN mission. During that time, people in the region faced almost as much violence from banditry as they had before the peace agreement was signed. Through a standing force, regional forces, or some other means, the international community must invest in peacekeeping capacity if the responsibility to protect is to be upheld. Perhaps the best hope is for the AU's proposal for an African Standby Force, provided this is properly supported by Northern governments.[197]

Time is usually of the essence: the signing of a peace agreement opens up a window of opportunity in which to build a sustainable peace by strengthening the fabric and confidence of society. If that opportunity is missed, the country can slide back into war or the kind of endemic social violence and crime that afflicted Central America after its civil wars came to an end in the 1990s. Forty-three per cent of negotiated settlements relapse into conflict within five years.[198]

The post-conflict period is also typically a moment for wider reform: political and social relations have been ruptured by the conflict, and new alliances and political possibilities appear in a moment of high fluidity. Many, perhaps most, major social and political changes occur during and immediately after conflicts, as discussed in the Annex.

Underpinning the UN's expanded role in peace operations, and the entire international security system, is the growing body of international law on conflict, known collectively as international humanitarian law (IHL). Best known for the 1949 Geneva Conventions (covering the treatment of non-combatants and prisoners of war), the Nuremberg Rules (for the prosecution of war criminals), and the 1948 Convention on the Prevention and Punishment of Genocide, IHL is designed to limit human suffering and to protect civilians in armed conflicts. The rules are to be observed not only by governments and their armed forces, but also by armed opposition groups and any other parties to a conflict.

The basic rules and obligations under international humanitarian law can be summarised as:

- **Distinction**: A distinction must be made at all times between the civilian population and those taking part in hostilities. Attacks must be directed only against military objectives. As such, indiscriminate attacks which fail to distinguish between military objectives and civilians are prohibited.
- **Precaution**: Not only must civilians and their possessions not be the object of attack, but also every precaution must be taken when attacking or locating military objectives to avoid, and in any event to minimise, incidental civilian losses and damage.
- **Proportion**: Warring parties are obliged to weigh carefully the direct military advantage of any attack against the potential for harming civilians. In no case shall such harm be excessive in relation to the concrete and direct military advantage anticipated.

A further key aspect of the Geneva Conventions ensures the ability of humanitarian organisations to operate impartially according to their mandates. Governments and warring parties must not allow their officials, allies, or citizens to disrupt life-saving aid. Despite this, attacks against civilians, including aid workers, are sadly still common occurrences. In Iraq, Oxfam was forced to close its office in 2004 due to the threat to its staff, although it continues to support Iraqi partners. In Afghanistan, 89 aid workers have been killed since 2003, compared with a very small number who were targeted in the preceding 14 years. Part of the problem has been the blurring of the boundaries between military and humanitarian activities when, for example, soldiers dress as civilians in order to deliver aid aimed at winning 'hearts and minds'.

International law can strengthen citizens' efforts to hold states to account. In Colombia, CCJAR, a lawyers' collective, was able to take the government to the Inter-American Court of Human Rights on behalf of the victims of a 1997 massacre in the village of Mapiripán by paramilitaries, with the collaboration and acquiescence of state security forces, in which at least 49 people were seized, tortured, and killed. The Court found that the government's investigation of the killings had been inadequate and that the government had failed in its responsibility to protect the community during the five days over which the massacre took place. It ruled that the authorities should pay compensation to the victims' families and guarantee their safe return to the village.

The growing influence of international humanitarian law was exemplified by the creation in 2002 of the International Criminal Court, which has global jurisdiction over genocide, crimes against humanity, and war crimes.[199] The ICC's mandate is to investigate crimes committed in conflicts currently under way. In the autumn of 2006, the Court issued arrest warrants in northern Uganda and the DRC, and in 2007 produced another set of indictments in Darfur. ICC warrants may complicate delicate peace negotiations, as has occurred in Uganda, and may not help provide immediate protection of civilians under threat but, over the long term, international legal experts believe that the prosecution of war criminals by the ICC will help deter violations of international humanitarian law.

## REFUGEES

People crossing borders to flee violence and persecution are protected under international law, and have a right to asylum. Including the 4.3 million Palestinian refugees under UN auspices, there are over 13 million refugees in the world today, the vast majority from developing countries. Developing countries provide asylum to over two-thirds of them.[200] Only 336,000 people claimed asylum in 50 industrialised countries in 2005, half as many as in 2001.[201]

Those seeking refuge often face a phalanx of border controls and interception methods, which can push them further into danger and abuse. If they manage to reach a territory and make their asylum claim, they frequently find a culture of hostility and disbelief, and often face destitution, detention, deportation, and denial of due legal process. Europe's air, sea, and land interception and border controls, for example, make no allowances for people who may be fleeing conflict and persecution. As ministers and civil servants admit, these are 'blunt instruments' that are blocking many people who have legitimate protection claims.[202]

There is a clear case for enhanced global governance in the field of humanitarian relief and conflict. International mechanisms and institutions are needed to ensure that costs are shared equitably and that all parties are treated fairly. These mechanisms are likely to include strengthened roles for the UN and ICC systems.

## THE ARMS TRADE

Conflict would not be so prevalent or so deadly without the open global trade in weapons. In November 2001 around Kisangani, the scene of intense fighting in the Democratic Republic of the Congo that involved many civilian deaths, Amnesty International found ammunition cartridges for North Korean, Chinese, and Russian heavy machine-guns, Russian revolvers, South African assault rifles, Chinese anti-aircraft weapons, and Russian, Bulgarian, and Slovak automatic grenade launchers. At the time, the DRC was subject to EU and UN arms embargoes, which should have prevented the sale of all of these weapons.[203]

International efforts at arms control have long focused on nuclear and other sophisticated weapons systems, yet small arms and light weapons are the true weapons of mass destruction, responsible for some 300,000 deaths in 2003.[204] And these are unregulated by international law. The UN has imposed arms embargoes but they are very difficult to enforce, given the nature of the industry.

Many weapons are now produced by global supply chains spread across a number of different countries, similar to those found in the electronics industry. This enables companies to circumvent national controls on arms exports to human rights violators, an exercise in which governments North and South are colluding. Austrian pistol-maker Glock, for instance, plans to set up production facilities in Brazil, from where exports would not be subject to the EU's Code of Conduct on Arms Exports, while in 2002 the Indian government scrapped its 'blacklist' of countries barred from buying its weapons. India has subsequently exported to Myanmar and Sudan, both of which, according to the UN and Amnesty International, systematically violate human rights and are now subject to EU and UN arms embargoes.[205]

National governments by themselves have been unable or unwilling to rein in this deadly trade, not least because of the lobbying power of large arms firms, both in their home countries and in their main markets. For most of the last century, the world's major arms exporters were the USA, Russia, the UK, and France. In the past decade, however, the big four have been joined by China, India, Israel, South Korea, and South Africa.

Arms firms are typically backed up by large public subsidies in the form of official 'export credit guarantees' against non- or late payment. In the UK, while arms deliveries made up only 1.6 per cent of all visible UK exports from 2000–03, they accounted for 43 per cent of the government's export credit guarantees.[206]

Collectively, countries in Asia, the Middle East, Latin America, and Africa spent $22.5bn on arms during 2004, a sum sufficient to put every child in school and to reduce child mortality by two-thirds by 2015.[207] In the face of the extraordinary levels of death and waste, governments and citizens' groups are increasingly taking action. In West Africa in 2006, the 15 countries of the Economic Community of

West African States (ECOWAS) signed the world's first regional arms trade treaty. The treaty, in large part the result of a public campaign led by a number of NGOs (including Oxfam), included controls on international arms transfers and a ban on arms sales to non-state actors – a first.[208] With the support of ECOWAS members, that same year the UN General Assembly voted overwhelmingly to launch talks on a global Arms Trade Treaty. Based on the principles of international human rights and humanitarian law, such a treaty would create minimum global standards for arms transfers, preventing those likely to be used to violate human rights or hinder development. The success of similar moves on landmines (see page 403) shows what can be achieved through co-ordinated international action. It may take another 20 years before such a treaty comes to fruition and is then rigorously enforced, but it will be essential for the international system for peace and security to function effectively.

## NATURAL RESOURCES

Global action is also essential to prevent the export of natural resources from financing wars, as occurred with rough diamonds, known more evocatively as 'blood diamonds', in the devastating conflicts in Angola, Côte d'Ivoire, the DRC, and Sierra Leone. The joint efforts of government, civil society, and the international diamond industry to certify 'clean diamonds' successfully stemmed the flow of blood diamonds. By 2007, the Kimberley Process, as it is known, covered 99.8 per cent of the global production of rough diamonds.[209] In the DRC, legitimate diamond revenues have more than doubled since the country began to implement the Kimberley recommendations. At the same time, it appears that the illegal trading routes across the DRC's eastern borders have indeed been closed.

The success of the Kimberley Process points to the need for further efforts by other industries to close down the market for those exploiting resources to fund conflict, whether by growing opium in Afghanistan or mining coltan, a raw material for the cell phone industry, in the DRC.[210] In parallel with curbing such trade, alternative livelihoods must be found for the poor people who rely on it, or conflict is likely to flare up again. Ending the black market in exports from conflict zones is only a start towards transparency across all industries that invest in conflict zones. The international community must also get to grips with those international banks, engineering companies, and private security firms that seek to profit from continued conflict.

## SECURITY AND THE 'WAR ON TERROR'

The aftermath of the attacks on the USA of 11 September 2001 has had a profound, and in many ways disastrous, impact on international efforts to prevent and resolve conflict. The political agendas in many of the most powerful countries have shifted away from addressing causes towards policing consequences, and the West has slipped back into a Cold War-style paradigm of protracted war. In retrospect, the 1990s look like a brief interlude in a bleak panorama dominated by an overwhelming focus on military security. Moreover, the struggle against terrorism has itself become another vicious circle, with terrorism, the global 'war on terror', and other brutal counter-insurgency campaigns each fuelling one another.

The 'war on terror' confronts a genuine threat. However, it has relaxed controls on arming human rights abusers in countries such as Georgia and Pakistan, has increased restrictive measures in developed countries against asylum seekers and refugees, and has exacerbated xenophobic reactions to immigration.[211] People fleeing terror are finding themselves denied protection, in the very name of the 'war on terror'. Relief agencies also find their ability to provide assistance without interference from combatants in conflicts curtailed in many countries, along with the freedom of civil society organisations to operate.

The 'war on terror' has also undermined attempts to improve human rights and governance, as the US government and others have lost the moral high ground, as well as their interest in the problem. In 2005 it became clear that the use of torture was effectively US policy.[212] Signing up to the 'war on terror' has given governments carte blanche to ignore challenges on human rights and governance, a loophole that has been exploited by governments from Chechnya to Israel to Zimbabwe.

Because the 'war on terror' sees conflict as a military struggle to vanquish enemies, it fails to address the political, social, and economic drivers of conflict. Fighting terrorism certainly requires effective police and related security measures – but since 2001, terrorism has become a justification for seeking military solutions to problems that are more than military in nature, and poor people are paying a terrible price.

Conflicts, as Part 4 showed, have local roots that require largely local solutions aimed at achieving peace and strengthening the combination of active citizens and effective, accountable states that holds the key to development. The international system can provide aid and diplomacy to support local efforts at conflict prevention and to relieve the terrible human toll when conflicts do break out. It can do more to support regional efforts at peacekeeping, especially in Africa. In exceptional circumstances, when governments are unable or unwilling to protect their own citizens, the international community should be ready to step in militarily. However, powerful countries must also address their own roles as drivers of conflict, whether through the arms they sell or as financiers of war through the purchase of natural resources.

Just as risk and vulnerability at an individual or community level often require a level of social protection and safety nets to prevent shocks turning into long-term disaster, so at a global level countries need support, if natural disaster or conflict is not to overwhelm their ability to guarantee rights and dignity to their citizens. That support must be co-ordinated, based on need, and be built on robust and impartial international institutions, particularly the UN and the International Criminal Court. In turn, powerful governments need to show the same vision at a global level, as the founders of welfare states have done in the national arena, recognising that both morality and long-term self-interest require not only leadership, but a readiness to set aside short-term advantage and to put their own house in order on issues such as aid and the arms trade.

## HOW CHANGE HAPPENS:
## LANDMINES, AN ARMS-CONTROL SUCCESS STORY

Until recently, governments and military commanders saw antipersonnel mines as a cheap, low-tech, and reliable weapon. Landmines were killing or injuring 26,000 people every year, and were stockpiled by some 125 countries. Now, thanks to an international treaty banning their use, that number has fallen to between 15,000 and 20,000 people a year. In 2005, only three governments – those of Myanmar, Nepal, and Russia – acknowledged using landmines (rebel groups used them in a further ten countries). The number of countries producing landmines had fallen from 50 to 13, despite the fact that a quarter of the world's governments had not yet signed or ratified the treaty.

The 1997 Mine Ban Treaty, and the 'Ottawa Process' that led to it, broke new ground in the annals of diplomacy, riding a wave of post-Cold War optimism, which allowed governments and NGOs to look at security issues with fresh eyes. Global civil society, led by NGOs in the International Campaign to Ban Landmines (ICBL), put the issue on the international agenda and built the extraordinary momentum needed to ban weapons that most governments considered to be as common and acceptable as bullets.

The ICBL mobilised public opinion and influenced governments across the globe with a clear and concise message: that nothing can justify the human cost of landmines. Its founding members were NGOs engaged in clearing mines, providing prosthetics for victims, and documenting the impact of mines on civilians. Governments immediately recognised their unmatched expertise on the issue. The diversity of ICBL's member-ship and its flexible structure (it has never had a secretariat, and it only became a legally registered entity after receiving the Nobel Peace Prize in 1997) added to the movement's strength.

Perhaps the key factor in the success of the movement was the close co-operation between the ICBL and a handful of like-minded govern-ments (especially Canada, Norway, Austria, and South Africa), as well as with UN agencies (especially UNICEF) and the International Committee of the Red Cross. In the face of opposition from the great powers, this core

CASE STUDY

group created a new form of international diplomacy, built upon a willingness to operate outside the UN system, extensive NGO participation, leadership from small and medium-sized countries, rejection of consensus rules, and avoidance of regional blocs.

The movement provided essential expertise to the diplomatic process and played a major role in the actual drafting of the treaty. At the first formal diplomatic conference in Ottawa in 1996, for example, Canadian diplomats and the ICBL worked together to ensure maximum government attendance. ICBL was given a seat at the table, while governments as yet unwilling to support a total ban were relegated to observer status. Campaigners helped to draft the language of the final declaration and the action plan. At the end of the conference, Canadian Foreign Minister Lloyd Axworthy stunned the delegates by announcing that his country would host a treaty-signing conference in a year's time.

Campaigners and core government supporters had learned from the failure of the UN-sponsored negotiations on a Landmines Protocol in 1995–96, when formal structures led by consensus gave the great powers infinite opportunities to delay and dilute, and traditional alignments and regional loyalties undermined progress. With the strong support of the then Secretary-General Kofi Annan, they took the process outside the UN and, rather than allow consensus to water down the treaty to the lowest common denominator, stressed the concept of 'like-minded' participation, whereby only those who believed in a total ban should take part. The negotiating rules required a two-thirds majority to make changes to the text, effectively undercutting efforts by the USA and others to weaken it through amendments.

Signed in December 1997 by 122 governments meeting in Ottawa, the Mine Ban Treaty was an agreement of the willing, not of all governments. But, as the figures above suggest, it has even affected the behaviour of some non-signatory governments. Like other parts of international humanitarian law that have not been universally agreed, it created an international norm of good behaviour that almost all governments now follow.

The campaign had certain advantages that may not be present in other cases: a focus on a single weapon, an easy-to-grasp message, and highly emotive content. The weapon itself was neither economically important nor militarily vital. However, the campaign proved that governments and civil society working together can rapidly address a major humanitarian concern, overcoming the opposition of the world's biggest and seemingly most uncompromising states.

*Sources:* International Campaign to Ban Landmines (2001, 2005) 'Landmine Monitor Report' (www.icbl.org); International Campaign to Ban Landmines (2006) 'Global Success, Big Challenges: Mine Ban Treaty Turns 7', press release, 1 March 2006; R. Muggah and S. Batchelor (2002) 'Development Held Hostage: Assessing the Effects of Small Arms Availability', UN Development Programme, Bureau of Crisis Prevention and Recovery, New York (this report mentions a figure of 25,000 casualties a year); S. Goose (2000) 'The Campaign to Ban Antipersonnel Mines – Potential Lessons', paper presented at the conference Human Security: New Definitions and Roles for Global Civil Society, Montreal International Forum.

CASE STUDY

# CLIMATE CHANGE

Climate change is no longer merely a potential threat, the distant consequence of continued pollution. Scientific analysis of the European heat-wave of 2003 that killed over 30,000 people showed it to be more clearly attributable to global warming than any previous disaster – climate change finally had its smoking gun.[213] In 2007, a year of climatic crises included Africa's worst floods in three decades, unprecedented flooding in Mexico, massive floods in South Asia, and heat waves and forest fires in Europe and Australia. Each disaster reaffirmed the shift from potential to actual impacts reflected in the Intergovernmental Panel on Climate Change's 2007 report. The challenge this presents the international community has never been clearer or more urgent.

In the rich countries, governments are already responding – the UK has nearly doubled spending on flood control and coastal erosion[214] – and insurance premiums are rising in tandem with the added risks. As discussed in Part 4, developing countries face far greater risks from climate change, because they are exposed to more intense climate-related hazards and because poor people and communities are less well equipped to withstand such shocks. Without urgent action, climate change will undermine decades of development and will increase poverty and inequality at both global and national levels. Even rich countries are not immune to such dramatic impacts – but poor countries are being affected first, and worst.

Scientists have been aware of the threats posed by climate change for decades, but the international apparatus for addressing the problem is more recent and is still largely incomplete. Beyond the scattered initiatives of some national governments, what currently exists is an agreement on the reduction of greenhouse gas emissions (known as 'mitigation') by some wealthy nations, carbon trading schemes to assist in that task, and several small international funds set up to assess and help pay for the additional costs of coping with climate change (known as 'adaptation') in developing countries.

These responses, organised under the 1992 UN Framework Convention on Climate Change and its 1997 Kyoto Protocol, are as yet entirely inadequate relative to the ultimate objective of the Convention: to stabilise the global climate within a timeframe that allows ecosystems to adapt naturally, ensures food production is not threatened, and enables sustainable development to take place.[215] Scientists estimate that we have less than ten years to turn things around.

## WHAT'S FAIR: STOP HARMING, START HELPING

Meeting this challenge will be a Herculean task, on the scale of global wartime mobilisation. Because the world economy is entirely dependent upon the fossil fuels that are the worst culprits in causing global greenhouse gas emissions, the need to tackle these emissions has far-reaching implications. Few economic sectors will be untouched, and the political, managerial, and organisational challenges of driving the rapid changes needed are massive. Further, the spillover effects of both impacts of, and responses to, growing emissions will affect all other aspects of the international system, including regimes governing trade and financial flows, aid and humanitarian relief, and conflict and security.

However, the challenge for the international climate regime is not just to ensure that global emissions of greenhouse gases are cut radically and fast: this must be done in a way that redresses the deep injustices that lie at the heart of climate change. Poor people least responsible for climate change are now most at risk from its impacts (see Part 4). Climate change will force developing countries not only to prepare for unprecedented natural disasters and adapt agriculture to significantly drier or wetter conditions (or both), but to build modern economies

407

without heavy dependence on fossil fuels – something no country has ever done before. And all this on top of the pressing need to overcome poverty and inequality.

Since industrialised countries bear an overwhelming historical responsibility for the excess carbon currently in the atmosphere, they have a duty to lead in both mitigation and adaptation efforts, at home and abroad. This is part of the 'ecological debt' rich countries owe poor countries, which has been estimated to exceed the entire developing world's actual debt of $1.8 trillion.[216] In other words, the international regime must ensure that the richest, most responsible countries stop harming and start helping.

The principles of equity that underpin this view are written into the international climate regime, which states that rich countries 'should take the lead in combating climate change and the adverse effects thereof'.[217] In addition to the importance of justice in its own right is the practical relevance of fairness and equity. Developing countries are unlikely to commit to take action under an international climate regime that is patently unfair. So far, the feeble pledges of rich countries fall far short of requirements. The enormous political challenge that this represents can be seen in the resulting stand-off in international climate negotiations.

In order to secure an effective international climate regime, rich countries must move quickly to reduce their own emissions (i.e. stop harming), which still continue to rise year-on-year more than 15 years after the UN Climate Convention was signed. In addition, rich countries must finance both adaptation and mitigation efforts – including development and deployment of relevant technologies – required in developing countries (i.e. start helping), to encourage sustainable development and poverty reduction. In turn, developing countries must put these incentives to work by taking steps to build their resilience to unavoidable climate change, and by moving to low-carbon development paths themselves.

## JUST ADAPTATION

Early on in the climate negotiations, the Alliance of Small Island States (AOSIS) – gravely concerned that climate change could see many of its countries swallowed up by rising sea levels – raised the prospect of compensation for climate change damages under international environmental law.[218] Climate change could one day be treated as the equivalent of a gigantic industrial accident – an atmospheric *Exxon Valdez*. But perhaps the closest parallel is with the tobacco industry, which has found itself forced to answer the question, 'Why did you continue trading and concealing evidence, when you knew your activities would lead to millions of deaths?'. Much the same could be asked of both companies and governments that, despite the increasing strength of the evidence, fail to rein in carbon emissions. Uganda's President Yoweri Museveni has described climate change as 'an act of aggression by the rich against the poor'.[219] Will the courts one day agree with him?

In large part, the answer will depend upon the extent to which rich countries deliver on their commitments, and the principles underpinning these, such as the 'polluter pays' principle, which establishes the duty of polluters – rather than victims – to pay for the costs of their pollution. Since the worst impacts of climate change can be greatly reduced through effective preventive steps – preparing for floods, anticipating dry spells and heat-waves, building infrastructure to withstand unprecedented frequency and scale of climate-related disasters – paying for adaptation rather than damages is a much more efficient and humane approach for polluters to deliver on their obligations. Apart from helping to avoid a chaotic welter of litigation, it can save lives and boost, rather than undermine, human development.

How much will adaptation in developing countries cost? While calculating such costs is a complicated and inexact science, setting a ball-park figure is critical to provide guidelines for the international community. Building on early World Bank estimates, but adding in community-level costs, Oxfam estimates the cost as a total of at least $50bn each year, and far more if greenhouse gas emissions are not cut rapidly.[220] The 2007 *Human Development Report* called for $86bn annually by 2015 in order to avoid 'adaptation apartheid' – a gulf between rich countries, where massive adaptation outlays are already planned, and poor countries, currently being left to (literally) sink or swim.

Studies are already under way to sharpen the economics of climate adaptation. While critical for better understanding how adaptation investments should be calculated and directed, it is already clear that unless the worst-hit countries – already strapped for cash – receive international compensatory financing, fighting climate change will stymie long-term efforts to reduce poverty. Equally, unless adaptation financing is additional to international aid commitments needed to achieve poverty reduction goals, developing countries will be unable to address both challenges.

Who should pay, and on what basis? The UN Climate Convention's principle of 'common but differentiated responsibilities and respective capabilities' (Article 3.1) provides a guide that still holds valid. Assuming that countries that are both *responsible* for producing excessive emissions and *capable* of providing assistance should bear the costs, Oxfam has developed an 'Adaptation Financing Index' as an indication of what each country should pay. On this basis, Oxfam has calculated that the USA, the EU, Japan, Canada, and Australia are responsible for over 95 per cent of the financing needed. It estimates that the USA is responsible for over 40 per cent, the EU for over 30 per cent, and Japan for over 10 per cent. Within the EU, the top five contributors to adaptation financing should be Germany, the UK, Italy, France, and Spain.[221]

The international climate regime must become a strong and orderly global system to address both adaptation costs and the mitigation of carbon emissions. Rich countries have so far pledged a mere $250m to international funds for developing-country adaptation – less than 0.5 per cent of what is needed.[222] Even the most promising new source of funding, the Climate Change Adaptation Fund, which will fund adaptation measures in developing countries, initially with funds from a 2 per cent levy on carbon credits generated under the Clean Development Mechanism (CDM), discussed below, is only expected to raise another $80m–$300m annually from 2008–12.

While the Adaptation Fund could become the primary channel for directing resources for adaptation in developing countries, its funding base needs to be massively expanded in order to meet the scale of need. One approach that is consistent with incentives to reduce emissions is to earmark proceeds from the auction of emissions permits in domestic carbon markets, such as the EU Emissions Trading Scheme or similar markets proposed in the USA and Australia. Germany announced its intention to set aside more than a quarter of proceeds for adaptation in developing countries in late 2007. Whatever approach is finally adopted, fairness demands that rich countries explain how they will make good on their obligations and commitments to help the vulnerable countries meet the costs of climate adaptation.[223]

## THE MITIGATION CHALLENGE

When the UN Climate Convention was signed at the Rio Earth Summit, in 1992, the international community looked forward to action by rich countries that would bring their emissions back down to 1990 levels by 2000. Today, as daily news reports chronicle how climate change is beginning to threaten food supplies and overrun the adaptive capacity of natural ecosystems, it is clear that the international community's efforts to address the climate threat are failing – at least relative to the ultimate objective of the Convention.

Globally, greenhouse gas emissions must fall sharply and fast. Ultimately, the questions, 'How far?' and 'How fast?' are political questions that the international community must answer, mindful that with each answer political leaders accept a degree of risk that poor people will bear most directly. Global cuts in the vicinity of 80 per cent below 1990 levels by mid-century are necessary in order to preserve a reasonable chance of keeping global warming below 2°C. Even with this dramatic drop in emissions, the world still faces as much as a one-in-three chance of catastrophic climate change.[224] Each day, week, month, and year that passes while emissions continue to rise is a step closer to potentially irreversible changes that lie across the 2°C threshold. Each delay in beginning to bend the emissions curve downwards makes reaching the 80 per cent target more expensive – and more unlikely.

In 2006, former World Bank chief economist Sir Nicholas Stern estimated the costs of stabilising carbon emissions at around 1 per cent of global GDP by 2050 – an enormous amount, but ultimately tolerable, and dwarfed by the 5–20 per cent of global output that Stern estimated would be the cost of *inaction*.[225] His influential review made a strong case for urgent action, arguing that mitigation 'must be viewed as an investment, a cost incurred now and in the coming few decades to avoid the risks of very severe consequences in the future'. The report concluded that: 'Tackling climate change is the pro-growth strategy for the longer term, and it can be done in a way that does not cap the aspirations for growth of rich or poor countries. The earlier effective action is taken, the less costly it will be.'

Discussions to date have often degenerated into an unproductive stand-off in which rich countries argue that fast-growing nations such as China and India need to accept curbs on their emissions while making only feeble progress in doing so themselves, whereas the poorer, more populous countries point to their much lower emissions per capita and the historic culpability of the rich countries in squandering the planet's carbon tolerance levels, and stress the developmental need for growth.

Bridging this divide is clearly a pre-condition for progress towards the level of global cuts necessary, as well as an indicator of the extent to which any future climate regime is perceived to deliver justice. Requiring poor countries and communities to forego prosperity in order to save the planet is tantamount to asking them to pick up the tab for centuries of pollution by developed countries. It is both unjust and unlikely to work. The question of how contributions to global mitigation efforts should be shared across countries lies at the heart of post-2012 negotiations.

While the options for slicing up global emissions obligations are many, the ethical principles that must underpin any viable burden-sharing agreement boil down to:

- **Equal emissions per capita**: No one person has a greater right to the global atmosphere's carbon cycling capacity that anyone else.
- **Responsibility and capability**: People and countries must take action on the basis of their responsibility for causing the problem (historical emissions) and their capability to assist.
- **The right to development**: The current level of poverty in a country must be taken into account in determining its obligation to pay towards mitigation and adaptation.

Critically, the burden-sharing framework embodied in the post-2012 climate regime must be defensible according to objective application of these principles *and* must satisfy more subjective ideas of justice and fairness. One approach that does this is captured in the Greenhouse Development Rights framework, in which national obligations to make – or pay for – carbon cuts are based on past responsibility for emissions and current capacity to pay, while guaranteeing the right to development of poor countries. In contrast with other approaches, it takes intra-national inequality (of income and emissions) into account by exempting the income and emissions of people who fall below a minimal 'global middle class' threshold of about $9,000 per capita. It argues that rich countries bear responsibility for current climate change and so should pay for the lion's share of global adaptation and mitigation efforts, allowing developing countries to focus on poverty reduction and development.[226]

However the burden is shared, reversing centuries of rising carbon emissions will not be an easy task. How can governments, companies, and individuals ensure that emissions peak, and then fall, within the next ten years? This question lies at the heart of the increasingly urgent debates on how to respond to climate change. The three main options use traditional tools of government policy:

**Standards**: Governments could reach global and/or national agreements setting emission standards for different industries, and agree a regime to enforce these rules. Examples include quality standards on vehicle emissions or legal requirements that new housing be carbon-neutral.

**Subsidies**: Rich-country governments could subsidise carbon reduction efforts – for example research into new technologies in fields such as renewable energy or carbon capture – or they could support companies or individuals producing or adopting existing low-carbon equipment. All countries should also end perverse subsidies that actually encourage fossil fuel use. Rich countries collectively subsidise domestic fossil fuel production and consumption in the range of $10bn–$57bn each year in tax breaks and direct support. If redirected, this could finance developing-country adaptation.[227]

**Taxes**: By ensuring that the true cost of carbon emissions is reflected in the prices paid by consumers, governments can create a system-wide incentive for low-carbon solutions and encourage innovation to meet this new demand. A tax on carbon emissions could curb greenhouse gases and at the same time raise funds for adaptation or other purposes. Taxes on air travel are increasingly justified as carbon taxes. However, although simpler to implement, taxes will not necessarily reduce the quantity of emissions, which is the critical factor in combating global warming.

Another approach that has gained great momentum combines standards and taxes to use price pressures to drive down carbon use via a regional, national, or global market for carbon emissions reductions. Modelled on US efforts to reduce sulphur dioxide emissions under the Clean Air Act, carbon trading allows companies to buy and sell 'carbon permits' so that those who find it easiest to reduce emissions do so, and make a profit by selling the resulting carbon savings to other companies who find it harder to cut their carbon footprint.

While individual governments have used all of the above approaches to reducing emissions, carbon trading has been adopted as a central tool for driving the global response, and it is evolving quickly. In 2006, international carbon markets turned over around $30bn (1.6bn tonnes of carbon emissions, or $CO_2e$[228]) and volumes were expected to double in 2007.[229] The largest markets are the European Union's Emission Trading Scheme (EU ETS), which was worth $24bn in 2006 (1bn tonnes of $CO_2e$) and the Kyoto Protocol's Clean Development Mechanism (CDM), worth $5bn (520m tonnes). The remaining carbon markets – incipient domestic markets in Australia, Japan, Canada, and the USA – form a tiny fraction of total volumes.[230] Unlike the EU scheme or the CDM, these are not tied to the Kyoto commitments. There is also a small but growing voluntary market in offsets ($100m/20m tonnes of $CO_2e$ in 2006).

The two main types of carbon trading that make up today's markets are emissions trading and offset trading. In the former, also known as 'cap and trade', the government sets a ceiling (or cap) on emissions from a particular economic sector and a schedule for lowering that ceiling over time. Companies in that sector are allocated a tradeable permit (or allowance) for their emissions, and must pay a fine if their emissions exceed that amount. Companies that find it cheaper to reduce their emissions can do so and sell their permits to other, dirtier, companies. The EU Emissions Trading Scheme is an early example of this kind of carbon market.

Trading in carbon offsets involves reducing emissions from projects outside of an economy that has an established mandatory cap on emissions. For example, by funding an energy efficiency project in a developing country, a company can earn credits for the reductions achieved and apply them to its own emissions allowance. The Clean Development Mechanism, run by the United Nations, involves trading offsets, while the EU Emissions Trading Scheme is a hybrid involving both kinds.

The carbon market is a construct of government policy, and its effectiveness hinges on the will and resolve of governments to set tough limits on emissions and reduce them over time. This is what creates market scarcity, driving the carbon price higher, creating the incentive for private sector actors to deliver more efficiency gains and greater reductions in emissions. Most observers and market players expect that there will be an extension and that trading schemes will be expanded to other countries and sectors.[231]

So far, however, carbon markets remain fragile, unproven, and hugely controversial. They are also relatively small, covering less than 5.5 per cent of global carbon emissions in 2006. On the plus side, they have established market institutions, rules, and a price for carbon. That much constitutes an impressive piece of institutional innovation, and discussions about the future of carbon trading under a post-2012 framework are buzzing. But the real test is whether this market will lead to rapid and significant emissions reductions and low-carbon investments, in both North and South. And therein lie significant drawbacks:

- Thanks to industry lobbying, caps were initially set far too high in Europe's flagship scheme, and the price of carbon duly collapsed, removing incentives to cut emissions. Ongoing industry lobbying threatens to undercut proposals to introduce auctioning of emissions permits into the ETS.
- The price of carbon has been too volatile to prompt the long-term investments in areas such as renewable energy that are required if emissions are to be reduced.[232]
- Because carbon trading seeks reductions in greenhouse gas emissions at the lowest possible overall cost, it channels private sector efforts toward the cheapest reductions rather than those that are vital in the long-term, such as changes to infrastructure, new technologies, and dispersed emissions sources (for example, transport and housing).

The CDM is beset with other problems: severe doubts surround the credibility of monitoring and verification of carbon reductions in some countries; the poorest countries are effectively excluded by their low levels of emissions and lack of concentrated sources; and the initiative may even deter governments from curbing pollution, as they wait for a chance to 'cash in' under the CDM. In such circumstances the offsetting option within the EU scheme constitutes a major leakage, offering firms the chance to buy their way out of carbon constraints on the cheap, with few net benefits in curbing overall emissions.

There is also a real tension between the CDM's twin aims of reducing overall emissions and transferring funds for low-carbon investments in the South. The market suits big, cheap emissions reduction projects, such as overhauling outdated chemical plants, rather than the dispersed investments that benefit poor people directly.

The strength and utility of these markets depends on how existing policy frameworks are reformed to make them more stringent, predictable, and credible.[233] Some potential key developments under allowance-based cap-and-trade systems include extended geographic scope and linking between markets in different countries; inclusion of new sectors, such as aviation; and more auctioning of permits, instead of free handouts to polluters (the leading allocation method in the past). In the longer term, more radical exponents of market solutions have even floated the possibility of personal carbon permits, providing incentives for individuals to save energy and sell their savings to inveterate SUV-driving, flight-hopping carbon hogs.

To date, however, carbon markets have not delivered either significant emissions reductions or progress towards more sustainable development models. The risks of failure are enormous. By the time we know how effective carbon trading really is, billions more tonnes of carbon will have been pumped into the atmosphere and irreversible changes may well be under way.

The reliance on carbon trading betrays a mix of ideological bias and perhaps the influence of lobbying from traders always keen to create another profitable (and preferably volatile) market. Trying to apply a market solution like carbon trading to every problem can entail seemingly endless contortions, when often a simple regulation or tax would be both more direct and more effective.[234] Other approaches, such as regulation, subsidy, and taxation, must be included if the global response is to match up to the urgency of the challenge.

Regardless of the instruments employed, the global mitigation effort will require big changes in the way that high-consumption societies live, and in the distribution of finance and technology across the globe. Just as with adaptation, successful mitigation will require the transfer of clean energy technologies and finance to tailor and deploy these in developing-country contexts on a massive scale. An innovation fund for clean development to finance an environmental equivalent of national poverty reduction strategies would be essential to allow developing-countries to curb their emissions while also addressing poverty and inequality.

The Intergovernmental Panel on Climate Change (IPCC) shows what good global governance can achieve. Set up in 1988 by the UN's World Meteorological Organisation and the UN Environment Programme, the IPCC has since released four comprehensive assessments of the available scientific, technical, and socio-economic knowledge relevant to climate change, in 1990, 1995, 2001, and 2007. Policy makers refer to these reports as the definitive word on the state of climate-related science.

The impressive authority and influence of the IPCC stem from the body's carefully conceived procedures and governance structure. Critically, the IPCC does not carry out any new scientific research itself; its reports are nothing but expert reviews of all of the published, peer-reviewed scientific findings available. It is expressly barred from making policy recommendations on the basis of its reviews – conclusions must be 'policy-relevant, not policy-prescriptive'.

Most importantly, as an intergovernmental body, the IPCC's conclusions must be agreed by all member governments before publication. This means that the IPCC's findings reflect not only the considered judgement and interpretation of around 1,000 scientists, but also a consensus of governments around the world.[235] It also means that its findings tend to be presented in the most conservative possible form, since governments that maintain an active interest in muzzling inconvenient scientific findings have some sway over decision-making.

Accused variously of 'scientific activism' or of being overly beholden to powerful government interests, the IPCC has worked relentlessly to consolidate, update, and communicate knowledge about human-induced climate change, in spite of intense political pressures. These efforts earned the IPCC the 2007 Nobel Peace Prize (shared with former US Vice President turned climate campaigner, Al Gore).

In contrast, an array of foot-draggers and deniers, ranging from genuine opponents to self-serving lobbyists, have put up a determined opposition. The Global Climate Coalition (GCC), set up in 1989 by the energy and automotive industries, opted for tactics employed by the tobacco lobby – one of whose lobbyists had the private slogan 'doubt is our product' – to, in the words of one leaked internal memo, 'reposition global warming as theory rather than fact'. Its most important victory was perhaps the US Senate's 95-to-0 vote in 1997 to oppose US participation in any agreement (i.e. the Kyoto Protocol) that imposed mandatory greenhouse gas reductions on the USA.

The GCC ran a $13m advertising campaign against Kyoto ('It's not Global and it won't work'), arguing it would damage competitiveness and unfairly let China and other developing countries 'off the hook'.[236] Eventually the accumulation of evidence led BP to resign from the GCC in 1996, to be followed by Shell and Ford. In 2002, the coalition closed down, but its legacy is a public debate in the USA (the world's largest emitter) that lags years behind that in Europe. Precious years have been wasted that increase both the urgency and difficulty of responding and the damage that is already under way.[237]

On the other side of the debate, environmental and, increasingly, development organisations have been joined by some unusual allies from the private sector. Some business sectors with 30-year investment horizons, such as pension funds or oil companies, naturally think along a longer timescale than the four-year electoral cycles of many politicians. The banking, insurance, and reinsurance industries meanwhile have become alarmed at the spiralling costs of environmental disasters, or interested in the potential returns from climate-friendly energy sources, technologies, and production systems. Other long-term investors fear another type of 'climate risk', namely the risk that oil companies and others responsible for climate change could lay themselves open to future litigation, along similar lines to the tobacco and fast food industries, for failing to anticipate regulation of emissions.[238]

A dwindling band of economists still question whether the benefits justify the costs in terms of foregone growth and poverty reduction, taking the view that future costs and harm are much less important than current costs.[239] (This view ignores the possibility or impact of irreversible damage that cannot be meaningfully costed). The Stern Report effectively countered such arguments. Progress has also been hampered by the intellectual gulf between the natural scientists who have so far dominated the climate change debate and the social scientists who lead discussions on development. The two academic tribes speak different languages, and so have struggled to build a common front.

Technology is bound to play a central role in the transition to a low-carbon economy that drastically reduces reliance on fossil fuels for transport, agriculture, and energy production. Technology is seen by some as a form of 'get out of jail free' card that will allow both rich and poor countries to keep growing their market economies while simultaneously achieving the reductions in carbon emissions needed to avoid catastrophic climate change. But is this techno-optimism justified?

One possibility is a new technology that transforms the world's reliance on carbon – for example, clean nuclear fusion that produces carbon-free energy. Nothing of that kind appears imminent, however (scientists have been trying to tame fusion for some 50 years, with little success), and even were such a technology to be discovered, it would take decades to commercialise and disseminate. With the global economy growing, and carbon emissions rising, the world cannot afford to wait any longer for such a painless technological fix to the problem.

Existing technology could in theory buy us some time, but only if the most advanced, cleanest techniques were rapidly to spread to all countries. If the whole world was able rapidly to become as carbon efficient (in terms of tonnes of carbon per unit GDP) as the more efficient, but not exceptional, developed countries (Germany, Italy, Japan, UK, Switzerland), global carbon emissions would fall by some 43 per cent. That, together with existing technological trends (global carbon efficiency has improved by about 1.6 per cent per annum since 1975), would buy us about ten extra years in which to find a techno- logical and development pathway that would allow us to cut global emissions by 80 per cent by 2050 compared to 1990 levels (the level of reductions required to minimise the risk of catastrophic climate change).[240]

Such a wholesale switch to new and existing clean technologies would require a massive effort on a global scale, overriding intellectual property rules and short-term commercial self-interest, and backed by appropriate funding. It also ignores issues such as the rapidly rising use of air travel, which is becoming increasingly significant as a source of greenhouse gases, without any low-carbon alternative in sight. It may well be that patterns of consumption have to change as much as patterns of production. These are huge challenges, but the alternatives are equally unpalatable: cross your fingers and hope for some technological magic bullet to emerge, or accept lower global rates of growth in the market economy.

In practice, avoiding catastrophic climate change is likely to require a mix of solutions, including accelerated technology transfer, innovation, and reduced emissions in the big polluter countries. It remains an open question whether this will include lower growth rates in some or all countries, or whether a combination of human ingenuity and political leadership will be enough.

For the poorest countries, the transition to a low-carbon economy may not be so urgent – after all, with the exception of the giant and rapidly growing economies of China and India, their carbon footprint remains very small. Eventually, however, they will have to find a path to development that does not rely on massive fossil fuel consumption, either because prices are simply too high or because (in a manner analogous to the nuclear proliferation treaty) those countries that have already used huge reserves of carbon to industrialise their own economies will deny that option to others. Another key consideration is whether poor countries can afford to be 'locked out' of new, low-carbon energy systems that will inevitably become a driver of competitiveness in the future.

In effect, poor countries will have to make transitions to carbon-efficient economies earlier in their development paths than today's developed countries did, just as they are currently doing in terms of transitions to literacy, low child mortality rates, and lower birth rates. At the very least, this will require a change of mindset among elites in developing countries, who tend to aspire to US models of conspicuous consumption.

What if there is no technological fix, and a planned and publicly agreed rebalancing of growth fails to occur? Then, economic adjustments can only occur chaotically in a scramble for carbon based on brute force rather than reason. A complicating factor is the possibility that the world will hit 'peak oil' in the near future, leading to rapidly rising prices and further tensions over access to carbon reserves. While rising prices would help push the world towards cutting carbon emissions (indeed that is part of the reason behind carbon trading and carbon taxes), they are likely to be a disaster for equality. Take away political leadership, and any price-driven or even military struggle over resources between the world's poor people and its gas-guzzling elites can have only one outcome – the exclusion of those without the power or wealth to gain access to carbon.

At a global level, a power struggle between carbon 'haves' and 'have-nots' could bring an abrupt end to the period of rapid global development that followed the end of colonialism. In its place we might see the fall of a 'carbon curtain' separating a wealthy, high-tech group of countries (or populations within countries), able to protect themselves from the ravages of climate change and control access to carbon, from poor countries and communities living through a new Dark Age, prone to increasingly erratic and devastating climate conditions, unable to afford the carbon needed to join the wealthy group.

These are apocalyptic thoughts, and environmentalists have been accused of crying wolf in the past, only to be proved wrong by new technologies and further discoveries of natural resource deposits. But as Jared Diamond's book *Collapse* graphically shows, environmental damage, and the nature of society's response to it, explain the sudden disappearance of some of history's greatest civilisations.[241] It should be remembered that in Aesop's fable, the wolf did indeed attack the shepherd boy's flock, and no one came to his aid.

While the EU and the USA remain locked in stand-off over how the international climate regime should evolve, the biggest gulf lies between rich, industrialised countries and developing countries. Complicating matters further, developing-country governments are themselves divided on climate change. Low-lying countries such as

Bangladesh and a number of small island states face national disaster if sea levels continue to rise, and are vociferous in their demands for action. Others are in the middle of huge economic growth spurts, heavily dependent on rising fossil fuel use, and are rapidly becoming some of the largest greenhouse gas emitters in the world.

Such governments remain suspicious of calls to curb their emissions, pointing out that the rich North has industrialised on the basis of fossil fuels, and now wants to deny poor countries that same opportunity. They also argue that it is natural for large countries such as China or India to have large aggregate emissions: true 'carbon equity' should be on a per capita basis. On that reckoning, emissions from the industrialised nations still dwarf those from emerging powers.

They have a point, but global warming is a reality, and large developing countries will eventually have to accept disciplines on their emissions. However, the terms of such disciplines, in particular the justice or injustice with which the pain is distributed between countries and between groups within them, will be hotly disputed. The transition to a low-carbon economy will be greatly eased if the rich countries move first and fastest (after all, they genuinely need to make deep cuts, while even the fastest-growing developing countries only need to stabilise at or around current levels), provide the technology and additional funding needed to reduce reliance on fossil fuels, and provide the large-scale financing needed urgently by developing countries to adapt and prevent the worst impacts in coming decades.

Climate change represents one of the greatest ever challenges to global governance: it is a turbo-charged version of the other threats that the international system was created to counter, such as war or financial crises. Somehow, the international community must work together to drastically reduce carbon emissions, while ensuring the right to development for poor women and men in a carbon-constrained world. And the challenge is time-bound: inadequate action will determine an irreversible shift within the next 15 years.

Powerful interests profit from the lack of regulation, in this case of $CO_2$ emissions rather than the arms trade or capital flows. Global institutions are weak or are dominated by governments in thrall to those vested interests. The benefits from preventive measures will only accrue in a relatively far-off future, and often in different countries altogether. The political reality is that floods in New Orleans or Central Europe are much more likely to prompt action in Washington or Brussels than cyclones in Bangladesh or droughts in Niger.

New institutions of the kind required by climate change have come about in the past as the result of a shock that galvanises allies and convinces waverers, such as war or depression. Such shocks have enormous costs, especially for poor people. In this case, waiting for a major systemic shock will probably entail irreversible tipping points. In that, it resembles nuclear warfare, where global agreements must be reached *before* a major shock occurs.

Convincing the public of the need for short-term sacrifice in the interest of long-term solutions is always difficult: witness the glacial pace of pension reform in many countries. Achieving all this with equity is even harder – as in the Doha trade talks, where rich countries have resisted granting additional flexibility to any poor country that might become a competitor. Politicians may hope that a less costly path comes along in the shape of technological fixes that can obviate the need for difficult trade-offs. However, technological solutions could well end up increasing inequality, while the wilder visions of geo-engineering – such as sprinkling the oceans with iron filings to encourage algal growth or launching giant reflectors into space – are likely to have serious unintended consequences.

The political obstacles are great, but the scale of the threat is almost unimaginable: climate change could make large parts of the globe uninhabitable, triggering a species loss comparable to the end of the dinosaurs. One of those species might be our own. Perhaps more plausible is a disintegration of civilisation, catapulting society back centuries, if not millennia. The global governance of the international system faces no sterner test in the decades to come.

# GLOBAL GOVERNANCE IN THE
# TWENTY-FIRST CENTURY

The twenty-first century will be characterised by growing economic integration and shifting power balances among nations: the slow decline of the post- Second World War powers; the inexorable rise of new powers such as China and India; the increased role of regional and sub-regional blocs such as the African Union, Comesa (East and Southern Africa), Caricom (Caribbean), or ASEAN (East Asia); and the sometimes precipitate collapse of poor countries on the margins of these tectonic shifts. The institutions of global governance were built on an order that is rapidly eroding, and will have to evolve to keep pace with new challenges.

With all its limitations, global governance holds out the promise of building some fairness and predictability into international relations by reining in the powerful, ensuring that poor nations have sufficient policy space and resources to work their way out of poverty, and helping the most vulnerable. The challenge is to make sure that global governance resembles a safety net more than it does a trap.

The current institutions of global governance fall far short of fulfilling that hope: the UN struggles to reform itself into the kind of effective organisation that can implement its newly agreed 'responsibility to protect'; the World Bank and the IMF remain in the grip of a largely outdated and ideological economic doctrine that does great harm in many countries, and the same goes for the WTO; aid agencies move slowly to overcome their inefficiencies and to spend new aid money in ways that strengthen, and do not undermine, fledgling democracies.

Moreover, from a development point of view, there are gaping holes in the fabric of global governance. Issues of vital importance to poor countries, such as migration or access to knowledge, receive only the lightest of touches, whereas the issues that matter to the powerful countries, such as access to markets, capital movements, or protecting their technological edge, are rigorously enforced. Thus far, the profound systemic challenge posed by climate change and the need for rich and poor countries alike to move to a low-carbon model of development dwarf the response.

Yet in spite of all this, recent developments provide grounds for optimism that global governance can do better. The dismal failure in Iraq has led to untold suffering for the Iraqi people, but it has also driven home the folly of a return to gunboat diplomacy in a multi-polar world. The creation of the International Criminal Court should deter future generations of dictators and torturers who might previously have banked on remaining immune from prosecution. Resurgent developing countries have created new coalitions to challenge the West's dominance in organisations such as the WTO. Public awareness in the West of global poverty and inequality has never been higher, and politicians from all parties appear increasingly concerned about those global issues, such as climate change, that require global responses. The upsurge in civil society organisation worldwide provides a strong impetus for further progress.

Beneath the froth of news and events, attitudes and beliefs are changing. International human rights laws and treaties are slowly acquiring weight and traction in the minds of governments and citizens. Even the most egregious dictators now pay lip service to the rhetoric, if not the practice, of rights and democracy; international rules on weapons and trade have mitigated some of the worst predatory behaviour of the powerful; and international co-operation has motiv-ated investment in global public goods. And perhaps most important of all, international systems have provided a vehicle for solidarity with the struggles of poor women and men. Nevertheless, the urgency and scale of the challenge means that global governance needs to go much further.

Prediction and ambition invariably fall short of what history actually delivers. In 1808, few foresaw the end of slavery; in 1908,

New Zealand was the sole nation with universal suffrage (and even there, women could not yet stand for parliament). What changes of comparable magnitude will this new century bring? Will it, as some predict, be the 'Asian Century' and see China and India eclipse the old powers of Europe and the USA? Is the rise of a global 'middle class' of emerging nations akin to the rise of national middle classes that heralded the downfall of autocracy and the rise of democracy and, if so, will we move towards a system of 'one country, one vote' or (much more radical, but more justifiable in terms of rights) of 'one person, one vote' in global institutions? Either would be preferable to the 'one dollar, one vote' system that prevails today in institutions such as the IMF.

And what of the UN? Will it come of age as something akin to a form of global government, perhaps with the UN Security Council expanding its remit from political to economic and environmental security (a process that is already under way, following its discussions on climate change)?

As international institutions, laws, and treaties proliferate, something resembling a global government is starting to rise from the morass, but its shape is unclear and its progress is beset with reversals. It looks like a saviour to some, a monster to others. In some lights it appears to be ruled by principles of the survival of the fittest, in others of global co-operation – Darwin or Gandhi, we do not yet know who will prevail. But we do know that the outcome will be critical in shaping the environment in which citizens and states struggle to eradicate poverty and tackle inequality, suffering, and the threat of environmental collapse over the course of this century.

# PART SIX

# CONCLUSION

## A NEW DEAL
## FOR A NEW CENTURY

# A NEW DEAL FOR A NEW CENTURY

This book sets out a vision of women and men in communities everywhere who are equipped with education, enjoying good health, with rights, dignity, and voice – in charge of their own destinies. Effective, accountable states and a dynamic economy propel countries forward, ensuring a fair distribution of assets, opportunities, and power. A democratic system of global governance manages the inevitable tensions and impacts of one country on another, and seeks to prepare for what increasingly looks like an approaching environmental storm.

The alternative – a world of ever-deepening gulfs between 'haves' (of wealth, technology, water, soil, carbon) and 'have-nots', a dualistic world of insiders and outsiders – portends the needless suffering of continents, nations, and excluded groups within otherwise wealthy countries. Such a dystopia is not only morally repugnant, but unstable and self-defeating, for the 'uppers' (in Robert Chambers' terminology) will spend much of their time fending off the legions of 'lowers' hammering at the gates of privilege.

How did we get to this historic fork in the road? The twentieth century was a breathtaking drama, generating unprecedented bloodshed, but also extraordinary progress in terms of decolonisation, economic growth, the emancipation of women, and technological innovation. In retrospect, however, it missed an unrivalled opportunity to use that technological and material progress to end poverty and promote a 'New Deal' that would make poverty history.

It is not too late to remedy this, but the environmental constraints imposed by climate change and finite natural resources bring an added urgency to the effort. The old ways (low-intensity democracy, trickle-down economics, dirty growth, inept global governance) have been found wanting. At the heart of the effort must be a recognition of the central role for active citizens and effective states. They alone can deliver the kinds of social and political structures needed to make development serve the poorest individuals and communities.

New approaches and analytical tools are also needed. In the effort to reform growth in an increasingly carbon-constrained world, the discipline of economics must change its frame of reference, allowing policy makers to see the full social, political, and environmental impact of their decisions, if the economies of the world are to move from dirty, inefficient (in terms of poverty reduction) growth to clean, smart growth that redistributes wealth to poor people. The idea of security must be reclaimed as 'human security' – a combination of empowerment and protection that targets the manifold vulnerabilities that particularly afflict poor communities and individuals. 'Security' must no longer mean armed, gated communities and endless war.

The drive to end poverty and tackle inequality and suffering will take place in an ever more globalised, multipolar world. Contrary to the views of globo-optimists, nation states will not wither away, but their actions will be increasingly constrained (for good or ill) by global rules and realities. Rich-country governments and their citizens need to help build a system of global governance that ensures that the powerful countries and corporations 'stop doing harm', while supporting national development efforts based on the combination of effective states and active citizens – women and men living in poverty, exclusion, and insecurity, but struggling for a better future. They are in the driving seat of development, but rich countries and their citizens can help by clearing the road of obstacles and supporting the struggle for development.

It is hard to imagine a more worthwhile cause. The fight against the scourges of poverty, inequality, and the threat of environmental collapse will define the twenty-first century, as the fight against slavery or for universal suffrage defined earlier eras. Fail, and future generations will not forgive us. Succeed, and they will wonder how the world could have tolerated such needless injustice and suffering for so long.

ANNEX

# HOW CHANGE HAPPENS

# HOW CHANGE HAPPENS

There is nothing permanent except change.

HERACLITUS, SIXTH CENTURY BC

In the 1780s some half-a-million African slaves were being worked to death growing sugar cane in British colonies in the West Indies. The idea that slavery was legitimate and 'normal' was deeply entrenched in public consciousness in Britain and the other slaving nations, and it was generally accepted that the British economy could not survive without slavery and the slave trade. 'If you had proposed, in the London of early 1787, to change all of this,' writes the historian Adam Hochschild, 'nine out of ten people would have laughed you off as a crackpot'.[1] Yet by 1807 the British parliament had banned the slave trade, and on 1 August 1838 almost 800,000 slaves throughout the British Empire became free when slavery itself was abolished.

How did such a momentous social change take place? Across the Caribbean, Latin America, and southern USA, a wave of slave rebellions challenged the institution of slavery, achieving their most notable success in the creation of the independent black republic of Haiti in 1804. But slavery was also challenged in the heart of the empire. A coalition of extraordinary and dedicated individuals formed, led by the Anglican deacon Thomas Clarkson and the parliamentarian William Wilberforce. They were backed by the Quakers, a radical religious group, many of whom were influential businessmen. The abolitionists used public

432

meetings, speaker tours, petitions, posters, and demonstrations in perhaps the first mass campaign that would be recognisable to today's activists. Over the next 250 years, their actions inspired mass movements for women's suffrage and for the right to form a trade union, and for numerous other struggles and campaigns that continue to shape the modern world and the lives and possibilities of its people.

Mass campaigning, however, is only one source of change. Not all change is consciously pursued: the inventors of barbed wire did not foresee that its impact on troop mobility would contribute to the horrors of trench warfare in the First World War. Nor is it achieved only by political activism. New technologies, from lightbulbs to the Internet; the demographic trends of ageing or urbanisation; the boom and bust of the commodity trade; the spread of literacy; and the slow grind of political change, punctuated by the sudden 'tipping points' of war and rebellion, all contribute to Heraclitus's vision of constant upheaval.

Nor is all change positive, of course. History is studded with collapses, pogroms, and disasters, many of which involve the same kinds of actors and dynamics as those changes normally deemed to be progressive. Indeed, the Rwandan genocide of 1994 could be seen as a particularly barbaric version of the combination of active citizens and effective states that so often drives national change. Sometimes what is most notable is the *lack* of change – countries, groups of people, or processes that 'get stuck' while the rest of the world changes around them.

The various actors in the drama can be studied to explain why change is absent as well as present. Change is intimately bound up with power. The many dimensions of power (power over others, power to act, 'power with' in the form of collective organisation, and 'power within' – self-confidence and a sense of legitimacy) determine the nature of the interaction between the different components of change. Power determines who wins, and how: peacefully or not, legally or not, enduringly or not. Achieving change is often about shifting the balance of power between different players, and positive change often involves shifting it in favour of poor people and their organisations.

How change happens is a central issue in almost every field of academic inquiry. Historians debate how National Socialism emerged in Germany. Economists investigate the drivers of economic growth. Sociologists examine the rise of radical Islam. Psychologists discuss the incentive structures that alter human behaviour. Geographers study the role of climate in the rise and fall of civilisations.

It is therefore striking that there is no academic discipline of 'change studies' (the work of Jared Diamond, such as *Guns, Germs and Steel* (1997) probably comes closest to the genre). Instead, the development of independent academic disciplines over the past century has resulted in isolation and over-specialisation. Economists, for example, have learned very little from sociologists about human motivation, and generally maintain simplistic assumptions about human nature. Political scientists focus primarily on institutional processes, and rarely draw on the insights of social psychologists about the determinants of individual and group behaviour. Some disciplines have focused on quantitative research, and consider qualitative research to be lacking in rigour and objectivity. Others engage mainly with current, observable phenomena, and do not possess the long view encountered amongst historians. Experts in one discipline frequently find it impossible to penetrate the abstruse language or mathematical formulae contained in the journal articles of another.

The lack of conversations between disciplines has limited our understanding of how change happens. In particular, the 'development world' of government, academics, and NGOs has suffered from an over-reliance on the single and limited prism of orthodox economics to understand the nature and challenges of development, impoverishing its understanding both of real lives and of the processes that lead to change. These failings matter, because achieving positive change (such as pro-poor economic growth or ending discrimination) and preventing negative change (such as conflict or climate change) are central to tackling poverty, inequality, and suffering.

This annex sketches some ideas for improving our understanding of change. These have been used to analyse the various change episodes discussed in this book, notably the eight case studies that illustrate how change actually happens.

## THE COMPONENTS OF CHANGE

A change process, whether at national or local level, typically involves a combination of four different components: context, institutions, agents, and events (see Figure 7.1).[2] Disentangling any change process into its components in this way can help to identify the different actors and processes involved:[3]

**Context** describes the environment within which changes take place. This can be the most important determinant of the nature and direction of change. Context includes:

- Demographic change: urbanisation, migration, ageing, changing family structures, shifts in the ethnic mix, etc.;
- Globalisation: constraints and opportunities arising from integration into the global economy;
- Environment: change in availability of natural resources, climate, etc.;
- Technological change: introduction of new technologies such as the mobile phone or GM crops, and the more slow-moving adaptation and dissemination of existing technologies such as electricity, vaccines, or the internal combustion engine.

**Institutions**: the organisations and rules (both formal and informal) that establish the 'rules of the game' governing the behaviour of agents. These include:

- Culture, caste, and religion: these to a large extent determine the common perceptions of what is right and wrong, what is socially acceptable, and what is 'normal' in areas such as gender roles, or the acceptability of protest and rebellion. The shifting tides of religious belief in particular are one of the most fundamental drivers of social and political change (as any glance at the evening news will confirm);
- Besides religious belief, the evolution of other ideas and knowledge determines what is seen (by both rulers and ruled) as normal, acceptable, or unacceptable. NGOs and policy makers talk endlessly about 'debates' precisely because, over the long term, such discussions shape the landscape of politics and power;

- Family structures;
- Formal institutions such as the civil service, the rule of law, etc.;
- Government systems: for example democracy, whether inclusionary or exclusionary, autocracy, military rule, etc.;
- The nature of the private sector (small vs large, national vs foreign);
- Patron–client networks.

**Agents**: organisations and individuals actively involved in promoting or blocking change. Examples include:

- Social movements;
- Political parties;
- Political and business elites, whether for or against;
- Military and police;
- Inspirational leaders;
- Social entrepreneurs.

**Events**: one-off events which trigger wider change, such as wars, pandemics, civil conflict, natural disasters, or economic collapse. Elections and election campaigns are often catalysts for social and political change. At a local level, events such as marches and repression by authorities can be key catalysts to popular organisation.

These categories are inevitably approximate and the boundaries between them are blurred. 'Agents' overlap with 'institutions' when institutions become actively engaged in a change process: the civil service is both an institution and an agent, often being in the driving seat in blocking, or promoting, different kinds of change. Wars are often started deliberately by governments, while revolts and civil wars may stem from armed uprisings by previously excluded groups.

How does this framework link to the underlying theme of this book: that sustainable development requires a combination of active citizenship and an effective, accountable state? In terms of change components, active citizens are agents and an effective state an important institution. As Figure 7.1 shows, these two elements can be seen as an inner circle, surrounded by wider components of change such as context and events, which are less susceptible to political or public action. The dotted arrows between the inner and outer circles show that institutions and agents have some limited (especially in developing countries) control over these contextual factors, while the solid arrows show that such factors have an immediate and important impact on institutions and agents. Understanding these wider components helps us understand the constraints and possibilities for building active citizenship and an effective, accountable state.

## FIGURE 7.1: HOW CHANGE HAPPENS

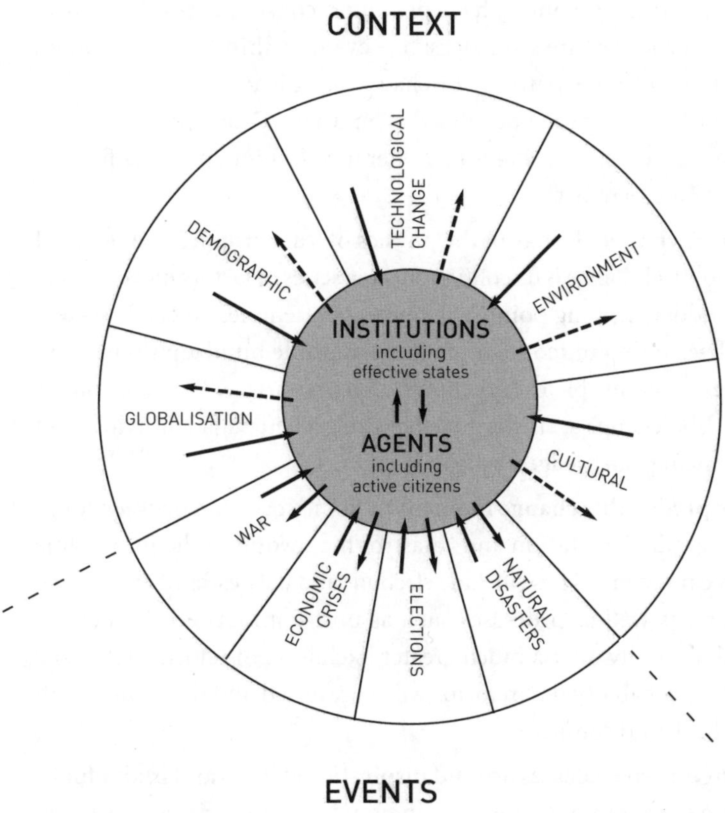

CONTEXT

EVENTS

## THE DYNAMICS OF CHANGE

The components of change combine and interact, creating a complex pathway that involves peaks and troughs of activity and different combinations of context, institutions, agents, and events. Change processes are highly complex and unpredictable, but some of the following dynamics may well be involved:

**Cumulative and sequential progress**: Much change is slow and, from close up, may appear inconsequential. Over the longer term, however, changes such as the evolving notion of human rights, or attitudes to violence against women, have profound consequences. Moreover, change processes are sequences: one event or shift leads to another, creating a unique 'pathway of change' that is usually very hard to predict, but which can be analysed in hindsight. Often, citizens' organisations interact with states in an iterative fashion, pressing for and responding to reforms.

**Chaotic change**: Just as in the physics of 'catastrophes', some social and political change is discontinuous, as a series of factors move matters to a sudden 'tipping point'.[4] The process resembles an earthquake – the devastating outcome of an imperceptible build-up in pressure between tectonic plates far below the Earth's surface. The question for would-be 'change agents' is how they can get better at identifying (and influencing) such 'edge of chaos' situations.

**More predictable change moments**: On the spectrum between long-term, gradual evolution and catastrophic revolution lie foreseeable change moments. These include elections and the deaths of entrenched leaders, as well as processes such as post-conflict reconstruction, which typically offer a much greater likelihood of reform, but also a greater probability that reforms will be reversed and the country will slide back into conflict.[5]

**Change often coalesces around inspirational ideas and individuals**: Oxfam's programme experience in numerous countries attests to the importance of leadership at all levels. Leaders can give words and direction to broad discontent or to desire for change. Ideas and words can play a similar catalytic role, which is why campaigners and politicians devote such attention to what are often decried as soundbites and slogans.

**Organisations often hold the key to shifting the balance of power**: Organisation brings safety in numbers and strengthens the ability to influence change. Often the powerful are among the best-organised groups in society – for example, the business associations and political lobby groups set up by large landowners or firms. However, when poor people get organised, as in Tikamgarh (see page 146), they can transform power relations and trigger deep change.

**Demonstration effects**: At all levels, people's behaviour is powerfully influenced by their points of reference. At a global level, Hollywood exerts a powerful attraction on the minds of most of the world's cinemagoers, while the rise of China has emboldened many developing-country leaders to question the policies espoused by the 'Washington Consensus'. At a local level, change in one community or country often provides a source of inspiration (or alarm) to neighbours.

**Change through price signals**: Pressures for change are often signalled through changes in prices, which themselves are the result of action by governments and companies and the shifting tides of supply and demand. Such changes can be sudden, as with the jump in oil prices that triggered global economic chaos in the 1970s, or a gradual shift in relative prices that alters the nature of economic activity. Processes such as the response to climate change are likely to take place to a large degree through price signals.

## THE POLITICS OF CHANGE

Many change processes require action from those in power. For campaigning organisations such as Oxfam, understanding how such action occurs is crucial in designing strategies to influence decision-makers. A key factor is the degree of pain involved in any given change. Whether a change is easy or difficult determines how much political heat it is likely to generate. A relatively painless change is more likely to be achievable through evidence and argument, whereas a change that seriously harms one group or another is less amenable to argument and more likely to be contentious and possibly violent.

**Champions, shifters, and blockers**: Most social and political change processes excite support, opposition, and apathy, depending on how they affect different groups and individuals. For any organisation seeking change, neutralising opponents or winning over the undecided can be just as important as finding champions.

**Alliances and coalitions**: Most political change is messy, involving building and maintaining coalitions of often-disparate groups, many of whom may disagree on many issues. However, experience suggests that coalitions are often essential to gain the political and social critical mass necessary to effect change. Often the most effective are those that involve sympathetic officials and politicians within the state apparatus and 'experts' willing to challenge received wisdom on a given issue.

**Pre-emptive reforms by the powerful**: Systemic breakdown and revolution are comparatively rare. If simply blocking change does not work, governments and elites typically hold onto power by making the limited reforms necessary to adjust to the forces of change – be they social, economic, or political – without surrendering power. This is not necessarily a cynical process: genuine reformers within a government can acquire more influence because their proposals are seen to be in the interest of the party as a whole. Such reforms typically concede only part of the changes being demanded by their pro-ponents, placing heavy strains on pro-change coalitions, who often disagree over whether to welcome or reject the reforms.

## IMPLICATIONS FOR NGOS AND OTHER CAMPAIGNERS FOR CHANGE

How do the thinking and action of development practitioners such as the World Bank or bilateral aid donors (or NGOs such as Oxfam) match up to this analysis of how change happens? Much current thinking is characterised by a linear model of cause and effect, caricatured by one author as a 'project approach': 'In a situation that needs changing we can gather enough data about a community and its problems, analyse it and discover an underlying set of related problems and their cause, decide which problems are the most important, redefine these as needs, devise a set of solutions and purposes or outcomes, plan a series of logically connected activities for addressing the needs and achieving the desired future results, as defined up front, cost the activities into a convincing budget, raise the funding and then implement the activities, monitor progress as we work to keep them on track, hopefully achieve the planned results and at the end evaluate the project for accountability, impact and sometimes even for learning.'[6]

Such an approach may work for specific tasks such as building a school or sinking a well, but it is ill-suited to describing or influencing the kind of chaotic and complex changes that often characterise development.

More broadly, NGOs abhor violence and suffering: indeed, reducing the prevalence of these is one of the main reasons for their existence. But recognising the role of, say, conflict in change need not require endorsing it. If the only change that NGOs can even think about is economic growth without Schumpeter's 'creative destruction' – innovation without risk and change without conflict – then they risk ignoring some of the most important drivers of change. A pale change model that considers only slow and painless progress can end up looking very much like support for the status quo.

Roman Krznaric points to several flaws in development thinking on change:[7]

**Excessive reformism without politics or history**: Most development thinking is essentially reformist, attempting to work within existing institutions and systems. It therefore ignores the possibility of sudden shifts, and struggles to understand the link between social and political upheaval and change. Development organisations limited to a reformist agenda would have found it difficult to support the African National Congress during apartheid because of its policy of armed struggle; liberation movements in 1980s Central America; or the more than two decades of illegal land occupations by Brazil's Landless Rural Workers Movement.

This raises difficult questions for our understanding of change. If we eschew violence in all but the most extreme situations, as most NGOs do, we remove from the equation one of the most omnipresent forces of change. Heraclitus believed that 'war is the father of all things'. Modern observers might not be so militaristic, but war is undoubtedly a major source of political and social upheaval, not all of which is negative, as the creation of the European welfare states following the Second World War demonstrates.

441

Within many development organisations there is often something of a divide, with staff on the ground in different developing countries having a sophisticated grasp of local politics and history (albeit often in their heads rather than on paper). However, this knowledge rarely makes it into the overall thinking of the organisation. One seasoned NGO observer noticed that, almost invariably, serious political discussions with staff around the world took place only in the restaurant or bar after the formal business of the day had ended.[8]

**Ignoring the impact of sudden change and 'shocks':** Shocks such as wars or natural disasters are perhaps the most powerful forces for change, and yet development organisations largely respond to them solely in terms of humanitarian aid, such as food, water, or shelter. These undoubtedly save lives, but ignore the opportunities for positive change created by such shocks. Major changes (both good and bad) that would normally take decades to happen may occur in the weeks and months after a war, disaster, or political upheaval. How could development practitioners respond more effectively to these 'silver linings' to promote wider systemic change (for example new laws and constitutions, political actors, movements for change)?

**Lack of multi-disciplinary agility:** Development practitioners tend to look at change through the lens of a single discipline. In 2006, when the World Bank commissioned an external evaluation of its research department, it appointed a group of 20 eminent economists, to the chagrin of the non-economists in its research team. Such disciplinary blinkers also afflict NGOs. This may explain why development advocates have a weakness for magic bullets – whether on the neoliberal wing, (de Soto's work on property rights, discussed on page 71) or on the left (popular participation, social movements).

**Underestimating contextual limitations:** There are an enormous number of contextual factors that affect change or are an obstacle to it. Development strategies tend to underestimate the importance of such contexts, and hence overestimate the possibilities for successful change. Sometimes advocates of change default to 'If I ruled the world' visions of Utopias, with little analysis of how such visions could be achieved given the existing distribution of power and influence. Such apolitical thinking can be self-defeating, swinging between feelings of omnipotence, frustration, and powerlessness.

**Technological literacy**: Science and technology are central to development (with both good and bad impacts). Debates on the use of IT, mobile telephony, intellectual property rights, technology transfer, GM, nanotechnology, and a host of other issues are only likely to increase in importance in the coming years. Nevertheless, many NGOs have a serious blind spot on science and technology, either ignoring them altogether or focusing purely on their downsides, as in the case of GM or TRIPS.

**Disregarding the environment**: Most development strategies fail to situate their approach within a sustainable development paradigm (see page 113). This will have to change to take into account factors such as climate change and the loss of biodiversity.

**Overlooking personal relationships and mutual understanding**: Development strategies display an overwhelming focus on individual actors, organised social groups, and institutions, with little acknowledgement that societies and institutions are composed of human relationships that are a potential locus of change. There is much greater scope for development organisations to pursue strategies that encourage mutual understanding, empathy, and trust by creating personal relationships between those who have and those who have not, and which contribute to changing the attitudes and beliefs of those in power.

## DOES COMPLEXITY INVALIDATE THINKING ABOUT CHANGE?

If all change is unpredictable and complex, if we can never tell which beat of which butterfly's wing will trigger the hurricane, is there any point in trying to analyse unforeseeable events? One possible answer is, 'No': given such complexity, all international NGOs can reasonably do is to show solidarity with poor people and their organisations engaged in unpredictable struggles, accompanying them without trying to foresee the future or 'pick winners'. However, there are several flaws with this argument. First, 'solidarity' itself involves a choice: NGOs select who to work with and who to support as partners on the basis of criteria that involve implicit assumptions about what is important for development and how change happens – for example, 'the best path to change for poor people is through social movements'.

Second, because processes are complex it does not mean that they are entirely unforeseeable; indeed, modern washing machines are designed on the basis of mathematical theories of complexity. What it *does* mean is that a simplistic 'input–output' model of change is never likely to work. NGOs need to be more flexible, nimble, and willing to take risks and to experiment, even if it means failing more often than when 'playing safe'. In his book *The Bottom Billion*, Paul Collier proposes that large aid donors should adopt a 'venture capitalist' model, funding 20 initiatives in the knowledge that most of them will fail, but that in the one or two that succeed the results will outweigh the costs. This could equally well apply to NGOs – although they are unlikely to relish the comparison.

# NOTES

## PART 1: INTRODUCTION

1    The infant mortality rate in Norway is one in 250. UNDP (2007)
     *Human Development Report 2007.*

2    UNDP (2005) *Human Development Report 2005.*

3    The risk to women of dying from pregnancy-related causes ranges from one
     in 18 in Nigeria to one in 8,700 in Canada. In poor countries, as many as
     30 per cent of deaths among women of reproductive age (15–49 years) may be
     from pregnancy-related causes, compared with rates of less than 1 per cent in
     developed countries. Sources: UNDP (2005) *op. cit.*; UN Department of
     Economic and Social Affairs (2006).

4    Per capita spending on health ranges from an average of more than $3,000 in
     high-income OECD countries with the lowest health risks to an average of $78
     in low-income countries with the highest risks. It is far less in many of the
     poorest countries. UNDP (2005) *op. cit.*

5    Department of Health, UK (2005).

6    A. Ciconello (2007).

7    Scheduled castes have been known as 'untouchables', although the term is not
     in current use.

8    DFID (2005) 'Reducing Poverty by Tackling Social Exclusion'.

9    UNDP (2005) *op. cit.*

10   L. Kruzenga (2004); J.S. Frideres (1998).

11   ODI (2006) 'Overview', Inter-Regional Inequality Facility.

12   In 2004, the richest 1 per cent of Americans held 34.4 per cent of all net worth
     and 42.2 per cent of all net financial assets, while the bottom 90 per cent held
     only 28.7 per cent of all net worth and 19.1 per cent of all financial assets.
     Economic Policy Institute (2006).

13   ODI (2006) *op. cit.*

14   Chronic Poverty Research Centre (2004); UNDP (2005) *op. cit.*

15    For a more detailed discussion of the nature, extent, and current trends in inequality, see D. Green (2006) 'Equality, Inequality, and Equity'.

16    E. Anderson and T. O'Neill (2006).

17    Gender parity in education is the only aspect of inequality explicitly addressed in the MDGs.

18    See the following reports for a summary of the literature on changing views of equality: World Bank (2005) *World Development Report 2006*; UNDP (2005) *op. cit.*; UN Department of Economic and Social Affairs (2006) *op. cit.*

19    A. Verschoor, A. Covarrubias, and C. Locke (2006) *Women's Economic Empowerment: Gender and Growth.*

20    Chronic Poverty Research Centre (2004) *op. cit.*

21    PPP$, UNDP (2007) *Human Development Report 2007/2008.*

22    UNDP (2005) *op. cit.*

23    R. Chambers (1997).

24    R. Chambers *et al.* (2000).

25    The MDGs were agreed by the international community in 2000, and set a number of targets for improvements in areas such as health, education, and poverty. See: www.un.org/millenniumgoals.

26    UN (2007) *The Millennium Development Goals Report.*

27    UNDP (2005) *op. cit.* Following the World Bank's recalculation of purchasing power parity estimates for individual countries in December 2007, which drastically reduced (in PPP terms) the GDP of countries such as China, poverty numbers in China and India, among others, were likely to be revised sharply upwards. However, figures were not available at the time of writing. See B. Milanovic, 'Developing countries worse off than once thought', YaleGlobal, 11 February 2008.

28    UN Department of Economic and Social Affairs (2006) *op. cit.*

29    J. Beall and S. Fox (2006).

30    UN Department of Economic and Social Affairs (2006) *op. cit.*

31    UN (2007) *The Millennium Development Goals Report.*

32    WHO (2007) 'Malaria'.

33    UNDP (2005) *op. cit.*

34    UNICEF (2008).

35    UNDP (2005) *op. cit.*

36    UN Department of Economic and Social Affairs (2006) *op. cit.*

37    UNAIDS and WHO (2007).

38    P. Kantor and P. Nair (2005).

39    Chronic Poverty Research Centre (2008).

40    UN Department of Economic and Social Affairs (2006) *op. cit.*

41    F.H.G. Ferreira *et al.* (2005).

42    IPEA (undated).

43    www.oxfam.org/en/about/accountability/strategic_plan

44    www.fp2p.org

45    M.L. King (1968).

## PART 2: POWER AND POLITICS

1  J. Rowlands (1997).
2  B. De Jouvenel (1949).
3  Quoted in J. Rowlands (1997) *op. cit.*
4  M.H. Khan (2002).
5  Interview with Oxfam Australia/Community Aid Abroad, cited in 'Advocacy for the Eradication of Poverty', internal paper, Oxfam Novib.
6  For a proposed list of basic capabilities, see M. Nussbaum (1999).
7  See introduction to P. Gready and J. Ensor (2005).
8  P. Uvin (2004). See www.business-humanrights.org/Home for more on businesses and human rights.
9  R.C. Offenheiser and S.H. Holcombe (2003).
10 UNDP (2000) *Human Development Report 2000.*
11 See www.righttofoodindia.org and www.righttoinformation.info.
12 M. Brouwer *et al.* (undated).
13 DFID (2005) 'Reducing Poverty by Tackling Social Exclusion'.
14 R.C. Offenheiser and S.H. Holcombe (2003) *op. cit.*
15 R. Chambers (2006).
16 Author interview, 2006.
17 R. Chambers (2006) *op. cit.*
18 D. Green (2006) *Faces of Latin America.*
19 World Bank (2006) *World Development Report 2007.*
20 G. Mulgan (2006).
21 World Bank (2006) *op. cit.*
22 E. Reis and M. Moore (2005).
23 R. Chambers *et al.* (2000) *op. cit.*
24 W. Tyndale (1998).
25 E. Tomalin (2007).
26 P. Watt (1999).
27 S. Mehrotra and R. Jolly (1997).
28 Author interview, November 2006.
29 Oxfam International (2007) 'Paying for People'.
30 I. Goldin and K. Reinert (2006).
31 IPEA (undated) *op. cit.*
32 UNESCO (2006).
33 *Ibid.*, p.3.
34 *Ibid.*, p.4.
35 *Ibid.*, p.12.
36 www.campaignforeducation.org
37 Oxfam International and WaterAid (2006).
38 *Ibid.*, p.35.
39 UN (2006) *The Millennium Development Goals Report.*
40 Figure specifies economic losses associated with health spending and productivity losses. UNDP (2006) *Human Development Report 2006.*

41   WaterAid (2007).

42   S. Singh *et al.* (2004).

43   *Ibid.*

44   A. Sen (1999).

45   For a fuller discussion, see Oxfam International and WaterAid (2006) *op. cit.*

46   Public Services International Research Unit, 2003.

47   ODI (2007).

48   Oxfam International and WaterAid (2006) *op. cit.*

49   *Ibid.*, p.8.

50   *Ibid.*, p.86.

51   www.ifpri.org/2020/focus/focus06/focus06_11.htm

52   E. Reis and M. Moore (2005) *op. cit.*

53   Oxfam International (2006) 'Serve the Essentials', p.33; R. Jenkins and A.M. Goetz (1999); BBC, 14 November 2006, 'Information law lifts Indian poor', http://news.bbc.co.uk/2/hi/south_asia/6124898.stm

54   Development Studies Association, UK (2007).

55   www1.worldbank.org/prem/PREMNotes/premnote93.pdf, October 2004.

56   Committee to Protect Journalists, 2006.

57   DFID (2005) 'Reducing Poverty by Tackling Social Exclusion'.

58   World Bank (2005) *World Development Report 2006.*

59   www.internetworldstats.com/stats.htm

60   www.freedomhouse.org/pfs2000/sussman.html

61   J. McMillan and P. Zoido (2004).

62   C. Kenny (undated).

63   UNDP (2001).

64   M. Leach and I. Scoones (2006).

65   UNDP (2001) *op. cit.*

66   CGIAR, see: www.cgiar.org; M. Leach and I. Scoones (2006) *op. cit.*, p.33.

67   UNDP (2001) *op. cit.*, p.75.

68   D. Green (2006) *Faces of Latin America.*

69   DFID (2007) 'Civil Society and Good Governance'.

70   G. Mulgan (2006) *op. cit.*, p.237.

71   J. Howell and J. Pearce (2001).

72   UNDP (2000) *Human Development Report 2000.*

73   J. Howell and J. Pearce (2001) *op. cit.*, p.31.

74   Freedom House (2005).

75   S. Hopkins Leisher (2003).

76   B. Knight *et al.* (2002).

77   The word democracy comes from the Greek 'demos' (people) and 'kratos' (power).

78   http://viacampesina.org/main_en/index.php

79   www.socialwatch.org/en/portada.htm

80   J. Howell and J. Pearce, *op. cit.*, p.237.

81   IDS (2003).

82    J. Beall and S. Fox (2006) *op. cit.*

83    J. Beall and S. Fox (forthcoming, 2008).

84    M.H Khan (2006).

85    M.H Khan (2002) *op. cit.*

86    H. de Soto (2000).

87    B. Cousins *et al.* (2005).

88    M. Bourke (2005).

89    'The mystery of capital deepens', *The Economist*, 24 August 2006.

90    D. Green (2003).

91    The International Institute of Environment and Development *et al.* (2005).

92    UNFPA (2005).

93    J. Rodin (2007).

94    Oxfam GB (2006).

95    In the UK, for example, the Married Women's Property Act of 1884 permitted women bringing property to their marriages to keep ownership rights over it. Previously these had passed automatically to their husbands.

96    C. Nyamu-Musembi (2006).

97    The International Institute of Environment and Development *et al.* (2005) *op. cit.*

98    J. Gaventa (2005).

99    UNDP (2005) *op. cit.*

100   UNDP (2002) *Human Development Report 2002.*

101   B. Knight *et al.* (2002) *op. cit.*, p.76.

102   Gallup, 2005.

103   Afrobarometer (2006); Latinbarometro, quoted in C. Graham and S. Sukhtankar (2004).

104   E.D. Mansfield and J. Snyder (2005).

105   G. Mulgan (2006) *op. cit.*

106   *Ibid.*

107   *Ibid.*

108   T. Mkandawire (2004).

109   N. Birdsall (2007).

110   N. Bobbio, translated by M. Ryle and K. Soper (1990).

111   H.-J. Chang (2007).

112   International Women's Democracy Centre, www.iwdc.org/resources/fact_sheet.htm

113   www.quotaproject.org/system.cfm

114   M. Lockwood (2005).

115   World Bank (2003) *World Development Report 2004.*

116   M. K. Sparrow (2006).

117   H. Elshorst and D. O'Leary (2005).

118   Oxfam International and WaterAid (2006) *op. cit.*

119   www.transparency.org/policy_research/surveys_indices/cpi/2007

120   Paul Wolfowitz, World Bank, quoted in *The Observer*, 5 November 2006.

121   UNDP (2007) *Human Development Report 2007/2008.*

122   P. Collier (2006).

123   E. Galeano (1973).

124   www.eitransparency.org

125   DFID (2007) 'Governance, Development and Democratic Politics'.

126   S. Pradhan (2006).

127   C. Tilly (1990).

128   G. Mulgan (2006) *op. cit.*, p.168.

129   OECD (2007) 'OECD in Figures 2007'.

130   G. Mulgan (2006) *op. cit.*

131   IDS (2006).

132   T. Mkandawire (2001).

133   G. Mulgan (2006) *op. cit.*

134   A strong positive correlation is evident between the scores on the two indices of the ten developing countries that are comparable on both the CIVICUS Civil Society Index (a proxy for active citizenship) and the World Bank's Resource Allocation Index (a proxy for effective states).

135   M.H. Khan (2002).

136   P. Evans (1995).

137   J.-J. Rousseau (1762).

138   DFID (2005) 'Reducing Poverty by Tackling Social Exclusion'.

139   Author interview with Wendy Isaack, POWA (People Opposing Women's Abuse), South Africa, 2007.

140   P. O'Brien (2001).

141   G. Hesselbein *et al.* (2006).

142   J. Di John (2006).

143   IDS (2005).

144   J. Beall and S. Fox (forthcoming, 2008) *op. cit.*

145   Oxfam GB (2005).

146   H. Wainwright (2003).

147   B.S. Baviskar (2003); Centre for Women's Development Studies (1999).

148   H.-J. Chang (2007) *op. cit.*

149   G. Hesselbein *et al.* (2006) *op. cit.*

150   G. Mulgan (2006) *op. cit.*

## PART 3: POVERTY AND WEALTH

1   A. Sen (1999).

2   J. Stiglitz (2000).

3   There are, however, sub-schools of neoclassical economics that seek to explain institutions such as marriage and behaviour using the tools of economics. See, for example, G. Becker (1992).

4   Many influential neoclassical thinkers are, however, classical liberals with a firm belief that markets are the best way to deliver democracy and individual rights. See, for example, M. Friedman (1980) or F. Hayek (1944).

5   There has, however, been increasing interest in equity in recent years:
    see World Bank (2005) *World Development Report 2006* for references.
6   See, for example, N. Folbre (1994).
7   L. Goldschmidt-Clermont and E. Pagnossin-Aligisakis (1995).
8   A. Latigo (2005).
9   J. Bruce (1989).
10  N. Çağatay and K. Ertürk (2004).
11  G.H. Brundtland (1987).
12  W.M. Adams (2006).
13  World Bank (2006) 'Where is the Wealth of Nations? Measuring Capital for
    the 21st Century'.
14  J. Liu and J. Diamond (2005).
15  World Bank (2006) 'Where is the Wealth of Nations?', *op. cit.*
16  A phenomenon known as the 'environmental Kuznets curve'.
17  World Wide Fund For Nature (2006).
18  UNDP (2006) *Human Development Report 2007*.
19  UN (2004) 'The Impact of AIDS'.
20  OECD (2006) *Development Cooperation Report 2006*.
21  World Bank (2007) *World Development Report 2008*.
22  A. Dorward *et al.* (2004).
23  World Bank (2007) *op. cit.*
24  *Ibid.*
25  *Ibid.*
26  A. Dorward *et al.* (2004) *op. cit.*
27  F. Kasryno (2004).
28  World Bank (2007) *op. cit.*
29  Nestlé, Philip Morris-Kraft Foods, Procter & Gamble, and Sara Lee/ Douwe
    Egberts.
30  Cargill, ADM, Barry Callebaut, and Hosta.
31  BASF, Bayer, Dow, DuPont, Monsanto, and Syngenta.
32  B. Vorley (2003).
33  M. Prowse (2007).
34  S. Singh (2005).
35  I. Delforge (2007).
36  T. Reardon *et al.* (2006).
37  T. Reardon and J.A. Berdegué (2002).
38  K. Kelleher and M.L. Weber (2006).
39  World Bank (2004).
40  FAO (2005) 'The State of Food Insecurity in the World 2005'.
41  M. Allain (2007).
42  D. Boyer (2001).
43  D. Pauly *et al.* (2004); D. Pauly *et al.* (2005).
44  L. Van Mulekom (1999); STREAM (2004).
45  www.agra-alliance.org/work/seeds.html

46   R. Offenheiser (2007).

47   IPCC (2007).

48   www.etcgroup.org/article.asp?newsid=486

49   Meridian Institute (2007).

50   World Bank (2007) *World Development Report 2008.*

51   J. Pretty (2006).

52   World Bank (2007) *op. cit.* Zero tillage maintains a permanent or semi-permanent organic soil cover (e.g. a growing crop or dead mulch) that protects the soil from sun, rain, and wind. It allows soil micro-organisms and fauna to take on the tasks of 'tilling' and soil nutrient balancing – natural processes disturbed by mechanical tillage. Source: FAO (2001).

53   Oxfam International (2007) 'Bio-fuelling Poverty'.

54   FAO (2008) 'Crop Prospects and Food Situation No 1'.

55   World Bank (2007) *op. cit.*

56   For an overview of the issues facing producer organisations, see C. Penrose-Buckley (2007).

57   J.L. Arcand (2004).

58   Research by Leuven University cited in Proceedings Report, Corporate Governance and Co-operatives, Peer Review Workshop, London, 8 February 2007.

59   U.S. Awasthi (2001).

60   C. Penrose-Buckley (2007) *op. cit.*

61   This view is supported largely by anecdotal evidence and theoretical expectations rather than by significant statistical analysis (e.g. B. Shiferaw *et al.* (2007); E. Chirwa *et al.* (2005); and J. Hellin *et al.* (2006). However, in Tanzania only around 3 per cent of rural households are estimated to be affiliated to POs, and the vast majority of these are smallholders producing cash crops, with above-average farm holdings.

62   www.acdivoca.org/acdivoca/CoopLib.nsf/whycoopsandassociations/malawinasfam?opendocument

63   E. Kaganzi *et al.* (2006).

64   J. Hellin and S. Higman (2003).

65   J. Coulter *et al.* (1999).

66   A study in Central America and Mexico concluded that POs established by and directly linked to supermarkets fared better than others, for example those set up by NGOs. J. Hellin *et al.* (2007).

67   M. Chen (2006).

68   FLO Annual Report (2006), p.6.

69   A number of studies and anecdotal evidence indicate a relatively high failure rate for POs, suggesting a high turnover in some parts of the world. See G.F. Ortmann and R.P. King (2007); R. Stringfellow *et al.* (1997); A.W. Shepherd (2007).

70   DFID (2005) 'Growth and Poverty Reduction: The Role of Agriculture'.

71   World Bank (2007) *World Development Report 2008.*

72   www.leftbusinessobserver.com/Stiglitz.html

73   See also DFID (2005) 'Growth and Poverty Reduction: The Role of Agriculture' and CIDA (2003).

74   http://econ.worldbank.org/WBSITE/EXTERNAL/EXTDEC/EXTRE-SEARCH/EXTWDRS/EXTWDR2008/0,,menuPK:2795178~pagePK:64167702~piPK:64167676~theSitePK:2795143,00.html

75   A. Dorward *et al.* (2004) 'A policy agenda for pro-poor agricultural growth'.

76   M. Stockbridge (2006).

77   G. Denning and J. Sachs (2007).

78   World Bank (2007) *op. cit.*

79   L.O. Fresco (2003).

80   DFID (2004).

81   A. Dorward *et al.* (2005). These figures may be highly contingent on the context in Africa, although the *World Development Report 2007* estimates that, overall, more than half of rural households are net food purchasers.

82   A. Dorward *et al.* (2004) 'Institutions and Economic Policies for Pro-Poor Agricultural Growth'.

83   Directorate of Economics and Statistics, Ministry of Agriculture, Government of India, http://dacnet.nic.in/eands/At_A_Glance/as.htm

84   A. Dorward *et al.* (2004) *op. cit.*

85   D. Green *et al.* (2004).

86   International Food Policy Research Institute (2004).

87   Author interview from D. Green (1998) *Hidden Lives.*

88   New Economics Foundation (2006) 'A Long Row to Hoe'.

89   www.oxfam.org.au/oxfamnews/march_2006/rags.html

90   World Bank (2007) *op. cit.*; International Labour Organization, Facts on Agriculture, www.ilo.org/public/english/bureau/inf/download/wssd/pdf/agriculture.pdf

91   ILO (2006).

92   ILO (2008).

93   ILO (2002).

94   ILO (2005).

95   Despite the rapid rise in opportunities for women in low-productivity jobs in agriculture and services, over the past ten years women's share of the total global paid workforce has remained at 40 per cent, following decades of rising women's employment. See ILO (2007).

96   Oxfam International (2004) 'Trading Away Our Rights'.

97   *Ibid.*, p.18.

98   *Ibid.*, p.27.

99   M. Chen *et al.* (2005).

100  See N. Folbre and M. Bittman (2004).

101  Oxfam International (2004) 'Trading Away Our Rights', p.29.

102  M. Chen *et al.* (2005) *op. cit.*, p.40.

103  'The flicker of a brighter future', *Economist*, 7 September 2006.

104  D. Green (2003).

105  J. Beall and S. Fox (forthcoming, 2008) *op. cit.*

106   M. Rama (2003).

107   M. Chen *et al.* (2005) *op. cit.*, p.39.

108   UN Department of Economic and Social Affairs (2006) *op. cit.*

109   UN (2006) 'Report of the Secretary-General on International Migration and Development'; ILO (2002) *op. cit.*, p.26.

110   See ILO (2002) *op. cit.* for their definition of 'informal employment'.

111   G. Standing (1999).

112   J.M. Ramirez-Machado (2003).

113   Oxfam International (2004) 'Trading Away Our Rights'.

114   World Bank (2002).

115   www.doingbusiness.org; personal correspondence, Peter Bakvis, ICFTU, October 2006.

116   N. Sekhamane (2004).

117   Oxfam International (2004) 'Trading Away Our Rights', p.52.

118   Author interviews, Bangladesh, quoted in D. Green (1998) 'Fashion Victims'.

119   Oxfam International (2004) 'Trading Away Our Rights', p.68.

120   Author interviews, quoted in D. Green (1998) 'Fashion Victims'.

121   D. Gallin (2004).

122   ILO (2001).

123   http://web.worldbank.org/WBSITE/EXTERNAL/NEWS/0,,contentMDK: 20091655~menuPK:34463~pagePK:34370~piPK:34424~theSitePK:4607, 00.html

124   Fatima Shabodien, executive director, Women on Farms Project (WFP), personal communication February 2008.

125   M. Chen (2006) *op. cit.*

126   For further examples of organising in the informal economy, see: www.wiego.org

127   'Wal-Mart backs down and allows Chinese workers to join union', *The Guardian*, 11 August 2006, http://business.guardian.co.uk/story/0,,1842080,00.html

128   Oxfam International (2004) 'Trading Away Our Rights'.

129   *Ibid.*, p.77.

130   www.ethicaltrade.org

131   T. Moran (2002).

132   'An ugly side of free trade: sweatshops in Jordan', *New York Times*, 3 May 2006.

133   www.oxfam.org.hk/one/200710/index.html

134   S. Polaski (2004). For more details on the Cambodia example, see D. Wells (2006).

135   M. Chen *et al.* (2005) *op. cit.*, p.96.

136   Some analyses draw a distinction between 'micro-enterprises', employing fewer than ten staff, small enterprises with 10–50 staff, and medium enterprises up to 250 staff.

137   M. Ayyagari *et al.* (2003). As discussed in the previous section, the boundaries between formal and informal companies are becoming blurred, as formal firms make more use of 'flexible' labour contracts to drive down costs.

138   UNDP (2004) 'Unleashing Entrepreneurship'.

139    Author interview, December 2007.

140    G. Gereffi and D.L. Wyman (1990) and (2001); and Taiwanese government
       website, Ministry of Economic Affairs,
       www.moeasmea.gov.tw/np.asp?ctNode=260&mp=2

141    J. Clay (2005).

142    World Bank (2007) *Global Development Finance 2007*. In 2004–05,
       62 developing countries carried out 400 privatisations, worth $90bn.
       See World Bank (undated).

143    World Bank (2007) *Global Development Finance 2007*; UNDP (2007)
       *Human Development Report 2007/ 2008*.

144    UNCTAD (2006) *World Investment Report 2006*.

145    A. Goldstein (2005).

146    http://news.bbc.co.uk/2/hi/africa/3694043.stm

147    World Bank (2005) 'FDI Trends'.

148    http://news.bbc.co.uk/2/hi/business/7180396.stm

149    OECD (2006) 'Developing Country Multinationals'.

150    D. Brown (2007).

151    S. Hart (2005).

152    A.A. Picard (2001).

153    B.S. Javorcik (2004).

154    World Bank (2007) *Global Development Finance 2007*.

155    UNCTAD (2005) *World Investment Report 2005*.

156    J. Brigmann and C.K. Prahalad (2007).

157    J. Clay (2005) *op. cit.*

158    Author interview, Martin Kalungu-Banda, 2007.

159    Figures for 2003, from UNDP (2005) *Human Development Report 2005*.

160    UNDP (2006) 'China, Country Programme Document 2006–10'.

161    Commission on Growth and Development (2008).

162    Estimates of the proportion of poverty reduction accounted for by economic
       growth vary widely: see, for example, A. Kraay (2006).

163    M. Ravallion (2004).

164    S. Wiggins, with K. Higgins (2008).

165    www.growthcommission.org

166    Michael Spence, chair of Commission on Growth and Development, personal
       communication, January 2008.

167    J. Schumpeter (1975).

168    GDP measured at purchasing power parity, at 1993 prices. Calculations are by
       New Economics Foundation (2006) 'Growth Isn't Working'.

169    R. Layard (2005).

170    This pattern emerges when countries are weighted by population. For an
       unweighted distribution, the finding is slightly different: at any given income,
       there is a range of reported levels of life satisfaction, with both 'content' and
       'uncontented' countries, but as income rises, the dispersion decreases and
       countries converge on a higher level of life satisfaction. Source: New
       Economics Foundation, personal communication.

171    New Economics Foundation (2007).

172   P. Chaudhry (2007).

173   ECLAC (various years).

174   L. Taylor and R. von Arnim (2007).

175   D. Rodrik (2004).

176   D. Rodrik (2003).

177   M. Spence (2007).

178   H.-J. Chang (2005).

179   China reduced levels of $1-a-day poverty from approximately 32 per cent of its
population in 1990 to 10 per cent in 2004, and Viet Nam from approximately
51 per cent in 1990 to 10 per cent in 2004. An important caveat to the poverty
reduction story is that economic growth in both China and Viet Nam has
driven (and been driven by) an enormous expansion of the informal urban
industrial sector, where migrants are employed in often poor and dangerous
conditions, with no social protection measures and poor wages in comparison
with workers in the formal economy. Recent urban migrants are invisible in
national poverty surveys, which measure only those with registered residents'
status, and so 'new' urban poverty is likely to be significantly under-represented
in official poverty data.

180   WTO (2007).

181   The actual figure is 37 per cent for 2005: 2005 figures, World Bank (2007)
*World Development Indicators 2007*.

182   S. Laird *et al.* (2006).

183   M. Stockbridge (2006) *op. cit.*

184   H.-J. Chang (2001) *Kicking Away the Ladder*.

185   For a pre-commodity boom analysis of the commodity trade, see D. Green
(2005).

186   J. Banister (2005); R. Kaplinsky (2005) 'Asian Drivers: China, India And
The Global Labour Force'.

187   World Wide Fund for Nature (2006).

188   H. Lopez (2006).

189   M. Spence (2007) *op. cit.*

190   R. Layard (2005) *op. cit.*

## PART 4: RISK AND VULNERABILITY

1    R. Chambers *et al.* (2000) *op. cit.*

2    D.F. Bryceson and J. Fonseca (2006).

3    Oxfam International (2006) 'Causing Hunger: an Overview of the Food Crises
in Africa'.

4    UNDP (2005) *op. cit.*

5    P. Suarez (2006).

6    UNISDR (2004).

7    R. Chambers *et al.* (2000) *op. cit.*, p.175.

8    For a more recent formulation, see the Final Report of the UN Commission
on Human Security (2003).

9    See D. Green (1998) *Hidden Lives*.

10    Sources for Figure 4.2: Children under 5, UNICEF (2007) *State of the World's Children 2007*; tobacco, child undernutrition, and overweight & obesity, WHO, www.who.int/dietphysicalactivity/publications/facts/en/gsfs_ppt_rf. pdf; air pollution, WHO (2006) 'Global Burden of Disease and Risk Factors'; HIV and AIDS, UNAIDS and WHO (2007) 'AIDS Epidemic Update 2007'; alcohol, WHO (2007) 'Alcohol and Injury in Emergency Departments'; water-borne diseases, UNDP (2005) *Human Development Report 2006*; road-traffic accidents, armed conflict, and suicide, WHO (2002) 'Global Burden of Disease 2002'; interpersonal violence and crime, WHO (2002) *World Report on Violence and Health*; childbirth or pregnancy-related disease, UNDP (2005) *Human Development Report 2005*; small arms, calculated from Small Arms Survey (2004) and Small Arms Survey (2005), www.smallarmssurvey.org/files/sas/publications/; terrorism, US Department of State (2007) 'Country Reports on Terrorism', www.state.gov/s/ct/rls/crt/2006/

11    S. Devereux and R. Sabates-Wheeler (2004).

12    Vusimuzi Madonsela, Director-General, South African Department of Social Development, lecture, Oxford, November 2007.

13    1996 Constitution of the Republic of South Africa, Section 27, 1c.

14    Inter-Regional Inequality Facility (2006).

15    A. Shepherd *et al.* (2005).

16    www.sewa.org

17    Quoted in Oxfam GB *et al.* (2006).

18    S. Wiggins (2005).

19    Oxfam International (2006) 'Causing Hunger: an Overview of the Food Crises in Africa'.

20    Oxfam GB, internal project monitoring report, August 2007.

21    Commission for Africa (2005).

22    Center for American Progress (2007).

23    The initiative was developed by the Network for the Citizens' Basic Income (Rede Brasileira da Renda Básica de Cidadania (RBRBC)), set up the previous year.

24    Based on calculation in UNDP (2005) *op. cit.*

25    L.-H. Piron (2004).

26    D. Coady *et al.* (2002).

27    Microcredit Summit Campaign (2006).

28    Based on Oxfam America's Saving for Change Scheme in Mali, Senegal, Burkina Faso, and Cambodia, which now reaches 100,000 members, www.oxfamamerica.org/whatwedo/issues_we_work_on/saving_for_change

29    M. Chen (2006) *op. cit.*

30    Taken from C.K. Prahalad (2005).

31    www.procreditbank.com

32    World Bank (2001).

33    *The Guardian*, 20 March 2007.

34    World Bank (2003).

35    T. Dichter (2006).

36    B. Popkin (2003).

37    FAO (2007).

38    FAO (2006) *The State of Food Insecurity in the World 2006.*

39    World Food Programme (2007).

40    FAO (2003).

41    There is no universally accepted definition of a food crisis or of acute food insecurity, but a working definition would be 'a situation of unusually severe food insecurity that threatens peoples' lives and/or livelihoods'. This happens when people experience a large reduction in their major source of food due to external shock, and are unable to make up the difference through new strategies; when the prevalence of malnutrition is abnormally high for the time of year, and this cannot be accounted for by either health or other factors; when a large proportion of the population or group is using marginal or unsustainable coping strategies; or when people are using coping strategies that are damaging their livelihoods in the longer term, or engage in illegal or immoral activities to gain food. Famine is when people are unable to meet their needs through survival strategies or are displaced into camp environments, and malnutrition and deaths increase.

42    UN OCHA.

43    African Union (2005); Civil Society Organisations for Peace in Northern Uganda (2006).

44    FAO (2004) 'The State of Food Insecurity in the World 2004'.

45    'Cheap no more' *Economist*, 6 December 2007.

46    FAO (2004) 'The State of Agricultural Commodity Markets'.

47    Oxfam International (2005) 'Food Aid or Hidden Dumping?'.

48    FAO, 'Crop Prospects and Food Situation', December 2007.

49    Unfortunately, the term 'mitigation' means contradictory things according to the risk being discussed. In climate change it is about reducing emissions, while in discussions on natural disasters it is about reducing potential impact.

50    A. Sen (1999) *op. cit.*

51    Ministry of Health and Family Welfare, Government of India (2007).

52    Author interview, 2007.

53    UNAIDS (2006) 'Global Facts and Figures'.

54    UNAIDS (2006) 'Report on the Global AIDS Epidemic'.

55    www.who.int/hiv/mediacentre/universal_access_progress_report_en.pdf

56    UNAIDS (2006) 'Report on the Global AIDS Epidemic'.

57    UNICEF (2007).

58    S. Lewis (2005).

59    The UN Special Rapporteur on the Right to Health has recognised this fact, and has developed a draft set of guidelines which apply provisions on the right to health to pharmaceutical companies' policies and practices.

60    F. Farley, 'At AIDS disaster's epicenter, Botswana is a model of action; during U.N. conference, leader speaks of national "extinction", but country plans continent's most ambitious programs', *Los Angeles Times*, 27 June 2001.

61    T. Rosenberg (2001).

62    WHO press release, March 2007, www.who.int/tb/features_archive/wtbd07_press/en/index.html

458

63   WHO (2006) 'Cumulative Number of Confirmed Human Cases of Avian Influenza'.

64   C.J.L. Murray *et al.* (2006).

65   UN (2005) *Millennium Development Goals Report 2005*.

66   WHO (2007) 'Lifetime Maternal Mortality Risk'.

67   www.unfpa.org/mothers/facts.htm

68   M.D. Layton *et al.* (2007).

69   S. Maxwell (2005).

70   J. Senderowitz (1995).

71   UNDP (2005) *op. cit.*

72   However, 26 million children worldwide were still not immunised by DTP3 in 2006: WHO (2007) 'Progress Towards Global Immunization Goals'.

73   WHO (2005).

74   www.who.int/reproductive-health/publications/cervical_cancer_gep/text.pdf

75   WHO (2006) *World Health Report 2006*.

76   Oxfam International and WaterAid (2006) *op. cit.*

77   UNDP (2004) 'Reducing Disaster Risk: A Challenge for Development'; International Federation of Red Cross and Red Crescent Societies (2004).

78   In 2005, an unusually bad year because of the Asian tsunami of 26 December 2004, the numbers tripled to a total of 244,577 people killed and over 150 million affected.

79   UNISDR (2004) *op. cit.*

80   T. Vaux and F. Lund (2003).

81   N. Fariba (2006).

82   AFP, 'Tsunami calamity highlights key protective role of coral, mangroves', Asia Pacific News, Channel News Asia, 6 January 2005, www.channelnewsasia.com/stories/afp_asiapacific/view/125966/1/.html

83   In February 2005, Japan Bank of Industrial Cooperation conducted a study on the role of mangrove afforestation in mitigating the damage caused by the tsunami, which confirmed that it provided a beneficial screen against wind and sand, www.jbic.go.jp/english/environ/report/2005/pdf/08.pdf

84   G. Venkataramani (2004).

85   According to the Global Platform for Disaster Risk Reduction in its *Disaster Risk Reduction: 2007 Global Review* (June 2007), using data from the CRED-CRUNCH EM-DAT emergency disaster database (www.cred.be or www.em-dat.net).

86   Oxfam International (2007) 'Climate Alarm: Disasters Increase As Climate Change Bites'.

87   Oxfam International (2007) 'Sink or Swim'.

88   J. Cosgrave *et al.* (2007).

89   Oxfam International (2008) 'Rethinking Disasters'.

90   Oxfam America (2003).

91   UNDP (2004) 'Reducing Disaster Risk: A Challenge For Development'; G. Venkataramani (2004).

92   K. Annan (1999).

93   WMO (2006).

94   IPCC (2007).

95   S. Dasgupta *et al.* (2007).

96   www.ipcc.ch/SPM2feb07.pdf

97   R. Roach (2007).

98   www.nature.com/nature/journal/v438/n7066/abs/nature04188.html

99   G. Mutangadura *et al.* (1999).

100   M. Boko *et al.* (2007); M.L. Parry *et al.* (2007).

101   UNEP (2006).

102   Stern Review (2006) 'What is the Economics of Climate Change?'.

103   WHO (2002).

104   UNHCR (2003)
     www.neweconomics.org/gen/uploads/igeebque0l3nvy455whn42vs
     19102004202736.pdf

105   Further warming is now inevitable; even if atmospheric concentrations
     of greenhouse gases remained at 2000 levels, the IPCC estimates that we would
     have to expect further warming of approximately 0.6°C this century. IPCC
     (2007).

106   Tyndall Centre for Climate Change (2004).

107   P. Suarez (2005).

108   ActionAid (2006).

109   Oxfam interview, February 2007.

110   P. Chaudhry and G. Ruysschaert (2007).

111   Stern Review (2006) *The Economics of Climate Change*.

112   J. Davies and R. Hatfield (2006).

113   Much of this work draws on the 'new range ecology' of Scoones, Benkhe,
     Kerven, and others, which developed during the 1990s. Their work
     demonstrated that the underlying assumptions of equilibrium range ecology
     (such as fixed carrying capacities) and consequent solutions (such as
     destocking) were inappropriate to many parts of Africa. The spatial
     distribution of livestock rather than their number is what must be managed
     to avoid overgrazing, thus highlighting the critical importance of mobility in
     dry-land resource management. A more opportunistic approach to ecosystem
     management is essential in areas with high co-efficients of variation in rainfall.
     (Drawn from I. Birch and R. Grahn (2007).)

114   J. Davies and R. Hatfield (2006) *op. cit.*

115   N. Brooks (2006).

116   C. Hesse and J. MacGregor (2006).

117   Documented by IUCN, www.unep-wcmc.org/forest/restoration

118   Human Rights Watch (2007).

119   Niger (1993), Guinea (1995), Mauritania (2000), Mali (2001), and Burkina
     Faso (2003).

120   M.C. Gning (2004).

121   Quoted in African Union and Interafrican Bureau for Animal Resources
     (2007).

122   J. Swift (undated).

123   J. Davies and M. Nori (2007).

124 K. Annan (2005) 'In Larger Freedom: Towards Development, Security and Human Rights for All'.

125 Human Rights Research and Advocacy Consortium (2004).

126 US Department of Justice – Federal Bureau of Investigation (2006).

127 UN (2005).

128 UNFPA (2000).

129 'Uganda Demographic and Health Survey 2000–2001'; *Gender and Development*, November 2006, p.411.

130 www.wecanendvaw.org/index.htm

131 UNDP (2005) *op. cit.*, p.153.

132 L. Harbom and P. Wallensteen (2005). This uses a definition of armed conflict as 'a contested incompatibility that concerns government or territory or both, where the use of armed force between two parties results in at least 25 battle-related deaths' a year. In general, this paper has inadequate data, especially comparable year-on-year or very up-to-date data, on many security issues, and a note of caution should be attached to most of the figures it contains.

133 Human Security Centre (2005).

134 Figure for IDPs from World Refugee Survey 2006, www.refugees.org/data/wrs/06/docs/key_statistics.pdf; figures for refugees and asylum seekers from World Refugee Survey 2006, Table 3, www.refugees.org/data/wrs/06/docs/refugee_and_asylum_seekers_worldwide.pdf

135 UNDP (2005) *op. cit.*, p.154.

136 B. Lacina and N.P. Gleditsch (2005).

137 'A More Secure World', Report of the UN High-Level Panel on Threats, Challenges and Change, 2004, p.20, quoting M. Humphreys and A. Varshney (2004).

138 P. Collier (2007).

139 *Ibid.*, p.12.

140 International Rescue Committee (2004).

141 Norwegian Refugee Council (2007).

142 UNDP (2005) *op. cit.*, p.155.

143 K. Annan (2005) 'Report on the Protection of Civilians in Armed Conflict'.

144 Physicians for Human Rights (2002).

145 UNDP (2005) *op. cit.*, p.160.

146 Human Security Centre (2005) *op. cit.*, p.9.

147 UNDP (2005) *op. cit.*, p.163.

148 D. Smith and J. Vivekananda (2007).

149 Control Arms Campaign (2003).

150 P. Collier (2004).

151 UNDP (2005) *op. cit.*, p.166–7.

152 'The pastor and the imam: from rivals to partners', *Conflict Prevention Newsletter* 9(1) 18–19.

153 'A More Secure World: Our Shared Responsibility', UN High Level Panel Report.

154 A. Bonwick (2006).

155   UN OCHA (2007) 'Israeli-Palestinian Fatalities since 2000: Key Trends'.

156   UN OCHA (2007) 'The Humanitarian Impact on Palestinians of Israelis
      Settlements and Other Infrastructure in the West Bank'. See also M. Asser
      (2007) 'Obstacles to peace: water,' BBC Online,
      http://news.bbc.co.uk/2/hi/middle_east/6666495.stm. Israel takes 80 per cent
      of the ground water and also surface water from the Jordan River, equating to
      about 90 per cent of available water resources.

157   Human Security Centre (2006) 'Human Security Briefing 2006'.

158   C. Cramer (2006).

## PART 5: THE INTERNATIONAL SYSTEM

1     President Amadou Toumani Touré, opening speech at a Development
      Cooperation Forum in Washington, cited in Oxfam International (2006)
      'Kicking the Habit'.

2     Oxfam International (2006) 'Kicking the Habit' *op. cit.*; Oxfam International
      (2007) 'Pricing Farmers out of Cotton'; Direction de Production
      Agricole/Compagnie Malienne de Développement des Fibres Textiles
      (CMDT), estimates as at 31 December 2007.

3     One exception is the arm of the World Bank that lends to low-income countries,
      the International Development Association (IDA). Technically, this has a
      different structure from the main board of the Bank, and poor countries get
      41 per cent of the vote in decisions made by the IDA board. However, only a
      few of these countries are involved in setting the agreements that decide the
      IDA's policies, a process that takes place every three years. Here, as everywhere
      at the IFIs, it is the large donors who really make all the significant decisions.

4     N. Woods (2006).

5     N. Woods (2007).

6     World Bank (2007) *World Development Indicators 2007.*

7     J. Stiglitz (2006).

8     J. Williamson (2003).

9     The conclusions can be found on the SAPRI website (www.saprin.org).
      According to the document summarising the project's findings, even though
      the Bank funded the exercise, it 'went to extraordinary lengths to bury SAPRI
      and its findings within the institution, as well as to lower its profile to the
      outside world. After insisting on joint actions throughout the exercise,
      management decided to write its own final report, which focused as much on
      its own in-house research as on SAPRI field work…At the conclusion of the
      forum, it immediately closed down the SAPRI process without any commit-
      ment to follow-up or any trace of the multi-year SAPRI analysis in any of its
      internal documents'.

10    Agricultural liberalisation played a part in all major World Bank lending
      during the 1990s (see for example Fiscal Restructuring and Deregulation
      Programmes 1–3). Lending conditions relating to agriculture, for example
      the abolition of the state marketing board in Zambia and the reform and
      privatisation of the Agricultural Development and Marketing Corporation
      (ADMARC) in Malawi, also played a part in IMF lending during this time.
      The sequence of agricultural liberalisation in Zambia is detailed in
      N. McCulloch *et al.* (2000). The main lending instruments were the Policy

Framework Paper drawn up between the government of Zambia and the IMF in 1990 and the two related Enhanced Structural Adjustment Facilities in 1991 and 1995. The sequence of adjustment for Malawi is detailed in S. Devereux (1997). The first key commitment was in the second Structural Adjustment Loan in the 1980s. In 1994 the country's currency was devalued, leading to a massive increase in fertiliser prices, and all fertiliser subsidies were removed a year later as a result of World Bank and IMF lending conditions. In both countries, the influence and responsibility of the major bilateral donors on this issue was also very relevant, and particularly 'the shortsighted and erratic activities which characterise…what the major donors term as policy' (M. Blackie, personal communication).

11   Oxfam International (2002) 'Death on the Doorstep of the Summit'.

12   Oxfam International (2007) 'Blind Spot: The Continued Failure of the World Bank and IMF to Fully Assess the Impact of their Advice on Poor People'.

13   Oxfam International (2004) 'From 'Donorship to Ownership?'.

14   *Ibid.*

15   World Bank (2005) 'Review Of World Bank Conditionality'.

16   Seventeen of the 42 countries with IMF-supported programmes during 2003–05 included a wage ceiling (D. Goldsbrough 2007). The IMF has now introduced a new policy that wage bill ceilings will only be used in 'exceptional circumstances', although it has failed to specify what such circumstances would be.

17   J. Stiglitz (2006) *op. cit.*

18   IMF, *IMF Survey Magazine*, 20 July 2007.

19   See, for example, World Bank (2005) 'Economic Growth in the 1990s: Learning from a Decade of Reform', and R. Chambers *et al.* (2000) *op. cit.*

20   N. Woods (2006) *op. cit.*

21   Bretton Woods Project, 'Just Say No: Vocal Rejection of Bank, Fund Increasing', 2 July 2007.

22   N. Birdsall and D. Kapur (2005).

23   A. Banerjee *et al.* (2006).

24   Y. Akyüz (2006).

25   N. Birdsall and D. Kapur (2005) *op. cit.*

26   D. Green (2003).

27   Heavily Indebted Poor Countries (HIPC) Initiative and Multilateral Debt Relief Initiative (MDRI) – Status of Implementation Report, September 2007.

28   www.jubileedebtcampaign.org.uk/?lid=1103

29   'Nestlé And Ethiopian Government Reach Settlement', Nestlé press release, 24 January 2003.

30   Jubilee Debt Coalition (undated) 'Vulture Funds and Zambia'; C.F. Gueye *et al.* (2007).

31   Full details from the Norwegian Development Ministry at: www.odin.dep.no/ud/english/news/news/032171-070886/dok-bn.html

32   M.F. de Castro, University of Brasilia, author interview, 1998.

33   Calculated from WTO (2006). The daily trade in more obscure financial products, such as derivatives, stood at a further $1.2 trillion. Source: Bank of International Settlements, www.bis.org/publ/rpfx07.htm

34   UN (2006) 'World Economic and Social Survey 2006'.

35   J.M. Keynes (1941).

36   *Wall Street Journal*, 24 May 1985.

37   N. Birdsall (2006).

38   J. Kimmis (2005).

39   Quoted in D. Green (1999).

40   NGOs (including Jubilee 2000) had serious reservations about the IMF model – not least that it excluded the IMF itself from having to be subject to any such mechanism.

41   NatWest Group Financial Review, p.34.

42   J. Williamson *et al.* (2003).

43   J. Stiglitz (2006) *op. cit.*, p.4.

44   'The invasion of the sovereign-wealth funds', *Economist*, 19 January 2008.

45   A. Cobham (2005).

46   'Report Of Investigation Of Enron Corporation And Related Entities Regarding Federal Tax And Compensation Issues, And Policy Recommendations', www.gpo.gov/congress/joint/jcs-3-03/vol1/ index.html

47   R. Baker (2005).

48   J. Kimmis (2005) *op. cit.*

49   This has been proposed by the Tax Justice Network; see: www.taxjustice.net/cms/front_content.php?idcat=2

50   Landau Commission Final Report, www.diplomatie.gouv.fr/en/IMG/pdf/LandauENG1.pdf

51   Named after the Nobel prize-winning economist James Tobin, who first proposed it.

52   US International Trade Commission, www.usitc.gov

53   OECD (2007) 'Agricultural Policies in OECD Countries'.

54   Oxfam International (2005) 'A Round for Free'.

55   H.-J. Chang and D. Green (2003).

56   Oxfam International (2007) 'Signing Away The Future'.

57   Since the accession of China in 2001, the WTO is essentially a global body. Only a few transition economies, notably Russia and the Ukraine, and a few others such as Saudi Arabia, have yet to join.

58   See Oxfam International (2002) 'Rigged Rules and Double Standards'; the Oxfam International website carries numerous papers on trade issues: www.oxfam.org/en/policy

59   Oxfam America (2007) 'Paying the Price'.

60   Oxfam International (2005) 'Truth or Consequences'.

61   Oxfam International (2005) 'Kicking Down the Door'.

62   N. Schrijver and F. Weiss (2004).

63   SUNS #5784, 20 April 2005.

64   H.-J. Chang (2001) *Kicking Away the Ladder*.

65   R. Falvey and N. Foster (2006). The same study also found that weak IP protection has actually stimulated R&D activity in many countries by encouraging knowledge spillovers from transnational corporations and other domestic firms.

66    H.-J. Chang (2001) 'Institutional Development in Developing Countries'.
67    This figure includes royalties from other developed, as well as developing
      countries. US ODA came to $27.6bn in 2005. World Bank (2007)
      *World Development Indicators 2007.*
68    www.who.int/healthinfo/bodgbd2002revised/en/index.html
69    EQUITAP Project (2005).
70    J.O. Lanjouw and I.M. Cockburn (2001).
71    The decision to de-register the medicines means that new medicines to treat
      HIV, cardiovascular disease, and other diseases are no longer available in
      Thailand. This includes a heat-resistant version of Kaletra that is needed in
      poor, rural settings, where there is infrequent access to electricity.
72    UNESCO 'Barbed wire in the research field', www.unesco.org/courier/
      2001_11/uk/doss14.htm
73    T. Apte (2006). See also the annual 'Captain Hook Awards' for bio-piracy on
      www.captainhookawards.org
74    www.bloomberg.com/apps/news?pid=10000086&sid=agv_ HExYkgKk&refer
      =latin_america
75    P. Drahos (2004).
76    This section is largely based on Oxfam Intermón (2007).
77    www.ohchr.org/english/law/cmw.htm
78    D. Massey (2003).
79    R. Winder, *New Statesman*, 7 April 2003.
80    World Bank (2006) *Global Economic Prospects 2006.*
81    Ç. Özden and M. Schiff (2007).
82    D. Ratha and W. Shaw (2007).
83    World Bank (2007) 'Remittance Trends 2007'.
84    World Bank (2006) 'Migration and Development Brief 2'.
85    Oxfam Intermón (2001).
86    *Financial Times*, 30 August 2007.
87    Ç. Özden and M. Schiff (2007) *op. cit.*
88    World Bank (2006) *Global Economic Prospects 2006.*
89    UNFPA (2006).
90    World Bank (2006) *op. cit.*
91    www.la-moncloa.es/NR/rdonlyres/62B6B50E-AE7B-455A-85A5-600EF4
      EA9281/80516/InmigracionYEconomiaEspaniola12NovResumen.pdf
92    P. Legrain (2006).
93    L. Pritchett (2006).
94    'The Right to Food', Note by the Secretary-General, A/62/289, 22 August 2007.
95    L. Pritchett (2006) *op. cit.*
96    www.iom.int/jahia/jsp/index.jsp. The idea of a World Migration Organisation
      has been proposed by Professor Jagdish Bhagwati, among others.
97    M. Chen (2006) *op. cit.*
98    *Ibid.*
99    *Los Angeles Times*, 11 September 2007.
100   World Bank (2006) *World Development Report 2007.*

101   M. Chen (2006) *op. cit.*

102   UNCTAD (2006) *World Investment Report 2006.*

103   *Ibid.*

104   J. Stiglitz (2006) *op. cit.*

105   D. Hartridge (1997).

106   www.ethicalcorp.com/content.asp?ContentID=1323

107   FAO (2004) 'The State of Agricultural Commodity Markets'.

108   Néstor Osorio, Executive Director, ICO (2002) 'The Global Coffee Crisis'.

109   R.M. Locke *et al.* (2007).

110   World Bank, www.worldbank.org/wbi/governance/pdf/icac_hk_survey_
      results_5_06.pdf

111   S. Hawley (2003).

112   'UK criticised for axeing BAE probe', *Financial Times*, 18 July 2007.

113   *New York Law Journal*, 4 January 2007.

114   'The invasion of the sovereign-wealth funds', *Economist*, 17 January 2008.

115   J. Clay (2005) *op. cit.*

116   www.globalreporting.org/Home

117   www.ethicaltrade.org

118   J. Ruggie (2007).

119   http://eitransparency.org

120   Oxfam America (2007) 'Newmont Mining Company: Background'.

121   Oxfam International and WaterAid (2006) *op. cit.*

122   'Has the 2005 measles mortality reduction goal been achieved? A natural
      history modelling study', *Lancet*, Volume 369,
      http://dx.doi.org/10.1016/S0140-6736(07)60107-X

123   W. Easterly (2006).

124   'NGO' is a clumsy and imprecise term, describing what an organisation is
      not rather than what it is. It usually refers to the sub-set of 'third sector' or
      'voluntary' organisations involved in development, human rights, and
      environmental activism. While most of these remain local in scope, some
      (like Oxfam or the Save the Children Fund) have become international.

125   D. Lewis (2007).

126   OECD DAC (2006).

127   J. Court (2006).

128   OECD DAC International Development Statistics Online Database.

129   Oxfam International (2006) 'The View from the Summit'.

130   www.oecd.org/dataoecd/7/20/39768315.pdf

131   Speech at the Chicago Council of Foreign Relations, 26 June 2002.

132   Oxfam International (2007) 'The World is Still Waiting'.

133   *Financial Times*, 10 December 2007.

134   M. Klein and T. Harford (2005).

135   S. Bazzi *et al.* (2007).

136   I. Kuziemko and E. Werker (2006).

137   S. Burall *et al.* (2006).

138　Information gathered from an Oxfam research trip to Mali and Senegal in October 2006.

139　S. Burall *et al.* (2006) *op. cit.*

140　There have been some moves to introduce longer-term commitments, for example in the UK's aid agreement with Rwanda and to bring longer timescales into IMF programmes.

141　A. Bulir and J. Hamann (2005).

142　OECD DAC (2005).

143　OECD DAC (2006).

144　Technical assistance is aid spent on consultants, research, and training; it accounted for $21.3bn of global aid in 2005, around one-fifth of the aid total. OECD DAC (2006) *op. cit.*

145　Oxfam International and WaterAid (2006) *op. cit.*

146　L. Whitfield and E. Jones (2007).

147　EFA Global Monitoring Report (2006).

148　The Paris Declaration outlines five principles for aid effectiveness: ownership, alignment, mutual accountability, harmonisation, and managing for results.

149　D. Bräutigam and S. Knack (2004).

150　So called because the Netherlands experienced a decline in its competitiveness following the discovery and subsequent export of natural gas reserves in the 1960s.

151　M. Foster and T. Killick (2006).

152　Cited in T. Moss *et al.* (2006).

153　G. Maipose *et al.* (1996).

154　Oxfam International (2007) 'Paying for People', based on OECD DAC International Statistics Online Database (2004 figures).

155　IDD and Associates (2006).

156　Chris Adam, Queen Elizabeth House, Oxford, personal communication.

157　http://blogs.odi.org.uk/blogs/main/archive/2006/01/16/109.aspx

158　The proportion of total NGO funds in a country that are drawn from official sources varies very widely, from 85 per cent in Sweden to about 10 per cent in the UK (1995 figures, Lewis (2007) p.136).

159　Oxfam defines its work in terms of five basic rights: the right to a sustainable livelihood; the right to basic social services; the right to life and security; the right to be heard; and the right to equity.

160　Such services reach 35 per cent of the functionally landless population of the country (which numbers half of Bangladesh's 130 million people).

161　A. Fowler (1994).

162　Michael Edwardes, speech, June 2005.

163　W. Easterly (2006) *op. cit.*, p.5.

164　These included identifying lead donors in each sector and setting minimum amounts of donor financing to be pooled in budget support or trust funds. P. de Renzio and A. Rogerson (2005).

165　www.oxfam.org.uk/about_us/legitimacy.htm?searchterm=accountability

166　www.ingoaccountabilitycharter.org/about-the-charter.html

167　Quoted in R. Hayman (2007).

168   D. Rodrik (2005).

169   R. Chambers (1997) *op. cit.*

170   'NGO Futures: Beyond Aid', *Third World Quarterly*, August 2000.

171   Gebreselassie Yosief Tesfamichael, see: www.thepeninsulaqatar.com/commentary/commentaryother.asp?file=augustcommentary842005.xml

172   These include UNDP (UN Development Programme, whose mandate is crisis prevention and recovery); UNICEF (UN Children's Fund, responsible for protection of victims of war and disasters); UNHCR (UN High Commissioner for Refugees); and WFP (World Food Programme, which provides emergency food aid.)

173   Global Humanitarian Assistance (2006).

174   Global Humanitarian Assistance (2004).

175   www.reliefweb.int/fts

176   The Joint Evaluation of Emergency Assistance to Rwanda (1996); Telford *et al.* (2006).

177   See: www.un.org/aboutun/chartlg.html

178   UK Government (2006).

179   *New York Times*, 30 December 2005.

180   In non-emergencies, food aid is often not even given to the hungry, but goes directly to governments to sell on local markets in order to raise revenue. This is known as 'monetisation', and has the effect of forcing down local prices.

181   Oxfam calculations from Canadian International Development Agency.

182   FAO (2006) 'The State of Food and Agriculture 2006'.

183   OECD (2005).

184   P. Creti and S. Jaspars (2005).

185   Australia now permits up to 67 per cent of its food aid to be procured locally; the EC permits unlimited procurement under specified circumstances from a list of developing countries; and in September 2005 Canada agreed to permit up to 50 per cent of its government food aid budget to be used for local or regional procurement, up from the previous 10 per cent. See Canadian Foodgrains Bank/Oxfam Canada (2005). The UK, Belgium, Germany, Sweden, and the Netherlands also source their food through local purchase and unrestricted tendering (OECD 2004, *op. cit.*).

186   Oxfam International (2007) 'The UN Central Emergency Response Fund One Year On'.

187   UN (2006) 'Delivering as One: Report of the Secretary-General's High Level Panel'.

188   www.goodhumanitariandonorship.org

189   Humanitarian Accountability Partnership (HAP): www.hapinternational.org; Active Learning Network for Accountability and Performance in Humanitarian Action (ALNAP): www.alnap.org; The Sphere Project: www.sphereproject.org

190   www.icrc.org/web/eng/siteeng0.nsf/htmlall/57JMNB

191   H. Slim (2007).

192 United Nations (2005) 'World Summit Outcome', Items 9 and 10, p.2. The summit also set up a global Peacebuilding Commission that brings together the UN, individual governments, and international financial institutions to work together in supporting countries at risk of sliding into conflict, and to support countries more effectively after peace agreements are reached.

193 Global decisions have been echoed at regional level. In 2001, the African Union acknowledged for the first time that it could intervene in member states in the event of war crimes, genocide, or crimes against humanity, leading to the presence of AU peacekeepers in Darfur. Reality of Aid Project (2006) 'Reality of Aid', p.28.

194 Center on International Cooperation (2007).

195 OI Policy Compendium Note on Disarmament, Demobilisation and Reintegration (DDR), 2007.

196 Center on International Cooperation (2007) *op. cit.*

197 www.africa-union.org/root/au/AUC/Departments/PSC/Asf/asf.htm

198 Centre for Humanitarian Dialogue (2007).

199 Although the ICC Statute was agreed in Rome in 1998, it only formally came into existence when the treaty had been ratified by a minimum of 60 states, which took a further four years. Definitions from 1949 Geneva Conventions, Nuremberg Rules, in Agreement for the Prosecution and Punishment of the Major War Criminals of the European Axis, and Articles II and III of the 1948 Convention on the Prevention and Punishment of Genocide.

200 UNHCR (2002) 'Developing Countries Host Most Refugees According to Statistical Yearbook from UNHCR', UNHCR press release, 8 November 2002.

201 UNHCR (2006); UNHCR (2005).

202 UK Home Affairs Select Committee Report on Immigration Controls, www.publications.parliament.uk/pa/cm/cmhaff.htm

203 Control Arms Campaign (2003) *op. cit.*

204 Small Arms Survey (2005).

205 Control Arms Campaign (2006) 'Arms Without Borders'.

206 www.caat.org.uk/issues/jobs-subsidies.php

207 Control Arms Campaign (2006) *op.cit.*

208 For a full account of the ECOWAS arms trade treaty, see M. Coulibaly (2007) 'From Moratorium to a Convention on Small Arms'.

209 www.kimberleyprocess.com

210 Of course, the Kimberley process has not ensured that the many poor diamond diggers receive a decent income, but it has helped to undercut a primary motivator of the war.

211 Oxfam International (2008) 'For a Safer Tomorrow: Protecting Civilians in a Multipolar World'.

212 Human Rights Watch (2006) *World Report 2006*.

213 P.A. Stott *et al.* (2004).

214 UK spending rose from £436m to £600m in 2007/08, rising to £800m by 2010/11. DEFRA News Release '2007 Pre-Budget Report and Comprehensive Spending Review', 9 October 2007, www.defra.gov.uk/news/2007/071009e.htm

215  UN Framework Convention on Climate Change (UNFCCC), Article 2 (Objective).

216  www.universityofcalifornia.edu/news/article/17184

217  UNFCCC, Article 3.1.

218  International law holds that countries may not do each other harm, either intentionally or through neglect. See, for example, Principle 21 of the Stockholm Declaration (1972 UN Conference on the Human Environment) and Principle 2 of the 1992 Rio Declaration on Environment and Development. P. Sands (1995).

219  Quoted by the then UK Foreign Secretary Margaret Beckett in a speech to the UN Security Council, 17 April 2007.

220  Oxfam International (2007) 'Adapting to Climate Change'. Similarly, the UNFCCC estimates adaptation costs at between $28bn–$67bn annually by 2030 (and this only covers a sub-set of needs).

221  Oxfam International (2007) 'Adapting to Climate Change'.

222  Global Environmental Facility, September 2007, www.gefweb.org

223  'The developed country Parties and other developed Parties included in Annex II shall also assist the developing country Parties that are particularly vulnerable to the adverse effects of climate change in meeting costs of adaptation to those adverse effects.' UNFCCC, Article 4.4.

224  P. Baer et al. (2007).

225  www.hm-treasury.gov.uk/media/4/3/Executive_Summary.pdf, pp.ix–x. Note that Stern's estimate assumed stabilisation at 500–550ppm $CO_2$e by 2050, which represents less than 80 per cent below 1990 levels ($CO_2$e, or carbon dioxide equivalent, is an internationally recognised measure of greenhouse gas emissions).

226  P. Baer et al. (2007) op. cit.

227  UNEP and International Energy Agency (2002); A. De Moore (2001). The Canadian government spent $1.4bn on subsidies – mainly tax breaks – for the oil and gas sector in 2002 (Pembina Institute 2005). The US 2005 Energy Bill gave fossil fuel producers a five-year royalty break worth an estimated $7bn–$28bn on oil and gas from the Gulf of Mexico (Offices of the Democratic Leaders Harry Reid and Nancy Pelosi 2006). In 2005, the German government's direct subsidy to coal production was an estimated €2.8bn ($3.7bn) (Newman 2003). This estimate excludes pension fund deficit payments.

228  $CO_2$e: equivalent mass of carbon dioxide ($CO_2$) that would have the same global warming potential.

229  C. Hepburn (2007); World Bank (2007) State and Trends of the Carbon Market 2007.

230  These include Japan's Voluntary Emissions Trading Scheme, the New South Wales Abatement Scheme in Australia, and the Regional Greenhouse Gas Initiative and the Chicago Climate Exchange in the USA.

231  K. Hamilton (2006); C. Cundy (2007); and World Bank (2007) State and Trends of the Carbon Market 2007.

232  M. Lockwood (2007).

233  For a detailed proposal of the reforms required to the CDM, see J. Cozijnsen et al. (2007).

234 In the UK, for example, the Carbon Reduction Commitment is a complex cap-and-trade scheme for UK commercial and retail companies (plus large public sector organisations) not currently covered by the EU trading scheme, with auctioning of permits and revenue recycled according to an obscure formula. Much of the emissions reduction will come about anyway under new building regulations. Although the scheme will draw the issue to the attention of CEOs, the same result could arguably have been achieved simply by passing a few statutory regulations on carbon emissions, or knocking a few heads together in boardrooms (Matthew Lockwood, IPPR, personal communication).

235 The 2001 Third Assessment Report was prepared by 122 co-ordinating lead authors and lead authors, 515 contributing authors, 21 review editors, and 337 expert reviewers. www.ipccfacts.org/how.html

236 K. Hamilton (2005) *Business and post-2012: A Political Analysis.*

237 M. Hertsgaaard 'While Washington slept', *Vanity Fair*, May 2006.

238 The Investor Network on Climate Risk, which represents more than $4 trillion in assets managed by 65 institutional investors, lobbies governments to require more rigorous disclosure of emissions and other information by companies. The Carbon Disclosure Project, whose members have an extraordinary $41 trillion under management (close to the value of global GDP) seeks information on the business risks and opportunities presented by climate change and greenhouse gas emissions data from the world's largest companies – 2,400 in 2007.

239 See, for example, B. Lomborg (2006).

240 R. King (2007).

241 J. Diamond (2005).

## ANNEX: HOW CHANGE HAPPENS

1 A. Hochschild (2005).

2 See also DFID's 'Drivers of Change' work: www.gsdrc.org/go/topic-guides/drivers-of-change

3 There are many alternative frameworks for analysing change in more specialised areas, such as gender (see C. March *et al.* 1999), sustainable livelihoods (see www.livelihoods.org/info/info_guidancesheets.html), or markets. For a summary of frameworks for analysing political context, see R. Nash *et al.* (2006).

4 M. Gladwell (2000).

5 P. Collier (2007).

6 D. Reeler (undated).

7 R. Krznaric (2007).

8 Matthew Lockwood, personal communication.

# BIBLIOGRAPHY

ActionAid (2006) 'Climate Change, Urban Flooding and the Rights of the Urban Poor in Africa: Key Findings from Six African Cities', London: ActionAid.

Active Learning Network for Accountability and Performance in Humanitarian Action (ALNAP) (undated) www.alnap.org/

Adams, W.M. (2006) 'The Future of Sustainability: Re-thinking Environment and Development in the Twenty-first Century', Gland, Switzerland: The International Union for Conservation of Nature (IUCN).

African Union (2005) 'Status of Food Security and Prospects for Agricultural Development in Africa', Addis Ababa: African Union.

African Union and Interafrican Bureau for Animal Resources (2007) 'Pastoralism In Africa: Introducing a Pastoral Policy Framework for the Continent', Addis Ababa: African Union.

Afrobarometer (2006) www.afrobarometer.org/index.html

Akyüz, Y. (2006) 'Reforming The IMF: Back To The Drawing Board', Penang: Third World Network.

Allain, M. (2007) 'Trading Away Our Oceans: Why Trade Liberalization of Fisheries Must Be Abandoned', Amsterdam: Greenpeace.

Anderson, E. and T. O'Neill (2006) 'A New Equity Agenda?', London: Overseas Development Institute (ODI).

Annan, K. (1999) 'Annual Report on the Work of the Organization of the United Nations', New York: United Nations.

Annan, K. (2005) 'In Larger Freedom: Towards Development, Security and Human Rights for All', New York: United Nations.

Annan, K. (2005) 'Report on the Protection of Civilians in Armed Conflict', New York: United Nations.

Apte, T. (2006) 'A Simple Guide to Intellectual Property Rights, Biodiversity and Traditional Knowledge', London: International Institute for Environment and Development (IIED).

Arcand, J.L. (2004) in M.R. Mercoiret and J.M. Mfou'ou (2006) 'Rural Producers' Organizations for Pro-poor Sustainable Agricultural Development', paper for World Development Report 2008 Workshop, Paris 2006, Washington DC: World Bank.

Awasthi, U.S. (2001) 'Resurgence of co-operative movement through innovations', *Co-op Dialogue* 11( 2): 21–6.

Ayyagari, M., T. Beck, and A. Demirgüç-Kunt (2003) 'Small and Medium Enterprises Across the Globe: a New Database', Washington DC: World Bank.

Baer, P., T. Athanasiou, and S. Kartha (2007) 'The Right to Development in a Climate Constrained World: The Greenhouse Development Rights Framework', www.ecoequity.org/docs/TheGDRsFramework.pdf

Baker, R. (2005) *Capitalism's Achilles Heel*, Chichester: Wiley.

Banerjee, A., A. Deaton, E. HSU, N. Lustig, and K. Rogoff (2006) 'An Evaluation of World Bank Research, 1998–2005', Washington DC: World Bank.

Banister, J. (2005) 'Manufacturing employment in China', *Monthly Labor Review*.

Baviskar, B.S. (2003) 'The Impact of Women's Participation in Local Governance in Rural India', paper presented at conference 'A Decade of Women's Empowerment Through Local Government in India', ISS/South Asia Partnership Canada/ International Development Research Centre, 20–21 October 2003, New Delhi.

Bayne, N. (2007) 'Overcoming evil with good: impressions of the Gleneagles Summit, 6–8 July 2005', in M. Fratianni, J.J. Kirton, and P. Savona (eds.) *Financing Development: The G8 and UN Contribution*, Aldershot: Ashgate.

Bazzi, S., S. Herrling, and S. Patrick (2007) 'Billions for War, Pennies for the Poor: Moving the President's FY2008 Budget from Hard Power to Smart Power', Washington DC: Center for Global Development (CGD).

Beall, J. and S. Fox (2006) 'Urban Poverty and Development in the 21st Century: Towards an Inclusive and Sustainable World', Oxfam Research Reports, Oxford: Oxfam GB.

Beall, J. and S. Fox (forthcoming, 2008) *Cities and Development*, London: Routledge.

Becker, G. (1992) 'The Economic Way of Looking at Life', Nobel Prize lecture, http://nobelprize.org/nobel_prizes/economics/laureates/1992/becker-lecture.html

Behnke R.H., I. Scoones, and C. Kerven (1993) 'Rethinking range ecology: implications for rangeland management in Africa', in R.H. Behnke, I. Scoones, and C. Kerven (eds.) *Range Ecology at Disequilibrium: New Models of Natural Variability and Pastoral Adaptation in African Savannas*, London: Overseas Development Institute (ODI).

Birch, I. and R. Grahn (2007) 'Background Note on Pastoralism', Input Paper for *Human Development Report 2007*, unpublished.

Birdsall, N. (2006) 'Stormy Days on an Open Field: Asymmetries in the Global Economy', Washington DC: Center for Global Development (CGD).

Birdsall, N. (2007) 'Do No Harm: Aid, Weak Institutions and the Missing Middle in Africa', Washington DC: Center for Global Development (CGD).

Birdsall, N. and D. Kapur (2005) 'The Hardest Job In The World: Five Crucial Tasks For The New President Of The World Bank', Washington DC: Center for Global Development (CGD).

Bobbio, N., translated by M. Ryle and K. Soper (1990) *Liberalism and Democracy*, London: Verso.

Boko, M., I. Niang, A. Nyong, C. Vogel, A. Githeko, M. Medany, B. Osman-Elasha, R. Tabo, and P. Yanda (2007) *Africa Climate Change 2007: Impacts, Adaptation and Vulnerability*, Cambridge: Cambridge University Press.

Bonwick, A. (2006) 'Protection in Colombia: A Bottom-up Approach', London: Overseas Development Institute (ODI).

Bourke, M. (2005) 'Agricultural production and customary land in Papua New Guinea', in J. Fingleton (ed.) 'Privatising Land in the Pacific – A Defence of Customary Tenures', Discussion Paper, Australia Institute.

Boyer, D. (2001) 'Trade: The Connection Between Environment and Sustainable Livelihoods', Boston MA: Oxfam America.

Bräutigam, D. and S. Knack (2004) *Foreign Aid, Institutions and Governance in Sub-Saharan Africa*, Chicago IL: University of Chicago Press.

Brigmann, J. and C.K. Prahalad (2007) 'Co-creating business's new social compact', *Harvard Business Review*, February.

Brooks, N. (2006) 'Climate Change, Drought and Pastoralism in the Sahel', discussion note for the World Initiative on Sustainable Pastoralism, www.iucn.org/wisp/documents_english/climate_changes.pdf

Brouwer, M., H. Grady, V. Traore, and D. Wordofa (undated) 'The Experiences of Oxfam International and its Affiliates in Rights-Based Programming and Campaigning', The Hague: Oxfam Novib.

Brown, D. (2007) 'Globalization and Employment Conditions', Social Protection discussion paper, Washington DC: World Bank.

Bruce, J. (1989) 'Homes divided', in *World Development* 17(7).

Brundtland, G.H. (1987) *Our Common Future*, Oxford: Oxford University Press, for the World Commission on Environment and Development.

Bryceson, D.F. and J. Fonseca (2006) 'Risking death for survival: peasant responses to hunger and HIV/AIDS in Malawi', *World Development* 34(8).

Buckner, L.J. and S.M. Yeandle (2007) 'Valuing Carers – Calculating the Value of Unpaid Care', Leeds: University of Leeds.

Bulir, A. and J. Hamann (2005) 'Volatility of Development Aid: From the Frying Pan into the Fire?', Washington DC: International Monetary Fund (IMF).

Burall, S. and S. Maxwell with A.R. Menocal (2006) 'Reforming the International Aid Architecture: Options and Ways Forward', London: Overseas Development Institute (ODI).

Caceres, E. (2007) 'Territories and Citizenship: the Revolution of the Chiquitanos', background paper for Oxfam International.

Çağatay, N. and K. Ertürk (2004) 'Gender and Globalization: a Macroeconomic Perspective', Geneva: International Labour Organization (ILO).

Canadian Foodgrains Bank/Oxfam Canada (2005) 'Increasing Local Purchase Flexibility in Canadian Food Aid Procurement – An Idea Whose Time Has Come', Ottawa: Oxfam Canada.

Canadian International Development Agency (CIDA) (2003) 'Promoting Sustainable Development through Agriculture,' www.acdi-cida.gc.ca/CIDAWEB/acdicida.nsf/En/REN-2181377-PRU

Castillo, G. and M. Brouwer (2007) 'Reflections on Integrating a Rights-Based Approach in Environment and Development', Gland, Switzerland: International Union for the Conservation of Nature (IUCN).

Center for American Progress (2007) 'Iraq By the Numbers', www.american-progress.org/issues/2007/03/iraq_by_the_numbers.html

Center on International Cooperation (2007) 'Annual Review of Peace Operations 2007: Briefing Paper', New York: New York University.

Centre for Humanitarian Dialogue (2007) 'Charting the Roads to Peace: Facts, Figures and Trends in Conflict Resolution', Geneva: Centre for Humanitarian Dialogue.

Centre for Women's Development Studies (1999) 'From Oppression to Assertion: A Study of Panchayats and Women in Madhya Pradesh, Rajasthan and Uttar Pradesh', New Delhi: Centre for Women's Development Studies.

Chambers, R. (1997) *Whose Reality Counts?: Putting the First Last*, Bourton on Dunsmore: Intermediate Technology Publications.

Chambers, R. (2006) 'Transforming Power: From Zero-Sum to Win-Win?', *IDS Bulletin*, November 2006, p.108.

Chambers, R., D. Narayan, M.K. Shah, and P. Petesch (2000) *Voices of the Poor: Crying Out for Change*, Oxford: Oxford University Press for World Bank.

Chang, H.-J. (2001) 'Institutional Development in Developing Countries in a Historical Perspective: Lessons from Developed Countries in Earlier Times', paper presented at the European Association of Evolutionary Political Economy, Siena, Italy, November 2001.

Chang, H.-J. (2001) *Kicking Away the Ladder*, London: Anthem Press.

Chang, H.-J. (2005) 'Why Developing Countries Need Tariffs', Geneva and Oxford: South Centre and Oxfam International.

Chang, H.-J. (2007) *Bad Samaritans*, London: Random House.

Chang, H.-J. and D. Green (2003) 'The Northern WTO Agenda on Investment: Do As We Say, Not As We Did', Geneva: South Centre.

Chaudhry, P. (2007) 'Why Has Viet Nam Achieved Growth With Relative Equity, and China Hasn't?', background paper for Oxfam International.

Chaudhry, P. and G. Ruysschaert (2007) 'Climate Change and Human Development in Viet Nam', Occasional Paper, *Human Development Report 2007/2008*, New York: United Nations Development Programme (UNDP).

Chen, M. (2006) 'Empowerment of Informal Workers: Legal and Other Interventions', WIEGO, www.wiego.org/publications/

Chen, M., J. Vanek, F. Lund, and J. Heintz with R. Jhabvala and C. Bonner (2005) 'Progress of the World's Women 2005: Women, Work and Poverty', New York: UNIFEM.

Chirwa, E., A. Dorward, R. Kachule, I. Kumwenda, J. Kydd, N. Poole, C. Poulton, and M. Stockbridge (2005) 'Walking Tightropes: Supporting Farmer Organizations for Market Access', *Natural Resource Perspectives* 99, November 2005, Overseas Development Institute (ODI).

Chronic Poverty Research Centre (2004) *Chronic Poverty Report 2004–05*, CPRC.

Chronic Poverty Research Centre (2008) *Chronic Poverty Report 2008–09*, CPRC.

Ciconello, A. (2007) 'The Challenge of Eliminating Racism in Brazil: the New Institutional Framework for Fighting Racial Inequality', background paper for Oxfam International.

Civil Society Organisations for Peace in Northern Uganda (2006) 'Counting the Cost, Twenty Years of War in Northern Uganda', Kampala: CSOPNU.

Clark Leith, J. (2006) *Why Botswana Prospered*, McGill: Queen's University Press.

Clay, J. (2005) 'Exploring the Links Between International Business and Poverty Reduction: A Case Study of Unilever in Indonesia', Oxford and The Hague: Oxfam GB, Oxfam Novib, Unilever.

Coady D., M. Grosh, and J. Hoddinott (2002) 'Targeting Outcomes Redux', paper commissioned by the Social Protection Anchor unit for the Safety Nets Primer series, World Bank, www1.worldbank.org/sp/safetynets/Primers/Targerting_Article.pdf

Cobham, A. (2005) 'Tax Evasion, Tax Avoidance and Development Finance', Queen Elizabeth House, University of Oxford.

Collier, P. (2004) 'Development and Conflict', Centre for the Study of African Economies, Department of Economics, Oxford University, 1 October 2004.

Collier, P. (2006) 'The Resource Curse, Democracy and Growth', talk at Centre for Islamic Studies, Oxford, 15 November 2006.

Collier, P. (2007) *The Bottom Billion: Why the Poorest Countries are Failing and What Can Be Done About It*, Oxford: Oxford University Press.

Commission for Africa (2005) 'Our Common Interest', Final Report of the Commission for Africa.

Commission on Growth and Development (2008) 'Final Report', www.growthcommission.org/index.php

Control Arms Campaign (2003) 'Shattered Lives: the Case for Tough International Arms Control', Oxford and London: Oxfam International and Amnesty International.

Control Arms Campaign (2006) 'Arms Without Borders: Why Globalized Trade Needs Global Controls', London and Oxford: Amnesty International, IANSA, Oxfam International.

Cosgrave, J., C. Goncalves, D. Martyris, R. Polastro, and M. Sikumba-Dils (2007) 'Inter-Agency Real Time Evaluation of the Response to the February 2007 Floods and Cyclone in Mozambique', Inter-Agency Humanitarian Standing Committee, Humanitarian Country Team, Mozambique.

Coulibaly, M. (2007) 'From Moratorium to a Convention on Small Arms: a Change in Politics and Practices for the 15 Member Countries of the Economic Community of West African States (ECOWAS)'.

Coulter, J., A. Goodland, A. Tallontire, and R. Stringfellow (1999) 'Marrying Farmer Cooperation and Contract Farming for Service Provision in a Liberalising Sub-Saharan Africa', London: Overseas Development Institute (ODI).

Court, J. (2006) 'Policy Engagement for Poverty Reduction – How Civil Society Can be More Effective', London: Overseas Development Institute (ODI).

Cousins, B., T. Cousins, D. Hornby, R. Kingwill, L. Royston, and W. Smit (2005) 'Will Formalising Property Rights Reduce Poverty in South Africa's "Second Economy"? Questioning the Mythologies of Hernando de Soto', Cape Town: Programme for Land and Agrarian Studies, University of the Western Cape.

Cozijnsen, J., D. Dudek, K. Meng, A. Petsonk, J.E. Sanhueza (2007) 'CDM and the Post-2012 Framework', Environmental Defense Discussion Paper prepared for Vienna Intersessionals, 27–31 August 2007.

Cramer, C. (2006) *Civil War is Not a Stupid Thing: Accounting for Violence in Developing Countries*, London: C Hurst.

Creti, P. and S. Jaspars (2005) *Cash Transfer Programming in Emergencies*, Skills and Practice series, Oxford: Oxfam GB.

Cundy, C. (2007) 'Carbon funds: paying up to cut emissions', *Environmental Finance*, July–August 2007, 20–2.

Dasgupta, S., B. Laplante, C. Meisner, D. Wheeler, and J. Yan (2007) 'The Impact of Sea Level Rise on Developing Countries: A Comparative Analysis', World Bank Policy Research Working Paper 4136, Washington DC: World Bank.

Davies, J. and M. Nori (2007) 'Change of Wind or Wind of Change? Climate Change, Adaptation and Pastoralism', summary of an online conference prepared for the World Initiative for Sustainable Pastoralism, Nairobi: The International Union for Conservation of Nature (IUCN).

Davies, J. and R. Hatfield (2006) 'Global Review of the Economics of Pastoralism', prepared for the World Initiative for Sustainable Pastoralism, Nairobi: The International Union for Conservation of Nature (IUCN).

De Jouvenel, B. (1949) *On Power*, New York: Viking Press.

De Moore, A. (2001) 'Towards a Grand Deal on Subsidies and Climate Change', *Natural Resources Forum* 25 (2).

De Renzio, P. and A. Rogerson (2005) 'Power to Consumers? A Bottom-up Approach to Aid Reform', London: Overseas Development Institute (ODI).

De Soto, H. (2000) *Mystery of Capital*, New York: Basic Books.

Delforge, I. (2007) 'Contract Farming in Thailand: A View from the Farm', Focus on the Global South.

Denning, G. and J. Sachs (2007) 'The rich world can help Africa', *Financial Times*, 29 May 2007.

Department of Health, UK (2005) 'Tackling Health Inequalities: Status Report on the Programme for Action', London: Department of Health.

Development Prospects Group (2006) 'Migration and Development Brief 2', Migration and Remittances Team, Remittance Trends 2006, Washington DC: World Bank.

Development Studies Association, UK (2007) 'Mobiles and Development: Infrastructure, Poverty, Enterprise and Social Development', Information, Technology and Development Study Group workshop summary and papers, www.sed.manchester.ac.uk/research/events/conferences/mobile.htm

Devereux, S. (1997) 'Household Food Security in Malawi', IDS Discussion Paper 362, Institute of Development Studies, University of Sussex.

Devereux, S. and R. Sabates-Wheeler (2004) 'Transformative Social Protection', IDS Working Paper 232, Institute of Development Studies, University of Sussex.

Dey, N., J. Drèze, and R. Khera (2006) *Employment Guarantee Act: A Primer*, New Delhi: National Book Trust.

DFID (2004) 'Agriculture, Hunger and Food Security', London: Department for International Development (DFID).

477

DFID (2005) 'Growth and Poverty Reduction: The Role of Agriculture', London: Department for International Development (DFID).

DFID (2005) 'Reducing Poverty by Tackling Social Exclusion', London: Department for International Development (DFID).

DFID (2007) 'Civil Society and Good Governance', London: Department for International Development (DFID).

DFID (2007) 'Governance, Development and Democratic Politics: DFID's work in building more effective states', London: Department for International Development (DFID).

Di John, J. (2006) 'The Political Economy of Taxation and Tax Reform in Developing Countries', United Nations University World Institute for Development Economics Research (UN WIDER).

Diakonia, La Paz (2006) 'Género, etnicidad y participación politicia', García Linera.

Diamond, J. (2005) *Collapse: How Societies Choose to Fail or Survive*, New York: Viking.

Dichter, T. (2006) 'Hype and hope: the worrisome state of the microcredit movement', www.microfinancegateway.org/content/article/detail/31747

Dorward, A., J. Kydd, and C. Poulton (2005) 'Beyond liberalisation: development coordination policies for African smallholder agriculture', *IDS Bulletin* 36(2).

Dorward, A., J. Kydd, J. Morrison, and I. Urey (2004) 'A policy agenda for pro-poor agricultural growth', *World Development* 32(1): 73–89.

Dorward, A., S. Fan, J. Kydd, H. Lofgren, J. Morrison, C. Poulton, N. Rao, L. Smith, H. Tchale, S. Thorat, I. Urey, and P. Wobst (2004) 'Institutions And Economic Policies For Pro-Poor Agricultural Growth', Washington DC: The International Food Policy Research Institute (IFPRI).

Drahos, P. (2004) 'Access to Knowledge: Time for a Treaty?', *Bridges*, April 2004.


Easterly, W. (2006) *White Man's Burden: Why the West's Efforts to Aid the Rest Have Done So Much Ill and So Little Good*, London: Penguin.

ECLAC (various years) *Statistical Yearbook for Latin America and the Caribbean*, www.eclac.cl/publicaciones/

Economic Policy Institute (2006) *State of Working America 2006–2007*, Washington DC and New York: The Economic Policy Institute and Cornell University Press.

EFA Global Monitoring Report (2006) 'Literacy for Life', Paris: UNESCO.

Elshorst, H. and D. O'Leary (2005) 'Corruption in the Water Sector: Opportunities for Addressing a Pervasive Problem', Berlin: Transparency International, www.siwi.org/downloads/WWW-Symp/Corruption_in_the_water_sector_Elshorst.pdf

EQUITAP Project (2005) 'Paying Out-of-Pocket for Health Care in Asia: Catastrophic and Poverty Impact', Working Paper #2.

ETC Group (2003) 'From Genomes to Atoms, The Big Down – Atomtech: Technologies Converging at the Nano-scale', www.etcgroup.org/upload/publication/171/01/thebigdown.pdf

Evans, P. (1995) *Embedded Autonomy: States & Industrial Transformation*, Princeton NJ: Princeton University Press.

Ferreira, F.H.G., P.G. Leite, and J.A. Litchfield (2005) 'The Rise and Fall of Brazilian Inequality: 1981–2004', World Bank Policy Research Working Paper.

Falvey, R. and N. Foster (2006) 'The Role of Intellectual Property Rights in Technology Transfer and Economic Growth: Theory and Evidence', Vienna: United Nations Industrial Development Organization (UNIDO).

FAO (2001) 'Zero Tillage: When Less Means More', Rome: Food and Agriculture Organization (FAO).

FAO (2003) 'The State of Food Insecurity in the World 2003', Rome: Food and Agriculture Organization (FAO).

FAO (2004) 'The State of Agricultural Commodity Markets', Rome: Food and Agriculture Organization (FAO).

FAO (2004) 'The State of Food Insecurity in the World 2004', Rome: Food and Agriculture Organization (FAO).

FAO (2005) 'The State of Food Insecurity in the World 2005', Rome: Food and Agriculture Organization (FAO).

FAO (2006) 'The State of Food and Agriculture 2006', Rome: Food and Agriculture Organization (FAO).

FAO (2006) 'The State of Food Insecurity in the World 2006', Rome: Food and Agriculture Organization (FAO).

FAO (2007) 'The State of Food and Agriculture 2007', Rome: Food and Agriculture Organization (FAO).

Fariba, N. (2006) 'How the West short-changed Afghanistan', Times Online, 29 October 2006.

FLO (2006) 'Annual Report 2006', Bonn: Fairtrade Labelling Organizations International (FLO).

Folbre, N. (1994) *Who Pays for the Kids? Gender and the Structure of Constraint*, London: Routledge.

Folbre, N. and M. Bittman (2004) *Family Time: The Social Organization of Care*, London and New York: Routledge.

Foster, M. and T. Killick (2006) 'What Would Doubling Aid Mean for Macroeconomic Management in Africa?' Working Paper 264, London: Overseas Development Institute (ODI).

Fowler, A. (1994) 'Capacity Building and NGOs: A Case of Strengthening Ladles For The Global Soup Kitchen?', *Institutional Development* 1(1), Delhi: PRIA.

Freedom House (2005) 'How Freedom Is Won: From Civic Resistance to Durable Democracy', Washington DC: Freedom House.

Fresco, L.O. (2003) 'Which Road Do We Take? Harnessing Genetic Resources and Making Use of Life Sciences, a New Contract for Sustainable Agriculture', paper presented to EU Discussion Forum 'Towards Sustainable Agriculture for Developing Countries: Options from Life Sciences and Biotechnologies', Brussels, 30–31 January 2003.

Frideres, J.S. (1998) *Indigenous Peoples of Canada and the United States of America: Entering the 21st Century*, Ottawa: University of Ottawa Press.

Friedman, M. (1980) *Free to Choose*, Fort Washington PA: Harvest Books.

Galeano, E. (1973) *Open Veins of Latin America*, New York: Monthly Review Press.

Gallin, D. (2004) 'Organizing in the Global Informal Economy', paper presented to the Bogazici University Social Policy Forum: Changing Role of Unions in the Contemporary World of Labour, Istanbul, 26–27 November 2004, cited at: www.global-labour.org/workers_in_the_informal_economy.htm

Gaventa, J. (2005) 'Triumph, Deficit or Contestation? Deepening the "Deepening Democracy" Debate', Institute of Development Studies, University of Sussex.

Gereffi, G. and D.L. Wyman (1990) *Manufacturing Miracles: Paths of Industrialization in Latin America and East Asia*, Princeton NJ: Princeton University Press.

Gereffi, G. and D.L. Wyman (2001) 'Rethinking East Asian industrial policy – past records and future prospects', in P.-K. Wong and C.-Y. Ng (eds.), *Industrial Policy, Innovation and Economic Growth: The Experience of Japan and the Asian NIEs*, Singapore: Singapore University Press.

Gladwell, M. (2000) *The Tipping Point: How Little Things Can Make a Big Difference*, London: Little, Brown.

Global Humanitarian Assistance (2004) 'Updated Trends November 2004', www.globalhumanitarianassistance.org/ghqafrNov2004update.htm

Global Humanitarian Assistance (2006) www.globalhumanitarianassistance.org/

Global Platform for Disaster Risk Reduction (2007) 'Disaster Risk Reduction: 2007 Global Review'.

Gning, M.C. (2004) 'Trade, Political Influence and Liberalization: Situating the Poor in the Political Economy of Livestock in Senegal', PPLPI Working Paper No 8, Pro-Poor Livestock Policy Facility.

Goldin, I. and K. Reinert (2006) 'Globalization For Development', Washington DC: World Bank.

Goldsbrough, D. (2007) 'Does The IMF Constrain Health Spending In Poor Countries?', Washington DC: Center for Global Development (CGD).

Goldschmidt-Clermont, L. and E. Pagnossin-Aligisakis (1995) 'Measures of Unrecorded Economic Activities in Fourteen Countries', Human Development Report Office Occasional Papers 20, New York: United Nations Development Programme (UNDP).

Goldstein, A. (2005) 'Emerging Multinationals in the Global Economy: Data Trends, Policy Issues, and Research Questions', Paris: OECD Development Centre.

Gonsalves, C., P.R. Kumar, and A.R. Srivastava (2005) 'Right to Food', New Delhi: Human Rights Law Network.

Graham, C. and S. Sukhtankar (2004) 'Does economic crisis reduce support for markets and democracy in Latin America? Some evidence from surveys of public opinion and well being', *Journal of Latin American Studies* 36: 349–77.

Gready, P. and J. Ensor (2005) *Reinventing Development?: Translating Rights Based Approaches, from Theory to Practice*, London: Zed Books.

Green, D. (1998) 'Fashion Victims: Together We Can Clean up the Clothes Trade', London: CAFOD.

Green, D. (1998) *Hidden Lives: Voices of Children in Latin America and the Caribbean*, London: Cassell.

Green, D. (1999) 'Capital Punishment: Making International Finance Work for the World's Poor', London: CAFOD.

Green, D. (2003) *Silent Revolution: The Rise and Crisis of Market Economics in Latin America*, London: Cassell.

Green, D. (2005) 'Conspiracy of Silence: Old and New Directions on Commodities', Oxford: Oxfam GB.

Green, D. (2006) 'Equality, Inequality, and Equity', background paper for Oxfam International.

Green, D. (2006) *Faces of Latin America*, London: Latin America Bureau.

Green, D., J. Morrison, and S. Murphy (2004) 'Agricultural Trade and Poverty Reduction: Opportunity or Threat?', London: Department for International Development (DFID).

Gueye, C.F., M. Vaugeois, M. Martin, and A. Johnson (2007) 'Negotiating Debt Reduction In The HIPC Initiative And Beyond', Debt Relief International Ltd.

Hamilton, K. (2006) 'Business Views on International Climate Policy: Summary and Key Observations', Business Council for Sustainable Energy and The Climate Group.

Harbom, L. and P. Wallensteen (2005) 'Armed Conflict and its International Dimensions, 1946–2004', Uppsala Conflict Data Programme, *Journal of Peace Research* 42(5) 624–34.

Hart, S. (2005) *Capitalism at the Crossroads*, Philadelphia PA: Wharton School Publishing.

Hartridge, D. (1997) 'What the General Agreement on Services Can Do', speech at the Conference Opening Markets for Banking Worldwide: The WTO Agreement on Trade in Services, 8 January 1997, UK.

Hawley, S. (2003) 'Underwriting Bribery: Export Credit Agencies and Corruption', Corner House Briefing.

Hayek, F. (1944) *The Road to Serfdom*, Chicago IL: University of Chicago Press.

Hayman, R. (2007) 'Milking the Cow: Negotiating Ownership of Aid and Policy in Rwanda', Global Economic Governance Programme, University College Oxford.

Hellin, J. and S. Higman (2003) *Feeding the Market*, Bourton on Dunsmore: ITDG Publishing.

Hellin, J., D. White, and R. Best (2006) 'High-Value Agricultural Products: Can Smallholder Farmers Also Benefit?', *CIAT Annual Report*, http://gisweb.ciat.cgiar.org/SIG/download/Annual_Report_2006.pdf#page=56

Hellin, J., M. Lundy, and M. Meijer (2007) 'Farmer Organization, Collective Action and Market Access in Meso-America', Washington DC: Consultative Group on International Agricultural Research (CGIAR).

Hepburn, C. (2007) 'Carbon trading: a review of the Kyoto Mechanisms', *Annual Review of Environment Resources*, 32: 375–93.

Hesse, C. and J. MacGregor (2006) 'Pastoralism: Drylands' Invisible Asset? Developing a Framework for Assessing the Value of Pastoralism in East Africa', IIED Issues paper number 142, London: International Institute for Environment and Development (IIED).

Hesselbein, G., F. Golooba-Mutebi, and J. Putzel (2006) 'Economic and Political Foundations of State-Making in Africa: Understanding State Reconstruction', London: London School of Economics.

Hochschild, A. (2005) *Bury the Chains: The British Struggle to Abolish Slavery*, New York: Houghton Mifflin.

Hopkins Leisher, S. (2003) 'A Case Study of Donor Impact on Political Change at the Grassroots in Vu Quang District, Ha Tinh Province, Viet Nam', London: Department for International Development (DFID).

Howell, J. and J. Pearce (2001) *Civil Society and Development: A Critical Exploration*, Boulder CO: Lynne Rienner Publishers Inc.

Human Rights Research and Advocacy Consortium (2004) 'Take the Guns Away: Afghan Voices on Security and Elections', see www.cmi.no/pdf/?file=/afghanistan/doc/TaketheGunsAwayEnglish.pdf

Human Rights Watch (2006) *World Report 2006*, http://hrw.org/wr2k6/introduction/2.htm

Human Rights Watch (2007) 'Get the Gun! Human Rights Violation by Uganda's National Army in Law Enforcement Operations in Karamoja Region', Human Rights Watch, 19(13A).

Human Security Centre (2005) *The Human Security Report 2005*.

Human Security Centre (2006) 'Human Security Briefing 2006', University of British Columbia.

Humphreys, M. and A. Varshney (2004) 'Violent Conflict and the MDGs: Diagnosis and Recommendations', paper prepared for the MDG Poverty Task Force Workshop, Bangkok, June 2004.

IDD and Associates (2006) 'Joint Evaluation of General Budget Support 1994–2004', Birmingham: University of Birmingham.

IDS (2003) 'Safe as houses: securing urban land tenure and property rights', IDS Insights Issue 48, October 2003, Institute of Development Studies, University of Sussex.

IDS (2005) 'Signposts to More Effective States Responding to Governance Challenges in Developing Countries', Institute of Development Studies, University of Sussex.

IDS (2006) 'Building Effective States: Taking a Citizen's Perspective', Institute of Development Studies, University of Sussex.

ILO (2001) 'Reducing the Decent Work Deficit: A Global Challenge', Report of the Director General, International Labour Conference 89th Session, Geneva: International Labour Organization.

ILO (2002) 'Decent Work and the Informal Economy', Report VI to the International Labour Conference, 90th Session, Geneva: International Labour Organization.

ILO (2005) 'Promoting Fair Globalization in Textiles and Clothing in a post-MFA Environment: Report for Discussion at the Tripartite Meeting on Promoting Fair Globalization in Textiles and Clothing in a Post-MFA Environment', www.ilo.org/public/english/dialogue/sector/techmeet/tmtc-pmfa05/tmtc-pmfa-r.pdf

ILO (2006) 'Global Employment Trends Brief', January 2006, Geneva: International Labour Organization.

ILO (2007) 'Global Employment Trends for Women', Geneva: International Labour Organization.

ILO (2008) Global Employment Trends 2007, www.ilo.org/trends

International Campaign to Ban Landmines (2001, 2005) 'Landmine Monitor Report', www.icbl.org

International Federation of Red Cross and Red Crescent Societies (2004) *World Disasters Report 2004*, Geneva: IFRC.

International Food Policy Research Institute (IFPRI) (2004) 'Ending Hunger In Africa, Prospects for the Small Farmer', Washington DC: The International Food Policy Research Institute (IFPRI).

International Institute for Environment and Development (IIED), Natural Resources Institute (NRI), Royal African Society (RAS) (2005) 'Land in Africa: Market Asset of Secure Livelihood?'.

International Monetary Fund (2002) 'Article IV Consultation, Chile', www.imf.org/external/pubs/cat/longres.cfm?sk=1523.0

International Rescue Committee (2004) 'Mortality in the Democratic Republic of the Congo: Results from a Nationwide Survey', New York: International Rescue Committee (IRC).

Inter-Regional Inequality Facility (2006) 'Overview', London: Overseas Development Institute (ODI), www.odi.org.uk/inter-regional_inequality/overview.html

Inter-Regional Inequality Facility (2006) 'Social Grants in South Africa', Inter-Regional Inequality Facility case study, London: Overseas Development Institute (ODI).

IPCC (2007) 'Summary for policymakers' in 'Climate Change 2007: The Physical Science Basis', Contribution of Working Group I to the Fourth Assessment Report of the Intergovernmental Panel on Climate Change, S. Solomon, D. Qin, M. Manning, Z. Chen, M. Marquis, K.B. Averyt, M.Tignor, and H.L. Miller (eds.), Cambridge, UK and New York: Cambridge University Press.

IPEA (undated) 'On the Recent Fall in Income Inequality in Brasil', Florence MA: Institute for People's Education and Action (IPEA).

Jarman, M. (2007) *Climate Change*, Small Guides to Big Issues series, Oxford and London: Oxfam GB and Pluto Press.

Javorcik, B.S. (2004) 'Does foreign direct investment increase the productivity of domestic firms? In search of spillovers through backward linkages', *American Economic Review* 94(3): 605–27.

Jenkins R. and A.M. Goetz (1999) 'Accounts and accountability: theoretical implications of the right to information movement in India', *Third World Quarterly* 20(3): 603–22.

Joint Learning Initiative (2004) 'Human Resources for Health: Overcoming the Crisis', Boston, MA: Harvard University Global Equity Initiative.

Jubilee Debt Coalition (undated) 'Vulture Funds and Zambia', London: Jubilee Debt Coalition.

Kaganzi, E., S. Ferris, A. Abenakyo, P. Sanginga, and J. Njuki (2006) 'Sustaining Linkages to High-value Markets through Collective Action in Uganda: The Case of the Nyabyumba Potato Farmers', paper for Research Workshop on Collective Action and Market Access for Smallholders, 2–5 October 2006, Cali, Colombia.

Kantor, P. and P. Nair (2005) 'Vulnerability to Crisis in Lucknow, India: The Role of Assets in Mitigating Risk', New Delhi: Oxfam GB.

Kasryno, F. (2004) 'The linkage between agriculture development, poverty alleviation and employment', www.jajaki.or.id/data/publications/Faisal%20Kasryno.pdf

Kelleher, K. and M.L. Weber (2006) 'Towards sustainable management of world fisheries and aquaculture', in V.K. Bhargava (ed.), 'Global Issues for Global Citizens', World Bank Report No. 29090-GLB 2006, Washington DC: World Bank.

Kenny, C. (undated) 'Information and Development', unpublished.

Keynes, J.M. (1941) 'The Post-War Currency Policy', in Keynes papers Volume XXV, Basingstoke, UK: Macmillan.

Khan, M.H. (2002) 'State Failure in Developing Countries and Strategies of Institutional Reform', paper for World Bank ABCDE Conference, Oslo, 2002.

Khan, M.H. (2006) presentation at Overseas Development Institute (ODI), www.odi.org.uk/events/states_nov06/index.html

Kimmis, J. (2005) 'Financial Markets', background paper for Oxfam International.

King, M.L. (1968) *Where Do We Go From Here: Chaos or Community,* Boston MA: Beacon Press.

King, R. (2007) 'Carbon Dioxide Emissions, Technology, and Economic Growth', background paper for Oxfam International.

Klein, M. and T. Harford (2005) *The Market for Aid,* Washington DC: World Bank.

Knight, B., H. Chigudu, and R. Tandon (2002) *Reviving Democracy: Citizens at the Heart of Governance,* London: Commonwealth Foundation.

Kraay, A. (2006) 'When is growth pro-poor? Evidence from a panel of countries', *Journal of Development Economics* 80(1) 189–227.

Kruzenga L. (2004) 'Report confirms health disparities for aboriginals, poor; comparisons with Third World continue', *The First Perspective* 13(3).

Krznaric, R. (2007) 'How Change Happens: Interdisciplinary Perspectives for Human Development', Oxfam Research Reports, Oxford: Oxfam GB.

Kuziemko, I. and E. Werker (2006) 'How much is a seat on the Security Council worth? Foreign aid and bribery at the United Nations', *Journal of Political Economy* 114(5): 905–30.


Lacina, B. and N.P. Gleditsch (2005) 'Monitoring Trends in Global Combat: A New Dataset of Battle Deaths', *European Journal of Population* 21: 145–66.

Laird, S. and S. Fernández de Córdoba (2006) *Coping With Trade Reforms: A Developing Country Perspective on the WTO Industrial Tariff Negotiations,* Basingstoke: Palgrave.

Lanjouw, J.O. and I.M. Cockburn (2001) 'New pills for poor people? Empirical evidence after GATT', *World Development* 29(2): 265–89.

Latigo, A. (2005) 'A New Round of Time-use Studies for Africa: Measuring Unpaid Work for Pro-poor Development Policies', paper presented at UNDP/Levy Economics Institute Global Conference on Unpaid work and the Economy, 1–3 October 2005, www.levy.org/undp-levy-conference/papers/ paper_Latigo.pdf

Layard, R. (2005) *Happiness, Lessons from a New Science,* London: Penguin.

Layton, M.D., B.C. Carrete, I. Ablanedo Terrazas, and A.M. Sánchez Rodríguez (2007) 'Mexico Case Study: Civil Society and the Struggle to Reduce Maternal Mortality', unpublished.

Le Quang, B. (2006) 'What Has Made Viet Nam a Poverty-Reduction Success Story?', background paper for Oxfam International.

Leach, M. and I. Scoones (2006) 'The Slow Race: Making Technology Work for the Poor', London: Demos.

Legrain, P. (2006) *Immigrants: Your Country Needs Them,* London: Little, Brown.

Lewis, D. (2007) *The Management of Non-Governmental Development Organizations,* 2nd edition, London: Routledge.

Lewis, S. (2005) *Race Against Time,* Toronto ON: House of Anansi Press.

Liu, J. and J. Diamond (2005) 'China's environment in a globalizing world: How China and the rest of the world affect each other', *Nature* 435, 1137–286.

Locke, R.M., F. Qin, and A. Brause (2007) 'Does monitoring improve labor standards? Lessons from Nike', *Industrial and Labor Relations Review* 61(1): 3–31.

Lockwood, M. (2005) *The State They're In*, Bourton on Dunsmore: ITDG Publishing.

Lockwood, M. (2007) 'A rough guide to carbon trading', *Prospect*, January 2007.

Lomborg, B. (2006) *How to Spend $50 Billion and Make the World a Better Place*, Cambridge: Cambridge University Press.

Lopez, H. (2006) 'Did Growth Become Less Pro-Poor in the 1990s?', Washington DC: World Bank.


MacAuslan, I. (2007) 'India's National Rural Employment Guarantee Act: A Case Study for How Change Happens', background paper for Oxfam International.

Maipose, G., G. Somolekae, and T. Johnston (1996) 'Effective Aid Management: The Case of Botswana', Foreign Aid to Africa, Nordic Africa Institute.

Mansfield, E.D. and J. Snyder (2005) *Electing to Fight: Why Emerging Democracies Go to War*, Cambridge MA: MIT Press.

March, C., I. Smyth, and M. Mukhopadhyay (1999) *A Guide to Gender Analysis Frameworks*, Oxford: Oxfam GB.

Massey, D. (2003) 'Patterns and Processes of International Migration in the 21st Century', paper prepared for Conference on African Migration in Comparative Perspective, Johannesburg, South Africa, 4–7 June, 2003.

Maxwell, S. (2005) 'Should We Provide a Guarantee That No Child will be Brain-Damaged by Malnutrition in Africa if Money Can Prevent It?', ODI Opinions, No 39, London: Overseas Development Institute (ODI).

McCulloch, N., B. Baulch, and M. Cherel-Robson (2000) 'Poverty, Inequality and Growth in Zambia During the 1990s', IDS Working Paper 114, Institute of Development Studies, University of Sussex.

McMillan, J. and P. Zoido (2004) 'How to subvert democracy: Montesinos in Peru', *The Journal of Economic Perspectives* 18(4): 69–92.

Mehrotra, S. and R. Jolly (1997) *Development with a Human Face: Experiences in Social Achievement and Economic Growth*, New York: UNICEF.

Meridian Institute (2007) 'Global Dialogue on Nanotechnology and the Poor: Opportunities and Risks', background paper for the Meridian Institute International Workshop on Nanotechnology, Commodities, and Development, Rio de Janeiro, 29–31 May 2007.

Microcredit Summit Campaign (2006) 'Report of the Microcredit Summit Campaign', www.microcreditsummit.org

Milanovic, B. (2003) 'Why we all do care about inequality (but are loath to admit it)', Washington DC: World Bank.

Ministry of Health and Family Welfare, Government of India (2007) 'National Family Health Survey, 2007'.

Mkandawire, T. (2001) 'Thinking About Developmental States in Africa', *Cambridge Journal of Economics* 25: 289–314.

Mkandawire, T. (2004) 'Disempowering New Democracies and the Persistence of Poverty', in M. Spoor (ed.), *Globalisation, Poverty and Conflict*, Dordrecht: Kluwer Academic Publishers.

Moran, T. (2002) *Beyond Sweatshops: Foreign Direct Investment and Globalization in Developing Countries*, Washington DC: Brookings Institution Press.

Moss T., G. Pettersson, and N. van de Walle (2006) 'An Aid-Institutions Paradox? A Review Essay on Aid Dependency and State Building in Sub-Saharan Africa', Washington DC: Center for Global Development (CGD).

Muggah, R. and S. Bachelor (2002) 'Development Held Hostage: Assessing the Effects of Small Arms Availability', Bureau of Crisis Prevention and Recovery, New York: United Nations Development Programme (UNDP).

Mulgan, G. (2006) *Good and Bad Power,* London: Allen Lane.

Murray, C.J.L., A.D. Lopez, B. Chin, D. Feehan, and K.H. Hill (2006) 'Estimation of potential global pandemic influenza mortality on the basis of vital registry data from the 1918–20 pandemic: a quantitative analysis', *Lancet* 368: 2211–18.

Mutangadura, G., D. Mukurazita, and H. Jackson (1999) 'A Review of Household and Community Responses to the HIV/AIDS Epidemic in Rural Areas of Sub-Saharan Africa', Geneva: UNAIDS.

Nash, R., A. Hudson, and C. Luttrell (2006) 'Mapping Political Context: A Toolkit for Civil Society Organisations', London: Overseas Development Institute (ODI).

New Economics Foundation (2006) 'A Long Row to Hoe: Family Farming and Rural Poverty in Developing Countries', London: New Economics Foundation (NEF).

New Economics Foundation (2006) 'Growth Isn't Working: The Unbalanced Distribution of Benefits and Costs from Economic Growth', London: New Economics Foundation (NEF).

New Economics Foundation (2007) 'Towards a New Economics Paradigm for Poverty Eradication in a Carbon-Constrained World', London: New Economics Foundation (NEF).

Newman, J. (2003) 'Environmental Benefits of Subsidy Removal in the German and United States Energy Sectors', OECD Technical Expert Meeting on Environmentally Harmful Subsidies, 3–4 November 2003, Paris.

Norwegian Refugee Council (2007) 'Internal Displacement: A Global Overview of Trends and Developments in 2006', Global IDP Project: Geneva. Prepared for the 3rd Expert Consultative Meeting on Gender and Early Warning, London, 11 February 2002.

Nussbaum, M. (1999) *Sex and Social Justice*, Oxford: Oxford University Press.

Nyamu-Musembi, C. (2006) 'Breathing Life into Dead Theories about Property Rights: de Soto and Land Relations in Rural Africa', IDS WP272, Institute of Development Studies, University of Sussex.

O'Brien, P. (2001) 'Fiscal Exceptionalism: Great Britain and Its European Rivals', Working Paper 65/01, Department of Economic History, London School of Economics.

ODI (1996) 'The Joint Evaluation of Emergency Assistance to Rwanda', London: Overseas Development Institute (ODI).

ODI (2004) 'Inequality in Developing Countries', London: Overseas Development Institute (ODI).

ODI (2007) 'Community-Based Workers: A Possible Solution to More Services, Reaching Many Communities and Within Budget', London: Overseas Development Institute (ODI).

ODI (undated) 'Inequality in Developing Countries', Policy Briefing Pack, London: Overseas Development Institute (ODI).

OECD (2006) 'The Development Effectiveness of Food Aid. Does Tying Matter?', www.oecd.org/document/59/0,3343,en_2649_33721_35423803_1_1_1_1,00.html#food

OECD (2006) 'Developing Country Multinationals: South–South Investment Comes of Age', Paris: Organisation for Economic Co-operation and Development (OECD).

OECD (2006) *Development Cooperation Report 2006*, Paris: Organisation for Economic Co-operation and Development (OECD).

OECD (2007) 'Agricultural Policies in OECD Countries: Monitoring and Evaluation 2007', Paris: Organisation for Economic Co-operation and Development (OECD).

OECD (2007) 'OECD in Figures 2007', Paris: Organisation for Economic Co-operation and Development (OECD).

OECD DAC (2005) 'Making Poverty Reduction Work: The OECD's Role in Development Partnerships', Paris: Organisation for Economic Co-operation and Development (OECD).

OECD DAC (2006) 'Implementing the 2001 DAC Recommendations on Untying Official Development Assistance to the Least Developed Countries', Paris: Organisation for Economic Co-operation and Development (OECD).

Offenheiser, R. (2007) 'A 21st Century Green Revolution that Works for the Poor', unpublished memo to the Gates Foundation.

Offenheiser, R. and S.H. Holcombe (2003) 'Challenges and opportunities in implementing a rights-based approach to development: an Oxfam America perspective', *Nonprofit and Voluntary Sector Quarterly* 32(2): 268–301.

Offices of the Democratic Leaders Harry Reid and Nancy Pelosi (2006) 'For and By Big Oil', A Special Joint House and Senate Democratic Report.

Ortmann, G.F. and R.P. King (2007) 'Agricultural cooperatives II: can they facilitate access of small-scale farmers in South Africa to input and product markets?', *Agrekon* 46(2): 219–44.

Osorio, N. (2002) 'The Global Coffee Crisis: A Threat To Sustainable Development', Néstor Osorio, Executive Director, ICO, Submission to the World Summit on Sustainable Development, Johannesburg.

Oxfam America (2003) 'Weathering the Storm: Lessons in Risk Reduction from Cuba', www.oxfamamerica.org/newsandpublications/publications/research_reports/art7111.html

Oxfam America (2007) 'Newmont Mining Company: Background', unpublished.

Oxfam America (2007) 'Paying the Price: How US Farm Policies Hurt West African Cotton Farmers – and How Subsidy Reform Could Help', Boston MA: Oxfam America.

Oxfam GB (2005) 'Decentralization Learning Guide', internal paper.

Oxfam GB (2006) 'Overcoming Poverty and Suffering through Land Rights: Oxfam's Policy and Practice', internal paper.

Oxfam GB, World Vision, Care, RHVP, and OVHA (2006) 'Food Security in Southern Africa: Changing the Trend?'.

Oxfam Intermón (2001) 'La realidad de la ayuda 2001–02', Barcelona: Ed. Intermón Oxfam.

487

Oxfam Intermón (2007) 'Puertas al mar. Por qué todos deberíamos estar interesados en una política migratoria más justa e inteligente', Barcelona: Ed. Intermón Oxfam.

Oxfam International (2002) 'Death on the Doorstep of the Summit', Oxford: Oxfam International.

Oxfam International (2002) 'Rigged Rules and Double Standards: Trade, Globalization, and the Fight Against Poverty', Oxford: Oxfam International.

Oxfam International (2004) 'From Donorship to Ownership?: Moving Towards PRSP Round Two', Oxford: Oxfam International.

Oxfam International (2004) 'Trading Away our Rights: Women Working in Global Supply Chains', Oxford: Oxfam International.

Oxfam International (2005) 'A Round for Free: How Rich Countries are Getting a Free Ride on Agricultural Subsidies at the WTO', Oxford: Oxfam International.

Oxfam International (2005) 'Food Aid or Hidden Dumping?: Separating Wheat from Chaff', Oxford: Oxfam International.

Oxfam International (2005) 'Kicking Down the Door: How Upcoming WTO Talks Threaten Farmers in Poor Countries', Oxford: Oxfam International.

Oxfam International (2005) 'Truth or Consequences: why the EU and USA Must Reform Their Subsidies or Pay the Price', Oxford: Oxfam International.

Oxfam International (2006) 'Causing Hunger: an Overview of the Food Crises in Africa', Oxford: Oxfam International.

Oxfam International (2006) 'Kicking the Habit: The World Bank and IMF Still Addicted to Economic Policy Conditionality', Oxford: Oxfam International.

Oxfam International (2006) 'Serve the Essentials: What Governments and Donors Must Do to Improve South Asia's Essential Services', Oxford: Oxfam International, p.33.

Oxfam International (2006) 'The View from the Summit – Gleneagles G8 One Year On', Oxford: Oxfam International.

Oxfam International (2007) 'Adapting to Climate Change: What's Needed in Poor Countries, and Who Should Pay', Oxford: Oxfam International.

Oxfam International (2007) 'Bio-fuelling Poverty: Why the EU Renewable Fuel Target May Be Disastrous for Poor People', Oxford: Oxfam International.

Oxfam International (2007) 'Blind Spot: The Continued Failure of the World Bank and IMF to Fully Assess the Impact of Their Advice on Poor People', Oxford: Oxfam International.

Oxfam International (2007) 'Climate Alarm: Disasters Increase As Climate Change Bites', Oxford: Oxfam International.

Oxfam International (2007) 'Paying for People: Financing the Skilled Workers Needed to Deliver Health and Education Services For All', Oxford: Oxfam International.

Oxfam International (2007) 'Policy Compendium Note on Disarmament, Demobilisation and Reintegration (DDR)' , Oxford: Oxfam International.

Oxfam International (2007) 'Pricing Farmers out of Cotton: The Costs of World Bank Reforms in Mali', Oxford: Oxfam International.

Oxfam International (2007) 'Signing Away The Future: How Trade and Investment Agreements Between Rich and Poor Countries Undermine Development', Oxford: Oxfam International.

Oxfam International (2007) 'Sink or Swim: Why Disaster Risk Reduction Is Central To Surviving Floods In South Asia', Oxford: Oxfam International.

Oxfam International (2007) 'The UN Central Emergency Response Fund One Year On', Oxford: Oxfam International.

Oxfam International (2007) 'The World is Still Waiting: Broken G8 Promises Are Costing Millions of Lives', Oxford: Oxfam International.

Oxfam International (2008) 'For a Safer Tomorrow: Protecting Civilians in a Multipolar World', Oxford: Oxfam International.

Oxfam International (2008) 'Rethinking Disasters: Why Death and Destruction Are Not Nature's Fault But Our Failure', New Delhi: Oxfam International.

Oxfam International and WaterAid (2006) 'In the Public Interest: Health, Education, and Water and Sanitation For All', Oxford and London: Oxfam International and WaterAid.

Özden, Ç. and M. Schiff (2007) 'International Migration, Economic Development and Policy', Washington DC: World Bank.

Parry, M.L., O.F. Canziani, J.P. Palutikof, P.J. van der Linden, and C.E. Hanson (2007) 'Contribution of Working Group II to the Fourth Assessment Report of the Intergovernmental Panel on Climate Change', Cambridge: Cambridge University Press.

Pauly, D., R. Watson, and J. Alder (2005) 'Global trends in world fisheries: impacts on marine ecosystems and food security', *Philosophical Transactions of the Royal Society* 360(1453): 5–12.

Pauly, D., V. Christensen, S. Guenette, T.J. Pitcher, U. Rashid Sumaila, and C.J. Walters (2004) 'Towards sustainability in world fisheries', *Nature* 2002: 418.

Pembina Institute (2005) 'Government Spending on Canada's Oil and Gas Industry: Undermining Canada's Kyoto Commitment'.

Penrose-Buckley, C. (2007) *Producer Organisations: A Guide to Developing Collective Rural Enterprises*, Oxford: Oxfam GB.

Physicians for Human Rights (2002) 'War-Related Sexual Violence in Sierra Leone: A Population-Based Assessment', Boston MA: Physicians for Human Rights (PHR).

Picard, A.A. (2001) 'Resultados del Tratado de Libre Comercio de America del Norte en Mexico', Mexico: RMALC.

Piron, L.-H. (2004) 'Rights Based Approaches to Social Protection', London: Overseas Development Institute (ODI).

Polaski, S. (2004) 'Protecting Labour Rights Through Trade Agreements – An Analytical Guide', Stanford CA: Carnegie Foundation.

Popkin, B. (2003) 'The nutrition transition in the developing world', *Development Policy Review* 21(5/6): 581–97.

Pradhan, S. (2006) Presentation and background papers from 'Consultation on the World Bank's Approach to Governance and Anti-Corruption', 4 December 2006, World Bank.

Prahalad, C.K. (2005) *The Fortune at the Bottom of the Pyramid: Eradicating Poverty Through Profits*, Philadelphia PA: Wharton School Publishing.

Pretty, J. (2006) 'Agroecological Approaches to Agricultural Development', background paper for *World Development Report 2008*, Washington DC: World Bank.

Pritchett, L. (2006) 'Let Their People Come: Breaking the Gridlock on Global Labor Mobility', Washington DC: Centre for Global Development (CGD).

Prowse, M. (2007) 'Making Contract Farming Work With Co-operatives', London: Overseas Development Institute (ODI).

Rama, M. (2003) 'Globalization and Workers in Developing Countries', World Bank Research Working Paper 2958, Development Research Group, Washington DC: World Bank.

Ramirez-Machado, J.M. (2003) 'Domestic Work, Conditions of Work and Employment: A Legal Perspective', Conditions of Work and Employment Series No. 7, Geneva: International Labour Organization (ILO).

Ratha, D. and W. Shaw (2007) 'South–South Migration and Remittances', Development Prospects Group, Washington DC: World Bank.

Ravallion, M. (2004) 'Pro-Poor Growth: A Primer', Washington DC: World Bank.

Reardon, T. and J.A. Berdegué (2002) 'The rapid rise of supermarkets in Latin America: challenges and opportunities for development', *Development Policy Review* 20(4): 317–34.

Reardon, T., P. Pingali, and K. Stamoulis (2006) 'Impacts of Agrifood Market Transformation During Globalization on the Poor's Rural Nonfarm Employment: Lessons for Rural Business Development Programs', Michigan State University.

Reeler, D. (undated) 'A Theory of Social Change and Implications for Practice, Planning, Monitoring and Evaluation', Cape Town: Community Development Resource Association.

Reis, E. and M. Moore (2005) *Elite Perceptions of Poverty and Inequality*, London: Zed Books.

Republic of South Africa (1996) Constitution of the Republic of South Africa, Section 27, 1c.

Riad El-Ghonemy, M. (1999) 'The Political Economy of Market-Based Land Reform', Discussion Paper 104, Geneva: United Nations Research Institute for Social Development (UNRISD).

Ricardo, D. (1817) *The Principles of Political Economy and Taxation*, London: John Murray.

Roach, R. (2007) 'Two Degrees, One Chance', London: Tearfund, www.tearfund.org/webdocs/website/Campaigning/Policy%20and%20research/Two_degrees_One_chance_final.pdf

Rodin, J. (2007) Speech to National Association of Women Judges' Annual Conference, November 2007.

Rodrik, D. (2003) *In Search of Prosperity: Analytic Narratives on Economic Growth*, Princeton NJ: Princeton University Press.

Rodrik, D. (2004) 'Rethinking Growth Policies In The Developing World', Harvard University.

Rodrik, D. (2005) 'Making Globalisation Work for Development', lecture at London School of Economics, 18 November 2005.

Rosenberg, T. (2001) 'Look at Brazil', *The New York Times Magazine*, www.nytimes.com/library/magazine/home/20010128mag-aids.html

Rousseau, J.-J. (1762) Social Contract, I, 9.

Rowlands, J. (1997) *Questioning Empowerment*, Oxford: Oxfam GB.

Ruggie, J. (2007) 'Report of the Special Representative of the Secretary-General on the Issue of Human Rights and Transnational Corporations and Other Business Enterprises', New York: United Nations.

Sachs, J. (2005) *The End of Poverty: How We Can Make It Happen in Our Lifetime*, London: Penguin.

Sands, P. (1995) *Principles of International Environmental Law, Volume I: Frameworks, Standards and Implementation*, Manchester: Manchester University Press.

Schrijver, N. and F. Weiss (2004) *International Law and Sustainable Development: Principles and Practice*, Martinus Nijhoff Publishers.

Schumpeter, J. (1975) *Capitalism, Socialism and Democracy* (originally published 1942), New York: Harper.

Sekhamane, N. (2004) 'Impact of Urban Livelihoods on Women's Caregiving Behaviours, Household Food Security and Nutrition of Children in Lesotho: A Community Case Study', unpublished.

Sen, A. (1999) *Development as Freedom*, New York: Knopf.

Senderowitz, J. (1995) 'Adolescent Health: Reassessing the Path to Adulthood', World Bank Discussion Paper No. 272, Washington DC: World Bank.

Shepherd, A., R. Marcus, and A. Barrientos (2005) 'Policy Paper On Social Protection', London: Overseas Development Institute (ODI).

Shepherd, A.W. (2007) 'Approaches to Linking Producers to Markets: A Review of Experience to Date', Agricultural Management, Marketing and Finance Occasional Paper 13, Rome: Food and Agriculture Organization (FAO).

Shiferaw, B., G. Obare, G. Murich, and H. Mukhong (2006) 'Building Market Linkages: Experiences from Commercialization of Smallholder Production', International Crops Research Institute for the Semi-Arid Tropics (ICRISAT).

Singh, S. (2005) 'Contract Farming for Agricultural Development: Review of Theory and Practice with Special Reference to India', CENTAD Working Papers, New Delhi: India, www.centad.org/cwp_02.asp

Singh, S., J.E. Darroch, M. Vlassof, and J. Nadeau (2004) 'Adding It Up: The Benefits of Investing in Sexual and Reproductive Health Care', Washington DC and New York: The Alan Guttmacher Institute and United Nations Population Fund (UNFPA).

Slim, H. (2007) *Killing Civilians: Method, Madness and Morality in War*, Oxford: Signal Books Ltd.

Small Arms Survey (2005) www.smallarmssurvey.org/files/sas/publications

Smith, D. and J. Vivekananda (2007) 'A Climate of Conflict: The Links between Climate Change, Peace and War', London: International Alert.

Sparrow, M. K. (2006) 'Corruption in Health Care Systems: The US Experience', in *Global Corruption Report 2006*, Berlin: Transparency International.

Spence, M. (2007) Presentation to Commission on Growth and Development, London.

Standing, G. (1999) *Global Labour Flexibility*, New York: St. Martins.

Stern Review (2006) *The Economics of Climate Change*, Cambridge: Cambridge University Press, www.hm-treasury.gov.uk/media/4/3/Executive_Summary.pdf

Stern Review (2006) 'What is the Economics of Climate Change?', discussion paper, www.hm-treasury.gov.uk/media/213/42/What_is_the_Economics_of_Climate_Change.pdf

Stiglitz, J. (2000) 'What I learned at the world economic crisis', New Republic, April 2000.

Stiglitz, J. (2006) *Making Globalization Work*, London: Penguin.

Stockbridge, M. (2006) 'Agricultural Trade Policy in Developing Countries During Take-Off', Oxfam Research Reports, Oxford: Oxfam GB.

Stott, P.A., D.A. Stone, and M.R. Allen (2004) 'Human contribution to the European heatwave of 2003', *Nature* 432, 610–14.

STREAM (2004) 'System Requirement Report for Level 2 – National Management Institutions', Bureau of Fisheries and Aquatic Resources in the Philippines.

Stringfellow, R., J. Coulter, T. Lucey, C. McKone, and A. Hussain (1997) 'Improving the Access of Smallholders to Agricultural Services in Sub-Saharan Africa: Farmer Cooperation and the Role of the Donor Community', Natural Resources Perspectives No. 20, London: Overseas Development Institute (ODI).

Suarez, P. (2005) 'Predictions, decisions and vulnerability: theoretical explorations and evidence from Zimbabwe', in 'Decision-Making for Reducing Vulnerability Given New Climate Predictions: Case Studies from Merto Boston and Rural Zimbabwe', Boston MA: Boston University.

Suarez, P. (2006) 'Combined Effect of Climate Change and HIV/AIDS on Subsistence Farmers in Monze District, Zambia', unpublished.

Swift, J. (undated) 'Pastoralism and Mobility in the Drylands', New York: United Nations Development Programme (UNDP).


Taylor, L. and von Arnim, R. (2007) 'Modelling the Impact of Trade Liberalisation: A Critique of Computable General Equilibrium Models', Oxfam Research Reports, Oxford: Oxfam GB.

Telford, J., J. Cosgrave, and R. Houghton (2006) 'Joint Evaluation of the International Response to the Indian Ocean Tsunami: Synthesis Report', London: Tsunami Evaluation Coalition.

Tilly, C. (1990) *Coercion, Capital and European States, A.D.990–1990*, Oxford: WileyBlackwell.

Tomalin, E. (2007) 'Sociology, Religion and Development: Literature Review', University of Birmingham, UK.

Tyndale, W. (1998) 'Key Issues for Development: A Discussion Paper for the Contribution by the World Faiths Development Dialogue (WFDD) to the World Bank's World Development Report 2001', World Faiths Development Dialogue.

Tyndall Centre for Climate Change (2004) 'Adaptive Research Notes No. 9'.


UK Government (2006) 'System-Wide Coherence – A Vision for the United Nations'.

UN (1994) 'Framework Convention on Climate Change (UNFCCC), Article 2 (Objective)', New York: United Nations.

UN (2004) 'A More Secure World: Our Shared Responsibility', Report of the UN High-Level Panel on Threats, Challenges and Change, New York: United Nations.

UN (2005) 'The Inequality Predicament: Report of the World Social Situation 2005', New York: United Nations.

UN (2005) 'The Millennium Development Goals Report', New York: United Nations.

UN (2006) 'Report of the Secretary-General on International Migration and Development', May 2006, General Assembly, 60th Session, New York: United Nations.

UN (2006) 'The Millennium Development Goals Report', New York: United Nations.

UN (2006) 'World Economic and Social Survey 2006: Diverging Growth and Development', New York: United Nations.

UN (2007) 'The Millennium Development Goals Report', New York: United Nations.

UN Commission on Human Security (2003) 'Final Report of the UN Commission on Human Security', www.humansecurity-chs.org/finalreport/index.html

UN Department of Economic and Social Affairs (2006) 'UN Report on the World Social Situation 2005: The Inequality Predicament', www.un.org/esa/socdev/rwss/media%2005/cd-docs/fullreport05.htm

UN OCHA (2007) 'Israeli-Palestinian Fatalities since 2000: Key Trends', www.ochaopt.org

UN OCHA (2007) 'The humanitarian impact on Palestinians of Israelis settlements and other infrastructure in the West Bank', www.ochaopt.org

UNAIDS (2006) 'Global Facts and Figures', www.who.int/hiv/mediacentre/ 200605-FS_globalfactsfigures_en.pdf

UNAIDS (2006) 'Report on the Global AIDS Epidemic', ww.who.int/hiv/mediacentre/ 2006_GR_ANN2_en.pdf

UNAIDS and WHO (2007) '07 AIDS epidemic update', http://data.unaids.org/pub/EPISlides/2007/2007_epiupdate_en.pdf

UNCTAD (2005) *World Investment Report 2005*, New York: United Nations Conference on Trade and Development.

UNCTAD (2006) *World Investment Report 2006*, New York: United Nations Conference on Trade and Development.

UNDP (2000) *Human Development Report 2000*, New York: United Nations Development Programme.

UNDP (2001) *Human Development Report 2001*, New York: United Nations Development Programme.

UNDP (2002) *Human Development Report 2002*, New York: United Nations Development Programme.

UNDP (2004) 'Reducing Disaster Risk: A Challenge for Development', New York: United Nations Development Programme.

UNDP (2004) 'Unleashing Entrepreneurship: Making Business Work for the Poor', Commission on the Private Sector and Development, New York: United Nations Development Programme.

UNDP (2005) *Human Development Report 2005*, New York and Oxford: United Nations Development Programme and Oxford University Press.

UNDP (2006) 'China, Country Programme Document 2006–10', New York: United Nations Development Programme.

UNDP (2006) *Human Development Report 2006*, New York: United Nations Development Programme.

UNDP (2007) *Human Development Report 2007/2008*, New York: United Nations Development Programme.

UNDP (2008) *Human Development Report 2008*, New York: United Nations Development Programme.

UNEP (2006) 'Climate Change Information Kit', www.unep.org/themes/climatechange/ PDF/infokit2003-E.pdf

UNEP and International Energy Agency (2002) 'Reforming Energy Subsidies', New York: United Nations Environment Programme.

UNESCO (2001) 'Barbed wire in the research field', www.unesco.org/courier/2001_ 11/uk/doss14.htm

UNESCO (2007) *EFA Global Monitoring Report 2007*, New York: UNESCO.

UNFPA (2000) *State of World Population 2000*, New York: The United Nations Population Fund.

UNFPA (2005) *State of World Population 2005*, New York: The United Nations Population Fund.

UNFPA (2006) *State of World Population 2006*, New York: The United Nations Population Fund.

UNHCR (2005) 'Asylum Levels and Trends in Industrialised Countries', New York: The Office of the UN High Commissioner for Refugees.

UNHCR (2006) 'Global Trends, UNHCR', New York: The Office of the UN High Commissioner for Refugees.

UNICEF (2007) *State of the World's Children 2007*, New York: UNICEF.

UNICEF (2008) *State of the World's Children 2008*, New York: UNICEF.

UNISDR (2004) 'Living With Risk: A Global Review of Disaster Reduction Activities', New York: United Nations International Strategy for Disaster Reduction.

US Department of Justice – Federal Bureau of Investigation (2006) 'Crime in the United States', US Department of Justice.

Uvin, P. (2004) *Human Rights and Development*, Sterling VA: Kumarian.


Van Mulekom, L. (1999) 'An institutional development process in community based coastal resource management: building the capacity and opportunity for community based co-management in a small-scale fisheries community', *Ocean & Coastal Management* 42: 439–56.

Vaux, T. and F. Lund (2003) 'Working women and security: Self Employed Women's Association's response to crisis', *Journal of Human Development* 4(2): 265–87.

Venkataramani, G. (2004) 'Mangroves can act as shield against tsunami', *The Hindu*, 28 December 2004, www.hindu.com/2004/12/28/stories/ 2004122805191300.htm

Vorley, B. (2003) 'Food, Inc.: Corporate Concentration From Farm to Consumer', UK Food Group.


Wainwright, H. (2003) *Reclaim the State: Experiments in People's Democracy*, Verso.

WaterAid (2007) 'Global Cause and Effect: How the Aid System is Undermining the Millennium Development Goals', London: WaterAid.

Watt, P. (1999) 'Social Investment and Economic Growth: A Strategy to Eradicate Poverty', Oxford: Oxfam GB.

Wells, D. (2006) 'Best Practice in the Regulation of International Labor Standards: Lessons of the US–Cambodia Textile Agreement', Hamilton ON: McMaster University.

Whitfield, L. and E. Jones (2007) 'Ghana, the Political Dimensions of Aid Dependence', Global Economic Governance Programme, University of Oxford.

WHO (2002) *World Health Report 2002: Reducing Risks, Promoting Healthy Life*, Geneva: World Health Organization.

WHO (2005) 'Immunisation Against Diseases of Public Health Importance', Fact Sheet No. 288, March 2005, Geneva: World Health Organization.

WHO (2006) 'Cumulative Number of Confirmed Human Cases of Avian Influenza A/(H5N1) Reported to WHO', www.who.int/csr/disease/avian_influenza/country/ cases_table_2008_01_24/ en/index.html

WHO (2006) *World Health Report 2006*, Geneva: World Health Organization.

WHO (2007) 'Lifetime Maternal Mortality Risk', from Maternal Mortality in 2005, Geneva: World Health Organization.

WHO (2007) 'Malaria', Fact Sheet 94, www.who.int/mediacentre/factsheets/fs094/en/index.html

WHO (2007) 'Progress Towards Global Immunization Goals – Summary Presentation of Key Indicators', www.who.int/immunization_monitoring/data/SlidesGlobal Immunization.pdf

Wiggins, S. (2005) 'Southern Africa's Food and Humanitarian Crisis of 2001–04: Causes and Lessons', Discussion Paper, Agricultural Economic Society Annual Conference, Nottingham, April 4–6 2005.

Wiggins, S. with K. Higgins (2008) 'Pro-Poor Growth and Development', London: Overseas Development Institute (ODI).

Williamson, J. (2003) 'The Washington Consensus and Beyond', *Economic and Political Weekly*.

Williamson, J., S. Griffith-Jones, and R. Gottschalk (2003) 'Should Capital Controls have a Place in the Future International Monetary System?', paper prepared for a meeting of the International Monetary Convention held by the Reinventing Bretton Woods Committee, Madrid, May 2003, unpublished, Institute of Development Studies, University of Sussex.

WMO (2006) 'Statement on the Status of the Global Climate in 2006', www.wmo.ch/pages/themes/wmoprod/documents/WMO_1016_E.pdf

Woods, N. (2006) *The Globalizers: The IMF, the World Bank and their Borrowers*, New York: Cornell University Press.

Woods, N. (2007)'Global economic governance: a programme of reform', in D. Held and D. Mepham (eds.), *Progressive Foreign Policy*, Cambridge: Polity.

World Bank (2001) 'Commercialization and Mission Drift: The Transformation of Microfinance in Latin America', Washington DC: World Bank.

World Bank (2002) 'Country Assistance Strategy – Mexico 2002', Washington DC: World Bank.

World Bank (2003) 'The Impact of Microfinance', donor brief, July 2003, Washington DC: World Bank.

World Bank (2003) *World Development Report 2004*, Washington DC: World Bank.

World Bank (2004) 'Saving Fish and Fishers: Toward Sustainable and Equitable Governance of the Global Fishing Sector', Washington DC: World Bank.

World Bank (2005) 'Economic Growth in the 1990s: Learning from a Decade of Reform', Washington DC: World Bank.

World Bank (2005) 'FDI Trends', *Public Policy for the Private Sector Journal*, September 2005, http://rru.worldbank.org/documents/publicpolicyjournal/273palmade_anayiotas.pdf

World Bank (2005) 'Review Of World Bank Conditionality', Washington DC: World Bank.

World Bank (2005) *World Development Report 2006*, Washington DC: World Bank.

World Bank (2006) *Global Economic Prospects 2006*, Washington DC: World Bank.

World Bank (2006) 'Where is the Wealth of Nations? Measuring Capital for the 21st Century', Washington DC: World Bank.

World Bank (2006) *World Development Report 2007*, Washington DC: World Bank.

World Bank (2007) *Global Development Finance 2007*, Washington DC: World Bank.

World Bank (2007) 'Remittance Trends 2007', Washington DC: World Bank.

World Bank (2007) *State and Trends of the Carbon Market 2007*, Washington DC: World Bank.

World Bank (2007) *World Development Indicators 2007*, Washington DC: World Bank.

World Bank (2007) *World Development Report 2008*, Washington DC: World Bank.

World Bank (undated) 'Public Policy for the Private Sector', Note Number 314, Washington DC: World Bank.

World Bank, www.worldbank.org/wbi/governance/pdf/icac_hk_survey_results_5_06.pdf

World Food Programme (2007) 'The Changing Face of Famine', Rome: World Food Programme (WFP).

World Refugee Survey (2006) 'Table 3', www.refugees.org/data/wrs/06/docs/refugee_and_asylum_seekers_worldwide.pdf

World Wide Fund For Nature (WWF) (2006) 'Living Planet Report 2006', www.panda.org/news_facts/publications/living_planet_report/index.cfm

WTO (2006) *World Trade Report 2006*, www.wto.org/english/res_e/booksp_e/anrep_e/wtr06-1a_e.pdf

WTO (2007) *World Trade Report 2007*, Geneva: World Trade Organization.

# BACKGROUND PAPERS AND CASE STUDIES

## THE UNEQUAL WORLD

Barber, C. (2005) 'Notes on Poverty and Inequality'.

Beghin, N. (2008) 'Inequality and poverty in Brazil: Current Situation and Challenges'.

Green, D. (2006) 'Equality, Inequality, and Equity: Where Do These Fit in the Poverty Agenda?'

King, R. (2007) 'Global Inequality'.

## POWER AND POLITICS

Beall, J. and S. Fox (2007) 'Urban Poverty and Development in the 21st Century: Towards an Inclusive and Sustainable World', Oxfam Research Reports, Oxfam GB.

Cerdeña, K.M. (2007) 'Indigenous People's Education: Mindanao, the Philippines'.

Ciconello, A. (2007) 'The Challenge of Eliminating Racism in Brazil: the New Institutional Framework for Fighting Racial Inequality'.

Ciconello, A. (2007) 'Social Participation as a Democracy-Consolidating Process in Brazil'.

Essoyan, C. (2007) 'Israel: The ADVA Center: an Equality and Social Justice NGO'.

Essoyan, C. (2007) 'The Centre for Trade Union and Workers' Services (CTUWS), Egypt'.

Fung, K. (2007) 'Oxfam Hong Kong's Advocacy Work on the Relocation of Rural Schools in China'.

Hine, C. and M. Cacace (2007) 'Armenia's community-based healthcare programme'.

Hine, C. and M. Cacace (2007) 'Israel: Advocacy on Employment Issues for Arab Women'.

Horner, L. (2006) 'Democracy and Building Political Voice'.

Judeh, R. (2007) 'Capacity Building in Serbia: Roma Organisations'.

Mahmoud, O., S. Aikman, and M. Kamal-Yanni (2006) 'Essential Services Background Paper'.

Oxfam Australia (2007) 'Land Rights in Papua New Guinea'.

Oxfam Australia (2007) 'Natural Resources and Forestry in the Solomon Islands'.

Oxfam GB (2007) 'Social Spending Advocacy in Guatemala'.

Pandjiarjian, V. (2001), adapted by Sweetman, C. (2006) 'Campaigning on Reproductive and Sexual Rights: CLADEM and the African Women's Protocol'.

Sweetman, C. (2006) 'Change Models: What Worked to Gain Suffrage for Women?'.

Sweetman, C. (2006) 'How Title Deeds Make Sex Safer: Women's Property Rights in an Era of HIV'.

Sweetman, C. (2007) 'Women's Political Participation and Leadership'.

van Tongeren, P. and M. Nahabedian (2007) 'The Georgian Young Lawyers Association (GYLA)'.

## POVERTY AND WEALTH

Borkenhagen, L. with N. Fenton (2006) 'Rural Realities, Now and in the Future'.

Chaudhry, P. (2007) 'Why Has Viet Nam Achieved Growth With Equity, and China Hasn't?'.

Gaye, M. (2006) 'Agricultural Reforms and Rural Poverty: the Case of the Peanut Industry in Senegal'.

Hine, C. and M. Cacace (2007) 'Rebuilding the Co-operative ethic in Albania'.

Hine, C. and M. Cacace (2007) 'Russia: Economic Marginalisation'.

Kidder, T. and M.S. Smiaroski (2006) 'Decent Work'.

Le Quang, B. (2006) 'What Has Made Viet Nam a Poverty-Reduction Success Story?'.

Raworth, K., S. Dhanarajan, and L. Wren-Lewis (2006) 'The Private Sector and Poverty Reduction'.

Raworth, K. and L. Wren-Lewis (2006) 'Private Sector Case Studies: How the Biggest Supermarket in Africa Started Buying Locally Grown Vegetables in Zambia'.

Stockbridge, M. (2007) 'Agricultural Trade Policy in Developing Countries During Take-off', Oxfam Research Reports, Oxfam GB.

Sweetman, C. (2006) 'Feminist Economics'.

Taylor, L. and R. von Arnim (2007) 'Modelling the Impact of Trade Liberalisation: A Critique of Computable General Equilibrium Models', Oxfam Research Reports, Oxfam GB.

Tórrez, B. (2007) 'Building Advocacy Capacity and Labour Rights in the Garment Industry in Honduras (CODEMUH)'.

van Mulekom, L. (2007) 'Reflections on Community-Based Coastal Resources Management (CB-CRM) in the Philippines and South-East Asia'.

Viñuales, D. (2007) 'Market Access for Indigenous Women Producers in Guatemala'.

## RISK AND VULNERABILITY

Cairns, E. (2006) 'Security Background Paper'.

Coulibaly, M. (2007) 'From Moratorium to a Convention on Small Arms: a Change in Politics and Practices for the 15 Member Countries of the Economic Community of West African States (ECOWAS)'.

Doran, A. (2006) 'Private Sector Microfinance'.

Fried, M. (2007) 'Somaliland: Local Resources for Development'.

Goulet, L. (2007) 'Ethiopia: the ABCD Project'.

Grootenhuis, F. (2007) 'Community Recovery Grants Supporting *Gotong Royong* in Indonesia'.

Henderson-Andrade, N. (2006) 'Health Risks'.

Hine, C. and M. Cacace (2007) 'Yemen: Advocacy on Violence Against Women'.

Ng, D. (2007) 'The All Ukraine Network of People Living With HIV (PLWH)'.

Oxfam GB (2007) 'Haiti: Community Information Campaigns for Disaster Risk Reduction'.

Oxfam GB (2007) 'Justice for Maria: Violence Against Women in Guatemala'.

Turnbull, M. with E. Smith and D. Walker (2006) 'From Vicious Spirals of Vulnerability to Virtuous Spirals of Disaster Risk Reduction'.

Viñuales, D. (2007) 'Nicaragua: A Tool Against Climate Change – and Hurricanes'.

## THE INTERNATIONAL SYSTEM

Barber, C. (2006) 'The Logic of Migration'.

Fenton, N. (2005) 'Aid and Middle-Income Countries'.

Fraser, A. (2006) 'International Finance Background Paper'.

Hill, A. (2006) 'Environment and Climate Change'.

Kimmis, J. (2005) 'Financial Markets and Developing Countries'.

King, R. (2007) 'Carbon Dioxide Emissions, Technology, and Economic Growth'.

Mulley, S. (2006) 'Global Governance'.

Prasopa-Plaizier, M. (2006) 'Improving the Provision of Humanitarian Assistance in Major Crises'.

## HOW CHANGE HAPPENS

Caceres, E. (2007) 'Territories and Citizenship: the Revolution of the Chiquitanos in Bolivia'.

Krznaric, R. (2007) How Change Happens: Interdisciplinary Perspectives for Human Development', Oxfam Research Reports, Oxfam GB.

MacAuslan, I. (2007) 'India's National Rural Employment Guarantee Act: A Case Study for How Change Happens'.

# GLOSSARY

**Accountability**  The means by which power is used responsibly. In the humanitarian context, accountability involves taking account of, and accounting to, beneficiaries of aid.

**Active citizenship**  The combination of rights and obligations that link individuals to the state, including paying taxes, obeying laws, and exercising political, civil, and social rights. Active citizens use these rights to improve the quality of political or civic life, often through collective action.

**Antiretrovirals**  Drugs used to treat retroviruses, primarily HIV. Different ARVs are used at different stages of the HIV life cycle and, typically, in combinations of three or four different drugs.

**Biofuels**  Most commonly, crops such as corn, sugar cane, or oilseed rape that are processed to make bioethanol, an alcohol that is blended with petrol, or biodiesel. Biofuels were initially hailed as a 'green' alternative to fossil fuels, but there is evidence that the rush to cultivate fuel crops is having adverse environmental impacts of its own and is also putting serious pressure on food production.

**Capital account liberalisation**  The removal of government barriers to international flows of capital, a policy recommended to many developing-country governments by institutions such as the International Monetary Fund and World Bank, in order to boost efficiency and growth.

However, in many cases it has also led to volatility and instability in financial markets.

**Carbon trading**  The two main types of carbon trading are emissions trading, or 'cap and trade', under which governments set a ceiling on emissions from a particular sector and companies are allocated a tradeable allowance for their emissions; and offset trading, which involves reducing emissions from projects outside an economy that has a mandatory cap on emissions (for example, in a developing country).

**Comparative advantage**  Theory advanced by nineteenth-century economist David Ricardo that countries can attain greater wealth by producing only goods that are relatively efficient to produce, then trading those goods with other countries, rather than trying to produce all goods for themselves.

**Corruption**  Corruption is the abuse of entrusted power for private gain. 'Corruption for need' refers to small-scale charges levied by officials who are themselves poorly paid; 'corruption for greed' is graft on a grander scale, typically involving senior officials, governments, or transnational corporations.

**Creative destruction**  Term popularised by economist Joseph Schumpeter (in his 1942 book *Capitalism, Socialism and Democracy*) to describe transformation and upheaval that leads to radical innovation. According to this concept, entrepreneurs play a particularly important role in stimulating economic growth.

**Debt/financial crisis**  Can take different forms: for example, in poor countries, governments may have unmanageable debts owed to creditor governments or to international financial institutions; in middle-income countries, mass default on private debt can destabilise the economy, or governments may be unable to repay public and private creditors. The first is typically a chronic problem (debt crisis); the second two tend to be sudden-onset crises linked to capital markets (financial crisis).

**Dumping**  In international trade, when a government or manufacturer in one country exports a product to another country at a price lower than the domestic price, or lower than the cost of production. The practice can distort international trade and hurt producers in poor countries.

**Effective state**    A state that can guarantee security and the rule of law, and can design and implement an effective strategy to ensure inclusive economic growth. Such a state should be accountable to citizens and able to guarantee their rights.

**Export-processing zone**    A special economic or free trade zone, typically in a developing country, that offers exemptions from bureaucracy, taxes, and tariffs, with the aim of attracting foreign investment. Although EPZs often succeed in this aim, their lack of regulation often also results in poor pay and conditions for the workers employed in them.

**Fairtrade**    Fairtrade products carry the FAIRTRADE Mark, which guarantees that the market chain for the product is certified by the Fairtrade Labelling Organization (FLO) to fulfil international social, economic, and environmental standards. A minimum price is paid to the producer in advance, plus an additional premium that must be spent on community development.

**Flexible labour**    'Flexibility' can sometimes benefit workers in terms of leave entitlement or working hours, but more commonly it involves low pay, temporary contracts, poor working conditions, and a lack of recognition of labour rights. It also makes it easier for employers to hire or fire staff.

**Free trade agreement**    Bilateral or regional trade agreements to reduce tariffs and regulation of trade and investment flows. FTAs can involve significant disparities in rights and benefits between parties (in market access, tariffs, intellectual property), particularly if one is a developing country and the other a powerful developed country or trading bloc.

**Full-cost accounting**    The pricing of goods and services to reflect their true costs, including cost of manufacture, cost of disposal, and impact on the environment. Also takes account of the value to the economy of unpaid work, which is undertaken largely by women.

**Generic medicines**  Copies of pharmaceutical products no longer protected by patent. They contain the same active ingredients as original branded drugs, though not necessarily in the identical formulation. They are cheaper than branded drugs as manufacturers do not incur the research and development costs associated with new medicines and, once a patent has expired, competition between manufacturers drives down market prices.

**Green Revolution**  Refers to the big increase in agricultural productivity in Asia in the 1960s and 1970s. It was led by techno-logical innovation based on new varieties of rice and wheat and the use of chemical fertilisers, coupled with state investment in irrigation, infrastructure such as roads, and new institutions to ensure stable crop prices.

**HIV and AIDS**  HIV (human immunodeficiency virus) is a virus, while AIDS (acquired immune deficiency syndrome) is a syndrome of opportunistic infections and diseases that can develop at the end stage of HIV infection. It is not possible to die from HIV itself. Indeed, many HIV-positive people, with a good diet and access to drugs, live a relatively normal life and may not develop AIDS for a very long time.

**International financial institutions**  The World Bank, the International Monetary Fund, and other supra-national financial bodies such as regional development banks.

**Keynesian economics**  Economic theory based on the work of British economist John Maynard Keynes (1883–1946). Keynes promoted a mixed economy in which both the state and the private sector play important roles.

**Microfinance**  Financial services designed to reduce poverty by giving poor people access to credit, insurance, savings, fund transfers, and so on. Microfinance can be organised at the community level among groups of community members, or can be provided more formally by microfinance institutions or NGOs.

**Mitigation**  When referring to climate change, 'mitigation' means reducing emissions of harmful greenhouse gases; when discussing natural disasters, it refers to reducing their potential impact.

| | |
|---|---|
| **Neoclassical economics** | An approach to economics, frequently embraced by institutions such as the World Bank and the International Monetary Fund, that relates supply and demand to the ability of individuals to maximise utility or profit. Typically based on mathematical modelling, it is often criticised for its reliance on hypothetical assumptions that fail to take account of complex human behaviour in the real world. |
| **Pastoralism** | Pastoral agriculture is based on the raising of animals such as cattle, camels, goats, and sheep, which typically represent the pastoralist's main economic resource. Pastoralism is found in many forms in different parts of the world, but commonly includes a mobile aspect, with pastoralists moving (often over long distances) in search of water and fresh pasture, according to season and environmental conditions. |
| **Remittances** | Money sent by migrant workers in foreign countries back to their families at home. Remittances make a significant contribution to the economies of developing countries. |
| **Rights-based approach** | An approach to human development that unites economic and social rights with political and civil rights, aiming to build a 'social contract' between state and citizen. At its core is the idea that all people are of equal dignity and worth, and have natural rights but also responsibilities towards their communities. |
| **Small and medium-sized enterprises** | In developing countries, SMEs typically play a much more important role in creating employment (and reinforcing local linkages) for poor people than do transnational corporations. |
| **Social capital** | The social resources that people draw on, including informal networks with individuals or institutions such as political or civic bodies; membership of formalised groups such as churches; and relationships of trust, reciprocity, and exchange. |
| **Social protection** | Consists of two components: *social assistance* transfers resources to vulnerable groups in the form of pensions, child-support grants, and so on, while *social insurance* allows individuals and households to protect themselves against risks by pooling resources with others. |

**Structural adjustment programme**
In the 1980s and 1990s, SAPs were agreed between many developing-country governments and the World Bank and the International Monetary Fund. In return for economic assistance, countries were frequently forced to accept conditions of economic restructuring that undermined their social services and their ability to develop viable industrial or agricultural sectors of their own.

**Sustainable development**
Defined by the Brundtland Report of 1987 as 'development that meets the needs of the present without compromising the ability of future generations to meet their own needs'.

**Terms of trade**
Economic term describing the rate of exchange between different kinds of goods, such as raw materials and manufactured goods; presented, for example, as the number of bags of coffee or barrels of oil needed to buy a truck.

**Transfer pricing**
A manoeuvre used by transnational corporations to minimise their tax liability. It involves either under- or over-charging for trade within different company affiliates to reduce the amount of tax liable in a particular jurisdiction.

**Vulnerability**
The reduced ability of communities or households to cope either with personal stresses such as death in the family, sickness, robbery, eviction, or the loss of a job or a crop, or a major event such as a drought or a conflict that affects the whole community.

**Vulture fund**
A private company that buys the debt of a developing-country government at a low price, and then attempts to sue the government for the full amount, plus interest.

**Washington Consensus**
Economic orthodoxy embraced by economists, politicians, and institutions such as the World Bank and the International Monetary Fund in the 1980s and 1990s. It held that developing countries could solve their economic problems by curbing inflation, reducing the power of the state, and unleashing market forces. It led to market liberalisation and the implementation of structural adjustment programmes in dozens of developing countries, often with negative outcomes for development.

# INDEX

Page numbers in *italics* refer to figures, tables, and boxes. Please note that *f*, *t*, and *b* after page numbers indicates material found in figures, tables, and boxes respectively

Pacific region 155–6, 323; Solomon Islands
Natural Resources and Rights Coalition
54
Pakistan 46, 63, *75t,* 97, 101, 276, 335
Palestine 50, 81, 284–5, 398
Paris Declaration on Aid Effectiveness
(2005) 28, 366–7, 375, 377, 378
Peru 54, *75t,* 99–100, 144–5, 260, 279, 309,
331
Philippines:
agricultural issues 129; civil society
activism 60, 307; on debt relief 307;
democratisation 79; as effective state 101;
employment issues 165; financial crisis
311; fishing industry *127b;* intellectual
property laws 330; land reform *75t,* 76;
migration 340; property rights issues 74
politics:
as change agent 439–40; civil society
involvement 60–1, 64–6, 84–5; and
effective states 95–7, 183; in international
humanitarian relief 386–7; political
parties 11, 21, 61, 80, 84–5; producer
organisation involvement 137; and
religion 38–9, 92; and trade unions 41,
160, 163; and violence 79, 81, 277;
women's involvement 83, 84; and young
people 35, 61; *see also* governments
poverty:
and access to information 53–4, 133, 204;
and agriculture 121–3, 133, 141, 144;
democracy and 80, 82–3; disease and
2–3, 9, 232; economic growth and 5, 6,
10, 179–81, 189–90, 191, 195–6; and
education 9, 10, 11, 40–1, 42–4; and
employment 148–9, 150, 157, 166; and
food production 9–10, 142–3, 227; health
and 7, 8, 9, 11, 40, 231–2; human rights
and 27–8, 208; justice system and 11,
97–8; markets and 7, 14, 108, 195–6, 220;
migration and 2, 333, 337; and powerlessness 7, 11, 27, 28, 86, 104; property
rights and 58–9, 70, 71–2; reduction
measures *see* poverty reduction; and risk
11, 120, 198, 199–200, 203, 245, 247, 248,
288; rural poverty 8, 119, 120, 121, 133,
196, 203; and transnational corporations
171, 176–7, 344; violence and 27, 200,
274, 277, 278–9, 280; vulnerability and
14, 120, 156, 199, 201, 203, 246, 247–8,
288

poverty reduction:
active citizenship and 20, 144, 429; civil
society involvement 61, 300, 301, 307;
and climate change 266, 408, 410, 413,
417, 419; from economic growth 110,
180, 204, 429; effective states' role 141–2;
global governance role 292–4, 429; and
international aid 354, *359b, 360b, 361b,
362b;* and international financial institutions 7, 300; international trade role
318; and redistribution of wealth
179–80, 429; social protection measures
207, 208, 211, 212–16, *214–15b*
power:
active citizenship 19, 20, 29, 439; change
and 433; democracy and 81, 103; and
elites 28, 29, 30; and global governance
293–4, 424; and human rights 23, 24,
28–30; nature of 28–9; and poverty 7, 11,
27, 28, 86, 104
private sector:
active citizenship and 14, 178; agriculture
and 56, 123–6, 128, 132, 133; biofuel
production 132; climate change strategies
267, 418–19; corruption 48, 86, 87; debt
relief involvement 308–9; developing
countries involvement 123–5, 313; in
economic growth 14, 163, 169–70, 196;
effective states and 14, 163–4, 169, 170–1,
178, 183; fast food chains 125–6, 137,
419; in financial crises 313, 314; financial
sector liberalisation 299, 313; in 'flexibilisation' of labour 157, *159f;* in HIV and
AIDS protection 234–5; international
humanitarian relief 391; labour rights
and 65, 163, 164–5, 169, 170, 299; microfinance and 221–3; 'race to the bottom'
166–7, 176, 351; regulation and 48, 57,
163, 170; small and medium-sized enterprises (SMEs) 169–71, 178; 'stop doing
harm' agenda 293, 429; supermarkets
125, 144, 164, 165, 177–8; supply chains
157, *159f,* 164–5, 345, 348, 350; technology and 14, 56–7, 128, 168, 170, 175,
176; vulture funds 308, 309; *see also*
markets; transnational corporations
producer organisations (POs) 134–5,
*135–6b,* 136–8, 139
property rights:
agricultural land 58–9, 72, 73, *75t,* 76–7,
*122f,* 142; civil society campaigns 58–9,
73, 74, 76; and development 71–3; and